HOLMAN
Old Testament Commentary

HOLMAN
Old Testament Commentary

Psalms 1-75

GENERAL EDITOR

Max Anders

AUTHOR

Steven J. Lawson

HOLMAN
REFERENCE

Nashville, Tennessee

Holman Old Testament Commentary
© 2003 Broadman & Holman Publishers
Nashville, Tennessee
All rights reserved

Bible versions used in this book:

ISBN 0-8054-9471-5
Dewey Decimal Classification: 223.2
Subject Heading: BIBLE. O.T. PSALMS 1–75

Psalms / Steven J. Lawson
p.   cm. — (Holman Old Testament commentary)
Includes bibliographical references. (p.).
ISBN
  1. Bible. Psalms Vol. 1—Commentaries.   I. Title.   II. Series.

—dc21

1 2 3 4 5 6 07 06 05 04 03
R

R. Albert Mohler

for his unwavering stance
in the evangelical cause
and whose indomitable leadership
as president of the
Southern Baptist Theological Seminary
has ignited a renewed commitment
to preaching the full counsel of God.

Contents

Contents

Contents

Editorial Preface

Today's church hungers for Bible teaching, and Bible teachers hunger for resources to guide them in teaching God's Word. The Holman Old Testament Commentary provides the church with the food to feed the spiritually hungry in an easily digestible format. The result: new spiritual vitality that the church can readily use.

Bible teaching should result in new interest in the Scriptures, expanded Bible knowledge, discovery of specific scriptural principles, relevant applications, and exciting living. The unique format of the Holman Old Testament Commentary includes sections to achieve these results for every Old Testament book.

Opening quotations stimulate thinking and lead to an introductory illustration and discussion that draw individuals and study groups into the Word of God. Verse-by-verse commentary interprets the passage with the aim of equipping them to understand and live God's Word in a contemporary setting. A conclusion draws together the themes identified in the passage under discussion and suggests application for it. Bible teachers and pastors will find the teaching outline helpful as they develop lessons and sermons.

Some of the major psalms are given additional treatment. A "Life Application" section provides additional illustrative material. "Deeper Discoveries" gives the reader a closer look at some of the words, phrases, and background material that illuminate the passage. "Issues for Discussion" is a tool to enhance learning within the group. Finally, a closing prayer is suggested.

It is the editors' prayer that this new resource for local church Bible teaching will enrich the ministry of group, as well as individual, Bible study and that it will lead God's people truly to be people of the Book, living out what God calls us to be.

Acknowledgments

I want to express my sincere thanks to several people who have aided in the preparation of this book:

Max Anders, editor of the Holman Commentary series, for graciously asking me to write the two volumes on the Psalms;

Stephanie Reeves and Julie Riley for diligently typing this manuscript;

Jason Allen, Justin Hughes, Susan Raborn, and Brandy Cagle, whose edits and suggestions have proven to be very helpful;

Thad Key, my assistant, who helped oversee this project and has provided strategic insight, helpful research, and a careful eye on this manuscript;

Anne, my wife, along with my four children—Andrew, James, Grace Anne, and John—who have encouraged me greatly throughout the writing of this commentary and enthusiastically supported me in the preaching of the Psalms.

Steven J. Lawson

Holman Old Testament Commentary Contributors

Holman New Testament Commentary Contributors

Vol. 1, Matthew
ISBN 0-8054-0201-2
Stuart K. Weber

Vol. 2, Mark
ISBN 0-8054-0202-0
Rodney L. Cooper

Vol. 3, Luke
ISBN 0-8054-0203-9
Trent C. Butler

Vol. 4, John
ISBN 0-8054-0204-7
Kenneth O. Gangel

Vol. 5, Acts
ISBN 0-8054-0205-5
Kenneth O. Gangel

Vol. 6, Romans
ISBN 0-8054-0206-3
Kenneth Boa and William Kruidenier

Vol. 7, 1 & 2 Corinthians
ISBN 0-8054-0207-1
Richard L. Pratt Jr.

**Vol. 8, Galatians, Ephesians,
Philippians, Colossians**
ISBN 0-8054-0208-X
Max Anders

**Vol. 9, 1 & 2 Thessalonians,
1 & 2 Timothy, Titus, Philemon**
ISBN 0-8054-0209-8
Knute Larson

Vol. 10, Hebrews, James
ISBN 0-8054-0211-X
Thomas D. Lea

Vol. 11, 1 & 2 Peter, 1, 2, 3 John, Jude
ISBN 0-8054-0210-1
David Walls and Max Anders

Vol. 12, Revelation
ISBN 0-8054-0212-8
Kendell H. Easley

Holman Old Testament Commentary

Twenty volumes designed for Bible study and teaching to enrich the local church and God's people.

Series Editor	Max Anders
Managing Editor	Steve Bond
Project Editor	Dean Richardson
Product Development Manager	Ricky D. King
Marketing Manager	Stephanie Huffman
Executive Editor	David Shepherd
Page Composition	TF Designs, Greenbrier, TN

Introduction to

Psalms

No other book of the Bible compares with the wonder of the sacred collection of inspired worship songs known as the Psalms. Considered by many to be the most loved portion of Scripture, the Psalms have been a bedrock of comfort and a tower of strength for believers in every experience of life. From the soul-stirring heights of praise to the heart-rending depths of despair, the full range of human emotion is captured in these magnificent anthems. Written some three thousand years ago in the days of ancient Israel, the Psalms remain just as vibrant and fresh today as when they were first written. They are able to lead the hearts of all believers to praise God. Because it directs its readers to this highest, God-assigned end, the collection of psalms occupies a unique place in the canon of Scripture.

Contained in this inspired hymnbook is the psalmists' passionate devotion to God as these wise men and worship leaders led God's people in exalting the name of him who alone is worthy to be praised. More than any other portion of Scripture, the Book of Psalms has influenced the public worship and private devotions of God's people through the centuries, leading them to seek him more diligently, to love him more deeply, and to trust him more fully. But in order for the Psalms to be rightly understood, a basic orientation to each psalm's historical background, literary style, and figures of speech is necessary. This brief introduction serves as an important prelude to the study of the Psalms.

UNIQUE FEATURES

The Psalms, it can be argued, is the most unusual book in the Bible. Many interesting features cause it to stand out as a truly one-of-a-kind book. Consider some of the following special aspects:

- Psalms is the largest book in the Bible, containing 150 psalms.
- If each psalm is considered a chapter, then Psalms contains the most chapters of any book in the Bible, with its 150 psalms. The Book of Isaiah is a distant second with 66 chapters.
- Psalm 119 is the largest chapter in the Bible, a unit of 176 verses, containing more verses than many other short books of the Bible.

- Psalm 117 is the shortest chapter in the Bible, containing only two verses.
- Psalm 117 is also the middle chapter of the Bible, the very center of the 1,189 chapters found in Genesis through Revelation.
- Psalm 118:8 is the absolute center of the 31,173 verses contained in the Scripture, the middle verse of the entire Bible.
- Psalms is written by more authors than any other book in the Bible. It is a literary collection claiming a multiple authorship of many men such as David, Asaph, the sons of Korah, Solomon, Moses, Heman, Ethan, and others.
- Psalms was a long-term project that was approximately nine hundred to one thousand years in the making, requiring the longest time period for its writing than all the canonical books.
- Psalms is the most quoted Old Testament book in the New Testament. Of the 360 Old Testament quotations or allusions in the New Testament, 112 are from the Psalms.
- Psalms contains more messianic prophecies than any other Old Testament book, other than possibly Isaiah. It reveals the Messiah as the Son of God (Ps. 2) and son of man (Ps. 8) in his obedience (Ps. 40:6–8), betrayal (Ps. 41:9), crucifixion (Ps. 22), resurrection (Ps. 16), ascension (Ps. 68:18), and enthronement (Ps. 110).

BOOK TITLE

The word *psalms* comes from a Greek word which means "the plucking of strings." It means a song to be sung to the accompaniment of a plucked or stringed instrument such as a harp or lyre. Thus, the Psalms is a collection of worship songs sung to God by the people of Israel with musical accompaniment. The collection of these 150 psalms into one book served as the first hymnbook for God's people, written and compiled to assist them in their worship of God. At first, because of the wide variety of these songs, this praise book was unnamed, but eventually the ancient Hebrews called it "The Book of Praises," or simply "Praises." This title reflects its main purpose—to assist believers in the proper worship of God.

HUMAN AUTHORS

While most other biblical books were written by one person, a few of them claim multiple authors, Proverbs being one such example. Psalms is one of the rare books in the Bible that was written by several people and, thus, is a joint effort of many authors who wrote from many diverse experiences of life. Familiarity with the varied writers of the Psalms is important.

- David, the second king of Israel and "sweet psalmist of Israel" (2 Sam. 23:1 KJV), is the chief author of the Psalms. He is credited with writing 75 of the 150 psalms, exactly half the Psalms (3–9; 11–32; 34–41; 51–65; 68–70; 86; 101; 103; 108–110; 122; 124; 131; 133; 138–145; also Ps. 2 is identified by Acts 4:25 as being written by David, as is Ps. 95 by Heb. 4:7).
- Asaph, a priest who served as the worship leader of ancient Israel, wrote twelve psalms (Ps. 50; 73–83).
- The sons of Korah, a guild of singers and composers of music, are credited with writing ten psalms (Pss. 42; 44–49; 84–85; 87).
- Solomon, David's son, the third king of Israel, accounted for two psalms (Pss. 72; 127).
- Moses, prophet of Israel and mighty leader of the exodus, wrote one psalm (Ps. 90).
- Heman, a wise man, musician, an Ezrahite, a son of Korah, and founder of the Korahite choir (2 Chr. 5:12; 35:15), wrote one psalm (Ps. 88).
- Ethan, a wise man and Ezrahite, probably a Levitical singer (1 Chr. 6:42; 15:17,19), wrote one psalm (Ps. 89).
- Anonymous authors account for the remaining forty-eight psalms.
- Ezra, scribe and priest of Israel, is thought to be the author of some of the anonymous psalms.

TIME PERIOD

Because many different authors wrote the Psalms, the writing of these sacred songs occurred at different times, spanning a period of about nine hundred to one thousand years. The time of their writing reaches from approximately 1410 B.C., when the first psalm was written, to around 500 B.C. to 430 B.C., when the last psalm was written, depending upon the identity of the author of Psalm 126.

- The first psalm written, Psalm 90, was composed by Moses during Israel's forty years of wilderness wanderings (1445–1405 B.C.), probably toward the end of this time of severe testing, perhaps around 1410 B.C.
- The vast majority of the psalms were written during the kingly reigns of David (1020–970 B.C.) and Solomon (970–931 B.C.), around 1000 B.C.
- The last psalm composed, Psalm 126, is thought to have been recorded after the time of Israel's Babylonian exile, during their

return to the land of Judah, around 500 B.C., or even earlier, about 430 B.C., if Psalm 126 was written by Ezra.

INTENDED PURPOSE

No matter where a person is in the Christian life, whether up or down, soaring or struggling, there is a psalm that speaks directly to the spiritual state of his heart. The psalms were written to guide believers in the proper worship of God and, used rightly, are to be sung devotionally (Eph. 5:19; Col. 3:16), prayed fervently (Acts 4:25–26), preached evangelistically (Acts 2:25–28,31,34–35; 13:33,35), and taught expositionally (Luke 24:44; Rom. 3:10–14,18; 1 Cor. 15:27; Eph. 4:8; Heb. 1:5). The primary purpose of the Book of Psalms is found in its intensely God-centered focus to direct our hearts toward him in every experience of life.

SUPERSCRIPTIONS AND NOTATIONS

More than three-fourths of the psalms, 116 to be exact, have a superscription added to the beginning of the psalm that provides an editorial notation identifying its author, historical context, and how it should be sung. All but thirty-four of the psalms have such titles. These were added after the time of their writing and were included to assist the worship leader and congregation in understanding and singing these praise songs. Although these superscriptions were not a part of the original text, they are, nevertheless, considered accurate and reliable. Among the various kinds of information that these editorial additions provide are:

Historical information. Most of these titles provide background information about authorship, historical occasion, or personal dedication, all of which is helpful in interpreting and applying the psalm. An example of such a historical notation is Psalm 3: "A psalm of David. When he fled from his son Absalom."

Musical instructions. Some of the titles were intended for the worship director, and they indicated what kind of song it was and how it was to be sung. These musical inscriptions accompany fifty-five psalms, possibly to aid in their use on special occasions. For example, such a superscription is found in Psalm 4: "For the director of music. With stringed instruments. A psalm of David."

Important pauses. The word *Selah* has been added seventy-one times to the Psalms, serving as a later editorial addition that signaled a brief interlude in the psalm, either for a change of musical accompaniment, a brief interlude with stringed instruments, a call to pause and reflect upon the truth just stated, or a notice to begin a new section. Most scholars agree that *Selah* was a form of musical notation. An example is Psalm 3:4: "To the LORD I cry aloud, and he answers me from his holy hill. *Selah*."

LITERARY TYPES

The various psalms can be categorized by literary types, indicating the different subject matters they addressed or the various styles in which they were written. It is most helpful, even necessary, to detect these classifications if they are to be rightly interpreted. The basic types of psalms are:

Wisdom psalms. These instructive psalms provide practical guidelines for godly living and give pointed direction for righteous living in the pursuit of God's will (Pss. 1; 37; 119).

Royal psalms. Describing the coming messianic rule of Christ, these regal psalms portray him as the undisputed sovereign King over heaven and earth (Pss. 2; 18; 20; 21; 45; 47; 68; 72; 89; 101; 110; 118; 132; 144).

Lament psalms. These highly emotionally charged psalms record the writer's heart cry to God for divine deliverance from the psalmist's trouble and pain (Pss. 3–7; 12–13; 22; 25–28; 35; 38–40; 42–44; 51; 54–57; 59–61; 63–64; 69–71; 74; 79–80; 83; 85–86; 88; 90; 102; 109; 120; 123; 130; 140–143).

Imprecatory psalms. Motivated by fiery zeal for God's glory, these provocative, often controversial, psalms invoke God's wrath and judgment upon the psalmist's adversaries who were God's enemies. The psalmist called upon the Lord to punish the wicked and defend him as he carried out God's work in the midst of his persecutors (Pss. 7; 35; 40; 55; 58–59; 69; 79; 109; 137; 139; 144).

Thanksgiving psalms. These psalms express a profound awareness of and deep gratitude for God's abundant blessings, whether individual or national (Pss. 8; 18; 19; 29; 30; 32–34; 36; 40; 41; 66; 103–106; 111; 113; 117; 124; 129; 135–136; 138–139; 146–148; 150).

Pilgrimage psalms. These festive psalms promote a celebrative mood of praise for God as Israel recalled his goodness to them as they traveled to Jerusalem for their annual feasts (Pss. 43; 46; 48; 76; 84; 87; 120–134).

Enthronement psalms. These awe-inspiring majestic psalms describe the majesty of God's sovereign rule over all his creation and the providential care by which he sustains, controls, and directs all he has made (Pss. 48; 93; 96–99).

BOOK DIVISIONS

The entire collection of 150 psalms, often called the Psalter, was assembled in progressive stages which covered an extended period of time. In other words, the Book of Psalms was originally collected by ancient compilers as a series of smaller books, five in all, in which the next book augmented the previous material. Psalm 72:20 makes this clear when it states, "This concludes the prayers of David son of Jesse." This verse, no doubt, marked the end of an earlier, smaller edition of the Psalms which once concluded at this point but later was supplemented with Psalms 73–150.

These five books are easily recognizable because each section concludes with a climactic doxology (Pss. 41:13; 72:18–19; 89:52; 106:48; 150:6). Some interpreters have maintained that these five books of the Psalms correspond to the first five books of the Bible, Genesis through Deuteronomy. Thus, the Book of Psalms has been called "The Pentateuch of David" because they are thought to mirror the books of the Law, known as the Pentateuch of Moses. These five divisions of the Psalms are as follows:

Book I: Psalms 1–41. The first forty-one psalms were probably gathered together during the early days of the Jewish monarchy by either David or Solomon. Psalm 1 is an anonymous psalm that serves as the logical introduction to the entire Book of Psalms. Psalm 2 is attributed to David (Acts 4:25). Psalms 9 and 10 were probably considered one psalm, and Psalm 33 is attributed to David in the Septuagint. These facts probably indicate that the entire content of Book I was basically assigned to David. Because this first book, Psalms 1–41, highlights God's power in creation (Pss. 8; 19) and is dominated by the theme of sin and redemption, it is easy to see how it could correlate with the Book of Genesis.

Book II: Psalms 42–72. These thirty-one psalms were collected and assembled at a later time to form Book II, possibly three hundred years after Book I was compiled during the reign of Judah's thirteenth king, Hezekiah (about 715–686 B.C.). If so, the "men of Hezekiah," an active Bible committee that collected many of the proverbs of Solomon (Prov. 25:1), probably organized these psalms into a literary unit and added them to Book I. This is certainly consistent with Hezekiah's efforts to bring revival to Judah (2 Chr. 29:30; 32:26), as he elevated the forgotten wisdom of David and Solomon (2 Chr. 29:30–31; 30:26).

It is also possible that these psalms were collected during the reign of King Josiah (640–609 B.C.). Interpreters have noted that this second book of psalms focuses upon Israel's ruin and redemption and, thus, can be said to relate to the Book of Exodus, which documents Israel's redemption from Egyptian tyranny.

Book III: Psalms 73–89. These seventeen psalms were subsequently compiled into Book III, probably during this same era by the men of Hezekiah as previously mentioned for Book II, or by Josiah, sixteenth ruler of the Southern Kingdom (640–609 B.C.). This third book begins with eleven consecutive psalms written by Asaph, a Levite who led one of the temple choirs (Pss.

73–83), and includes some written by David (Pss. 86; 101; 103). These psalms center primarily upon the holiness of Israel's sanctuary and, thus, coincides with the concern of the Book of Leviticus with the tabernacle and holiness.

Book IV: Psalms 90–106. This fourth cluster of seventeen psalms was collected about two hundred to three hundred years later and added to the first three books, probably during the postexilic days when Israel returned to her land under Ezra (458 B.C.) and Nehemiah (445 B.C.). This division of the Psalms focuses upon Israel's relapse and recovery in the wilderness, echoing the theme of the Book of Numbers. Appropriately, Book IV begins with Psalm 90, the only psalm written by Moses during Israel's forty years of wilderness wanderings. This was a severe time of testing recorded in Numbers. Book IV contains the recurring theme of God's sovereign kingdom which dominates the kingdoms of the nations just as Numbers documents Israel's relationship to the surrounding nations.

Book V: Psalms 107–150. These last forty-four psalms make up Book V. Like Book IV, they were probably collected and added to the Book of Psalms during the postexilic days of Ezra, almost six hundred years after Book I was collated. This fifth book focuses upon the sufficiency of God's Word (Ps. 119) and the universal praise due to the Lord's name (Pss. 146–150), much like the Book of Deuteronomy focuses on God and his Word.

LITERARY STYLE

The Psalms were written in a literary style called Hebrew poetry, a form of communication that is quite different from the other genres used in Scripture (i.e., narrative, prophecy, epistle, parable, legal writings). Using highly figurative language, Hebrew poetry conveys God's message in potent expressions that are colorful, emotional, vivid, picturesque, and concise. Unlike English poetry which is based upon rhyming and meter, Hebrew poetry is based upon rhythm and parallelism. Specifically, poetic parallelism states an idea in the first line and then reinforces it with an array of literary devices in the second line. The following are some of the literary devices used in Hebrew parallelism.

Synonymous parallelism. This is the most common type of Hebrew parallelism. The second line repeats or restates the central idea of the first line. The synonymous terms of the second line are used for emphasis and dramatic effect. Consider these examples: "Why do the nations conspire and the peoples plot in vain?" (Ps. 2:1). "O LORD, how many are my foes! How many rise up against me!" (Ps. 3:1).

Antithetical parallelism. This literary device states a truth in the second line that contrasts with the idea of the first line. The contrast is intended in order to drive home the point with additional impact by stating the direct opposite. The word *but* often signals the contrast that will begin the second line. Here are two examples of antithetical parallelism: "For the LORD watches over the way of the righteous, but the way of the wicked will perish" (Ps. 1:6). "For evil men will be cut off, but those who hope in the LORD will inherit the land" (Ps. 37:9).

Synthetic parallelism. After the proposition stated in the first line, the second line advances and develops this central idea further. Here are two examples: "Blessed is the man who does not walk in the counsel of the wicked or stand in the way of sinners or sit in the seat of mockers. But his delight is in the law of the LORD, and on his law he meditates day and night" (Ps. 1:1–2). "The law of the LORD is perfect, reviving the soul. The statutes of the LORD are trustworthy, making wise the simple. The precepts of the LORD are right, giving joy to the heart. The commands of the LORD are radiant, giving light to the eyes. The fear of the LORD is pure, enduring forever. The ordinances of the LORD are sure and altogether righteous" (Ps. 19:7–9).

Emblematic parallelism. This literary device portrays the main idea in the form of a figure of speech known as a simile. This type of parallelism is easy to detect because the words *as* or *like* are used: "As the deer pants for streams of water, so my soul pants for you, O God" (Ps. 42:1).

Climactic parallelism. A crucial word, phrase, or truth stated in the first line is expanded in the second line and brought to a dramatic climax: "Ascribe to the LORD, O mighty ones, ascribe to the LORD glory and strength. Ascribe to the LORD the glory due his name; worship the LORD in the splendor of his holiness" (Ps. 29:1–2).

Alternate parallelism. In this form of parallelism, the third line repeats the idea of the first, and the forth repeats the second in an A-B-A-B pattern: "For as high as the heavens are above the earth, so great is his love for those who fear him; as far as the east is from the west, so far has he removed our transgressions from us" (Ps. 103:11–12).

Chiastic parallelism. This parallelism employs an A-B-B-A pattern in which the second line advances the first, then restates the second line in the third, and finally returns to the truth of the first line. Here are two examples: "Blessed is the man who does not walk in the counsel of the wicked or stand in the way of sinners or sit in the seat of mockers. But his delight is in the law of the LORD, and on his law he meditates day and night" (Ps. 1:1–2). "But I, by your great mercy, will come into your house; in reverence will I bow down toward your holy temple" (Ps. 5:7).

FIGURES OF SPEECH

The language of the Psalms uses many illustrative expressions known as figures of speech or literary devices that paint pictures in the reader's mind. This highly potent form of communication conveys truth in vivid fashion and stirs the emotions. Thus, the language of the Psalms is a colorful display of the truth that attracts the attention of the reader. Among the figures of speech most often used in the psalms are the following.

Simile. This particular figure makes a direct comparison between two realities by using the word *like* or *as* (i.e., "like a tree," "like chaff"). "He is like a tree planted by streams of water, which yields its fruit in season and whose leaf does not wither. Whatever he does prospers. Not so the wicked! They are like chaff that the wind blows away" (Ps. 1:3–4).

Metaphor. This figure of speech makes a comparison between two realities, declaring one to be like another without using "like" or "as." "The LORD is my shepherd, I shall not be in want" (Ps. 23:1). "For the LORD God is a sun and shield; the LORD bestows favor and honor; no good thing does he withhold from those whose walk is blameless" (Ps. 84:11).

Allegory. This literary device develops a series of extended metaphors which are built around a central theme (i.e., Israel a "vine" "planted" that "took deep root"). "You brought a vine out of Egypt; you drove out the nations and planted it. You cleared the ground for it, and it took root and filled the land. The mountains were covered with its shade, the mighty cedars with its branches. It sent out its boughs to the Sea, its shoots as far as the River. Why have you broken down its walls so that all who pass by pick its grapes? Boars from the forest ravage it and the creatures of the field feed on it. Return to us, O God Almighty! Look down from heaven and see! Watch over this vine, the root your right hand has planted, the son you have raised up for yourself. Your vine is cut down, it is burned with fire; at your rebuke your people perish" (Ps. 80:8–16).

Metonymy. This manner of speech substitutes one figure for another as the two are closely related (i.e., "mouth" exchanged for "tongue"). "Their mouths lay claim to heaven, and their tongues take possession of the earth" (Ps. 73:9). "In vain you rise early and stay up late, toiling for food to eat—for he grants sleep to those he loves" (Ps. 127:2).

Synecdoche. This literary device represents the whole of a matter by one of its parts, or vice versa, a part by a whole (i.e., "tongue" substituted for "words"). "You love every harmful word, O you deceitful tongue!" (Ps. 52:4).

Hyperbole. This form of communication conveys a truth by making an exaggerated statement, intended for dramatic effect, in order to arrest the reader's attention to the greatness of a matter (i.e., "flood my bed . . . with tears"). "I am worn out from groaning; all night long I flood my bed with weeping and drench my couch with tears" (Ps. 6:6).

Personification. This figure of speech assigns humanlike qualities, such as intelligence or speech, to inanimate objects or abstract ideas (i.e., "my bones will say"). "My whole being will exclaim, 'Who is like you, O LORD? You rescue the poor from those too strong for them, the poor and needy from those who rob them'" (Ps. 35:10).

Apostrophe. This manner of expression addresses lifeless objects as though they were a living person, heightening the intensity of the communication (i.e., "O sea"). "Why was it, O sea, that you fled, O Jordan, that you turned back" (Ps. 114:5).

Anthropomorphism. This medium of communication speaks of God as having a human body in order to convey an important truth about his character in familiar, humanlike ways that can be easily understood, although God, a spirit, has no body parts (i.e., "your hand"). "Arise, LORD! Lift up your hand, O God. Do not forget the helpless" (Ps. 10:12).

ALAPHABETICAL ACROSTIC

Several of the psalms use a literary device known as an alphabetical acrostic. In this form of communication, the first letter of the first word of a line, verse, or stanza begins with the next, successive Hebrew consonant in the alphabet and advances progressively in sequential order through the twenty-two consonants of the Hebrew letters. This medium, no doubt, served to assist people in memorizing the psalms, especially when set to music. Likewise, it conveyed the ordered structure of the psalm and organized thought as recorded by the author. It also indicated the full breadth of the subject matter addressed, expressing comprehensive thought (i.e., from A to Z).

- Psalms 25; 34. These are the only two psalms which build with the acrostic of the entire Hebrew alphabet of all twenty-two letters.
- Psalms 9; 10. These psalms contain an irregular acrostic that runs through its verses.
- Psalms 111; 112. Each of these psalms has ten verses with twenty-two lines on which each letter builds.
- Psalm 145. The psalm has twenty-one verses, omitting the Hebrew letter *nun* between verses 13 and 14.
- Psalm 119. This is the most advanced psalm, having twenty-two stanzas of eight verses each, each stanza beginning with the next letter of the Hebrew alphabet, emphasizing the perfection of God's Word.

PSALMS: A LIFE-CHANGING BOOK

It is the purpose of this study of the Psalms to unlock the inexhaustible riches of this portion of inspired Scripture which is a vast storehouse of truth that Spurgeon called "the treasury of David." May God use this exposition to more fully establish in the reader's hearts and lives the timeless truths contained in these psalms. In turn, may God use this magnificent portion of Scripture to strengthen his church and all who call upon the name of the Lord. Through the centuries, the Book of Psalms has always been strategic and pivotal in the lives of God's people. May it be so again in this critical hour.

On October 31, 1517, Martin Luther posted his Ninety-Five Theses on the door of the castle church at Wittenberg and ignited the spark that began the Reformation. In years preceding the Reformation, Luther was chiefly studying and teaching two books of the Bible. Almost everyone associates Martin Luther with the Book of Romans, particularly Romans 1:17 which reads, "The just shall live by faith" (KJV). But Luther was converted not only by his study of Romans but also by his study of the Psalms. On August 16, 1513, he began lecturing on the first book of Scripture that he had ever taught—the Book of Psalms. These two books of inspired Scripture—Romans and Psalms—radically changed the direction of his life.

While Romans formulated Luther's doctrinal convictions about the purity of the true gospel, Psalms gave him the courage to proclaim these truths fearlessly. His personal study of the Psalms instilled within him such a high view of God that he developed a devil-defying boldness to stand alone against the world for the truth of the gospel of God's grace. The Psalms gave Luther an unconquerable spirit and indomitable will to trust God, no matter what happened to him.

In his latter years, during the traumatic days of the Reformation, Luther often became discouraged, suffering bouts of despair and even depression. The entire world, he felt, was against him. But in those dark and difficult hours, he would turn to his beloved coworker Philip Melanchthon and say, "Come, Philip, let us sing the psalms." They would often sing a version of Psalm 46 set to music:

> A sure stronghold our God is He,
> A timely shield and weapon;
> Our help He'll be and set us free
> From every ill can happen.

We know this song today as "A Mighty Fortress Is Our God," perhaps the greatest hymn of the church. A masterpiece of heart-moving truth written by Martin Luther, this famous hymn is drawn from the inspired text of Psalm 46.

"We sing this psalm," Luther reflected, "because God is with us and powerfully and miraculously preserves and defends his church and his word against all fanatical spirits, against the gates of hell, against the implacable hatred of the devil, and against all the assaults of the world, the flesh, and sin."

May God use this study of the Psalms to instill such bold, confident faith within his people. Though the earth moves and the mountains shake, though the seas roar and foam as a result of great upheaval, those who trust in the Lord will be immovable. It is the prayer of this author that these studies in the Psalms will fortify your hope in God and cause your heart to be filled with glorious adoration of him who alone is worthy to be praised.

Soli deo gloria.

Psalm 1
The Two Roads of Life

"*Walk* with God, and you cannot mistake the road; you

have infallible wisdom to direct you, permanent love to com-

fort you, and eternal power to defend you."

C h a r l e s   H .   S p u r g e o n

I. INTRODUCTION

The High Way and the Low

John Oxenham, the noted British author and hymn writer of the well-known classic "In Christ, There Is No East Nor West," wrote in his poem *The Ways:*

> To every man there openeth
> A Way, and Ways and a Way,
> And the High Soul climbs the High way,
> And the Low Soul gropes the Low,
> And in between, on the misty flats,
> The rest drift to and fro.
> But to every man there openeth
> A High way and a Low,
> And every man decideth
> The Way his soul shall go.

Penned with poignant language, this literary masterpiece states that there are many different paths before every person, a series of choices that open before each life. But amid these many different roads that could be taken, there are in reality only two paths—"a High way and a Low." Every person's life and, ultimately his destiny, is marked by the choice he makes regarding "the Way his soul shall go." So each life must choose wisely. Decisions determine destinies. The road a person chooses marks the course of his or her life, not only for the present but for the eternities that follow.

Psalm 1 differentiates between these two paths of life. One road leads to blessing, the other to cursing; one to salvation, the other to destruction. There are only two roads in life—the way of the godly and the way of the ungodly—and they lead to two opposite destinies—one to life, the other to death. Accordingly, this first psalm is considered a wisdom psalm, one that provides guidance for godly living. Like a clearly marked entrance to the path of righteousness, it serves as an introduction to the entire Book of Psalms, directing all travelers to the path of God's blessedness. This psalm, intentionally placed at the beginning, serves as a preface to the remaining 149 psalms.

II. COMMENTARY

The Two Roads of Life

> **MAIN IDEA:** *Blessed are the righteous who live insulated from the deceptions and defilements of this evil world and who internalize God's Word while, to the contrary, the wicked are unstable and will perish.*

The Way of the Godly (1:1–3)

> **SUPPORTING IDEA:** *The godly are abundantly blessed because they do not live according to the sinful philosophies, practices, or associations of fallen men but are deeply rooted in God's Word.*

1:1a. This psalm begins with the emphatic declaration that God's abundant favor will rest upon the person who lives a truly God-centered life. In the original language, **blessed** is repeated. This is the Hebrew method of indicating the plural, intensifying its meaning. Thus, the phrase should read, "O, how very happy" or "the happinesses!" In reality, this soul satisfaction is pleasure found in the Lord himself. This promise of blessing is precisely what Jesus announced in the Beatitudes (Matt. 5:3–12). True happiness is the experience of all who trust in the Lord (cp. Pss. 16:11; 21:6; 34:8). The righteous are genuinely satisfied in the Lord (Phil. 4:4).

1:1b,c,d. This God-blessed life is first described negatively, or what the godly person does *not* practice. First, He **does not walk in the counsel of the wicked**, meaning he refuses the secular philosophy and humanistic values of the godless. He refuses the worldview that places man at the center of the universe and entices him to live by his own standards of morality and pursuits of pleasure.

Second, neither does the righteous person **stand in the way of sinners.** This infers that his personal behavior resists the lure of the crowd to participate in their carnal activities and sensual living.

Third, the godly person does not **sit in the seat of mockers,** meaning he refuses to associate with those who scoff at God. He avoids close relationships with blasphemers, infidels, and atheists, no matter how prosperous they may be, because "bad company corrupts good character" (1 Cor. 15:33).

1:2. Positively, the **delight** of the godly **is in the law of the LORD.** The person who knows genuine joy reads and relishes God's Word. This hunger for the Bible is a clear indication of the new birth as his new nature longs for the truths of God. This new appetite for God's truth leads him to meditate upon the Word **day and night.** He constantly sets his mind on the truths of the Bible, throughout the day focusing on Scripture because it reveals the glory of God and his supremacy.

1:3. The person who delights in God's law will be like **a tree planted by streams of water** which draws its life-sustaining nourishment from a stream flowing through its roots. The God-centered life draws its spiritual vitality from God's Word, which is compared to many **streams.** This word *streams* is in the plural, representing the abundant, overflowing supply of strength and sustaining grace conveyed in God's Word. The godly sets down deep roots into a reservoir which will never run dry—one that refreshes, revives, renews, cleanses, and satisfies those who draw upon it (John 15:3; Eph. 5:26). God's Word can sustain the godly (cp. Ps. 19:7–10).

When indwelt by the living Word, the leaf of the righteous **does not wither,** meaning all that he does will have eternal value and lasting results. Furthermore, he is like a tree that **yields its fruit in season.** This pictures a continual fruitfulness in every season of life, whether good times or bad times, triumphs or trials. So potent is God's Word that **whatever he does prospers.** He will enjoy a spiritually enriched life, the fullest life imaginable.

B The Way of the Ungodly (1:4–6)

SUPPORTING IDEA: *By contrast, the person who lives without God is morally corrupt and will be condemned and damned forever.*

1:4. Are the ungodly blessed? **Not so!** Are they happy? Not so! Successful? Not so! Fruitful? Not so! They may sound gregarious and look successful, but they are not so! The ungodly actually do what God forbids in verse 1. They walk in the counsel of the wicked; they stand in the way of sinners; and they sit in the seat of mockers. Therefore, unlike the righteous who are like a tree whose leaf does not wither, the wicked are **like chaff that the wind blows away.** This is a picture drawn from harvest time. The part of the grain known as chaff was discarded as worthless and having no value. Accordingly, **the**

wicked are empty, void, futile, unsubstantial, shallow, worthless, and, in the end, to be burned in the fire.

1:5. As a result, **the wicked will not stand in the judgment**. They will not have God's acceptance when they stand before him in the last day. Rather, they will be exposed for what they really are (Rev. 20:11–15). They will be justly condemned in their sin, sentenced to eternal punishment in hell. Such corrupt sinners will not be allowed to remain **in the assembly of the righteous** but will be excluded from the joyful fellowship of the saints (Rev. 21:8; 22:15). They will be revealed in the final **judgment** as unworthy sinners, rightly condemned by Christ (Acts 17:31), and removed from the presence of the godly forever.

1:6. The last verse summarizes the two ways in life—**the way of the righteous** and **the way of the wicked**. The Lord **watches over** the way of the righteous, which means far more than that he is informed about their ways. Rather, he has a personal, intimate relationship with the godly and is involved with them in order to guard, guide, and grace them. But the way of the wicked **will perish**. The ungodly sinner, judged and condemned in the final judgment, will be damned forever. The wicked will suffer relentless torment in a real place called hell, always perishing, forever suffering the eternal wrath of God, never finding relief from God's just vengeance.

MAIN IDEA REVIEW: *Blessed are the righteous who do not participate in the deceptions and defilements of this evil world and who internalize God's Word.*

III. CONCLUSION

You *Can* Get There from Here!

Martyn Lloyd-Jones tells about a traveler in Ireland who once stopped a man working beside the road to ask directions. The traveler asked, "My friend, if you were going to Dublin, which way would you go?" The Irishman quipped, "I wouldn't go there from here." Many people want to start from some place other than where they are in order to be where they want to be. But the truth is, we must start where we are, *now,* if we are to reach our desired destination. So it is, spiritually speaking. Many people want to enter the way of the godly, but they procrastinate, putting it off for another time, waiting to be at some other place in life. They want to start from somewhere other than where they are.

But if a person is to enter the way of the Lord, he must enter from where he is. He must face his sin, confessing it for what it is, and turn to the Lord by faith. Anyone who travels the broad path of the wicked may enter the way of the righteous. But he must start where he is. He must repent of his sin and believe on Christ, who bore the sins of his people in his body upon the cross. This is the good news of the gospel. One may enter the way of the godly if he will trust Christ. But it begins where a person is—right now.

IV. LIFE APPLICATION

What Path Am I Traveling?

Every person must ask the soul-searching question, What path in life am I traveling? Have I entered through the narrow gate that leads to the path of the godly? Or am I traveling the broad road that is headed to destruction? These are the important diagnostic questions that each person must ask himself and answer carefully and accurately. If you say that you are walking the path of the righteous, this brings on another series of questions to determine the genuineness of your profession of faith. Is there clear evidence of a transformed life that authenticates such a claim? Are you experiencing the blessedness of God's favor? Are you living a separated life, distinct from the beliefs and behavior of the ungodly? Have you made the break from the world? Is your delight in the law of the Lord?

The answer to these questions will reveal which path you travel. Many people today point to a mystical feeling or emotional "experience" for the validity of their conversion, but we must look for the fruit of a changed life. The authenticity and validity of a person's faith is proven by the spiritual fruit he produces. Fruit is the test of salvation. This includes personal holiness (Rom. 6:22), Christlike character (Gal. 5:22–23), good works (Col. 1:10), ministry (Rom. 1:13), stewardship (Rom. 15:25–28), and praising God (Heb. 13:15).

V. PRAYER

God, we praise your magnificent name for blessing us so abundantly. Thank you for your abounding goodness which has been lavished upon us in Jesus Christ. We praise you that our hearts are most satisfied in you. May you insulate our souls from the temptations and deceptions of this world. Anchor us in your Word. Help us to draw the spiritual nourishment we need from the Scripture so that we may stand strong and live fruitful lives for the honor of your name. In Jesus' name. Amen.

VI. DEEPER DISCOVERIES

A. Blessed (1:1)

This word (Heb. *esher*) means an overflowing joy and full contentment in God, a satisfaction and happiness in the Lord. This noun occurs forty-four times in the Old Testament, twenty-five of which are found in the Psalms. The word *happy* is a good synonym, although it must be understood that this word conveys far more than feelings of peace and contentment. This word is in the plural which intensifies its meaning, expressing God's redemptive favor upon the person who fears the Lord and pursues his will. An alternate translation in Psalm 1:1 would be, "Oh the blessednesses." This blessedness is not deserved, but it is a gift of God, not dependent upon our circumstances but upon the vitality of our relationship with God.

B. Walk, Stand, Sit (1:1)

These words picture the way of the ungodly as devolving decadence into deeper strongholds of sin. This downward spiral descends from walking, to standing, to sitting. The power of evil always proceeds downward in the lives of wicked people—from bad to worse. To *walk* refers to the series of steps that the ungodly person takes in life, the decisions he makes, the direction he pursues. To *stand* pictures the commitments a person makes to various causes. To *sit* represents the settled attitudes of the heart, the fixed disposition of a person's heart.

Thus, the sinner descends from being one who is "wicked," meaning corrupt internally, to being a sinner, or one who practices sin, and finally, to being a mocker, one who scoffs at God and holy things. This downhill slide begins with "the counsel of the wicked," or ungodly thinking, digresses to "the way of sinners," which is the perverted practice of ungodly beliefs, and arrives at "the seat of mockers," or aligning oneself with the company of those who scoff at God.

C. Meditates (1:2)

See "Deeper Discoveries," 63:6.

D. Chaff (1:4)

This word pictures a threshing floor at the time of the grain harvest. The threshing floors of Palestine were on hills that received the best breezes. The grain would be gathered and brought up to the elevated place of the threshing floor and crushed by animals pulling heavy instruments over it. Then the ground grain would be pitched high in the air, and the wind would blow the chaff, consisting of husks and broken straw, leaving the heavier grain to fall back to the threshing floor. The worthless chaff was gathered and burned, so it would not be blown back into the grain (Job 21:18; Ps. 35:5; Isa. 17:13; 29:5; 41:15; Hos. 13:3; Zeph. 2:2). The wicked and evildoers will face God's judgment (Isa. 33:11; Matt. 3:12).

E. Perish (1:6)

This word (Heb. *abad*) means "to die" or "to undergo destruction." Among the various words which speak of destruction, *abad* is the most important. It is used to describe the loss of strength and knowledge, the decline of nations (Exod. 10:7; Num. 21:29–30), and is even applied to the destruction of pagan idols, images, and temples (Num. 33:52; Deut. 12:2–3). When used of people, the word generally refers to death and the cessation of life (Deut. 4:26; 11:4; Num. 16:33; Lev. 26:38; Josh. 23:16). Yet *abad* was also used of the eternal destruction of the wicked beyond physical death (Pss. 49:10,12,20; 73:27; 83:17; Prov. 10:28; 11:7; Ezek. 28:16). When used of destruction after death, *abad* was never used of a destruction that led into complete annihilation. Rather, it spoke of an unending, eternal destruction of the wicked that would never cease.

VII. TEACHING OUTLINE

A. The Way of the Godly (1–3)
  1. He is satisfied in the Lord (1a)
    a. Favored by God (1a)
    b. Fulfilled in God (1a)
  2. He is separated from the world (1b,c,d)
    a. Refusing secular beliefs (1b)
    b. Refusing sensual behavior (1c)
    c. Refusing shameful belongings (1d)
  3. He is saturated with the Word (2–3)
    a. Delighting in the Word (2a)
    b. Dwelling upon the Word (2b)
    c. Digging into the Word (3a)
    d. Drawing from the Word (3b-e)
      (1) Stability (3b)
      (2) Productivity (3c)
      (3) Constancy (3d)
      (4) Prosperity (3e)
B. The Way of the Ungodly (4–6)
  1. He is corrupted internally (4)
    a. The wicked are useless, life chaff (4a)
    b. The wicked are unstable, life chaff (4b)

2. He is condemned judicially (5)
   a. He will not stand in the judgment (5a)
   b. He will not stand with the righteous (5b)
3. He is damned eternally (6)
   a. The righteous will prosper (6a)
   b. The wicked will perish (6b)

VIII. ISSUES FOR DISCUSSION

1. How might I be in danger of walking in the counsel of the wicked?
2. In what ways might I be standing in the way of sinners?
3. Do I find myself reading and delighting in God's Word?
4. What fruit is God bearing in my life from the study of his Word?

Psalm 2
The Invincible Kingdom

Psalm 2

I. INTRODUCTION

Then Pull Down the Stars!

In the turbulent days of the French Revolution, a political revolutionary stormed the Bastille in Paris, seeking to remove every vestige of law and order from the eyes of his countrymen. He scaled the Cathedral of Notre Dame and tore down the cross from atop its spire, dashing it into pieces on the ground below. The cross, representing the authority of God, lay demolished on the ground for everyone to see. Turning to a poor peasant, the revolter boasted, "We are going to pull down all that reminds you of God!" But from the crowd came the challenging reply, "Citizen, then you might as well pull down the stars themselves!"

Such is impossible, and so are the arrogant attempts of sinful man to overthrow the sovereign rule of God. This cosmic revolt is as old as the garden of Eden when the first man, Adam, rose up against the supreme authority of God. Since then, the human race has gained momentum in its conspiracy to revolt against God. But no matter how determined and imaginative the apostasy of depraved humanity may be, it can never succeed in tearing down the authority of God. There are isolated times when this cosmic rebellion is more intense than at other times, but through it all, the puny efforts of man can never thwart the sovereign will of God.

Psalm 2 portrays this ongoing rebellion of a lost world against God and his Son. Although this second psalm has no title, Peter and John ascribed its authorship to David (Acts 4:25). According to the New Testament, it looks ahead to a future time in which the promised Messiah, the Lord Jesus Christ, will appear on the stage of human history (Acts 4:25–26; 13:33; Heb. 1:5; 5:5; Rev. 2:26–27; 12:5; 19:15). The world's rebellion against God is, in reality, a revolt against the reign of God's Son over all the earth. But all such attempts will falter and fail. All unbelievers are called upon by the Lord to bow before the Son before it is too late.

II. COMMENTARY

The Invincible Kingdom

MAIN IDEA: *In spite of the repeated attempts of man to resist God's kingdom, the Lord has established his Son as Lord over all and invites sinners to come and embrace him now before his wrath is unleashed.*

A The Insurrection Against God (2:1–3)

SUPPORTING IDEA: *The human race is united in its rebellion against God's rule, a revolt that was climaxed at the first coming of Jesus Christ.*

2:1. The first voice to be heard in this human drama is lost mankind crying out in defiance against God. Expressing his absolute amazement that the nations are seeking to overthrow the Lord, the psalmist asked, **Why do the nations conspire and the peoples plot in vain?** The conspiracy addressed was a global rebellion against God and his Anointed (v. 3). Such a plan was **vain**, meaning empty and destined to fail.

2:2. Leading this resistance against God were the political and national leaders of the world. **The kings of the earth take their stand and the rulers gather together**. The annals of human history have proven this to be true as the mighty world rulers—Nimrod, Pharaoh, Nebuchadnezzar, Antiochus Epiphanes, and countless others—have resisted God. This rebellion was demonstrated in Christ's arrest, trials, and condemnation at the hands of Annas, Caiaphas, Pilate, and Herod (Matt. 26:47–27:26; Mark 14:53–15:15; Luke 22:54–23:25; John 18:12–19:16). Ultimately, this riotous rebellion will come together again in the last days when the kings of the earth will stand **against the LORD** (Rev. 13:1–18; 17:8–18) and his Anointed One who is God's Son (v. 7), the Lord Jesus Christ.

2:3. The defiant voice of sinners declared, "**Let us break their chains . . . and throw off their fetters.**" Represented here as speaking with one voice, these rebels expressed their desire to be free of control by God. This is the heart of sin: a repudiation of God's rule in favor of one's own will which says, "We will not have this man to reign over us" (Luke 19:14 KJV). This is precisely how the rest of the Bible portrays the human race (Ps. 14:1–3; cp. Rom. 3:10–12), as totally depraved by the effects of original sin.

B The Indignation of God (2:4–6)

SUPPORTING IDEA: *In spite of man's sinful revolt against heaven, God remains the unrivaled sovereign Lord; he laughs at man's feeble attempts to thwart his eternal purposes.*

2:4. In response to man's arrogant boastings, **the One enthroned in heaven**, God the Father, merely **laughs**. This is not the laughter of hilarity but of divine derision, mockery, and contempt. Men are boldly shaking their fists against heaven, but such an attempted takeover is so bizarre, even insane, that **the Lord scoffs at them**, ridiculing and mocking their puny efforts.

2:5. But the divine laughter turns to fury. **Then he rebukes them in his anger** because his absolute holiness moves him to judge sinners. As the Lord speaks, he **terrifies them in his wrath**, speaking words of burning indignation. Lest we forget, God hates (rejects) all who commit sin (Ps. 5:5) and is angry with the wicked every day (Ps. 7:11).

2:6. In response to man's insane attempts to overturn God's eternal plans, the Lord thundered from heaven, "**I have installed my King on Zion, my holy hill.**" This confident statement expresses his unrelenting resolution to enthrone his chosen king, his own Son, upon Zion—a clear reference to the holy city Jerusalem (both the earthly and heavenly Jerusalem). Within Zion is his holy hill, a specific location that refers to the earthly temple area in Jerusalem, as well as to the elevated throne room in heaven. This declaration speaks first to the present enthronement of Christ at the right hand of God, following his ascension, bestowing upon him the place of highest privilege and authority (Ps. 110:1–2; Acts 2:34–35). Ultimately, these words anticipate the return of Christ to earth and his glorious enthronement during his one-thousand-year reign from Jerusalem (Rev. 20:1–10).

C The Intention of God (2:7–9)

SUPPORTING IDEA: *What God has decreed, his Son the Messiah will execute, leading to his Father's bestowal of a universal inheritance upon him.*

2:7. As the third stanza now begins, the speaker shifts again. This time, the voice of God's Son, Jesus Christ, is heard uttering, **I will proclaim the decree of the LORD**. All that the Father has planned and purposed in eternity past, the Son will proclaim and perform within time and history. In this eternal counsel, the Father spoke to the Son, **You are my Son; today I have become your Father**. This passage does not suggest that the second member of the Godhead, Jesus Christ, is a created being; this statement points to his incarnation (Heb. 1:5–6) and resurrection (Acts 13:33–34).

2:8. The fulfillment of this divine decree occurred in Christ's incarnation and became the basis on which the Father said to the Son, **Ask of me, and I will make the nations your inheritance**. Because of Christ's submission to the Father's will, God will bestow a rich legacy upon his Son—a vast inheritance that is now being progressively realized and will be fully transferred to him during the millennial kingdom.

The Father will give the Son **the ends of the earth** as his inheritance (Rev. 11:15). From among the nations, a large host of people previously given to him by the Father in eternity past (John 6:37,39; 17:2,24) will come to Christ and become his own possession.

2:9. Once enthroned at the Father's right hand, the Son is promised, **You will rule them with an iron scepter**. So supreme will be the Son's reign over his enemies that the execution of his final judgment is compared to a potter who will take an **iron scepter** and **dash them to pieces like pottery** (cp. Rev. 19:15). He will consign them to his relentless wrath in hell forever.

D The Invitation of God (2:10–12)

SUPPORTING IDEA: *All sinners are warned to give up their rebellion and to humble themselves in submission to the Son and to embrace him before it is too late.*

2:10. The identity of this speaker is not revealed; it is probably the voice of the Holy Spirit entreating through the psalmist. The invitation goes out, **Therefore, you kings, be wise; be warned, you rulers of the earth.** Those involved in this revolt against God must think carefully and cease from their long war with heaven.

2:11. Instead of resisting God, sinners must turn around and **serve the LORD with fear.** They must realign themselves with God. No longer should they serve themselves, but they should yield their service to God. This involves a changed heart that is filled with the fear of awe and reverence for God. Furthermore, they must **rejoice with trembling**, finding their greatest pleasure in God and submitting their deepest reverence to him.

2:12. Sinners must **kiss the Son**, a sign of humble submission to his sovereignty as a subject who lowers himself before his king (1 Sam. 10:1; 1 Kgs. 19:18). Loving devotion and loyal allegiance to Christ are required, **lest he be angry and you be destroyed in your way.** The choice is clear. It is better to bend than be broken. God urgently calls sinners to pay homage to the Son, **for his wrath can flare up in a moment.** While there is an opportunity to do so, sinners must turn from their wicked ways and embrace the Son by faith.

What will happen if they do? About all who submit to the Son, it can be said, **Blessed are all who take refuge in him**. To take refuge in the Lord is synonymous with having saving faith (John 5:24; Eph. 2:8–9). Sinners must kiss the Son today while God is speaking in grace; one day, he will speak in wrath.

> **MAIN IDEA REVIEW:** *In spite of the repeated attempts of man to resist God's kingdom, the Lord has established his Son as Lord over all and invites sinners to come and embrace him now before his wrath is unleashed.*

III. CONCLUSION

A Coffin for Your Empire

Ascending to the throne as Caesar of Rome in A.D. 360, Flavius Claudius Julianus reinstated pagan worship which had been abolished under the rule of Constantine. With diabolical fury this ruler opposed the followers of Christ whom he viewed as "powerful enemies of our gods." With fanatical resolve he sought to remove Christianity from the face of the earth. History records that Julianus did persecute many Christians and took the lives of many who stood for their faith in Christ.

In an attempt to entertain some friends, Julian taunted one believer named Agaton. With so many Christians being put to death, the emperor asked him, "How is your carpenter of Nazareth? Is he finding work these days?"

Without hesitation Agaton replied, "He is perhaps taking time away from building mansions for the faithful to build a coffin for your Empire."

Agaton was right. Centuries have passed; the Roman Empire has risen and fallen, but only one kingdom has withstood the test of time—the kingdom of God. The Son of God still takes time away from building his mansions to build coffins for those who reject his truth. Such rebellion by Julianus represents the pathetic attempts of sinful man to revolt against the authority of God and his Christ. But try as they may, mankind cannot overthrow God's eternal throne. His kingdom is invincible!

IV. LIFE APPLICATION

Kiss the Son

All unbelievers must give attention to the invitation offered by God in this pslam to come to Christ by faith. Such a step of commitment to believe upon God's Son involves acknowledging that one has been a part of sinful revolt against Almighty God. This confession of personal guilt is not a simple "owning up" to sin but a sober admission of one's sin and the wretchedness of those sins in the sight of a holy God. Then, with brokenness and godly sorrow, one must experience deep contrition for his sin. No one struts into the kingdom of God with his head held high. "God opposes the proud but gives grace to the humble" (1 Pet. 5:5).

Finally, this self-humiliation must lead a believer to embrace the Son of God by faith, or to "kiss the Son" (Ps. 2:12) in an act of homage and submission. The person who truly believes must shift his allegiance from self to Christ, submitting to him as king over all.

V. PRAYER

God, may those who read this psalm and remain in an unconverted state humble themselves this day and come to faith in the Lord's Anointed, Jesus Christ. May they surrender to you and accept your unconditional terms of peace before it is too late. May they grasp the seriousness of their rebellion against you and take refuge in your Son. May they believe and be saved. In Christ's name. Amen.

VI. DEEPER DISCOVERIES

A. Nations (2:1)

This word (Heb. *goy*) refers to a group of people which make up a tribe or nation. The word is often used of the non-Israelite, Gentile nations that surrounded the nation of Israel (Deut. 4:38; Josh. 23:13) which was defined by a political or territorial affiliation or by ethnicity. It was also used of Abraham's descendants, the nation of Israel (Gen. 12:2; 17:20). When used of other nations or groups of people, they were usually pagan and described as wicked (Deut. 9:4–5), without understanding (Deut. 32:21), detestable (Deut. 18:9; 1 Kgs. 14:24; 2 Kgs. 16:3; 2 Chr. 28:3), idolators (2 Kgs. 17:29), ruthless (Isa. 25:3), and uncircumcised (Jer. 9:26). The Lord scoffs at the nations (Ps. 59:8), yet it is the nations whom the promised Messiah would redeem (Isa. 2:2; 11:10; 42:6; 60:10).

B. Vain (2:1)

This word (Heb. *rig*) means "emptiness," "senseless," or "futility." It refers to the foolish plan of man to oppose God and to throw off his sovereign control. Such anarchy against God is insane and foolish.

C. The Anointed One (2:2)

The title "Anointed One" (Heb. *mashiah*) refers to any anointed king who was seated on the throne of David. Occurring about forty times in the Old Testament, it was used in reference to the office of the high priest (Lev. 4:3), kings (1 Sam. 24:6; Isa. 45:1), patriarchs (Ps. 105:15), and prophets (1 Kgs. 19:16). To be the Lord's anointed implied a special relationship with God, being chosen, consecrated, and commissioned by him for a special function or task. Nowhere is this demonstrated more clearly than when David stood before Samuel and the Lord said to Samuel, "Rise and anoint him; he is the one" (1 Sam. 16:12). It is from *mashiah* that the English word *Messiah* is derived.

But ultimately the title finds its fulfillment in the New Testament. In fact, "Christ" is the Greek equivalent of the Hebrew term *Messiah,* both meaning "the Anointed One." The psalmist's reference to the Anointed One goes beyond King David to the Lord Jesus, who is the Christ. The early church understood that this psalm was fulfilled by the Lord Jesus Christ (Acts 2:32; Heb. 1:5; 5:5).

D. Lord (2:4)

The word *Lord* (Heb. *adonay*) means "master" or "lord." *Adonay* signifies majesty or intensification and is always used of God. Found throughout the Hebrew Bible, in the Pentateuch it is used as a reverent way of addressing God (Exod. 4:10,13; Josh. 7:8). *Adonay* is prominent in the prophets and is used fifty-five times in the Psalms. Its use in certain passages, "Lord of all the earth" (Josh. 3:13; Ps. 97:5; Mic. 4:13), "Lord of lords" (Deut. 10:17), and the contexts of other passages alludes to the meaning of *adonay* as the sovereign Lord who has ultimate authority, power, and rule. It is used of the Messiah in Psalm 110:1.

E. Dash Them to Pieces (2:9)

This phrase or the word *break* (Heb. *raa*) means "to shatter into pieces" or "to be broken up" (Job. 34:24; Jer. 15:12). It is used of God afflicting judgment upon the righteous (Jer. 25:29; 31:28; Mic. 4:6; Zech. 8:14). Elihu used *raa* in a similar way to demonstrate the punishment of sinners by God (Job 34:24).

VII. TEACHING OUTLINE

A. The Insurrection Against God (1–3)
   1. Men are scheming vainly (1b)
   2. Men are standing defiantly (2)
   3. Men are speaking arrogantly (3)
      a. Let us break their chains (3a)
      b. Let us throw off their fetters (3b)
B. The Indignation of God (4–6)
   1. God scoffs in derision (4)
   2. God speaks in displeasure (5–6)
      a. He will terrify his adversaries (5)

      b. He will enthrone his anointed (6)
C. The Intention of God (7–9)
    1. My Son will rule the nations (7)
    2. My Son will inherit the nations (8)
    3. My Son will judge the nations (9)
       a. Breaking them with a rod (9a)
       b. Shattering them like pottery (9b)
D. The Invitation of God (10–12)
    1. Be wise (10a)
    2. Be warned (10b)
    3. Serve the Lord (11a)
    4. Rejoice with trembling (11b)
    5. Kiss the Son (12)
    6. Take refuge in him (12b)

VIII. ISSUES FOR DISCUSSION

1. How have I sought to resist God's rule over my life?
2. How should the sovereignty of God be a comfort to my heart as I live in a chaotic world?
3. Have I come to embrace God's Son?
4. To whom do I need to witness regarding the Messiah of God and the judgment he will bring?

Psalm 3

Triumphant Trust

I. INTRODUCTION

*E*very personal trial teaches believers to trust the Lord more fully. Even what others mean for evil, God intends for good. This was certainly the experience of the psalmist in Psalm 3, "a psalm of David." It is a hymn of individual lament, written to paint a clear picture of what triumphant faith looks like when it is tested in the fires of adversity. The superscription above this third psalm reveals that it was written when David "fled from his son Absalom" (2 Sam. 15–18).

Leading a political coup against his father, Absalom won over the hearts of many in the country, forcing David to flee from his palace. In the midst of this ordeal, surrounded by innumerable enemies, David called upon the Lord with absolute trust, believing that God would rescue him. This psalm clearly conveys that God is Lord over life, even in times of adversity. He always works for his glory and for the good of his people. Thus, Psalm 3 is a psalm of both lament and confidence.

II. COMMENTARY

MAIN IDEA: *In the midst of his trials, David turned to the Lord in absolute trust, knowing that faith in God leads to triumphant living.*

A David's Problems (3:1–2)

3:1. In one of the great trials of his life, the revolt of his son Absalom, David called out to God, **O LORD, how many are my foes!** The word *many* is repeated three times in verses 1–2 and represents the growing opposition against David that was led by Absalom and involved many enemies who were loyal to Absalom. What began as a secret, covert rebellion by David's son, Absalom, escalated into a full-blown, public revolt by many of Israel's citizens. During this time of international peace under David's reign (2 Sam. 7:1), his greatest danger came from *within* Israel, even from within his own household. **How many rise up against me!** Outnumbered, David found himself a part of a minority that seemed to be shrinking.

3:2. Quoting his oppressors, David lamented, **Many are saying of me, "God will not deliver him"** (cp. 2 Sam. 16:8). Their arrogant belittling of Israel's king implied that God had abandoned David. Worse, their taunting words attacked the honor of God himself because they claimed there was no salvation with God. A unique feature of this psalm is the threefold repetition of **selah** (vv. 2,4,8), a musical term that apparently indicated a pause, a crescendo, or an interlude, inviting the reader to stop and consider carefully the magnitude of what was being said.

B David's Protection (3:3–4)

3:3. In the crucible of this crisis, David made the right choice. Turning to the Lord, he boasted, **But you are a shield around me, O LORD.** Using the language of the battlefield, he asserted that God was his impenetrable defense. Many times in the past, David had used a shield in battle to turn away the deadly arrows, spears, and swords of his enemies. David exclaimed that this shield (Heb. *magen*, used in Ps. 5:12) is what God was to him—an unassailable protection in the midst of danger (cp. Pss. 7:10; 18:30; 28:7). Furthermore, he declared, **You bestow glory on me,** meaning that he trusted God to restore his crumbling life and grant deliverance in the midst of his humbling experience. Confidently, he claimed that the Lord would **lift up** his head with courage and peace that only God could provide (Ps. 9:13).

3:4. As a man after God's own heart, David affirmed, **To the LORD I cry aloud** (cp. 2 Sam. 15:30). This king looked to a greater king—heaven's sovereign Lord—and called upon him. With a decisive, resolute faith, he committed himself to the Lord, testifying, **He answers me from his holy hill**. The Lord's holy hill refers to the place of the Lord's sanctuary, Mount Zion, the temple mount in Jerusalem where David had brought the ark that represented the presence and power of God (cp. 2 Sam. 6). Ultimately, this refers to the heavenly throne room where God sits enthroned, presiding over his troubles. In marked contrast to his enemies' taunts, David knew that God heard and answered his plea for help from his throne room in heaven.

🄲 David's Peace (3:5–6)

3:5. Because he had committed his soul and this desperate situation to the Lord, David was at peace, confessing with confidence, **I lie down and sleep; I wake again, because the LORD sustains me**. Knowing that God was always awake to protect him, he slept the sleep of peace, able to awake refreshed. Left to his own strength, David would have tossed and turned through sleepless nights, agitated over his troubling circumstances. But because the Lord was his shield, quiet sleep was possible.

3:6. With a deep sense of security, David declared, **I will not fear the tens of thousands drawn up against me on every side**. Because a great multitude had followed Absalom in his revolt (2 Sam. 15:13; 17:11; 18:7), David was severely outnumbered (cp. "many," vv. 1–2), and he was joined by only a few loyal supporters. Nevertheless, David did not fear because he was fortified by the truth that God was his all-sufficient protector.

🄳 David's Petition (3:7–8)

3:7. David's heart cry was really a battle cry, a confident appeal to God to rally to his defense and defeat his enemies: **Arise, O LORD! Deliver me, O my God!** Likening his pursuers to wild animals, David called upon the Lord, **Strike all my enemies on the jaw; break the teeth of the wicked**. Motivated by righteous indignation and a zealous passion for God's glory, his prayer was an urgent plea for divine intervention (2 Sam. 15:31).

3:8. With a confident trust in the Lord, David confessed, **From the LORD comes deliverance**. This bold statement countered what his enemies were saying, but more than that David invoked God's blessing upon all who put their trust in him when he said, **May your blessing be on your people**. This request for deliverance was not only for himself but for the stability and greater good of the nation of Israel. As Israel's leader, God's rescue of him in this dark hour would result in divine blessing upon all the people.

III. CONCLUSION

In the midst of adversity, the believer should trust in God, knowing that deliverance comes from him. Even when a Christian suffers because of wrong choices in his past, God causes all things to work together for the good of those who love him (Rom. 8:28). In the torrent of life's storms, God speaks peace to troubled hearts and is able to calm the tempest. Whatever the trial, the righteous should lean upon the Lord, knowing he is a shield and strength to his people.

But when believers try to live in their own strength, they are easily defeated. The arm of the flesh can never save us from troubles. When the godly entrust themselves to God, however, he will empower them to stand strong in their troubles and deliver them to safety. In every trial and difficulty, believers need not fear. Instead, they should trust the Lord. Such faith, when tested and toughened in the flames of adversity, results in victory and deliverance.

IV. TEACHING OUTLINE

A. David's Problems (1–2)
  1. Many foes resist me (1)
  2. Many foes ridicule me (2)
B. David's Protection (3–4)
  1. God is my shield (3a)
  2. God is my sovereign (3b)
  3. God is my strength (3c)
  4. God is my savior (4)
C. David's Peace (5–6)
  1. God sustains me (5)
  2. God secures me (6)
D. David's Petition (7–8)
  1. Rise up, Lord (7a)
  2. Rescue me, God (7b,c,d)
  3. Restore us, Lord (8)

Psalm 4

Calm Assurance

"*T*he sovereignty of God is the pillow upon which the child of God rests His head at night, giving perfect peace."

C h a r l e s   H .   S p u r g e o n

I. INTRODUCTION

*L*ife should be lived with the assurance of God's sovereignty, knowing that he rules over everything for his glory. Even when it seems as if the ungodly have dominated the scene, believers should remember that God has chosen the godly for himself and will not forsake them. This is the central message of Psalm 4, a song that provides a Godward focus in the midst of life's storms.

Often called "the Evening Psalm," this "psalm of David" was a prayer of trust offered to God at the close of a long, trouble-filled day. Many interpreters believe that Psalms 3 and 4 once formed a single unit. The third psalm was a prayer expressed in the early morning (3:5), and the fourth psalm was to be offered up to God in the evening (4:8).

If this connection exists, the background of Psalm 4 is the same as Psalm 3—the revolt of Absalom against David (cp. 2 Sam. 15–18). The superscription reads, "For the director of music," a title directing the worship leader during the public worship service. As this psalm was sung, it was to be accompanied "with stringed instruments," the harp and lyre acting as an orchestra. This psalm expresses the psalmist's confidence in God during an hour of desperate need. The psalmist could rest secure because God reigned supreme.

II. COMMENTARY

> **MAIN IDEA:** *In the midst of persecution, David called upon God for relief, asking the Lord to bring repentance to his enemies and divine favor to his supporters.*

A David's Request (4:1)

4:1. In the midst of his painful ordeal, David called out to God, **Answer me when I call to you.** Passionately, David pleaded to be heard by his **righteous God.** David did not appeal to God on the basis of his own goodness or personal achievement but solely upon the Lord's perfect righteousness given to him by faith. He prayed, specifically, **Give me relief from my distress.**

The Hebrew word for *distress* means a "tight place"; the word for *relief* means an "open place." The psalmist had been encompassed on all sides by this trial, and he asked God to make a spacious place for him. **Be merciful to me**, he cried, **and hear my prayer.** Mercy is God's tender compassion demonstrated toward those who are afflicted, not according to what they deserve but according to what they need to survive this trial.

B David's Rebuke (4:2-3)

4:2. No longer addressing God, David spoke to his enemies, chiding them for their evil opposition against him. He rebuked them, **How long, O men, will you turn my glory into shame?** Confronting these adversaries, David challenged them by asking how much longer they would seek to destroy his glory, a reference to the success of his life lived for God. David asked, **How long will you love delusions**, pointing to their slanderous lies which they spoke to undermine his leadership. Likewise, how long would they **seek false gods**, referring to their wicked unbelief in the Lord. As a man after God's own heart, David opposed all that the Lord opposed.

4:3. As if speaking to his enemies directly, David prayed, **Know that the LORD has set apart the godly for himself.** Identifying himself as God's chosen servant, David challenged them. Why should they persist in their opposition against him whom God had chosen? To oppose David was to oppose God, who had sovereignly elected him and set him apart. Thus, he had deep assurance that the LORD would hear when he called to him. David knew he would be safe because the Lord would remember his servant and hear his plea.

C David's Rebuttal (4:4-5)

4:4. David also prayed for their change of heart, pleading, **In your anger do not sin.** Another translation has "tremble" (NASB). This was a direct appeal to God that his attackers would be made to fear the Lord which would, in turn, thwart their attempt to harm him. He added, **When you are on your beds, search your hearts and be silent**. In other words, they must be made by God to reconsider their personal attacks against him. At night, when their consciences had pondered their ways, the Lord would reveal their opposition to him as a treacherous sin.

4:5. Still as if addressing his enemies, David asked God to direct them to **offer right sacrifices and trust in the LORD**. They must abandon the hypocrisy of their empty worship and approach God with right sacrifices from a pure heart. David's enemies must cease their sinful opposition of him and worship God with the right sacrifices of a pure heart. Ultimately, only God could bring about such change in their hearts.

D David's Relief (4:6–8)

4:6. **Many** of those who were following David were **asking, "Who can show us any good?"** His followers were wanting to know that their now-deposed king would still lead them into a victorious future. The question among his followers was, "Will following David result in good?" In response to this uncertainty, David appealed to God, **Let the light of your face shine upon us, O LORD**. He called for God to bless his loyal supporters with the fullness of his grace. These words were drawn from the well-known benediction of Aaron (Num. 6:24–26). This was a request that the fullness of God's divine favor be directed toward them.

4:7. **You have filled my heart with greater joy** was the result of David's prayer. Before his prayer changed his circumstances, it had already changed him. His anxiety was transformed into assurance as he experienced more joy than **when their grain and new wine abound**. He found more joy in God than when a farmer enjoys a bountiful harvest—all because he put his trust in the Lord.

4:8. Finally, David testified, **I will lie down and sleep in peace**. Thus, he concluded, **for you alone, O LORD, make me dwell in safety**. Only God could cause his fearful heart to be calm and know genuine peace—a calm contentment in the fire of adversity.

III. CONCLUSION

No believer is immune from the trials and afflictions of life. In difficult times it is critical that we call upon God. Only he can deliver us out of our troubles. But too many Christians internalize their anxiety rather than rely upon God for relief and rescue. When deeply distressed, believers should pray to God, who is a very present help in time of trouble (Ps. 46:1–2). When Christians call upon God from a pure heart, they may have confidence that he hears them and will answer according to his perfect will.

Prayer is never an exercise in empty chatter, but it is the overflow of a living, dynamic relationship with the one true God who will hear in the day of trouble (Ps. 50:15). It is in the painful moments of life, when surrounded by mounting pressures, that God's people will find the comfort and consolation they need when they trust the Lord. The light of God's presence will shine upon them. He will bring a supernatural peace which will flood their hearts and souls with a calm assurance that transcends all human understanding (Phil. 4:7).

IV. TEACHING OUTLINE

A. David's Request (1)
  1. God, answer me! (1a)
  2. God, acquit me! (1b)
B. David's Rebuke (2–3)
  1. Men shame me (2)
  2. God sanctifies me (3)
C. David's Rebuttal (4–5)
  1. Search your hearts (4a,b,c)
  2. Silence your mouths (4d)
  3. Sacrifice your lives (5a)
  4. Submit your wills (5b)
D. David's Relief (6–8)
  1. Favor me with goodness (6)
  2. Fill me with joy (7)
  3. Flood me with peace (8)

Psalm 5

A God-Saturated Life

"*G*ive me 100 men; I care not whether they be clergy or laity, who fear nothing but sin and desire nothing but God, and I will shake this world for Christ."

John Wesley

I. INTRODUCTION

*W*ho is the person whom God uses? It is the one who lives a supremely God-saturated life, one who is fully devoted to God. This is the person whom the Lord uses—one who has a high view of God, one who is focused upon the holiness and sovereignty of God. He is a person who loves what God loves and hates what he hates, whose heart is one with God.

David, the author of Psalm 5, is a man who models for us a God-saturated life. In this psalm we catch a glimpse of what it means for a person to be dominated by a lofty, transcendent view of God and who, in turn, knew the fullness of his favor upon his life. Not a perfect man, David nevertheless was a passionate man who sought God's heart. In this psalm, an individual lament psalm, the distinguishing marks of the person whom God uses are revealed. A psalm of David, written when he was surrounded by many foes (vv. 5,6,8), the superscription of this psalm reads, "For the director of music. For flutes," meaning this particular psalm was to be sung in congregational worship with flute accompaniment. Here David proves to be a worthy model for believers today of a life totally abandoned to God.

II. COMMENTARY

> **MAIN IDEA:** *The person whom God uses lives with a high view of God.*

A David's Contrition (5:1–3)

5:1–2. With a passionate appeal David began this psalm by pleading, **Listen to my cry for help, my King and my God**. Intense emotion and energy poured out of David's heart in his relationship toward God as he pleaded with the Lord for a hearing. **Consider my sighing** reveals his strong devotion to and hunger for God. As the anointed king of Israel, David understood that God is king over all.

5:3. David's heart was eager and persistent as he rose early in the morning to pray. Before David could begin the day, he had to converse with God. He declared, **In the morning I lay my requests before you**. Seeking God in the early part of the day reveals an energetic heart that was aggressively pursuing the Lord. As he prayed, he waited **in expectation**, believing that God would answer him (Jas. 1:6) according to his perfect timing and will.

B David's Conviction (5:4–6)

5:4. Every person whom God uses is gripped with a high view of God in his holiness. Consider the examples of Moses (Exod. 3), Isaiah (Isa. 6), Peter (Luke 5), and John (Rev. 1). So it was with David. He wrote, **You are not a God who takes pleasure in evil**. David understood God to be infinitely holy, and he could not approve of, tolerate, or fellowship with sin. The prophet Habakkuk affirmed, "Your eyes are too pure to look on evil" (Hab. 1:13; 1 John 1:5).

5:5. Since he is perfectly holy, God must reject all sin and sinners. David declared, **The arrogant cannot stand in your presence**. Literally, the proud could not stand "before your eyes," meaning no sin would go undetected by God's searching eyes. Therefore, David said, God hates **all who do wrong**. Simply put, God rejects all who reject him. This is a Hebraism that contrasts love and hate which communicates acceptance and rejection (cp. Luke 14:26; Rom. 9:13).

5:6. This holy God must also judge sinners as an expression of his holiness. Confidently, David stated, **You destroy those who tells lies**. The reference is to David's enemies who were lying about him and slandering his character. They would be confronted by God in the final judgment because the Lord detests people who are **bloodthirsty and deceitful**.

C David's Consecration (5:7–8)

5:7. Sinners may find acceptance with God if they will come to him as David did. He wrote, **I, by your great mercy, will come into your house**. This great mercy is God's unconditional covenant love by which he receives sinners who repent and believe. Knowing how unworthy he was, David wrote, **In reverence will I bow down toward your holy temple**. Not claiming any self-righteousness, he trembled because he recognized that he approached God solely on the basis of God's grace.

5:8. Then David petitioned God, submitting to his will, by saying, **Lead me, O LORD, in your righteousness**. This was a prayer in which he sought divine guidance into God's will. The Lord will never lead people into sin but only down paths of righteousness. David asked that the way of God's guidance would be level and smooth, free from temptations and obstacles of sin: **Make straight your way before me**.

D David's Condemnation (5:9–10)

5:9. David realized that **not a word** from the mouth of his enemies could **be trusted**. They spoke destructive, slanderous lies about him, rallying others against him by twisting the truth. Their mouths were wicked because their hearts were **filled with destruction**. Jesus said that a destructive tongue speaks from a destructive heart (Matt. 12:35–37; 15:18–19). Even worse, **their throat is an open grave; with their tongue they speak deceit**. Persecution for the sake of righteousness is often suffered by the godly from the vicious attacks of the ungodly (Matt. 5:10–12; John 15:18–20; Col. 1:24).

5:10. With a burst of holy indignation, David called out, **Declare them guilty, O God! Let their intrigues be their downfall**. Far from a merely selfish request, this prayer was spoken with holy zeal. He wanted God to make right the wrongs he had suffered. Thus, David appealed, **Banish them for their many sins, for they have rebelled against you**. The driving issue in David's heart was not his enemies' opposition against him, but their rebellion against God.

E David's Celebration (5:11–12)

5:11. David's high view of God led him to high praise for the Lord. He concluded this psalm by calling on all the righteous to be glad in the Lord. He overflowed with excitement in God: **But let all who take refuge in you be glad; let them ever sing for joy**. The heart that loves God's holiness will hate man's sin and, thus, **be glad** and full of **joy**.

On behalf of those who supported him, David asked the Lord, **Spread your protection over them**. Like a mother eagle would spread her wings of protection over her young, David called for God's protecting love to be shown toward all who had stood with him during this turbulent time. To love God's **name** is to love the fullness of all he is. Those who truly know him **love** him and **rejoice** in him with hearts that overflow with wonder and praise.

5:12. David concluded by affirming the supreme goodness of the Lord toward all his saints: O LORD, **you bless the righteous.** He had every reason to rejoice in the Lord, no matter how fiery his trials had been. Addressing God, he declared, **You surround them with your favor as with a shield.** God's protective care not only overshadows his people, but he also surrounds them with his favor so they are safe from the enemy. This divine blessing is like a shield, forming an impenetrable wall around his godly ones.

III. CONCLUSION

Anyone who is to be used by God will be consumed with a holy passion for God. It is in being overshadowed by the greatness of God that a person feels his own helplessness and inadequacies. This drives him to seek God with desperate urgency and total abandonment. As long as a person thinks he can succeed by his own efforts, he will never pursue God with deep desperation. Only in our weakness will God's strength be made full in us.

Everything in life must be viewed from the perspective of the high and lofty character of God. Even when circumstances are threatening, the "uplook" of faith always remains triumphant. Such is the experience of a God-saturated life.

IV. TEACHING OUTLINE

A. David's Contrition (1–3)
1. Consider my sighing (1)
2. Listen to my crying (2)
3. Hear my speaking (3)

B. David's Conviction (4–6)
1. God rejects the wicked (4)
2. God refuses the arrogant (5)
3. God resists the deceitful (6)

C. David's Consecration (7–8)
1. I will fear God (7)
2. I will follow God (8)

D. David's Condemnation (9–10)
1. My enemies are godless (9)
2. My enemies are guilty (10)

E. David's Celebration (11–12)
1. Let the godly resound (11a)
2. Let the godly rejoice (11b–12)

Psalm 6
The Conquering Power of Confessing Sin

"*A* great part of our worthiness lies in an acknowledgment of our own unworthiness."

M a t t h e w   H e n r y

I. INTRODUCTION

*H*oliness is the chief attribute of God. The angelic host surrounding God have no trouble recognizing this truth as they cry out, "Holy, holy, holy is the LORD Almighty" (Isa. 6:3). In the same way, what God desires in the believer's life, more than anything else, is personal holiness. God says to his people, "Be holy, because I am holy" (Lev. 11:44–45; 19:2; 20:7; 1 Pet. 1:16). This call for holiness requires that the believer live a pure and separated life, rooted and grounded in God's Word (Ps. 1:1–3).

But what happens when a believer falls into sin? When he fails to acknowledge and confess his sin, God will apply his chastening rod to restore him to holiness (Heb. 12:3–11). This is the message of Psalm 6, a penetrating insight into the life of David. During an unspecified time of his life, he persisted without acknowledging his sin to God. The consequences of unconfessed sin in his life were devastating. This "psalm of David" does not record the actual confession of his sin, but it is a reality to be understood.

Psalm 6 was "for the director of music" and was to be played "with stringed instruments." The word *sheminith* occurs in Psalm 12 and 1 Chronicles 15:21. It may have referred to an eight-string instrument. This psalm is classified as a penitential psalm, one in which the psalmist turns to God for forgiveness. This is the first such psalm in the Book of Psalms (cp. Pss. 32; 38; 51; 102; 130; 143).

II. COMMENTARY

MAIN IDEA: *Unconfessed sin in David's life was painful and costly, but by acknowledging it to God, he found a renewed confidence in the Lord.*

A The Problem of Unconfessed Sin (6:1–7)

6:1. David knew he had lost favor with God: O LORD, **do not rebuke me in your anger**. He was painfully aware that he was under God's **rebuke, anger,** and **wrath,** which in reality was the Lord's loving **discipline** for unconfessed sin in his life. He was aware that God was displeased with him. David appealed to God to lighten the discipline.

6:2. Crying out for relief from God's painful discipline, David yearned, **Be merciful to me,** LORD, **for I am faint**. He was so physically weak that he was faint, suffering loss of energy, drive, and ambition. Knowing that he deserved what he was receiving from God, David asked for mercy, not justice. He asked for the undeserved relief and tender compassion of the Lord in the midst of his misery: **Heal me, for my bones are in agony**. The word *bones* was a poetic way of describing his inner turmoil.

6:3. Having forfeited inward peace, David mourned, **My soul is in anguish**. His soul, representing his entire inner being, was downcast, discouraged, and in deep dismay. With a heavy heart aching for relief, he cried out, **How long, O** LORD, **how long?** This time of anguish had existed for a long time. The question **how long?** appears sixteen times in the Psalms, and it always expresses the anguish of a weary soul seeking comfort from God.

6:4. Sensing that his once-close intimacy with God had been forfeited, David prayed, **Turn, O** LORD, **and deliver me**. The closeness of their relationship had been breached because of his unconfessed sin. He felt estranged from God, as if the Lord had turned his back on him and hidden his face. This had resulted in a loss of sweet fellowship between himself and the Lord.

Praying for deliverance from his ordeal, David asked the Lord, **Save me because of your unfailing love**. This salvation was God's deliverance from his present discipline. David wanted the Lord to set him free from his physical, emotional, and spiritual pain in accordance with his loyal, unconditional love.

6:5. If God did not deliver him from this time of punishment, David knew he would soon die. Realizing he was in danger of losing his life, David reasoned with God, **No one remembers you when he is dead. Who praises you from the grave?** In other words, he explained to God that he could not offer him public praise or service if he suffered the loss of his life. David knew that a believer who persists in unconfessed sin may be subject to a premature death (Acts 5:1–11; Jas. 5:20; 1 John 5:17).

6:6–7. Drowning in grief, David suffered from sleeplessness, tossing and turning in his bed. He declared to the Lord, **I am worn out from groaning; all night long I flood my bed with weeping and drench my couch with tears.** Having shed many tears, David cried out, **My eyes grow weak with sorrow.** His eyes were so swollen that they could not be closed in sleep. Throughout the night he thought about his **foes,** who were God's instruments of discipline.

B The Power of Confessed Sin (6:8–10)

6:8. Turning to his adversaries, who had been taunting him, David commanded them, **Away from me, all you who do evil.** Suddenly he was as bold as a lion, rebuking those who had threatened his life. Why the dramatic change? David explained it was because **the LORD** had heard his **weeping.** This weeping surely involved the confession of his sin, now acknowledged to God with godly sorrow.

David, the man after God's own heart, had sought forgiveness with the weeping of a broken heart. With remorse over his sins, he had been forgiven and had been given a new, holy boldness. Although it is not directly stated, this confession of sin is clearly implied by the words **the LORD has heard.**

6:9. With deep, inner assurance toward God, David boasted, **The LORD has heard my cry for mercy; the LORD accepts my prayer.** The reason David was suddenly bold before God is because he was newly right before God. This confidence was based upon his assurance that God had heard his cry for mercy, which was a prayer of confession of sin leading to forgiveness.

6:10. How the situation had changed! With renewed faith, David prayed, **All my enemies will be ashamed and dismayed.** Why? Because he had confessed his sin, David believed that God would intervene on his behalf and scatter his enemies. When the Lord acted, they would **turn back in sudden disgrace.** The dismay he had felt was now reversed, and his foes would be turned back in defeat. These enemies whom God had used to discipline David would surely be defeated by the Lord because David had confessed his sin.

III. CONCLUSION

Essential to every healthy Christian life is the spiritual discipline of confessing one's sin to God. Confession begins with the heart attitude in which a person is sensitive to the convicting ministry of the Holy Spirit. It is the Spirit's work to point out specific areas of a believer's life that are entangled in sin. Then, once convinced, the believer must acknowledge his sin to God, naming the offenses to the Lord (1 John 1:9).

Sin does not break a Christian's relationship with God. That is, when a Christian sins, he is still a Christian. But known sin does break fellowship with God. Scripture indicates that God is displeased when we do not repent of known sin. He may discipline us to bring us to repentance, just as a loving parent disciplines his child (Heb. 12:5–11).

The believer must deal honestly with God, openly confessing the sin, never minimizing or excusing the offense. A Christian should never go for long periods of time with unconfessed sin in his life (Eph. 4:26–27). He should keep short accounts with God, regularly acknowledging his iniquity to him and seeking his forgiveness. A believer must turn from his sin and pursue the path of obedience (Prov. 28:13).

God delights in forgiving his children for their sin. Just as it is man's nature to sin, so it is God's nature to forgive those who repent. Therefore, the people of God should be confident when they confess their sin, knowing they will find acceptance and pardon with the Lord and a restoration of fellowship.

IV. TEACHING OUTLINE

A. The Problem of Unconfessed Sin (1–6)
   1. Loss of divine pleasure (1)
      a. Do not rebuke me in anger (1a)
      b. Do not discipline me in wrath (1b)
   2. Loss of physical strength (2)
      a. Restore my strength (2a)
      b. Heal my bones (2b)
   3. Loss of emotional peace (3)
      a. My soul is anguished (3a)
      b. My soul is impatient (3b)
   4. Loss of spiritual intimacy (4)
      a. Turn to me (4a)
      b. Save me (4b)
   5. Loss of physical life (5)
      a. Deliver me from death (5a)
      b. Deliver me from the grave (5b)
   6. Loss of physical sleep (6-7)
      a. I groan all night (6a)
      b. I grow weary (6b)
B. The Power of Confessed Sin (8–10)
   1. Confidence toward men (8)
   2. Confidence toward god (9–10)
      a. The Lord accepts my prayer (9)
      b. The Lord attacks my enemies (10)

Psalm 7

A Heart Cry for Justice

"*The* Lord has a golden scepter and an iron rod. Those who will not bow to the one shall be broken by the other."

Thomas Watson

I. INTRODUCTION

*B*elievers are often called upon to suffer unjustly at the hands of evil people through no sin of their own. During such times of injustice, the righteous should call upon God to prevail on their behalf, leaving it with him to make right the wrongs. Psalm 7 is the record of such a time for David—an incident in which he had suffered wrongly at the hands of ruthless enemies. An individual lament as well as a fiery imprecation, this psalm invokes God's wrath and judgment upon David's threatening foes.

God is a righteous judge who will defend his people when they are attacked. The Lord will execute perfect justice against evil people who persecute the godly, whether it be in this life or in the final judgment.

This psalm is entitled a *shiggaion*, which may mean a poem written with intense emotion. It was written by David, Israel's king, and sung to the Lord in the form of a vocal solo. Regarding its background, it is concerning the words of "Cush, a Benjamite," a man mentioned only here in the Bible. He was probably one of Saul's henchmen sent to kill David. In this turbulent time of trouble, David found comfort in God's justice that would lead him to judge David's enemies.

II. COMMENTARY

> **MAIN IDEA:** *When David was persecuted and attacked, he was motivated to examine his life for sin, after which he called upon God to deliver him.*

A Save Me! (7:1–2)

7:1. In the midst of his distress, David called upon the Lord: **O LORD my God, I take refuge in you.** He placed himself in God's hands, since God was his stronghold of protection, his first line of defense. He cried out to God, **Save and deliver me from all who pursue,** knowing that his foes were threatening to do him great harm. God alone had the ability to save him.

7:2. Describing his fiery ordeal, David explained, **They will tear me like a lion and rip me to pieces.** If God did not **rescue** him, there would be no deliverance from this attack. Both "deliver" (v. 1) and "rescue" (v. 2) are from the same Hebrew verb, *natsal.* It conveys the idea of being removed from imminent danger and harm (for more on *natsal,* see "Deeper Discoveries," 34:4).

B Search Me! (7:3–5)

7:3–4. Searching his own heart, David prayed, **If . . . there is guilt on my hands.** He was referring to the sins of which he was being accused by his enemies. This guilt was a stain that would hinder his life if he had committed the charged offense. David continued, **If I have done evil to him who is at peace with me or without cause have robbed my foe.** From this, proceeds a general idea of the slanderous charges being brought against the character of David. He was being falsely accused of stealing from innocent people.

7:5. If their character assault was true, David reasoned, then may God's discipline come upon him: **Let my enemy pursue and overtake me.** He was not claiming sinlessness but blamelessness, stating to God that he was "not guilty" as charged by his accusers. If the accusations were true, then let David's chief rival **trample** his **life to the ground** and make him **sleep in the dust.** In other words, if the slanderous charges were true, David was willing for his enemies to succeed in their personal attack, even to the point of taking his life. But it was not true, he maintained. He was innocent.

C Support Me! (7:6–9)

7:6. Having affirmed his blamelessness, David appealed, **Arise, O LORD, in your anger; rise up against the rage of my enemies.** He called upon God who seemed to be unconcerned about this matter to rally to his defense. He cried, **Awake, my God; decree justice**, urging the Lord to carry out justice by punishing evil and defending good.

7:7–8. Picturing a public judgment scene, David pleaded, **Let the assembled peoples gather around you**. Then he implored the judge of heaven and earth to **rule over them from on high**. He was content to rest in God's verdict. Speaking to his own heart, he affirmed, **Let the LORD judge the peoples**, believing God's judgment would be fair and accurate. In a final examination of his own life, David put his own conscience under the scrutiny of God: **Judge me . . . according to my righteousness**. Such an unconditional acceptance of God's verdict initiated this second searching of David's heart.

7:9. By addressing God as **O righteous God, who searches minds and hearts**, David knew the Lord would judge rightly. David's call for justice was, **Bring to an end the violence of the wicked and make the righteous secure**, or in other words, punish evil (his enemies) and protect good (himself). He knew God would confirm his righteousness before his opponents.

Ⅾ Shield Me! (7:10–17)

7:10–11. Shifting to a battle motif, David described God as a victorious warrior. The Lord would deflect all fiery darts of false accusation hurled against him. He would protect his servants who were **upright in heart**. This **righteous judge** was not just sitting in a courtroom setting, but he was handing down the verdicts of his court. Not waiting until the final judgment, he was expressing **his wrath every day**.

7:12–13. In this display of vengeance, God would not **relent** or be turned back from pursuing wrath, but he sharpened his **sword**, and readied his **bow** with **flaming arrows**. All his deadly weapons were prepared, poised, and pointed at the enemies of his chosen ones. God is in a constant state of war against his enemies.

7:14–16. David next profiled the enemy who was the object of God's deadly aim. Pictured as a pregnant woman, the enemy conceived much **evil** and **trouble**, but this would lead to his own disillusionment. He would dig a hole intending to capture a wild animal, only to fall into it to his own destruction. Whatever evil action he took, it would recoil on himself.

7:17. In response to God's strong defense of the godly, David determined that he would **give thanks to the LORD** because his righteousness was judging his enemies and defending his innocence. God, not his enemies, would issue the verdict on his life. Therefore, David would **sing praise** to the Lord.

Notice that David referred to **the LORD Most High**, which in the Hebrew language is *Jehovah Elyon*. Jehovah, the God of covenant (see "Deeper Discoveries," 8:1), is also Elyon, the God of universal rule and control. The name *Elyon* (Most High) occurs thirty-six times in the Bible, here for the first time in the Psalms. The divine name emphasizes the sovereignty of God as the one who is in control.

III. CONCLUSION

Believers will often be unfairly criticized and even attacked by coworkers, family members, and friends for their Christian faith. How should they respond when under assault? In such tribulations, Christians should run to God who is their only safe fortress. They should take refuge in him who is their rock. He alone can deliver them from their adversaries.

When accused, the righteous must search their own hearts to determine if the charges are true. If there is merit in the accusations, repentance must occur. Nothing would be worse than defending oneself if the accusation has validity. But if the attack is unfounded and is for the sake of righteousness, one must leave this matter with the Lord. He is the righteous judge who will bring his justice to bear on behalf of his people.

Believers must not retaliate against their foes, but they should leave wrath with the Lord. God, the Christian's shield and Savior, is worthy to be praised because he deflects the enemy's arrows and protects his people.

IV. TEACHING OUTLINE

A. Save Me! (1–2)
  1. From my enemies (1)
  2. From all evil (2)
B. Search Me! (3–5)
  1. I invite your examination (3–4)
  2. I invite your correction (5)
C. Support Me! (6–9)
  1. Arise in your anger (6a)
  2. Attack my adversaries (6b–7)
  3. Arraign the peoples (7–8)
  4. Abolish the wicked (9a–b)
  5. Affirm the righteous (9c)
D. Shield Me! (10–17)
  1. With God's defense (10–11)
  2. With God's sword (12a)
  3. With God's bow (12b)
  4. With God's arrows (13)
  5. With God's enemies (14–16)
  6. With God's victory (17)

Psalm 8
Only God Is Great!

"*D*ivine sovereignty simply means that God is God."

A . W . P i n k

I. INTRODUCTION

The Great Monarch

*A*scending to the throne of France at age four to rule for the next seventy-two years, Louis XIV enjoyed the longest reign in modern European history. Intoxicated with his own power, this self-consumed emperor called himself the "Great Monarch" and declared, "I am the State!" But in 1715, King Louis XIV, like all other rulers, abdicated his throne to death.

His funeral, just as he had prescribed, was nothing short of spectacular as the great cathedral was packed with mourners to pay final tribute to their king in his solid gold coffin. To dramatize the deceased ruler's greatness, a solitary candle burned above his jewel-laden casket. Thousands waited in hushed silence, gazing at the solitary flame.

At the appointed time the funeral service began. Bishop Massillon, who presided over the state funeral, stood to address the mourners, which included the assembled clergy of France. When the bishop rose, he did something that stunned the nation. Bending down from the pulpit, he extinguished the lone candle that represented the greatness of Louis XIV. The people gasped. Then from the darkness echoed four gripping words, "Only God is great!"

Regardless of man's inflated view of himself, God alone is truly great. Not only is he the Creator of all; the Lord is the sustainer of all and thus sovereign over all. God, not man, is great, so he alone is to be praised. Psalm 8 is a magnificent hymn written by David under the inspiration of the Holy Spirit that testifies to the majesty of God's name. Throughout all creation, God's unsurpassed greatness and glory is clearly seen. From the vastness of the universe to the weakness of man who is enabled to overcome his enemies by God's strength, all the creation testifies, "Only God is great."

The superscription over this psalm begins, "For the director of music," meaning this is a hymn of praise to be sung "according to *gittith*," which is a guitarlike harp associated with Gath in Philistia. This is "a psalm of David," written by Israel's king, the sweet psalmist of Israel. Its exact historical background is not known, but it arose from David's heart in a contemplative moment when, perhaps, he stared up into the vast skies and pondered the greatness of God.

Compared to this awesome God, what is man? May this psalm cause hearts to look upward and consider the glory of God.

II. COMMENTARY

Only God Is Great!

MAIN IDEA: *The greatness of God is seen in the vastness of his creation, both in his power to use the weakness of man to overthrow the mighty and in his ability to manage his creation.*

A God's Splendor Over All (8:1)

SUPPORTING IDEA: *The greatness of God far exceeds that which creation can reveal.*

8:1. This psalm begins with a declaration of God's greatness: **O LORD, our Lord, how majestic is your name in all the earth!** The word *majesty* refers to the radiant, revealed splendor of who God is and what he says and does. God's perfect character is seen in the beauty of his created world. By the works of his hand, David declared, **You have set your glory above the heavens.** God's glory, the shining of the greatness of his character, cannot be contained by creation. His glory exceeds the heights of creation. The heavens and earth can only partially express his excellence because the Creator remains far greater than what he creates.

B God's Strength Over All (8:2)

SUPPORTING IDEA: *In his greatness God uses the weakness of men to overthrow his enemies.*

8:2. David continued, pointing to God's choice to use the weakness of men to defeat his enemies. **From the lips of children and infants you have ordained praise because of your enemies, to silence the foe and the avenger.** This means God uses the weak to defeat the mighty. In this, God's greatness is further revealed. His strength is more than sufficient to empower the weakest of men and to overturn the mightiest of foes.

God's Sovereignty Over All (8:3–8)

SUPPORTING IDEA: *God's greatness is seen in his sovereign rule over his creation because he has delegated authority to man as his representative to rule over the earth.*

8:3–4. David reasoned that man's position seems insignificant when compared to the majesty of God's creation: **When I consider your heavens, the work of your fingers, the moon and the stars, which you have set in place.** For God to create the universe, David understood, was just the work of God's fingers, a relatively easy project.

In light of this, **what is man that you are mindful of him?** Compared to God, man is an insignificant creature in the universe—small and weak. But God is mindful of man and exercises **care** toward him. This creating God is also a caring God. The greatness of God is seen in his loving attention toward people who are so miniscule when compared to him. Finite man, David said, is nothing compared to the infinite God.

8:5. Reflecting upon the high dignity God has assigned to lowly man, David marveled, **You made him a little lower than the heavenly beings and crowned him with glory and honor.** This declaration is a testimony not to the greatness of man, but to the glory of God (cp. vv. 1,9). The psalmist was astonished that the sovereign Creator of the galaxies would bestow such relative significance on those as insignificant as man.

8:6–8. As man was given dominion of creation, David continued, **You made him ruler over the works of your hands; you put everything under his feet.** The greatness of God is seen in the fact that he has entrusted so much, his creation, to man. Only the supreme God could elevate those so low to a position so high—dominion over creation. Describing the comprehensive nature of man's delegated rule, David detailed some of the borders of his rule as being over **all flocks and herds, and the beasts of the field, the birds of the air, and the fish of the sea, all that swim the paths of the seas.** From grass-grazing cattle to flesh-eating beasts and to fish, all living creatures are under man's dominion.

God's Supremacy Over All (8:9)

SUPPORTING IDEA: *The greatness of God is clearly seen in all the earth.*

8:9. Summarizing all that he had said, David concluded where he began by declaring God's greatness (cp. v. 1): **O LORD, our Lord, how majestic is your name in all the earth!** As this psalm began, so it ends with an affirmation of the majesty of the Lord. God, not man, is to be praised. God alone is majestic, full of glory, and he alone deserves our worship.

> **MAIN IDEA REVIEW:** *The greatness of God is seen in the vastness of his creation, both in his power to use the weakness of man to overthrow the mighty and in his ability to manage his creation.*

III. CONCLUSION

What Is Man?

Years ago, on the campus of Harvard University, Emerson Hall was in the process of being constructed. The architect's plan included an inscription that was to be chiseled in marble over the main entrance. After much thought the professors in the department of philosophy decided that the engraving should read, "Man is the measure of all things."

But such a man-centered worldview did not meet with the approval of the president. When the professors returned from summer vacation, they found the building complete, but cut into the stone was an entirely different philosophy: "What is man that thou art mindful of him?" (Ps. 8:4). Although man continues to have an inflated view of himself, fallen and finite is he. God alone must be recognized as great—the Lord over all. With humble hearts all people must bow before the greatness of God.

IV. LIFE APPLICATION

Glory and Honor to God

Psalm 8 is a compelling call to worship. This is every believer's ultimate priority—the giving of glory to God. As this psalm begins and ends with praise to God (vv. 1,9), so every believer's thoughts and words, even his entire life, must be filled with praise for God. Because God is Lord over all, his pre-eminence must be declared with an adoration that is personal and passionate, both public and private. Wholehearted worship will surely flood the believer's heart when he realizes God's unsurpassed greatness.

God's supremacy, rightly understood, should affect how his people conduct themselves in every facet of life. Contrary to popular thinking, people are not the center of the universe—God is. Thus, all believers are to live every moment of every day under the shadow of God's greatness, seeking to bring glory and honor to him. God is glorified when his power fills man's weakness, enabling him to rule over the works of his hand. In all that God has called his people to do, they are nothing but children and infants who need divine strength to propel them forward in his will. Apart from the Lord, they have no ability to do anything eternal and lasting (John 15:5).

There is a God-assigned reason for every life. The glory of God compels believer to carry out this high calling in God's surpassing power.

V. PRAYER

God, you and you alone are worthy to be praised. With eyes of faith, we see your majesty in every place. From the heights of heaven to the depths of the earth, your creative power and infinite wisdom have been put on display for all to see. In our weakness your strength is being perfected, and this points to your greatness. You are a jealous God, and you will not share your glory with another. So we give you greater glory because you have chosen to crown us with lesser glory. We lift up our voice to declare the excellence of your name. In Jesus' name. Amen.

VI. DEEPER DISCOVERIES

A. Lord (8:1)

This word (Heb. *yehovah*) is the personal proper name of God given to Israel who knew it as the "glorious and awesome name" (Deut. 28:58). Derived from the tetragrammaton (YHWH), *yehovah* occurs 5,321 times in the Hebrew Bible, the most frequent name of God in Scripture. God was considered to be so holy that the name *yehovah* was never to be even pronounced aloud. Instead, the vowels markings for *adonai* were inserted to direct the reader of Scripture to say *adonai* instead of *yehovah*. The meaning of *yehovah* has been debated, but it is safe to infer that it refers to God's underived self-existence. The ancient Hebrews connected the word with *hava*, which meant "to be" as when God instructed Moses from the burning bush, "God said to Moses, 'I AM WHO I AM'" (Exod. 3:14). In this instance the divine name implies God's eternality, autonomy, independence, and immutability.

This divine name was often used in reference to God's covenants with Israel (Gen. 15:18; Exod. 3:15; 6:2,4–5; Deut. 7:9; 2 Kgs. 17:34–35; Isa. 26:4). The name also signified God's personal relationship and nearness to his people, "I will take you as my own people and I will be your God" (Exod. 6:7; cp. Hos. 1:9). It was to this name that the worship of Israel was to be directed (Deut. 4:32–37; 32:9; Amos 3:2).

B. Lord (8:1)

See "Deeper Discoveries," 2:4.

C. Majestic (8:1,9)

This word (Heb. *addir*) is an adjective that is translated numerous ways: "excellent, glorious, famous, mighty, wide, great, high, noble, splendid, magnificent." In some passages it refers to nobles and princes (Judg. 5:13; 2 Chr. 23:20; Neh. 3:5; 10:29; Jer. 14:3). Sometimes, as in this case, it describes the excellence of God (cp. Pss. 76:4; 93:4; Isa. 33:21).

D. Son of Man (8:4)

The title "son of man" (Heb. *ben 'adam*) was deliberately chosen by the psalmist to underscore man's frailty, mortality, and weakness. *Ben* is used almost five thousand times in the Hebrew Bible, and it refers to the human male offspring. Sometimes *ben* is used as an idiom for children, descendants, remote descendants, and sons. "Man" (*adam*) is used more than five hundred times throughout the Hebrew Bible to speak of mankind, but it is also used of individuals.

"Son of man" is a poetic term that deliberately emphasizes man's frailty (Num. 23:19; Job 25:6; 35:8). It was used at times as a proper title. Ezekiel referred to himself ninety-three times with the phrase "son of man." It denoted the finiteness of the prophet against the infinite God. This title was often used in reference to the coming Messiah (Dan. 7:13, in Aramaic). Jesus used it to refer to himself in all four Gospels.

E. Heavenly Beings (8:5)

The term "heavenly beings" (Heb. *elohim*), although translated here to refer to angelic beings, is also used for God in many other passages (Gen. 1:1). Probably the main meaning in the context is that man has been made "lower than God" (NASB). It is better to follow the NIV margin note which has "God" instead of "heavenly being."

VII. TEACHING OUTLINE

A. God's Splendor Over All (1)
   1. In all the earth (1a)
   2. Over all the heavens (1b)
B. God's Strength Over All (2)
   1. In man's weakness (2a)
     a. Spoken by children (2a)
     b. Sung by infants (2a)
   2. Over man's wickedness (2b)
     a. Silencing his adversaries (2b)
     b. Silencing the avenger (2b)
C. God's Sovereignty Over All (3–8)

1. Creating the universe (3)
   a. Making the planets (3a)
   b. Positioning the planets (3b)
2. Creating all mankind (4–8)
   a. God cares for man (4)
   b. God crowns man (5)
   c. God commissions man (6–8)
      (1) Over the flocks and herds (7a)
      (2) Over the beasts (7b)
      (3) Over the birds (8a)
      (4) Over the fish (8b)
   D. God's Supremacy Over All (9)
      1. His name is excellent (9a)
      2. His majesty is everywhere (9b)

VIII. ISSUES FOR DISCUSSION

1. How can my heart be more continually directed to praise God?
2. What steps must I pursue for God's strength to be perfected in my weakness?
3. What has God asked me to do to serve him?
4. What things prevent me from pursuing God?

Psalm 9
Awaiting the Final Verdict

╟─── Q u o t e ───╢

"*The resurrection and the judgment will demonstrate before all worlds who won and who lost. We can wait!*"

A . W . T o z e r

I. INTRODUCTION

In a sin-marred world filled with violence and vice, believers often find themselves discouraged and deflated by injustices. In order to remain strong in the faith, they must realize that no matter how much evil may reign, a final judgment by God is coming. Psalm 9 is a dramatic announcement of this fact. In the last day God will preside over all unbelievers and inflict eternal wrath upon the unrighteous. In light of this coming hour, believers should remain focused on God, especially when persecuted, knowing that God will bring justice in the end.

According to the title, Psalm 9 is addressed "for the director of music," directing him to lead in the singing of this song "to the tune of 'The Death of the Son.'" Regarding its authorship, it is "a psalm of David." It was probably joined originally with Psalm 10 to form one hymn of praise. Several reasons can be offered for considering these two psalms a single poem.

First, the Septuagint, the ancient Greek translation of the Old Testament, treated them as one psalm. Second, an acrostic pattern connects these two psalms. The verses of Psalm 9 begin with the first eleven letters of the Hebrew alphabet (omitting *daleth* "D"), while the verses of Psalm 10 begin with the letters of the second half of the Hebrew alphabet (three letters are missing; two are reversed). Third, Psalm 10 lacks a superscription. This is the only such omission from Psalm 3 to Psalm 32, strongly suggesting it may have been originally joined with the previous psalm.

II. COMMENTARY

MAIN IDEA: *David rejoices in the Lord because he rules over all nations, judging ungodly peoples but delivering those who trust in him.*

A David's Praise (9:1–2)

9:1–2. David set the strong tone of this psalm by declaring four times that he would praise God for his greatness. He resolved, **I will praise you, O LORD, with all my heart; I will tell of all your wonders.** These wonders point to God's amazing interventions into history by his saving acts toward his people. With building intensity, he exclaimed, **I will be glad and rejoice in you.** All true joy, David said, is found in God. David called God, **O Most High** (Heb. *Elyon*), a name that reveals him to be exalted over all, reigning in sovereignty, enthroned in the heavens, and working wonders.

B David's Proclamation (9:3–12)

9:3–6. When Israel was attacked by hostile nations, King David observed, **My enemies turn back; they stumble and perish before you.** When God intervenes, his foes are routed and defeated in the day of battle.

Giving glory to God for such military victories, David gave a fivefold description of this day of divine triumph. The Lord has: (1) **upheld my right and my cause,** or undergirded David's fighting; (2) **rebuked the nations,** or confronted and reproved them; (3) **destroyed the wicked,** referring to their total defeat; (4) **blotted out their name for ever and ever,** meaning they were eternally defeated, never to be remembered; and (5) **uprooted their cities,** indicating they were so demolished that there was no possibility of their being rebuilt.

9:7–8. Reaffirming God's sovereignty, David stated, **The LORD reigns forever,** never to be impeached and never to be usurped by another ruler. Therefore, **he will judge the world in righteousness** as all the nations will stand before him in the final judgment and receive perfect justice. In that awful day no mercy would be extended to unbelievers, only inflexible justice (Acts 17:31).

9:9–10. But to the contrary, David testified, **The LORD is a refuge for the oppressed, a stronghold in times of trouble.** God is both a refuge and stronghold (same Hebrew word, *misgob*), describing a high place, as atop a mountain, that is safe from the enemy because it provides strong security and sure defense. The phrase **those who know your name** refers to those who had a personal, intimate relationship with God. They were the ones who would **trust in** God alone.

9:11–12. Those who intimately know God were entreated by David to **sing praises to the LORD.** This God who intervenes on behalf of his people, delivering them from harm, must be worshiped with loud singing. So fervent should their praise be that David invited God's people to **proclaim among the nations what he has done**. Even the unbelieving peoples of the nations should hear this celebration of God's greatness, leading to their salvation. God avenges the innocent blood of his people which is shed by these ungodly nations. He **does not ignore the cry of the afflicted** who trust in him; instead, he rescues the righteous from harm.

C David's Petition (9:13–18)

9:13–14. Directly addressing God, David passionately cried, **O LORD, see how my enemies persecute me**! He found himself surrounded by his many foes who were persecuting him. Thus, he called to God, **Have mercy and lift me up from the gates of death**. He was standing at the doorsteps of death in life-threatening dangers (cp. Job 17:16; 38:17), and he desperately needed God to rescue him. This urgent appeal for divine deliverance was offered so David might **declare your praises** and **rejoice in your salvation** at **the gates of the Daughter of Zion**. He would be able to offer public praise in Jerusalem to her citizens, he reasoned, if God would rescue him from these oppressing nations.

9:15–18. Contrasting the end of the wicked and the godly, David declared, **The nations have fallen into the pit they have dug**. Like a hunter who digs a hole to catch an animal, they had fallen prey to their own evil devices. They were self-destructing as if **caught in the net they have hidden . . . ensnared by the work of their hands**. Their doom was sure as **the wicked return to the grave**, dying without God. These vast multitudes who would be defeated were **all the nations that forget God**.

On the contrary, **the needy** are not self-reliant but God-trusting. They will be remembered by God. It may appear that these needy were forsaken by God, but they were not forgotten. Their hope of eternal life was rooted in God, and they would never perish.

D David's Passion (9:19–20)

9:19–20. Climaxing this passionate psalm, David pleaded, **Arise, O LORD, let not man triumph**. He called upon God to arouse himself and come to his rescue before evil men were victorious. He called upon those peoples who forget God to **be judged in your presence**. He appealed, **Strike them with terror** at the hand of God's fierce judgment, and **let the nations know they are but men**, frail, defenseless, and unable to stand against Almighty God.

III. CONCLUSION

Believers should know that when they are persecuted by the ungodly, God will come to their rescue and defeat their adversaries. Sometimes this retribution will be inflicted in this lifetime. But this wrath may also await the final judgment. Whether now or later, God *will* make right every injustice suffered by his people at the hands of their enemies. Therefore, believers should call on God when they are attacked, trusting him to be their stronghold.

The righteous should never seek personal vengeance, but instead be reminded that the battle belongs to the Lord (2 Chr. 20:15). In their day of trouble, they should humble themselves under the mighty hand of God. He, and he alone, is working all things according to the counsel of his eternal will (Eph. 1:11). Let all God's people bow before him, never relying upon the arm of the flesh, but trusting in the Lord. He alone is an unassailable refuge whose sovereign plans and eternal purposes cannot be thwarted.

IV. TEACHING OUTLINE

A. David's Praise (1–2)
  1. For God's great powers (1)
  2. For God's glorious person (2)
B. David's Proclamation (3–12)
  1. God defeats his enemies (3–6)
    a. He undertook my cause (3–4)
    b. He overtook my enemies (5–6)
  2. God directs the world (7–8)
    a. He reigns eternally (7a)
    b. He judges righteously (7b–8)
  3. God defends the oppressed (9–10)
    a. He always protects them (9)
    b. He never forsakes them (10)
  4. God deserves their praise (11–12)
    a. For who he is (11a)
    b. For what he has done (11b–12)
C. David's Petition (13–18)
  1. For God's deliverance (13–14)
    a. See my affliction (13a)
    b. Save my life (13b–14)
  2. For God's destruction (15–18)
    a. Rout the nations (15–17)
    b. Remember the needy (18)
D. David's Passion (19–20)
  1. Arise, O Lord (19)
  2. Attack, O Lord (20)

Psalm 10

God's Inevitable Triumph

Psalm 10

I. INTRODUCTION

*T*he cause of Christ often seems to falter and suffer defeat. But the kingdom of God is marching forward, inevitably and triumphantly. Sin and iniquity may gain the advantage temporarily, giving the appearance that God is indifferent toward these injustices. But such temporary losses should never be interpreted as God's ultimate defeat. God *will* have the last word. His eternal kingdom cannot fail; it must prevail!

In Psalm 10 David saw the many injustices and what seemed to be the indifference of God toward sinful mankind. The success of sin brought debilitating discouragement and despair to David. But as he shifted his focus from the earthly to the eternal, his anxiety turned to assurance, his confusion to confidence, and his perplexity to praise. No superscription is recorded for this psalm, possibly because it was originally joined to Psalm 9. If so, the title for Psalm 9 also applies to Psalm 10, identifying David as the author.

II. COMMENTARY

> **MAIN IDEA:** *When confronted by the spread of evil, David called out to God to protect the innocent and to judge the wicked, offering praise that God would eventually make right every wrong.*

A David's Perplexity (10:1–11)

10:1. Surrounded by the triumph of the wicked, David was utterly confused and he asked, **Why, O LORD, do you stand far off?** In the face of widespread perversity (vv. 2–11), God seemed to be indifferent and withdrawn: **Why do you hide yourself in times of trouble?** Even worse, God seemed to be hiding when believers were suffering affliction.

10:2–4. The problem for the psalmist was the ego-driven pride of the wicked: **In his arrogance the wicked man hunts down the weak.** Pictured as a haughty hunter stalking his prey, the wicked pursued the harm of the righteous as a sport, driven by their **arrogance**. As the wicked man set a trap for the righteous, he found himself **caught in the schemes** he was devising, in essence, hung by his own rope. With pride he boasted **of the cravings of his heart**, boasting about his evil desires. His heart was so inverted and perverted that he blessed the greedy and reviled the Lord.

Furthermore, the wicked did **not seek** God because his heart was so desperately depraved. **In all his thoughts**, meaning the entirety of his thinking, there was **no room for God.** His mind was thoroughly godless, void of all divine perspective and absolute truth.

10:5–6. From a human perspective, what was so confusing about this dilemma was that the ways of the wicked were **always prosperous**. The wicked appeared to have the blessing of God, while the righteous were being destroyed by the plots of the wicked. The wicked man was **haughty**, not humble; thus, God's laws were **far from him.** Truth and obedience had no part in his life. Full of sinful self-assurance and utterly self-deceived, he said to himself, **Nothing will shake me; I'll always be happy and never have trouble.** The wicked felt nothing could affect his sense of self-security and self-sufficiency, but in reality, nothing could be further from the truth. He did not realize that he was without real knowledge (cp. John 9:39–41).

10:7. Spewing out of his wicked heart was perverse speech, **full of curses and lies and threats.** The following are three destructive weapons of the tongue: **curses**, words which seek to bring down evil powers upon people; **lies**, meaning false testimony and slander; and **threats**, or intimidations toward others.

10:8–11. Driven to harm others, the wicked, David declared, **lies in wait near the villages; from ambush he murders the innocent, watching in secret**

for his victims. Lurking in the shadows, he looked for opportunities to prey on others. Like a stalking animal, the wicked waited **like a lion in cover . . . to catch the helpless**. Like a cunning hunter or skilled fisherman, he caught the helpless and dragged them off in his net.

Without the defense of God, his victims were crushed and then **fell under his strength**. Because the Lord did not rescue them, the wicked wrongly concluded that **God has forgotten; he covers his face and never sees**. But to the contrary, God does see and remember, as the wicked would discover.

𝔹 David's Plea (10:12–15)

10:12–13. With a passionate appeal the psalmist cried out, **Arise, LORD! Lift up your hand, O God** to strike the wicked. This was a battle cry (Num. 10:35) that sought to rally God to come and fight the wicked. **Do not forget the helpless**, he appealed, but remember their desperate plight. Realizing the utter insanity of moral rebellion against God, he reasoned, **Why does the wicked man revile God?** There was no reasonable explanation for this, yet he continued in his blasphemy. How insane! Why did the unbelieving wicked say, **He won't call me to account?** No logical explanation could be given for this but the foolishness of sin.

10:14–15. Restoring an accurate picture of God, the psalmist exclaimed, **But you, O God, do see trouble and grief**. He knew that nothing escapes the Lord's omniscient gaze. Still addressing God, he stated, **You consider it to take it in hand**. God would surely act and judge sin! Reassured of God's righteous rule, the psalmist called out, **Break the arm of the wicked and evil man**, or, destroy the power of the godless that they may no longer oppress the godly. In other words, call the wicked to account for his wickedness.

ℂ David's Praise (10:16–18)

10:16. With dramatic declaration of God's eternal reign, the psalmist affirmed, **The LORD is King for ever and ever**. Knowing that his prayer had been heard, he expressed confidence that the nations would **perish from his land**, meaning God would defeat and destroy evil aggressors who rose up against God's people.

10:17–18. With bold confidence, the psalmist affirmed, **You hear, O LORD, the desire of the afflicted** who cry to be rescued from the oppression of the ungodly. God hears and will answer, **defending the fatherless and the oppressed** who have suffered vicious, violent attacks unjustly at the hands of the wicked. God would act **in order that man, who is of the earth**, depraved and evil as he is, might **terrify** the godly **no more**. One day God will put an end to such terror and triumph over all evil. What a blessed hope!

III. CONCLUSION

In order to endure persecution by the wicked, the believer must stay focused on God. When surrounded by unbelief and the ungodly, it is easy for us to become distracted and lose sight of the inevitable triumph of God's invincible kingdom. In the midst of an evil world, the righteous must remain focused upon those things above where Christ is seated, not upon the unstable things of this earth (Col. 3:2). God's people must remain faithful to him, resisting the lure to become squeezed into the world's mold (Rom. 12:2). The truth is that this globe is a world under divine judgment (Rom. 1:18). One day it will fall into the hands of the living God.

So believers should find their greatest joy in God himself rather than in the passing pleasures of worldly pursuits. Seeing and savoring God is the greatest fulfillment in life and the greatest antidote to the lure of sin.

IV. TEACHING OUTLINE

A. David's Perplexity (1–11)
  1. God's seeming inactivity (1)
    a. Why remove yourself? (1a)
    b. Why hide yourself? (1b)
  2. God's seeming indifference (2–11)
    a. With the prideful heart (2–6)
    b. With the perverse mouth (7)
    c. With the plundering hands (8–10)
    d. With the profane mind (11)
B. David's Plea (12–15)
  1. Remember the weak (12–14)
    a. In their affliction (12–13)
    b. In their vexation (14)
  2. Reject the wicked (15)
    a. Break them (15a)
    b. Judge them (15b)
C. David's Praise (16–18)
  1. For God's majesty (16)
    a. He reigns forever (16a)
    b. He removes foes (16b)
  2. For God's mercy (17–18)
    a. He hears the oppressed (17)
    b. He helps the orphaned (18)

Psalm 11

When the Foundations Tremble

I. INTRODUCTION

*N*ever do believers experience God to be so sufficient as when they find themselves in the most difficult times, confronted with trials beyond their control. It is in man's extremities that he discovers God's sufficiencies. This was the personal experience of David in Psalm 11, a song of strong confidence in God in the midst of unsettling times.

David was facing a national crisis that threatened to overturn the stability of the nation of Israel. All around him, the moral foundations of the people were crumbling. This upheaval was caused by evil men who sought to do him harm. Adding to this ordeal, the people who were loyal to David panicked, counseling him to flee Jerusalem. But David remained calm and resolute, keeping his eyes on the Lord. In this hour of crisis, David determined to trust in God in spite of his circumstances. His faith, unshakable and unwavering, kept him steadfast in uncertain times.

The title of this psalm reads, "For the director of music," indicating that the specific historical setting of this psalm is unknown. All that is known is that David was the author, and he wrote while in desperate straits. In the midst of turmoil, he assured his followers that in spite of the threats of the wicked, God remained in control. David acted as an example to believers by remaining resolute and unflinching in the face of desperate circumstances.

II. COMMENTARY

MAIN IDEA: *David stood strong in faith, even when other believers gave him faulty counsel. He remained fixed upon God who controls all.*

A David's Trust (11:1a)

11:1a. David began the psalm with a declaration of his trust in God: **In the LORD I take refuge.** In the midst of great difficulties, even the potential loss of his life at the hands of his enemies, he remained confident in God who was his refuge. As he had done throughout his life, David fled to God as his unassailable fortress of protection as he faced this crisis. Not looking to others, or even to himself, David placed his trust exclusively in the Lord.

B David's Temptation (11:1b–3)

11:1b–2. David was surrounded by well-meaning but weak-willed supporters, people who advised him to leave Jerusalem and escape the encroaching danger. In response he said to them, **How then can you say to me: Flee like a bird to your mountain?** To David's advisers the opposition seemed too strong to resist. His aides looked with terror at **the wicked** who were bending **their bows** and setting **their arrows** to shoot at them, **the upright in heart.** They perceived that their enemies were lurking in **the shadows,** waiting for the right moment to spring their deadly ambush.

11:3. In the face of this danger, David's supporters were fearful, saying, **When the foundations are being destroyed, what can the righteous do?** The word *foundations* is a metaphor for social order (Ps. 82:5; Ezek. 30:4). The word *destroyed* describes the turbulent upheaval of the moral values and civil order of their day. These advisers sensed they could no longer live in a culture in which right failed and evil prevailed. This was the counsel that David heard from his supporters—an appeal to run and hide from his oppressors.

C David's Triumph (11:4–7)

11:4a. David replied to his fearful followers, redirecting their focus to the Lord. First, David affirmed God's sovereignty, testifying, **The LORD is in his holy temple.** The presence of God had not moved from the temple. The psalmist also reminded his fellow believers that God was still upon his **throne,** ruling and reigning over this painful trial. Nothing was out of control; God was in control!

11:4b–5a. Second, David affirmed God's scrutiny: **He observes the sons of men; his eyes examine them.** David assured his supporters that the eyes of God see all human hearts, examining the inner life of the righteous who trust the Lord, as well as probing the souls of the wicked who were attacking them because they loved violence. In light of this, believers must remain strong in faith, not cowering to their enemies because God sees their hearts as well as the hearts of their enemies.

11:5b–6. Third, David underscored God's severity: **On the wicked he will rain fiery coals and burning sulfur.** This imagery probably alluded to God's fatal judgment such as that which fell upon Sodom and Gomorrah (Gen. 19; Deut. 29:23; Ezek. 38:22). The wicked could expect that **a scorching wind** would **be their lot.** This refers to the hot blast associated with God's dreadful judgments.

11:7. Finally, David affirmed God's support of the righteous. His saints would be rewarded and the wicked would be destroyed because **the LORD is righteous.** God must act consistently with his holy character, and he will execute perfect **justice** in all his dealings with men. The fact is that he loves justice and will never let injustice go unpunished. Therefore, when **upright men** face trouble, they must remember that they **will see his face.** This expression denotes a loyal citizen's access to his king, in this case heaven's true king, the Lord.

III. CONCLUSION

All Christians will encounter many threatening trials in their lives, especially when they live in a manner worthy of the Lord (Matt. 5:10–12; John 15:18–20; 2 Tim. 3:12). This world is no friend of grace when God's people live for him. When the righteous are persecuted for the gospel, they must remain strong in the Lord, finding their strength in him. In the midst of such fiery trials, God's people must take refuge in him. They must do so with unwavering faith, firmly committed to resist the temptation without withdrawing from this world. The key is insulation, not isolation.

When opposition comes, close friends around us may weaken and cause us to panic when they urge us to run from trouble. But such counsel must be resisted. God is sovereign through every trial, and he reigns over all. God alone is the Lord, and he overrules all for our good and his glory.

IV. TEACHING OUTLINE

A. David's Trust (1a)
   1. An explicit trust in God (1a)
   2. An exclusive trust in God (1b)
B. David's Temptation (1b–3)
   1. He heard counsel to depart (1b–2)
   2. He heard counsel to despair (3)
C. David's Triumph (4–7)
   David declared:

1. God's sovereignty (4a)
   a. He resides in his holy temple (4a)
   b. He reigns on his heavenly throne (4a)
2. God's scrutiny (4b–5a)
   a. He observes all men (4b)
   b. He examines all men (4c–5a)
3. God's severity (5b–6)
   a. He rejects the wicked (5b)
   b. He judges the wicked (6)
4. God's support (7)
   a. He is righteous (7a)
   b. He loves justice (7b)
   c. He favors the upright (7b)

Psalm 12

The Moral Minority

"America is running on the momentum of a godly ancestry. When that momentum goes, God help America."

J .   G r e s h a m   M a c h e n

Psalm 12

I. INTRODUCTION

True believers find themselves in the minority in this fallen world— the few on the narrow path that leads to life. Consequently, they face a growing number of unbelievers who stand in firm opposition to the cause of righteousness. If the righteous are to remain strong, they must call upon the Lord. Only he can give them the strength to stand when they are outnumbered by the ungodly. In Psalm 12, David recognized this sobering reality.

The once God-fearing society in which he lived, previously built upon the moral absolutes of God's law, was now crumbling from within. In its place a culture built on pagan beliefs and secular humanism was becoming the prevailing worldview of his day. Godly people such as David were finding themselves in the minority. In light of such lawlessness, how were the godly to respond to the godless? Should they withdraw into isolation?

As David looked around, he observed the righteous remnant diminishing, society disintegrating, truth crumbling, and sin flourishing. In this hour of national decadence, David did what all believers must do. He turned to God and trusted in his promises. He found the strength he needed to live through the crisis.

II. COMMENTARY

> **MAIN IDEA:** *When believers are surrounded and outnumbered by the wicked, they should pray to God, trusting in his promises and his protection.*

A David's Predicament (12:1–2)

12:1–2. Surrounded by an increasingly sinful society, David cried out, Help, LORD, pleading for God's intervention. He despaired that **the godly** were **no more**, meaning they were fading from the scene into extinction. Likewise, the faithful who maintained moral integrity had all but **vanished from among men**. David lamented that, beginning with their national leaders, those who lived moral lives had steadily decreased and passed off the scene. In this moral struggle, truth was crumbling because everyone seemed to be lying to his neighbor. Honesty was waning as **their flattering lips** spoke **with deception**.

B David's Petition (12:3–4)

12:3–4. In the midst of this spiritual collapse, David called for God to cut off those who had flattering lips and who spoke with a boastful tongue. He mourned that the nation had become a society of braggarts. With sickening arrogance, the wicked boasted, **We will triumph with our tongues; we own our lips**. The wicked sensed no accountability to anyone, certainly not to God, whom they defied by asking, **Who is our master?**

C David's Protection (12:5–6)

12:5. David was assured that the Lord would deal with **the oppression of the weak and the groaning of the needy.** The weak and needy were suffering under the attack of the ungodly because of their holy character. With an abrupt transition, God spoke with certainty; he promised, **I will protect them from those who malign them.** David believed it! He was reminded that the Lord knows the plight of his people and pledges to rise up on their behalf.

12:6. In stark contrast to the profane words of sinners, God spoke **flaw-less** words that were pure and trustworthy, like **silver refined in a furnace of clay, purified seven times.** The Lord spoke without any mixture of error (Prov. 30:5; John 17:17). By his infallible word, God guaranteed that his people would be kept safe.

D David's Peace (12:7–8)

12:7–8. With renewed confidence David boasted: O LORD, **you will keep us safe and protect us.** God promised to protect his people as they journeyed on this evil road. David believed that God would safeguard him as well as other believers from the wicked who were strutting about. The ungodly assumed they were not accountable to God. This defiant attitude was bolstered because what was **vile** (Heb. *zullut,* "squandered, worthless") was **honored among men**.

III. CONCLUSION

How should the godly live in a godless society? Psalm 12 makes clear that believers should not look to the majority to formulate the direction of their lives. Truth will always be in the minority. Instead, they must fix their gaze upon God, who alone is truth. The Christian must be willing to stand alone, if need be, always looking to God to show the way. God plus one always makes a majority.

In looking to God, the believer must study the Scripture, knowing that when the Bible speaks, God speaks. In the midst of increasing apostasy, all Christians must be rooted and grounded in the Scripture. Only God's Word can make us strong in the faith and enable us to live holy lives in the midst of a godless culture. We must obey God's commands and put into practice what he requires. The Christian must live for God, walking daily in personal obedience and holiness.

IV. TEACHING OUTLINE

A. David's Predicament (1–2)
   1. The godly have decreased (1)
   2. The godless have increased (2)
B. David's Petition (3–4)
   1. Cut off flattering lips (3a)
   2. Cut off boastful tongues (3b–4)
      a. We have no match (3b–4a)
      b. We have no master (4b)
C. David's Protection (5–6)
   1. God will triumph (5)
   2. God speaks truth (6)
D. David's Peace (7–8)
   1. Believers are guarded (7)
   2. Unbelievers are guilty (8)

Psalm 13

From Sinking to Swimming

Psalm 13

I. INTRODUCTION

*C*harles H. Spurgeon in his classic work, *A Treasury of David*, has written, "Whenever you look into David's Psalms, you will somewhere or other see yourself. You never get into a corner, but you find David in that corner. I think that I was never so low that I could not find that David was lower; and I never climbed so high that I could not find that David was up above me." These insightful words are relevant to Psalm 13 because this psalm contains both the heights of ecstasy and the depths of despair. Both extremes were David's experience. In this individual lament psalm, David's soul is dramatically transformed from perplexity to praise, from sinking to singing. Joseph Parker remarked, "This psalm begins with winter and ends with summer; it begins with low muffled tones of sorrow and ends with a rapture of praise."

What caused this dramatic turnaround? The answer is found in the midst of the psalm—prayer. Casting his burdens upon God, David found his heart elevated out of the prison of worry to the paradise of worship. This psalm was intended "for the director of music," a praise song to be sung in public worship.

II. COMMENTARY

> **MAIN IDEA:** *When discouraged and perplexed, David called upon God for his deliverance and soon found his heart filled with rejoicing.*

A David's Sorrow (13:1–2)

13:1–2. Surrounded by his enemies and facing imminent death, David repeated the same rhetorical question to God four times, **How long**? With deep agony he questioned God's apparent absence. This overwhelming trial caused David to feel ignored, as if God had forgotten him and was hiding from him. Spiraling downward into deep emotional despair, he realized his inability to deal with his troubles. As his **enemy** triumphed over him, he was left to wrestle with his own haunting **thoughts** of imagined defeat that compounded his **sorrow**.

B David's Supplication (13:3–4)

13:3–4. In his despair David turned to God in prayer, crying out, **Look on me and answer**. He asked for God to rescue him from this desperate situation. If not, David believed, he would **sleep in death** because his enemy would overcome him and rejoice in his defeat. He asked, **Give light to my eyes**, requesting divine wisdom and understanding to see his situation from God's perspective.

C David's Singing (13:5–6)

13:5–6. With unwavering confidence David put his trust in God's **unfailing love** (Heb. *hesed,* "covenantal love"). Although his enemies longed to rejoice in his defeat (v. 4), David's heart rejoiced in God's **salvation**, or divine deliverance from the threats of his enemies. His strong belief that his prayer had been heard by God caused David to **sing** because God had been **good** to him. From the depths of sorrow (vv. 1–2), he was elevated to the heights of singing as he anticipated the end of his long wait for God's rescue.

III. CONCLUSION

How can a believer remain steadfast through difficult times? When endangered and discouraged, Christians must turn to God in humble prayer. Discouraged souls often internalize their struggles rather than casting their burdens on the Lord. This only leads to self-destruction and despair. Believers should call out to God. Only he can deliver them out of their troubles. In the storms of life, God must be the believer's first recourse, never a last resort. Then after praying, he must wait patiently for God to act. The Lord's timing is always perfect, never too late, never too early. True faith gives the Lord time to work.

As believers wait patiently upon God, they should do so by praising him, exulting in his grace, magnifying his goodness, and singing to the Lord, who is worthy to be praised. Because God's love is unfailing, the praise of believers for him who sustains them should also be unfailing.

IV. TEACHING OUTLINE

A. David's Sorrow (1–2)
1. How long will God forget? (1a)
2. How long will God hide? (1b)
3. How long must I be discouraged? (2a)
4. How long must I be defeated? (2b)
B. David's Supplication (3–4)
1. Remember me, God (3a)
2. Rescue me, God (3b–4)
C. David's Singing (5–6)
1. I will rely upon God (5)
2. I will rejoice in God (6)

Psalm 14

The Insanity of Depravity

"*I*n all unbelief there are two things: a good opinion of one's self and a bad opinion of God."

H o r a t i o   B o n a r

Psalm 14

I. INTRODUCTION

*H*aving a Christian worldview is critical if a person is accurately to assess the things around us. Only the right paradigm, a biblical truth, will result in the right perspective. Accordingly, only the vantage point revealed in Psalm 14 will correctly appraise the spiritual condition of the world in which we live. Lamenting the moral depravity of the human race, this psalm is a wisdom poem that reveals the utter foolishness of those who try to live apart from God.

In turning aside from God, people show themselves to be fools. Their problem is rooted in the sinful nature of their heart. The heart of the human problem is the problem of the human heart. Only God's Word provides the right diagnosis for the deadly plague that has infected the human race. The problem is sin, the futile attempt to live as if there is no God. This wisdom psalm assesses the sinful condition of man and longs for the salvation that only God can provide. Written by David, it was addressed to "the director of music" as a song that acted as a dirge on depravity.

II. COMMENTARY

> **MAIN IDEA:** *The entire human race is in moral rebellion against God, but his people long for the final establishment of his righteous kingdom on the earth.*

🄰 David's Assessment of Humanity (14:1–6)

14:1a. David began his diagnosis of the problem of the human race by saying, **The fool says in his heart, "There is no God."** The fool is a person who is morally perverse, not mentally deficient. The term is a synonym for *sinner*, and it describes everyone who has no place for God in his or her life. The fool's problem is that his heart refuses the knowledge of God. To be sure, he is not an intellectual atheist, denying the existence of God, but a *practical* atheist, living as if there were no God (Pss. 53:1; 74:18,22; Isa. 32:6). The words "there is" have been added to the English translation to make the psalm read smoothly. In the original Hebrew, the text actually reads, "The fool says 'No God!' or 'No God for me.'"

14:1b. Describing all mankind without God, David concluded that they were **corrupt**, meaning their human nature was rotten with sin; thus, their **deeds** were **vile**. This is to say, their depraved character bore the rotten fruit of wicked conduct. What they *did* (conduct) flowed out of who they *were* (character). The bottom line is that **there is no one who does good.** All humanity, David concluded, lived sinfully, turning aside from God.

14:2–3. As **the LORD** surveyed mankind from above, he searched hearts to determine if there were any who spiritually understood or who had spiritual affections to **seek God.** The sad reality is that **all** people have **turned aside** and are **corrupt** (Heb. *alah*, "sour like milk"). Sin has devastated their total personality, leaving their mind darkened, their emotions depraved, and their will deadened. Repeating his initial verdict (v. 1), David stated, **There is no one who does good.** The entire world is under sin, which leaves people incapable and unwilling to do good. The all-inclusive words **no one, any, any, all, no one, not even one** clearly convey the sad, universal reality of depravity (cp. Rom. 3:10–18).

14:4–5. David then turned to the outcome of such **evildoers.** He surmised, rightly so, that they devoured God's people as they would eat **bread** and failed to **call on the LORD** in saving faith or humble prayer. Surely, **God** would cause such sinners to be **overwhelmed with dread** because he would judge them for persecuting **the righteous.** To oppose God's people is to oppose God himself (Acts 9:4).

14:6. Shifting from the third person to the second person, David increased his intense confrontation of the ungodly. Addressing them directly, David proclaimd, **You evildoers frustrate the plans of the poor**. These evildoers might assail the poor who trust the Lord, but God would protect them because he was **their refuge**.

B David's Appeal to Heaven (14:7)

14:7. Expressing the heart cry of God's oppressed people, David cried out, **Oh, that salvation for Israel would come out of Zion!** David longed for God's deliverance of his people from evildoers who attack the righteous. He longed for the time when the Lord would establish God's kingdom upon earth, and restore **the fortunes of his people** (Ezek. 16:53; Zeph. 2:7). In anticipation of that final day, a day marked by divine conquest, God's people could **rejoice** and **be glad** because he would ultimately establish his righteous rule from **Zion**.

III. CONCLUSION

This psalm calls for a right understanding of God and man. The true spiritual state of the human race apart from divine grace is a condition of heart plagued by the corruption of sin. If anyone is to be acceptable to God, he must confess this problem of personal guilt and acknowledge his sin. Any presentation of the gospel must include a clear testimony about sin, the wages of which is death (Rom. 6:23).

This psalm also reveals that God is in heaven, high and exalted, looking down on all mankind, observing every life. He sees every heart, thought, deed, and life. He assesses the sinful depravity of human nature. One day he will bring his judgment on all who do not call upon him. He is holy, righteous, and just. God alone can save the sinner from the just punishment of his sin. Salvation comes out of Zion, not out of man's efforts to commend himself toward God. He alone is a refuge in the day of judgment. Let all people call upon him who is the Savior of his people.

IV. TEACHING OUTLINE

A. David's Assessment of Humanity (1–6)
  1. The insanity of the world (1a)
    a. Denying God (1a)
    b. Dismissing God (1a)
  2. The immorality of the world (1b)
    a. Destructive character (1b)
    b. Detestable conduct (1b)
  3. The inability of the world (2–3)

   a. None understand (2a)

   b. None seek God (2b)

  4. The ignorance of the world (4–6)

   a. They never learn (4)

   b. They never rest (5)

   c. They never win (6)

 B. David's Appeal to Heaven (7)

  1. For their salvation (7a)

  2. For their restoration (7b)

  3. For their celebration (7c

Psalm 15
Rightly Approaching the King

┌─────────────────┐
│   Q u o t e   │
└─────────────────┘

"*H*oliness is not something to be received in a meeting; it is a life to be lived in detail."

D .   M a r t y n   L l o y d - J o n e s

Psalm 15

I. INTRODUCTION

Reverencing Royalty

*M*any years ago Queen Elizabeth of England paid a visit to the United States. Accompanied by her royal entourage, she traveled through a poverty-stricken neighborhood of Los Angeles. As she was chauffeured through an impoverished project area, the monarch of England, wanting to see what life was like there, asked her limousine driver to stop the car. The queen got out and walked up to a shabby apartment. The lady of the house answered the knock and to her amazement found herself face-to-face with her majesty, the queen of England.

Unaware of the proper etiquette for addressing royalty, she did not curtsy. Nor did she properly address the queen as "her majesty." Instead, she naively approached England's monarch and wrapped both arms around the queen, giving her a hug. The royal entourage was appalled; the media was shocked; and the Secret Service was aghast. This common woman had no idea how to approach or address royalty. There was no reverence. No awe. No humility.

This is often true in the church today. Many of the Lord's servants have forgotten how to approach their Lord, the King of heaven and earth. There is a divinely prescribed manner in approaching God that is frequently forgotten in the present age. Believers must be careful not to enter his presence with a life filled with unholy thoughts, conduct, and words. Instead, they must prepare themselves with reverence, awe, and humble submission, knowing they are entering the presence of the King of kings.

This is the central message of Psalm 15, a "psalm of David." This psalm was probably quoted by ancient worshipers as they traveled to Jerusalem for one of the four annual festivals. Or perhaps it was designed to be recited as a worshiper arrived at the gate of the tabernacle court to worship God. In any case, this psalm is designed to prepare the worshiper to enter the holy presence of God.

II. COMMENTARY

Rightly Approaching the King

MAIN IDEA: *David describes the moral integrity and personal holiness of the person who worships God.*

A The Searching Question (15:1)

SUPPORTING IDEA: *Believers should search their hearts to determine if they are prepared to approach God in worship.*

15:1a. This psalm begins with David asking a single question which is posed in two parts. It is a searching question about who is eligible to come before the Lord and worship him: LORD, **who may dwell in your sanctuary?** The issue addressed here is the question of who may come before God and remain as a guest in his holy royal house.

The sanctuary was the appointed place where God chose to show his glory to Israel. This question may have been asked by a worshiper as he arrived at the gate to enter the tabernacle court to worship God, perhaps in one of the four great annual religious festivals. Or it may have been asked by a parent or teacher instructing children about those who might participate in the worship of God. This heart-searching question expresses a genuine question to anyone who wants to worship God. Who may enter God's house and be welcomed by the Lord as a guest in his house? It is a question that calls for meditation upon one's spiritual condition.

15:1b. The same searching question is asked a second time: **Who may live on your holy hill?** It is addressed to God by the person who came to worship him, asking who could draw near to him with acceptable worship? Who may come and abide in God's holy presence? God's "holy hill" refers to Mount Zion, on which the city of Jerusalem was built, the city of David where the temple would be built by David's son and the future king of Israel, Solomon. Who can come to this holy place in Jerusalem and have a living worship experience with God? Or put another way, Who may enjoy communion with God? Who may converse intimately with a holy God?

B The Spiritual Qualifications (15:2–5b)

SUPPORTING IDEA: *Personal holiness in the life of a believer is a prerequisite for worshiping God.*

15:2a–b. The sobering answer comes, and it is an answer that contains twelve injunctions. In reality it is six couplets. The answer is that the person who approaches God's holy hill must seek to be as holy as God is holy (cp. Heb. 12:14). Follows is a representative list that defines the life of a person who may worship God.

The first couplet focuses upon the holy conduct required of the worshiper of God. He must be one **whose walk is blameless**. The word *walk* describes the daily pattern of a person's life and the direction of a person's lifestyle. His ways must be marked as blameless, meaning whole or sound. A blameless person is one whose character is morally well-rounded. This person is not strong in certain areas of his life and weak in others. Every part of his life comes together to form a complete and balanced life of godly living.

Stated another way, the requirement of a worshiper is to be one **who does what is righteous**. Such moral integrity expresses itself in right actions that pursue what is right in the eyes of God. This is another way of saying obedience to God. The word *righteous* describes a person who leads a life marked by consistent conformity to the Word of God. He is not just a hearer of the Word, but one who does what is right, putting the truth into practice.

15:2c–3a. The second couplet focuses upon the tongue of the worshiper. It asks who may vocalize acceptable praise to God. Positively, he **speaks the truth from his heart**, meaning he is one who speaks what is consistent with his heart (cp. Matt. 12:34–35; 15:18). God despises hypocritical worship—worship that is given by the lips but from a heart that is far from him (Isa. 29:13; Matt. 15:8). As the truth of God stirs in his inner being, the genuine worshiper speaks to others nothing but the truth. He means what he says without being a double-tongued falterer who talks out of both sides of his mouth.

The true worshiper **has no slander on his tongue**, or he does not attack others maliciously with his mouth. The word *devil* means "slanderer," and a person is never more like the evil one nor more used by the prince of darkness than when he verbally attacks another person. If someone is to go into the presence of the Lord in Zion, he must be an obedient, truth-speaking servant. The double-tongued slanderer does not belong in the Lord's sanctuary.

15:3b–c. Furthermore, a genuine worshiper must maintain right relations with others, not harming or hurting them. Both parts of this couplet are presented in the negative, stating what the worshiper does not do. In order to be a guest in God's house, he must be a person who **does his neighbor no wrong**. In other words, he does not bring harm to anyone. His neighbor is anyone with whom he associates. Certainly doing the positive is implied.

Likewise, he **casts no slur on his fellowman**; he does not discredit his neighbor in the eyes of others. Instead, he lifts up others, saying what is truthful and affirming.

15:4a–b. In this fourth couplet the psalmist identifies the true worshiper in terms of the people whom he rejects or accepts. He is one who says no to the wicked and yes to the godly (cp. Ps. 1:1–3), rejecting those whom God rejects and accepting those whom God accepts. He is one **who despises a vile man**. A vile (Heb. *maas*) man is one who is worthless, polluted, dirty, or morally depraved. A genuine worshiper rejects the sinner, in the sense of rejecting his defiling influence, associations, and partnership. "Bad company corrupts good character" (1 Cor. 15:33). "A little leaven leavens the whole lump" (1 Cor. 5:6 NASB).

The true worshiper must reject all that is false and evil not only in his own life but specifically in the life of the vile man. The person who worships God in a close, vital relationship **honors those who fear the LORD**. This means that he affirms and associates with those who reverence God with a life of faith and obedience.

15:4c–d. The fifth couplet advances this profile of purity further, noting the firm, unwavering commitment of the person who genuinely worships God. A person who is allowed access to God is one **who keeps his oath**. He maintains the integrity of his word, standing for what he has promised to do, resisting the urge to bend or buckle under pressure. He keeps his word, meaning he holds fast to his commitments, no matter what the cost. This he does, **even when it hurts**, meaning he keeps his word when it means personal loss and pain.

15:5a–b. Finally, David lists the sixth couplet, focusing upon how the person who brings his tithe to God in worship uses his money. A genuine worshiper is one **who lends his money without usury**. He is a believer who does not take advantage of the person who must borrow. Taking interest from fellow Israelites was strictly forbidden by the Mosaic Law (Exod. 22:25; Lev. 25:36). Strict regulations on borrowing and lending money were instituted by the Lord (Deut. 23:19–20; 24:10–13). A genuine worshiper worships God by using his money to help others in need. At the same time, he **does not accept a bribe against the innocent**. True worshipers cannot be bought by this world's system. They do not let the potential for personal gain influence matters of principle.

The Strong Assurance (15:5c)

> **SUPPORTING IDEA:** *The person who walks in personal holiness will never be shaken because he has a refuge in God.*

15:5c. He who does these things will never be shaken. The correspondence of living one's life in the context of God's presence is that he is "like a tree planted by streams of water" (Ps. 1:3). The roots of a righteous and blameless life cause a person to stand secure and not slip or shake when the storms of life rage. Jesus noted this principle when he spoke of the wise and foolish builders (Matt. 7:24–27; Luke 6:47–49).

> **MAIN IDEA REVIEW:** *David describes the moral integrity and personal holiness of the person who worships God.*

III. CONCLUSION

God's Word Alone

A mother was visiting her son at college. Upon entering his dorm room, her eye swept across the walls which were covered with more than a dozen suggestive pictures. Her heart was grieved, but she said nothing. Several days later, the mailman delivered a package to the young man. It was a gift from his mother, a beautifully framed print illustrating the truth of Psalm 15:1–2. The boy hung the calligraphed Scripture on the wall above his desk, and the more he looked at the verses, the more he began to feel convicted by his other pictures. That night as he went to bed, he removed the pin-up picture which hung closest to the framed verses. Then, the next day, another picture was consigned to the wastebasket. Day after day the rest of the pictures began to disappear from the walls until only one frame remained—the illustrated print of God's Word.

The key to living a holy life is to live a Scripture-saturated life. When God's Word dwells within a person, sin diminishes. The light of his holiness always exposes areas of darkness, driving them away. Living a righteous life requires focusing and meditating upon the glory and majesty of the Word. The knowledge of the Scriptures, when united with faith, tends to drive out the practice of sin.

IV. LIFE APPLICATION

The Holiness of God

All who desire to worship God must have a right understanding of his holiness. God is "Holy, holy, holy" (Isa. 6:3), meaning he is transcendent, majestic, all-glorious, sinlessly perfect, and without any blemish or impurity (Exod. 15:11). A deep realization of the blazing holiness of God is essential for all who would rightly approach God. Not until a person has beheld the holiness of God is he able to understand the true state of his or her spiritual condition. Everyone must see himself in light of the holy character of God. Until he does, his self-knowledge is significantly flawed. Thus David prayed,

"Search me, O God, and know my heart; test me and know my anxious thoughts. See if there is any offensive way in me, and lead me in the way everlasting" (Ps. 139:23–24).

Such a preoccupation with this most central of God's attributes will lead to the realization of a person's own sin, as well as soul-searching confession of sorrow over sin. It was only after Isaiah saw the holiness of God that he became aware of his own sinfulness and the sinfulness of those around him (Isa. 6:5). A proper view of God, aided by the convicting work of the Holy Spirit, will drive a person to confess sin. This confession is not merely a formal acknowledgment of iniquity, as if done clinically or callously. Rather, true confession is seeing sin as God sees it (1 John 1:9) and hating it as God hates it. This results in the giving up of one's evil ways. Not until the holiness of God is seen is a person able to see sin as God sees it. Only after sins have been confessed is a believer ready to enter the presence of God in meaningful worship.

V. PRAYER

God, words fail to convey the magnitude of your holiness. You alone are holy! We declare our total depravity and your right to judge us because of our unholiness. We praise you that you have not left us to ourselves but you have provided us a way to be holy through the Lord Jesus Christ. Father, we beg you to conform us daily to the image of the Lord Jesus Christ so that we may be holy as you are holy. In his name we pray. Amen.

VI. DEEPER DISCOVERIES

A. Sanctuary (15:1)

This word is undoubtedly a reference to the tabernacle where the ark of the covenant rested. This is where God promised to dwell and to "meet" with Moses (Exod. 25:22). During David's reign this sanctuary was prepared by David for the ark of the covenant when he moved it to Jerusalem. The ark represented God's special presence within Israel and his protection of Israel against her enemies. Above the mercy seat, between the cherubim, was where God's shekinah glory radiated.

B. Holy (15:1)

The word *holy* (Heb. *qodesh*) means, in a primary sense, that which is "consecrated, sacred, set apart, dedicated, hallowed." In Leviticus 10:10 and Ezekiel 22:26, *qodesh* is set over against that which is "common" (Heb. *chol*). Like the Holy of Holies (Exod. 26:33–34; 2 Chr. 3:8,10) the temple (Ps. 20:2;

Dan. 8:14), and the holy tabernacle (Exod. 28:43; 29:30; 35:19; 39:1), the holy hill was holy because of God's intrinsic holiness (cp. Isa. 6:3). The presence of God made the objects near him holy (cp. Exod. 3:5). Because God is holy, his people must be holy (cp. Lev. 11:44; 19:2; 1 Pet. 1:16), which is the point of this psalm. In a secondary sense, the word *holy* means that which is "morally pure, sinless, without moral or ethical blemish." The holy hill was a pure place and without sin because it was set apart to God. Therefore, worshipers must be pure as they approach God.

C. Wrong (15:3)

This word (Heb. *ra*) is an adjective which means "that which is bad, evil, wicked, or corrupt." It is used of evil words (Prov. 15:28), evil thoughts (Gen. 6:5; 8:21), and evil actions (Prov. 2:14; Exod. 5:22–23; Deut. 17:5; Neh. 13:17; 2 Kgs. 3:2).

D. Shaken (15:5)

The word *shaken* (Heb. *mot*) means "to waver, slip, fall." This word is used fourteen times in the Psalms. In Psalm 55:22, David wrote, "Cast your cares on the LORD and he will sustain you; he will never let the righteous fall." In Psalm 62:2, David wrote, "He alone is my rock and my salvation; he is my fortress, I will never be shaken." In 62:6 he wrote, "He alone is my rock and my salvation; he is my fortress. I will not be shaken." Notice that these statements are conditional statements. In other words, the only way a person cannot be shaken when under attack is if God is the rock, salvation, and fortress of his or her life. In Psalm 93:1, *mot* is applied to the world that cannot be shaken because of God's sovereign rule.

VII. TEACHING OUTLINE

A. The Searching Question (1)
  1. Who may approach God? (1a)
  2. Who may abide with God? (1b)
B. The Spiritual Qualifications (2–5b)
  1. His character must be holy (2a–b)
    a. He pursues blamelessness (2a)
    b. He practices righteousness (2b)
  2. His conversations must be holy (2c–3a)
    a. He speaks truth (2c)
    b. He suppresses slander (3a)
  3. His contacts must be holy (3b–c)
    a. He restrains from sin (3b)
    b. He refrains from slurs (3c)
  4. His company must be holy (4a–b)

a. He rejects reprobates (4a)
b. He reveres believers (4b)
5. His commitments must be holy (4c–d)
a. He stands on his Word (4c)
b. He suffers for his Word (4d)
6. His commerce must be holy (5a–b)
a. He lends money without interest (5a)
b. He refuses money with interest (5b)
C. The Strong Assurance (5c)
1. He will be intimate with God (5c)
2. He will be immovable in God (5c)

VIII. ISSUES FOR DISCUSSION

1. Do I examine myself spiritually before I attempt to enter God's presence and worship him?
2. Am I living a blameless and righteous life?
3. In what ways have I attacked and slandered the character of others?
4. Do I speak the whole truth when interacting with others?
5. Do I use my money to help others and to glorify God?

Psalm 16

Living Hope

┤ Q u o t e ├

"*H*ope can see heaven through the thickest clouds."

T h o m a s   B r o o k s

Psalm 16

I. INTRODUCTION

*N*o one is ready to live until he is first ready to die. Only in facing the reality of death with a living faith in God is a person prepared to live boldly and courageously for him, even in the face of troubling adversity. This was true in the life of David as recorded in Psalm 16 as he faced another life-threatening trial. This psalm is a song of confident trust in God in which the psalmist was able to live life to the fullest because he was gripped with a living hope in God beyond the grave.

Psalm 16 was written at an unknown time when David was hard-pressed, perhaps when he faced threats to his life in the wilderness or severe opposition to his reign as king. David boldly declared that God had been his portion in life, so he would trust him even in death. No matter what David faced, his trust was anchored in the Lord, and this caused his heart to rejoice. David was gripped by a resolute reliance on God in the face of death. He looked beyond this life to the glories of the resurrection and glorification to come.

This psalm is a *miktam,* the meaning of which is uncertain. Verses 8–11 were quoted by Peter on the day of Pentecost (Acts 2:25–28), and verse 10b was cited by Paul at Antioch (Acts 13:35–37); both were used in reference to the resurrection of Jesus Christ.

II. COMMENTARY

> **MAIN IDEA:** *In the face of mounting adversity, David rejoices in the Lord, recounting the blessings of following him and the glory to come after death.*

A David's Prayer (16:1–2)

16:1–2. With a quiet confidence David began by praying, **Keep me safe, O God**, as he asked for God's protection. He reached out for the security that God alone can give. The basis of this request is that God was David's **refuge**. David had put his trust exclusively in God. Only he could protect David from the dangers of life. In this prayer of trust, David **said to the LORD, You are My Lord**, expressing total reliance on him. The Lord was the source of all that made life good and enjoyable for him. So David declared, **Apart from you I have no good thing**. God was his all and all, his security and satisfaction, his one and only good thing.

B David's Perplexity (16:3–4)

16:3–4. Turning his attention to the believers in the land, David rejoiced that they were **the glorious ones**, choice in the sight of God. With deep love for the godly citizens of Israel, King David wrote that they were those **in whom is all my delight**. But in stark contrast with these who, like David, trusted God, there were the ungodly who ran after **other gods** in a religious syncretism that would only **increase** their **sorrows**. With a compromising faith, they had weakened their loyalty to God. Thus, their **libations of blood** offered in worship were not poured out to God but to these false gods. David would have nothing to do with these **gods** or the people who worshiped them.

C David's Pledge (16:5–6)

16:5–6. Reaffirming his exclusive allegiance to the one true God, David prayed, **LORD, you have assigned me my portion and my cup**. The worship of other gods was no temptation to him because he had found total security and satisfaction in the Lord. His portion, referring to the inheritance a father leaves his son, and cup, or the goodness a host offers his guest, refer to the full life that he enjoyed in the Lord. His **lot** in life was **secure** because the Lord was his God. Spiritually speaking, David's **boundary lines** were expansive, allowing for a full provision of divine blessing. His **inheritance** was the Lord himself and all his overflowing goodness and provision.

D David's Praise (16:7–11)

16:7–8. Because of God's abundant favor, David offered **praise** to the Lord specifically because the Lord counseled him. So perfect was God's advice that it remained lodged in his **heart** even **at night**. He declared, **I have set the LORD always before me.** This was a place of undivided focus and exclusive preeminence. God was at his **right hand**, the position of highest exaltation, as his all-sufficient sustainer. Thus, David would **not be shaken** by any danger. God was unmovable; so was he.

16:9–10. Even in the face of life-threatening ordeals, David remained **glad**, and he rejoiced. He knew his **body** would also **rest secure**, even in death. With exuberant praise, he exulted, God **will not abandon me to the grave.** Not even death would separate him from God; he would not **see decay** by lying in the grave in a meaningless existence. God would forever be his portion.

16:11. Because the Lord was at David's right hand (v. 8), he would one day be at the Lord's **right hand**, where he would enjoy **eternal pleasures**. God had **made known** to him **the path of life**. This path would ultimately lead to God's presence in heaven where he would experience an overflowing, undiminishing **joy.**

III. CONCLUSION

Life in this world may end without warning. Death rarely sends its advance notice. Thus, believers should live every moment of every day as if it were their last. Richard Baxter once said, "Always preach as a dying man to dying men, as if never to preach again."

Only in living as dying men will believers live as God intends. Believers fix their hope on God, who is the only safe refuge from the deadly dangers which threaten the righteous. Like David, the believer must always set the Lord before him, constantly meditating upon his rock-solid character. Only with such a riveted focus upon God will the Lord become the believer's delight. Believers must continually remind themselves that the Lord has brought us to the path of life and he alone can bring joy and eternal pleasures. Therefore, the believer may confidently say with David, "We will not be shaken."

IV. TEACHING OUTLINE

A. David's Prayer (1–2)
  1. Save me! (1)
  2. Satisfy me! (2)
B. David's Perplexity (3–4)
  1. Saints are delightful (3)

      2. Sinners are disturbing (4)

C. David's Pledge (5–6)

      1. God Is my portion (5)

      2. God Is my inheritance (6)

D. David's Praise (7–11)

      1. For further instruction (7)

      2. For firm resolution (8)

      3. For future resurrection (9–10)

      4. For final glorification (11)

Psalm 17

Soul Survivor

"Prayer is a shield to the soul, a sacrifice to God, and a scourge for Satan."

John Bunyan

I. INTRODUCTION

*I*n every adversity of life, prayer is one of the believer's greatest weapons, a sure and trusted instrument that brings victory in the face of defeat. This proved to be true in David's life as he found himself in perilous situations, calling out to God to deliver him. David learned to put his trust in God, relying upon his presence and power to rescue him from harm.

The relevance of Psalm 17 is timeless, speaking to all believers who find themselves under attack from the unrighteous. Such persecution arises as a result of the spiritual warfare in which Christians find themselves, a clash between good and evil, light and darkness, heaven and hell. In the midst of such conflict, God must be the believer's first line of defense. This is precisely where the psalmist found himself in this "prayer of David."

This is the first psalm characterized as an intercession to God (cp. Pss. 86; 90; 102; 142). Prayer to God is the Christian's most powerful rebuttal when under attack by godless enemies.

II. COMMENTARY

> **MAIN IDEA:** *When persecuted for his faith, David turns to God in prayer, asking that he reveal any personal sin and supply perfect protection.*

A See Me! (17:1–2)

17:1–2. This psalm begins with the language of the courtroom as David pleaded his case before God, the ultimate chief justice, to **hear, O LORD, my righteous plea; listen to my cry.** This request expresses dire urgency for the **ear** of the Lord. This **righteous plea** is an urgent cry for justice in regards to the charges being brought against him. David asked for God's vindication because he believed he had done what was right.

B Search Me! (17:3–5)

17:3–5. Inviting God to **probe** his **heart** and **examine** and **test** him, David believed he was innocent of the charges made against him by his enemies. Not claiming sinless perfection, David did believe himself to be blameless. **You will find nothing,** he believed, of which he could be accused by God. Divine investigation would reveal that he had resolved not to sin and that he had restrained himself from **the ways of the violent.** His **steps** had followed God's **paths** without slipping. David believed that upon God's close scrutiny, his integrity would be preserved.

C Show Me! (17:6–7)

17:6–7. Again appealing to God for a response, David asked that the Lord **answer** him and show the **wonder** of his **great love.** Ultimately, the basis of his petition was not his own integrity, but God's loyal love (Heb. *hesed;* see "Deeper Discoveries," 23:6). He pleaded that God would deliver him from trouble by his **right hand.** David was confident that everyone who took refuge in God would be protected.

D Shield Me! (17:8–12)

17:8–9. In asking for God's protection, David prayed, **Keep me as the apple of your eye.** This expression refers to the protection of the pupil of a person's eyeball. **Hide me in the shadow of your wings,** he continued. This is a picture of welcomed protection from the blazing heat of the hot desert sun. As a mother bird's wing provides shade, so David requested God's protective care from those who would harm him. David petitioned God to be shielded from **the wicked** who assailed him, from his **mortal enemies** who surrounded him.

17:10–12. David described those vicious men from whom he needed to be saved. Insensitive and indifferent to what was right, they had closed up their **callous hearts**, literally, "closed their fat" (cp. Deut. 32:15; Job 15:27). Their dull hearts spoke with **arrogance**. In aggressive pursuit their feet had tracked him down to do him harm. They sought to throw David to **the ground** to devour him **like a lion hungry for prey.** David needed God's protection from such persecution.

E Save Me! (17:13–14a)

17:13. With urgent language David prayed, **Rise up, O LORD, confront them** (cp. 3:7; 9:19–20). This is the language of a person in battle, appealing to God as the divine warrior to intervene on his behalf and **bring them down.** He asked God to confront these enemies, to **rescue** him by wielding his **sword** against them. The battle belongs to the Lord!

17:14a. Encircled by such hatred, David pleaded to be saved from such **men** who desired to do him harm. He declared that such men were **of this world**, meaning a part of the evil system that is opposed to God and his people. Their **reward** was confined to **this world.** Believers need God's deliverance from such evil.

F Satisfy Me! (17:14b–15)

17:14b. Concluding with a confession of confidence in God, David testified to divine goodness. Addressing the Lord, he declared, **You still the hunger of those you cherish.** This means that God fully satisfies the hearts of believers whom he loves. So abundant are the Lord's earthly, temporal blessings that **their sons have plenty** as they **store up wealth for their children.** Certainly there are exceptions to this maxim.

17:15. God also promises eternal, spiritual blessings for those who trust him. One day, David knew, he would see God's **face.** Anticipating a greater reward that was based upon an imputed, divine **righteousness**, David looked ahead to the vision of God in heaven (Rev. 22:4). Beyond the grave he would be **satisfied with seeing** the Lord and, in that day, being glorified, or made fully in his **likeness** (1 John 3:2).

III. CONCLUSION

When attacked by the world, believers should look to God in prayer, asking his help in perilous times. Persecution should drive a person closer to the Lord, seeking his divine protection and sustaining grace. Someone said that "though the outlook is often bleak, the uplook is always bright." When opposed by the world, the believer should always examine his own heart and life to determine if the attack has been brought on by his own sin. Sometimes God uses the unrighteous to chasten the righteous.

Furthermore, believers must always look forward. The heat of adversity should always cause us to long for the glories of heaven and the beauties of the world to come. This world is passing away; heaven is eternal. Persecution is a reminder of this truth.

IV. TEACHING OUTLINE

A. See Me! (1–2)
  1. Hear my righteous plea (1)
  2. See my righteous life (2)
B. Search Me! (3–5)
  1. Examine my heart (3a)
  2. Examine my mouth (3b–4a)
  3. Examine my ways (4b–5)
C. Show Me! (6–7)
  1. Reveal your loyal love (6–7a)
  2. Reveal your deliverance (7b)
D. Shield Me! (8–9)
  1. Under divine care (8–12)
    a. As apple of God's eye (8a)
    b. Under shadow of God's wings (8b–9)
  2. From the wicked (9–12)
    a. Their hearts are callous (10a)
    b. Their mouths are arrogant (10b)
    c. Their feet are pursuing (11a)
    d. Their eyes are alert (11b)
    e. Their attacks are ravenous (12)
E. Save Me! (13–14a)
  1. Defeat my enemies (13a)
  2. Deliverer your servant (13b–14a)
F. Satisfy Me! (14b–15)
  1. With earthly blessings (14b)
  2. With eternal blessings (15)

Psalm 18

Anchored to the Rock

"One with God is a majority."

W i l l i a m   C a r e y

Psalm 18

I. INTRODUCTION

In every soul-testing trial, the believer must find strength in a refuge greater than himself. He must be anchored to a rock greater than the trial in which he finds himself. The only sure fortress is that rock which is highest of all—the Lord himself. This is the truth that David discovered and recorded in this psalm.

Psalm 18 is the fourth longest psalm in the Book of Psalms. It contains David's praise for repeatedly delivering him from all his enemies. The long title mentions that "the LORD delivered him from the hand of all his enemies and from the hand of Saul." Thus, this psalm celebrates David's victories over all his enemies rather than one specific triumph. Included in these many deliverances is one of his most noted victories—his rescue from Saul. This psalm also appears in 2 Samuel 22; it was recorded after the death of Saul.

Throughout this psalm, God is revealed as a rock (vv. 2,31,46), or the all-sufficient protection that David found in God. During the years he fled from Saul, and later Absalom, David escaped to the rocky cliffs, knowing he would be safe there. But in reality it was God who was his fortress of protection, a sure foundation for his soul.

II. COMMENTARY

MAIN IDEA: *David rejoices in God who has rescued him from all his enemies throughout his life.*

A David's Rejoicing (18:1–3)

18:1–3. David began with a vow to praise God. He was confident of divine protection for his life. He declared, **I love you, O LORD, my strength**, using a word for love (Heb. *raham*) that emphasizes the strong favor and tender intimacy of his heart toward God.

He used seven military metaphors to picture God's love: **my rock**, a foundation of stability and protection; **my fortress**, a high place of refuge and defense when under attack; **my deliverer**, a savior in the evil day; **my rock**, a different word than above, meaning a strong defense; **my shield**, a piece of heavy armor to deflect the enemies' arrows and swords; **horn of my salvation**, a description of power in battle; **my stronghold**, meaning God's care for his servant. God was all this to David. This prompted him to call on the Lord when his enemies attacked.

B David's Reasons (18:4–45)

18:4–6. David was in danger as the **cords of death** surrounded him as if he were tied down and unable to escape. Furthermore, the **torrents of destruction** overwhelmed him as if he were drowning. The **cords of the grave** coiled around him, entrapping him. So strong was their grip that the **snares of death** would not yield David, their helpless prisoner. In this perilous situation, he **cried to God for help**, confident that he would hear his **voice**.

18:7–15. The Lord came to David's rescue, intervening dramatically on his behalf. This bursting upon the scene is represented poetically as an earthquake. **The earth trembled and quaked** and **mountains shook** to overturn his circumstances. God **parted the heavens and came down** in wrathful vengeance to deal with David's enemies. Attended by **the cherubim**, God descended from heaven to answer David's prayer like a violent thunderstorm with **dark rain clouds, hailstones,** and **bolts of lightning.**

18:16–19. In this divine intervention, God **reached down** and **took hold** of David in order to deliver him **out of deep waters**. He rescued David from his enemies who were **too strong** for him—but not so for God. **The LORD was my support**, David testified. He released him out of this tight squeeze into a **spacious place.**

18:20–24. David also declared that the Lord rewarded him. This happened because he walked in **cleanness**, having refrained from **evil**, having kept God's law, and having been **blameless**. For this, the Lord **rewarded** him **according to** his **righteousness**. David did not make a claim for sinless perfection. He simply stated that he had devoted himself to following the Lord, and this had resulted in a godly life.

18:25–27. God rewards man according to his character. To those who are **faithful** to God, the Lord, in turn, is **faithful** (1 Sam. 2:30). Likewise, God shows himself to be **blameless** and **pure** to those who are the same. But those who are **crooked** find God to be **shrewd** to them, meaning that he will judge them in harsh ways. If a person insists on pursuing devious ways, God will reward him accordingly, giving him what he deserves. According to David, the Lord exalts the **humble** but will **bring low** the **haughty**.

18:28–36. Furthermore, David claimed that God caused his life to flourish by his favor. He claimed that the Lord would keep his **lamp burning**; God would cause his life to flourish. With the Lord's **help** he could **advance** against all opposition, even **scale a wall** in battle. Because God was his **shield** and **Rock**, the Lord enabled David **to stand** with **strength** on the **heights**, a place of victory. David could fight triumphantly because God empowered him supernaturally to **bend a bow of bronze**. God alone sustained him to make him **great** before his enemies. The Lord made David's footing sure on the **path** to victory so David would not fall.

18:37–42. Empowered by divine strength, David defeated all his **enemies and overtook them**; he even **destroyed** and **crushed them**. Clearly, it was God, he testified, who **armed** him **with strength** to utterly beat them. Every victory David won was due to God's empowering him.

18:43–45. Having routed his enemies, David was elevated by God to rule over them. He testified, **you have made me the head of nations**, a position of political and military superiority. These once-imposing foes were now **subject to** and obeyed him because God had given him the victory. So complete was this God-given triumph that they cringed before David and lost **heart**.

𝐂 David's Refrain (18:46–50)

18:46–50. With a concluding outburst of praise, David raised his voice to declare, **The LORD lives!** He had witnessed God's intervention in his life. This compelled him to shout, **Praise be to my Rock!** God vindicated David and subdued his foes who were violent men. David concluded, **I will sing praises to your name** because God had given great victories. So total were these triumphs that they extended not only to David but to **his descendants forever**.

III. CONCLUSION

David's example in this psalm calls out to every believer to make God his refuge in every trial, trusting him for deliverance. The Lord is an immovable rock who will save those who attach themselves to him. No threatening enemy can overcome God; he is a fortress to everyone who takes refuge in him. With unwavering hope, the righteous should rest in the Lord, assured of his ultimate victory. They should place all their faith in God, the rock who cannot fall or falter.

With no confidence in the flesh, the people of God should entrust themselves to the Lord, steadfast in their dependence on him. Even after God rescues from the day of attack, the believer should persevere, knowing that other enemies lurk in the shadows whom God alone can defeat. God alone is our hope and shield.

IV. TEACHING OUTLINE

A. David's Rejoicing (1–3)
  1. My regard for God (1a)
  2. My refuge in God (1b–3)
    a. My rock, fortress, deliverer (1b)
    b. My shield, salvation, stronghold (2–3)
B. David's Reasons (4–45)
  1. God rescued me (4–19)
    a. Personally from death (4–6)
    b. Powerfully from heaven(7–15)
    c. Perfectly from foes (16–19)
  2. God rewarded me (20–27)
    a. By my righteousness (20–24)
    b. By his faithfulness (25–27)
  3. God renewed me (28–42)
    a. Energizing me (28–29)
    b. Encouraging me(30–31)
    c. Empowering me (32–33)
    d. Equipping me (34–36)
    e. Enabling me (37–42)
  4. God restored me (43–45)
    a. Others are subject to me (43)
    b. Others shake before me (44–45)
C. David's Refrain (46–50)
  1. God subdues (46–47)
  2. God saves (48)
  3. God succeeds (49–50)

Psalm 19
Unveiled Glory

"*We* are all starved for the glory of God, not self. No

one goes to the Grand Canyon to increase self-esteem. . . .

There is greater healing for the soul in beholding the splen-

dor than there is in beholding self."

J o h n   P i p e r

I. INTRODUCTION

Your Chief Pursuit in Life

Approach ten people randomly on the street and ask them, "What is your chief pursuit in life?" A wide variety of responses will probably follow. Money, love, marriage, sex, freedom, security, status, pleasure, peace, and happiness would top the list. But there is only one main purpose for which man was created—and that is for the glory of God. This is God's chief pursuit in all he does—the magnification of his own glory. So this must be every believer's pursuit.

What is God's glory? A distinction must be made between his *intrinsic* glory and his *ascribed* glory. God's intrinsic glory is the sum total of all his divine attributes—his holiness, sovereignty, righteousness, grace, truth, goodness, mercy, justice, omnipresence, omniscience, omnipotence, and more. All these divine perfections constitute his intrinsic glory, and it is this that God desires to display in all his creation and works. Then, as God unveils this glory to man, man is to give him glory, which is *ascribed* glory, or the glory due his name. This is man's chief purpose in life. He is to live to make God's glory known in the world and to ascribe glory to him.

Psalm 19 is a magnificent psalm declaring that God's intrinsic glory is unveiled to man through two primary means: general revelation (vv. 1–6) and special revelation (vv. 7–14). General revelation is God's self-disclosure through creation. This revelation is available to all people, and it provides basic, foundational truths about God's existence and attributes. On the other hand, special revelation is God's manifested greatness to people through his inspired Word, the Bible. This revelation is special because it goes beyond the elementary truths of general revelation and testifies to how a person may know this great God and how he or she may live in a manner pleasing to him.

Psalm 19 records these two distinct means of divine revelation, both general and special. In this hymn of praise, "a psalm of David," the psalmist testifies that God has revealed himself to mankind through these two avenues—his world and his Word. David reflects on the glory of God in natural revelation and the glory God in special revelation which alone can save and sanctify.

II. COMMENTARY

Unveiled Glory

> **MAIN IDEA:** *God has made himself known to man through natural revelation in the physical creation and through supernatural revelation in the Scriptures.*

A God's Glory in His World (19:1–6)

> **SUPPORTING IDEA:** *The heavens proclaim the glory of God to all people around the world.*

19:1. First, God has revealed himself to all people through his creation, more specifically, through the universe. **The heavens**, referring to the sun, stars, and planets, **declare the glory of God**. This divine glory is the sum total of all God's holy character and attributes which are made known to man. **The skies**, referring to the lower atmosphere, clouds, weather, and so on, **proclaim the work of his hands**. The creation above testifies to the existence and excellencies of a Creator, God himself, who made it. The truth about God— that he is *who* and *what* he is—is made known through the skillful **work of his hands**.

19:2. This self-disclosing communication by God of himself to man is unceasing: **Day after day they pour forth speech; night after night they display knowledge**. This knowledge is the general revelation of God's character, especially his eternal power, goodness, genius, kindness, and faithfulness

(Rom. 1:20). This disclosure is a "soundless sermon" continually communicated in the skies.

19:3–4a. Even though creation does not speak audible words that can be heard, its **voice** reaches all nations and is equally accessible wherever human **speech** and **language** is spoken. No person anywhere is without God's self-revelation through creation. **Their voice goes out into all the earth,** literally, **to the ends of the world** as the entire globe is covered with the handiwork of God.

19:4b–5. David illustrated by pointing to **the sun.** He compared the sky and outer space to a **tent** in which he had placed the sun as a torch, lighting up the vast expanse above. Furthermore, this sun is like **a bridegroom coming forth from his pavilion,** radiant, glowing, beaming, and bright. Also, the sun is **like a champion rejoicing to run his course,** that is, strong, tireless, enduring, always moving forward, and never growing weary. God is like the noonday sun—bright and blinding in the radiance of his glory. He is high and exalted above man, unceasing and tireless in his work, powerful in all that he does, reaching out to the ends of the earth, enlightening and empowering all people.

19:6. Referring to the motion of the sun, David concluded, **It rises at one end of the heavens and makes its circuit to the other.** Rising in the east, it travels every day, humanly speaking, to set in the west, and **nothing is hidden from its heat.** In other words, the sun is always at work in all places, just like God its Creator. The glory of God is clearly seen in the sun. As it makes its daily journey across the skies, it pours out **its heat** on every creature, making its presence felt. So it is with God, making himself known through the sun.

B God's Glory in His Word (19:7–14)

> **SUPPORTING IDEA:** *God most fully reveals himself to man through his written Word, known as special revelation.*

19:7. Suddenly shifting focus, David gave attention to the glory of God revealed in his Word. He gave six descriptions of the sufficiency of God's written Word (vv. 7–9) which goes far beyond what natural revelation does. While the sun and the skies above reveal the existence and infinite power of God, Scripture reveals the only way to know God personally. **The law of the LORD is perfect** (Heb. *tamim*), meaning whole, complete, sufficient, lacking nothing, or comprehensive, **reviving the soul.** It is so perfect that it can convert, transform, and refresh the entire inner person.

The statutes of the LORD are trustworthy, meaning they are neither unstable nor fallible but unwavering and immovable. Not like shifting sands, God's commands cause a person to stand firm while **making wise the simple.** The Hebrew word for *simple* comes from a root meaning "an open door" or one who is gullible to false teaching, failing to shut his mind to error. Only Scripture can make a person **wise**, or skillful, in the issues of daily living.

19:8. Furthermore, **the precepts of the LORD are right**; they lay out the proper path through the intricate complexities of life, steering a person to the right course in life. God's Word always directs God's people in the right way, the way that pleases God. Thus, it gives **joy to the heart**, exciting and empowering the inner person with divine truth. **The commands of the LORD are radiant**, not dark and mysterious but clear and lucid, brightly shining, revealing truth, **giving light to the eyes**. They enlighten everyone who follows them; they are a lamp and light for life's travelers (Ps. 119:105).

19:9. Moreover, **the fear of the LORD is pure**; it has no impurity, filthiness, defilement, or imperfections. Scripture is flawless, unadulterated truth, without any error, **enduring forever**. The Bible will never pass away (Mark 13:31), nor will it ever need amending, updating, or editing. Instead, it will remain permanently relevant and eternally true. **The ordinances of the LORD are sure** (Heb. *emet*), meaning reliable, stable, **and altogether righteous**, presenting the divine standard for daily living and designed to cause believers to obey God with righteous lives.

19:10–11. Regarding the Scriptures, the psalmist declared, **they are more precious than gold**, even **pure gold**. This means God's Word is infinitely more desirable and valuable than anything this world has to offer. Likewise, the sacred writings are **sweeter than honey**, fully satisfying our spiritual hunger and a source of great pleasure and enrichment.

By the Scriptures, David declared, **is your servant warned** against temptation, sin, error, and every other spiritual threat to his spiritual well-being. Yet, positively, **in keeping them there is great reward**. Obedience to God's Word results in rich spiritual blessings (cp. John 13:17).

19:12–13. A rhetorical question, **Who can discern his errors?** implies an obvious answer: only the person who reads, studies, and meditates on God's Word. Scripture is a lamp that reveals **hidden faults** which must be confessed while asking God to **forgive**. Scripture is also a powerful restraint that prevents believers from participating in sin. Keep also your servant from willful sins, a preserving effect that the Word has upon the hearts of those who obey it.

19:14. David concluded this psalm by expressing to God, **May the words of my mouth and the meditation of my heart be pleasing in your sight**. Only the Word of God applied by the Spirit of God could make his mouth and heart so pleasing before God's all-knowing gaze. This God, in fact, was

David's LORD, **Rock**, and **Redeemer**. Such a great God demands obedience and personal holiness from all worshipers.

> **MAIN IDEA REVIEW:** *God has made himself known to man through natural revelation in the physical creation and through supernatural revelation in the Scriptures.*

III. CONCLUSION

The Right Response

In a PBS documentary entitled *Chariots of the Gods*, the well-known scientist and author Carl Sagan commented on the new optimism that there is life elsewhere in the universe. "It's nice to think that there is someone out there that can help us," he said. Unfortunately, this remark implied that he believed there was no God. His "religion" caused him to look out on the starry splendor of the universe and say, "The cosmos is all that is or ever was or ever will be." His hope to receive help from other beings in the universe is a blind hope.

The truth is God *does* exist and has revealed himself to mankind in ways that are unmistakable and undeniable. Natural revelation in the world has disclosed the fact of God's existence and his attributes. But more than that, the supernatural revelation in his Word has made known the way to know him through the plan of salvation. What is important is that every person should respond appropriately to this divine self-disclosure. This response, as required by Scripture, is for a person to repent of his or her sin and turn to God, believing on his Son, the Lord Jesus Christ.

IV. LIFE APPLICATION

The Living Book

Scripture is the sole instrument through which God has chosen to convict, convert, counsel, and comfort believers. It is the chief instrument through which God has revealed his character to the world. The Bible is a living book (Heb. 4:12a), full of divine and supernatural life, the very life of God himself. All other books are collections of dead words but not the Bible. Martin Luther said, "The Bible is alive, it speaks to me. It has feet, it runs after me. It has hands, it lays hold of me." Thus, the Bible is always relevant, always fresh, never obsolete, never stagnant.

So powerful is the Bible that it is a discerner of our hearts, possessing a living insight into our inner lives. Scripture contains a supernatural capacity to cut into the innermost recesses of a soul, penetrating far deeper than felt needs which lie on the surface. Only the Word can reveal the depths of human depravity and, in turn, lead to the true knowledge of God. Only the Word can convert the lost human soul to God (1 Pet. 1:23).

Furthermore, only the Word of God can sanctify a believer and transform him into the image of Christ. There can be no spiritual growth in our lives apart from the Word of God (1 Pet. 2:2). Scripture is also able to counsel believers, leading us into successful living (Ps. 119:24,98–100,105,130). The Bible touches every aspect of the Christian's life, giving sound instruction for holiness and righteousness.

V. PRAYER

God, our Father, you are the immortal, invisible, all-wise God. We thank you for giving us a glimpse of your great glory through the galaxies which dripped from your finger. We are forever grateful for your voice, which though not heard audibly, is crystal clear through the written Word of Scripture and the living Word, the Lord Jesus Christ. Father, for eternity we will praise you for all you have done for us. For from you, and through you and to you are all things. To you alone be the glory forever. Amen.

VI. DEEPER DISCOVERIES

A. Declare, Proclaim (19:1)

The verbs *declare* and *proclaim* are participial forms, expressive of the continuous revelations of the heavens, and they could be translated "keep on declaring" and "keep on proclaiming."

B. The Heavens (19:1)

The phrase "the heavens" (Heb. *shamayim*) is a plural noun form that literally means "the heights" or that which is raised up or lofty. It refers to the realms of outer space in which the stars, the moon, and the planets exist (Gen. 1:14–17). The phrase "the skies" (Heb. *raqia*) refers to the atmosphere surrounding the earth. This is the troposphere, or the region of breathable atmosphere that blankets the earth and contains the clouds, weather, birds, winds, and so on. This is where the hydrological cycle occurs (Ps. 147:8).

C. Titles of Scripture (19:7–9)

This psalm contains six titles for Scripture, each name emphasizing a different nuance of its ability to execute God's purposes. The first title, "the law (Heb. *tora*) of the LORD" (19:7), comes from a root meaning "to project" or "to teach" and refers to any direction or instruction flowing from the Word of

God that points out or indicates God's will to man. It refers not only to the moral, civil, or ceremonial law but to the whole teaching, instruction, or doctrine of Scripture.

The second title for Scripture, "the statutes (Heb. *edut*) of the LORD" (19:7), is derived from the root "to bear witness" and thus testifies to its divine author. It is a solemn attestation, a declaration of the will of God, the ordinances that became God's standard of conduct. Thus, it was used of the two tablets summarizing the law, the Ten Commandments, that were placed in the ark as a witness to the holy character of God.

A third title for the Bible, "the precepts (Heb. *piqqudim*) of the LORD" (19:8), is a poetical word for injunctions found only in the Book of Psalms, used only in the plural. It literally refers to an authoritative charge or order that is binding upon the recipient. In this instance, it is as from the sovereign Lord of the universe, directing and governing all men.

The fourth title for Scripture, "the commands (Heb. *miswa*) of the LORD" (19:8), signifies a definite, authoritative command or anything ordained by the Lord. It designates the general body of imperative commands contained in God's law.

The fifth title for Scripture, "the fear (Heb. *yira*) of the LORD" (19:9), refers to the parts of God's law that evoke fear (reverence), including passages that reveal God's holiness and awesome judgments. This term is a synonym for the law, since its purpose was to put fear into human hearts (Deut. 4:10). Thus, the Scripture is God's manual for worship, leading those who read it to reverence God, holding him in strictest awe. The Word of God also pronounces divine judgment on those who disobey its message, depicting God as angry at sin. Such passages inspire the fear of God.

The sixth title for Scripture, "the ordinances (Heb. *mishpat*) of the LORD" (19:9), represents a judicial decision that constitutes a precedent, a binding law. It denotes divinely ordered decisions on all kinds of issues in what might be called case-law applications to specific situations of the statutes, precepts, and commands of the law. In the Pentateuch it referred to the laws after the Ten Commandments. The word can also mean God's judgmental acts on the wicked.

VII. TEACHING OUTLINE

A. God's Glory in His World (1–6)
   1. His glory in creation is unmistakable (1)
   2. His glory in creation is unceasing (2)
   3. His glory in creation is unspoken (3)
   4. His glory in creation is universal (4a–b)

5. His glory in creation is undiminished(4c–5)
   a. Like a shining torch (4b)
   b. Like a glowing bridegroom (5a)
   c. Like a strong champion (5b)
6. His glory in creation is unresting (6)
   a. The sun is always rising (6a)
   b. The sun is always setting (6b)
B. God's Glory in His Word (7–14)
   1. Scripture is perfect (7–9)
      a. Reviving the soul (7a)
      b. Teaching the simple (7b)
      c. Rejoicing the heart (8a)
      d. Enlightening the eyes (8b)
      e. Reverencing the spirit(9a)
      f. Directing the life (9b)
   2. Scripture is precious (10)
      a. More valuable than gold (10a)
      b. Sweeter than honey (10b)
   3. Scripture is powerful (11–14)
      a. Rebuking sin (11)
      b. Revealing sin (12)
      c. Restraining sin (13–14)

VIII. ISSUES FOR DISCUSSION

1. Do I meditate on all that God has done to reveal himself to me?
2. Do I use God's Word as a source of restoration between God and myself?
3. Do I long for and desire God and his Word more than anything else in my life?
4. What rewards have I received by following God's Word?

Psalm 20
The Battle Belongs to the Lord

"One Almighty is more than all mighties."

William Gurnall

Psalm 20

I. INTRODUCTION

Only the Lord can lead his people into victory, and this he grants when prayer is offered to him, expressing total reliance on him. Thus, believers must always look to the Lord when they are confronted with conflict. The battle belongs to the Lord. In this psalm King David, the commanding general of Israel's military forces, was preparing to lead his armies into battle. To seek the Lord's favor, the people gathered in a holy convocation to pray for their leader. The people acknowledged their dependence on God, petitioning him for the victory. Such a public gathering involved prayer offered for David, their king-general (vv. 1–5), an expression of confidence in God (vv. 6–8), and a reaffirmation of their reliance on him (v. 9).

This psalm is "a psalm of David," written "for the director of music." Psalm 21 that follows is a celebration *after* the battle, as Israel rejoiced in the victory given by God. Psalm 20 may have been connected to Psalm 21 (see Introduction to Psalm 21). Of one thing they were sure: victory belonged to the Lord.

II. COMMENTARY

MAIN IDEA: *David describes the prayer for military victory offered for him by the people before he leads the armies of Israel into battle.*

A The Petitions for the King (20:1–5)

20:1. As David, Israel's king and commanding general, prepared to go into battle, the congregation of Israel, probably the national leaders, gathered to pray for him. Approaching God in prayer, they asked, **May the** LORD **answer you when you are in distress**, meaning, "May God hear your prayers for victory in the distress of battle." Throughout this prayer, *you* refers to the anointed King David. Likewise, **may the name of the God of Jacob protect you** was a request that the king's physical safety be preserved by divine providence and power.

20:2. Furthermore, they prayed, **May he send you help from the sanctuary** and **from Zion**. This aspect of their intercession acknowledged God's symbolic presence in the ark that David had recaptured and installed in the tabernacle (sanctuary) in Jerusalem (Zion). The people prayed for God's power to uphold, **support**, and sustain the king by granting him powers of leadership, character, reasoning, and decision making as the battle progressed.

20:3. Likewise, they prayed, **May he remember all your sacrifices and accept your burnt offerings**. They requested that David's offerings would be acceptable to God, a reflection that his spiritual life was strong. If the king's leadership in battle was to be strong, his spiritual life must be strong. So the people prayed for the spiritual well-being of their commander.

20:4. In addition, they prayed, **May he give you the desire of your heart and make all your plans succeed**. Since David was a man after God's own heart (1 Sam. 13:14; Acts 13:22), they assumed he would be seeking what God desired. In this sense they asked God to grant the desires of his heart, knowing that his ambitions were holy aspirations for God's kingdom.

20:5. Concluding this prayer, the assembly prayed, **We will shout for joy when you are victorious**. They anticipated shouting for joy over his triumph in battle when they would **lift up . . . banners in the name of our God**. These banners were the troop standards around which their units rallied in battle. Repeating their prayer, they interceded, **May the** LORD **grant all your requests**.

🅱 The Prayer of the King (20:6–8)

20:6. David announced with inner assurance that their prayers on his behalf had surely been heard and would be answered: **Now I know that the** LORD **saves his anointed**. In other words, God would surely grant military victory to David, who had been anointed years before to rule in the divine name (1 Sam. 2:4; 16:13; 2 Sam. 5:3). The word *anointed* was used by David of Saul and now of himself as king (1 Sam 24:6,10; 26:9,11,16,23; 2 Sam. 1:14). Victory over foreign armies was assured because God answered him in prayer **with the saving power of his right hand**. This was an expression of divine omnipotence.

20:7–8. On behalf of the nation, David confessed his trust in God: **Some trust in chariots and some in horses, but we trust in the name of the** LORD our God. David realized that, ultimately, "the battle is not yours, but God's" (2 Chr. 20:15). Those who trusted in their weapons instead of God would be **brought to their knees** and **fall** in defeat (cp. Ps. 33:16–17). But those who trusted in God would **rise up** against the enemy and **stand firm** in victory.

C The Pleadings for the King (20:9)

20:9. In a final reaffirmation the congregation interceded for David, their king-general, petitioning, **O LORD, save the king!** One last time, they asked God to bestow military victory on David as he went into battle.

III. CONCLUSION

Napoleon Bonaparte, the famed French military leader, was once asked, "Is God on the side of France?" Intoxicated with the power of his own success, he retorted, "God is on the side that has the heaviest artillery." Later this diminutive dictator boasted, "I make circumstances." But that was before the battle of Waterloo. In 1815, Napoleon's army advanced across Europe into Belgium to face the armies of Britain and Russia where, in spite of his superior weaponry, he lost both the battle *and* his empire. This humbled dictator was unseated from his throne and was exiled to the barren island of St. Helena. Napoleon changed his perspective about God and history. Quoting the words of Thomas à Kempis, this once-proud man acknowledged, "Man proposes, but God disposes."

Napoleon's fall is a valuable lesson for everyone. God is sovereign, and he rules over the affairs of all people, from the greatest to the least. This is the lesson that all of us must learn. God controls human history and destinies, and he is guiding them to their appointed end. God's sovereignty must be the confidence of all believers when faced with the opposition of spiritual forces. God is God, and victory belongs to him.

IV. TEACHING OUTLINE

A. The Petitions for the King (1–5)
1. For God's protection (1)
2. For God's power (2)
3. For God's prosperity (3–5)
    a. To accept David's sacrifices (3)
    b. To advance David's plans (4)
    c. To achieve David's victory (5)
B. The Prayer of the King (6–8)
1. God saves the king (6)

   2. God secures the victory (7–8)
        a. Not by man's resources (7a, 8a)
        b. But by his name (7b, 8b)
C. The Pleadings for the King (9)
    1. Save the king (9a)
    2. Answer our prayers (9b)

Psalm 21

Rejoicing in the Victory

"*There* can be no victory where there is no combat."

Richard Sibbes

Psalm 21

I. INTRODUCTION

The Lord who leads his people into battle is the same Lord who will lead them into victory. And when that triumph comes, believers should give thanks with grateful hearts to God who alone has won the day. Psalm 21 is a celebrative psalm, a song of jubilant praise offered to God for the victory he granted when David led Israel into battle against their enemies.

This psalm may have been connected originally with Psalm 20 because the structure and contents are similar. If so, Psalm 20 is a prayer offered *before* battle, a request for victory as David prepared to lead his armies into the conflict. Thus, Psalm 21 would be a prayer offered by David *after* this same battle after he, the Lord, defeated their enemies. In these verses David, the king and general of Israel, along with the people, rejoiced in the triumphs granted by God over their enemies. Likewise, David was encouraged to anticipate future victories in the Lord.

Addressed to "the director of music," this song is "a psalm of David," the same king mentioned in verses 1 and 7.

II. COMMENTARY

> **MAIN IDEA:** *David as the king and commander of Israel's forces rejoices in God's victories granted over his enemies.*

A David's Rejoicing (21:1–6)

21:1–3. The first six verses contain David's celebration for past victories given by God on the battlefield. David praised the Lord first for the divine **strength** he gave which led to **victories**. These **victories**, to be sure, were in direct response to the petitions David had made of God. Accordingly, God **welcomed him** back from battle **with rich blessings** that accompanied the victor. Perhaps this was a reference to spoils gathered from defeated enemies. Most specifically, David returned to exchange his warrior's helmet for the visible emblem of victory—**a crown of pure gold**, possibly the crown that had belonged to the defeated king.

21:4–6. The king had prayed for **length of days**, in essence requesting that his **life** be spared in battle. This prayer was answered, since God **gave it to him**. These military victories enhanced David's **glory, . . . splendor, and majesty** as Israel's king. God had given him prominence. Likewise, this regal honor would lead ultimately to the **eternal blessings** of God's reward in heaven **for ever**. But presently, David had been **made glad with the joy of** experiencing intimate fellowship with God in his holy **presence**. These battles, like all difficulties that believers face, drew David closer to God.

B David's Reliance (21:7)

21:7. Here is the underlying reason for David's great military victories— **the king trusts in the LORD**. Because he relied upon **the unfailing love** (see "Deeper Discoveries," 23:6) of God, he was granted success by God on the battlefield. Thus, he would **not be shaken** when attacked by the enemy but would stand immovable and secure.

C David's Reckoning (21:8–12)

21:8–12. As David and the people looked to the future, they rejoiced that more victories were certain to follow as they continued to rely on God. They believed that the Lord would capture their **enemies** and **seize** their **foes**. In the day of battle, God would **make them like a fiery furnace**, burning them up in his wrath. So complete would be his victory that **their posterity** would be utterly destroyed **from the earth**. David's enemies might **plot evil against** him, but they would not **succeed**. These foes would be forced to **turn their backs** in retreat and run away in the day of battle. Victory belongs to the Lord!

D David's Request (21:13)

21:13. In this final appeal, David entreated the Lord to assert his irresistible **strength** again to defeat his enemies. David and the people would **sing and praise** God, who was full of **might** to win all other conflicts.

III. CONCLUSION

In the battles of life, believers are attacked constantly by three great foes: the world, the flesh, and the devil. Spiritual warfare, like hand-to-hand combat, is difficult because behind these three evils are forces that seek to destroy believers (Eph. 6:12). It is critical that believers live with unshakable confidence in the Lord. "Thanks be to God who always leads us in triumphal procession in Christ" (2 Cor. 2:14). God promises victory wherever we go as we trust and follow him. As God has proven himself victorious in the past, he will grant similar spiritual victories in the present as his people rely on him.

IV. TEACHING OUTLINE

A. David's Rejoicing (1–6)
  1. For empowered fighting (1)
  2. For effectual prayers (2)
  3. For extended days (3–4)
  4. For earthly honor (5)
  5. For eternal blessing (6a)
  6. For enthusiastic joy (6b)
B. David's Reliance (7)
  1. His personal trust in God (7a)
  2. His powerful trust in God (7b)
C. David's Reckoning (8–12)
  That his enemies be:
  1. Captured (8)
  2. Consumed (9–10)
  3. Conquered (11–12)
D. David's Request (13)
  1. God, assert your power! (13a)
  2. God, accept our praise! (13b)

Psalm 22
A Prophecy of the Cross

"*The strongest objective argument for the validity of Scripture comes from fulfilled Bible prophecy.*"

John MacArthur

I. INTRODUCTION

The Amazing Proof of Prophecy

The greatest proof that the Bible is the inspired, inerrant Word of God is fulfilled prophecy. Only God knows the future. This is because only God ordains the future and only he can bring it to pass. Students of Scripture understand that many events were recorded in Scripture hundreds of years before they came to pass, and each one fulfilled brings indisputable confirmation that the Scripture is what it claims to be—the inspired, infallible Word of God.

Nowhere is this validation of the Bible more true than those prophecies which were fulfilled at the first coming of Jesus Christ. Although recorded many centuries before his incarnation, more than one hundred Old Testament prophecies concerning the life and ministry of Christ were perfectly fulfilled in the New Testament. Each one documents the authenticity of Scripture.

This is what makes Psalm 22 so amazing. Written one thousand years before the first coming of Christ, this psalm reads as if it were actually recorded by a person standing at the foot of the cross. The very words spoken by Christ from the cross, as well as his thoughts and the injuries he suffered, are recorded here. David, the sweet psalmist of Israel, set forth in this psalm a graphic portrayal of the cross hundreds of years before crucifixion was even invented as a form of capital punishment. With the precision of an eyewitness observing the crucifixion of the Lord Jesus Christ, David, under the direction of the Holy Spirit, wrote the most detailed description of the cross found anywhere in Scripture. Here is David's preview of the cross, a masterpiece that has been called "the fifth gospel," and "the gospel according to David."

It must be admitted that differing opinions exist about whether David wrote this psalm to describe a particular suffering that he himself experienced or as a prophetic psalm looking forward to the Messiah. Undoubtedly, this psalm was written primarily with a future event in mind, specifically the crucifixion of Jesus Christ. This interpretation is supported by several facts.

First, there are no recorded events in the life of David that correspond to this event. Second, the psalm has specific phrases that could only be used of someone undergoing crucifixion. Third, unlike other psalms, this psalm contains no mention of the psalmist's personal sin, confession of sin, or even regret for the pains that he was suffering. Fourth, there is no call to God for vindication of wrongs suffered. Surely if David were writing this psalm of himself, there would be some call for God's vengeance to fall on his enemies. But there is no cry for vindication on his behalf. Therefore, it is concluded that this psalm is a prophetic picture of the coming suffering Servant, the Messiah, who would suffer a grueling execution and would be forsaken of God so his people would know the Lord's forgiveness.

II. COMMENTARY

> **MAIN IDEA:** *The Son of God will be forsaken by God, put to death by evil men, yet remain fully confident in the faithfulness of God to deliver him. This the Lord did so he would declare his victory.*

A Prophecy of the Cross

A Christ's Separation from God (22:1–2)

> **SUPPORTING IDEA:** *God was distant from Jesus as he hung on the cross and did not answer his plea, yet he trusted God for his deliverance.*

22:1. The psalm begins with a poignant rhetorical question that is meant to show the rejection and abandonment suffered by the Son: **My God, my God, why have you forsaken me?** This was the fourth saying of Jesus uttered on the cross. It was the first statement spoken under the shroud of darkness. The intimate call by the Son was like the call of a lost child searching for the father whose face he longed to see again. Yet the absence of the words "my Father" and the use of the words "my God" in their stead indicate a breach in the relationship within the Godhead. This is followed by three statements in which the suffering one asks, **Why have you forsaken me?**

These were the exact words of Christ as quoted in the ninth hour of the day (3:00 p.m.) at the end of the three-hour period of darkness (cp. Matt. 27:46; Mark 15:34). This feeling of abandonment went further because the psalmist continued, **Why are you so far from saving me?** God purposely distanced himself from Jesus as he poured out his wrath on the sin bearer (Isa. 53:10) of his people. The Son cried out in desperation, "Why have you turned your back on me in the hour of my greatest need?" Yet the withdrawal was followed by God's refusal to listen to the Son's plea, **Why are you so far from the words of my groaning?**

No answer came because it was God himself who poured out his wrath on his suffering servant under the veil of darkness. The holiness of God forbade him from intervening in the death of Jesus Christ, since he became sin on behalf of his people (Isa. 53:4–6; 2 Cor. 5:21). This separation was the greatest hell known by Christ—to be utterly rejected by the Father with whom he enjoyed unhindered, intimate fellowship throughout all eternity. Furthermore, Jesus absorbed God's wrath for the sins of many.

22:2. This rejection came from one who was not detached from God. This is evident in the words, **O my God, I cry out by day, but you do not answer**. The desired answer did not come **by day**. This is a reference to the first three hours of the crucifixion of Jesus. As Jesus hung on the cross **by night**, he was **not silent**, yet he still failed to receive a response. The silence of heaven was an experience that Jesus had never known (John 11:41–42). The final three hours of darkness that veiled the earth (noon to 3:00 p.m.) before the death of Jesus is surely the **night** to which the psalmist referred (cp. Matt. 27:45).

Ⓑ Christ's Strength from God (22:3–5)

SUPPORTING IDEA: *Jesus affirms his trust in God to deliver him, knowing he will not be disappointed.*

22:3a. These questions that seem to convey doubt and confusion are followed by a strong assertion of trust in God and his sovereignty. Christ thought to himself, **Yet you are enthroned**, as an affirmation of his understanding that the silence of God did not mean that God had abdicated his position as the sovereign ruler over the affairs of men. Also, this was the answer to Christ's own question "Why?" When Jesus became sin for the many, **the Holy One**, God, hid his face from his own beloved Son. He understood that a holy God would not have fellowship with one who was sinful and unclean.

22:3b–5. Furthermore, the psalmist knew that God was **the praise of Israel**, and this was exemplified by the fact that the **fathers put their trust** in God. The psalmist remembered the faithfulness of God from his past witness when dealing with Israel. Three times in verses 4–5 the verb for *trust* (Heb. *batah*) is used as a synonym for faith in God. Realizing the past faithfulness of God, the psalmist could confidently assert, **They trusted and you delivered them** (cp. Ps. 44:1). God has always been faithful to deliver his people who put their trust in him. "Will God not therefore also be faithful to deliver me?" pictures the psalmist in desperation.

Christ was encouraged to persevere upon the cross, as he meditated on the character of God and his faithfulness to deliver his own in his darkest hour. If the nation of Israel **cried to** the Lord and **were saved**, how much more the Son of God? From the beginning of the nation through the lineage of Abraham (cp. Gen. 15:6), the nation originated with men and women who **trusted and were not disappointed** in God (cp. Heb. 11). Indeed, the Son of God would not be disappointed because the same Father who hid his face from his Son would raise him from the grave in three days.

𝐂 Christ's Scorn from God (22:6–8)

SUPPORTING IDEA: *The ridicule and derision hurled at Jesus Christ by evil men was countered by a trust in God that was active from the time he was in the womb of his mother.*

22:6. The rejection of the Anointed One was not restricted to God alone. Man seized the opportunity but not because of an inherit holiness. Jesus lamented, **I am a worm**, which is an expression of reproach and is used of a maggot that is utterly rejected. Moreover, he stated that he was **not a man**. The treatment that Jesus faced on the cross was inhumane. He was beaten so severely that a person who knew him probably could not recognize him (Isa. 52:14; 53:2–3). The scorn of man was shown in the ill treatment that Jesus suffered at the hands of satanic men who spit upon him (Matt. 26:67), struck him (Matt. 26:67–68), spoke blasphemous words against him (Luke 22:65), flogged him (Matt. 27:26; Mark 15:15; Luke 23:16; John 19:1), and beat him with a staff (Matt. 27:30). The hatred and reproach shown by those who crucified Jesus were prophesied by Isaiah (Isa. 53:3–4,7–8).

22:7–8. The crowd's reaction as they looked to the cross demonstrated the venom of hatred from those who crucified the Lord. Neither the crowds nor the religious leaders, having successfully pushed for the execution of Jesus, were satisfied in their thirst for blood. The phrase **all who see me mock me** indicates that the psalmist foresaw that as Jesus hung on the cross, many would **hurl** blasphemous **insults** while **shaking their heads**. This refers to a mocking gesture similar to jeering or sticking out the tongue. Beyond the outward actions of disgust were the **insults** that flowed from the mouths of his accusers (cp. Matt. 27:43; Mark 15:29–32; Luke 23:35–37).

Ⓓ Christ's Submission to God (22:9–10)

SUPPORTING IDEA: *Jesus remembers God's faithfulness to him at birth and throughout his life.*

22:9–10. Contrary to the accusations of the mockers, Jesus knew that God **brought** him **out of the womb**—a reference to the virgin birth—and that God had **made** him **trust** as a child. Like Job, Jesus could say of God, "Though he slay me, yet will I trust in him" (Job 13:15 KJV). Furthermore, while in his **mother's womb**, he declared, **you have been my God** (Jer. 1:5). Earlier, he meditated on God's faithfulness to others, but presently there was a shift to God's faithfulness to him. As Jesus suffered, he was sustained by meditating on how God had sustained him.

Ⓔ Christ's Suffering from God (22:11–18)

SUPPORTING IDEA: *The anguish and misery placed on the Lord Jesus when he was on the cross attest to the depraved condition of the human heart and the attitudes of men toward God and his Christ.*

22:11–15. The suffering Son asked God to bridge the distance between them: **Do not be far from me, for trouble is near.** Furthermore, Jesus pleaded, **There is no one to help** because his disciples and friends had deserted him. The trouble Jesus encountered on the cross is given in the imagery of being surrounded by a pack of wild, ravenous animals. The picture is one of base brutality. Note the metaphors used in comparing these people to beasts: **strong bulls** (v. 12), **roaring lions** (v. 13), dogs (vv. 16,20), wild oxen (v. 21). When people reject God, they act like animals. The crowd was like a bloodthirsty pack of beasts.

The Lord's strength upon the cross was waning as his heart **turned to wax** and **melted away within** him. This failing strength, mingled with the blistering heat, produced an extreme thirst for water. This is indicated by the phrase **my tongue sticks to the roof of my mouth.** The Lord Jesus Christ, the very one who created the rivers and lakes and who freely gives the water of life, thirsted on the cross (John 19:28). Even though evil men threatened, he realized that God is sovereign and the one who would **lay him in the dust of death** according to his eternal plan.

22:16–18. These **evil men** who crucified Christ were like wild **dogs** who **pierced** his **hands** and his **feet.** This is a prophetic reference to the wounds Jesus suffered in his crucifixion (cp. Isa. 53:5; Zech. 12:10). Although the original text is unclear, "like a lion, my hands my feet," this is a reference to the mauling he suffered or to the binding of his hands and feet. While on the cross, he thought, **I can count all my bones** because he could feel the pain of each one. He was aware that people stared and gloated over him. Here is the shame and indignity Christ felt because of his nakedness before the crowd, his mother, and the other women. The soldiers divided his garments and **cast lots** for his **clothing** (cp. Matt. 27:35; Mark 15:24; Luke 23:34; John 19:24), a phrase that documents his nakedness.

F Christ's Supplication to God (22:19–21)

> **SUPPORTING IDEA:** *As Christ was crucified, he implored the Father to come to his aid and to save him from those who sought to destroy him.*

22:19–20. This silent prayer offered by Christ as he hung on the cross begins with a plea to the Father to **be not far off**. For Jesus this dreadful distance from the Father, his **Strength**, was unbearable. So he cried, **come quickly to help me. Deliver my life from the sword, my precious life from the power of the dogs**.

22:21. Furthermore, Jesus pleaded, **Rescue me from the mouth of the lions; save me from the horns of the wild oxen.** Like the goring of the horns of a wild oxen, the nails pierced his hands and feet. Yet verse 21 ends on a note of triumph. The verb translated **save me** literally means, "you have heard me." Therefore, this section ends on an optimistic note and begins an important turning point in the mood of the psalm. As Christ died on the cross, he anticipated the Father's deliverance, believing his cry had been heard.

G Christ's Salvation for God (22:22–31)

> **SUPPORTING IDEA:** *Having fulfilled his work of redemption, Jesus declares his victory at the cross to his disciples who will proclaim it to the nations.*

22:22–24. There is a major shift at this point from a plea for deliverance to an affirmation of praise to God for his faithfulness. These verses imply a future resurrection of Christ in which he would announce his triumph over sin and death. From Hebrews 2:12, it is clear that Christ proclaimed, **I will declare your name to my brothers**. This verse is quoted in Hebrews 2:12 as referring to Christ. It tells us that Jesus is the speaker and will continue to be throughout the rest of this psalm. **In the congregation I will praise you** is a prophecy concerning Jesus' appearance in the upper room to his disciples, later to five hundred at once, and ultimately to those in heaven (cp. 1 Cor. 15:5–7).

All you descendants of Jacob is a reference to Jewish converts after his resurrection, beginning with Pentecost. Certainly the gospel was proclaimed to the Jews first (cp. Rom. 1:16) as the first church was planted in Jerusalem, the holy city. Jesus understood this as he sent his disciples out to the "lost sheep of Israel" (cp. Matt. 10:5–6). Before any other nation, Israel was chosen by God to **honor him**. At this point Jesus pleaded for his people to **revere him, all you descendants of Israel!** Christ wanted the people to know that, although he was despised by them, God had not **despised or disdained the suffering of the afflicted one**. Nor had God **hidden his face from him**. God had approved of the sacrifice Jesus offered to the Father for the reconciliation of his people.

22:25–29. In view of God's listening to his cry for help, the psalmist wrote, **From you comes the theme of my praise**. Not only was God the *object* of praise, but he was also the *source*. The **vows** were probably thank offerings vowed during his trouble. In such cases the flesh of the sacrifice offered was to be eaten (Lev. 7:16). This explains the imagery of a banquet or feast at which **the poor** would **eat and be satisfied**. Because of the great sacrifice offered by Christ, people may enter into his presence so that **they who seek the LORD will praise him**. The **great assembly** refers **to all the ends of the earth** who **will remember and turn to the LORD**.

Included in the gracious redemptive plan of God that was revealed to Abraham was the extension of God's grace to bless people from all nations (cp. Gen. 12:3). For God deemed in eternity past that **families of the nations** would **bow down before him** (cp. Pss. 72:8–11; 96:10–13; Rev. 5:9). This submission resulted from the **dominion** that **belongs to the LORD** as **he rules over the nations**.

And just as **the poor** would **eat and be satisfied** at this banquet, so the **rich of the earth** would **feast and worship** because there will be a banquet in the kingdom of heaven for all the people of God (cp. Isa. 25:6). The phrase **all who go down to the dust will kneel before him** was perhaps the phrase the apostle Paul had in mind when he wrote Philippians 2:10 as he thought of the exaltation of Christ by God the Father.

22:30–31. The word **posterity** refers to **future generations** yet unborn who would **serve** God because of the remnant's faithfulness to tell them **about the Lord** and **proclaim his righteousness**. This proclamation of the gospel hinges on the truth that **he has done it**. This is another way of stating that Christ has finished it (cp. Matt. 27:50; Mark 15:37; Luke 23:46; John 19:30). It is finished! Because the righteous demands of God were fully met by the atoning work of Christ on behalf of all who believe on Jesus, the righteousness of God will be applied to their account.

MAIN IDEA REVIEW: *The Son of God will be forsaken by God, put to death by evil men, yet remain fully confident in the faithfulness of God to deliver him. This the Lord did so he would declare his victory.*

III. CONCLUSION

The Wondrous Cross

Isaac Watts is considered one of the greatest and most prolific hymn writers in church history. From his pen flowed over six hundred inspiring hymns, the most famous being "When I Survey the Wondrous Cross." Charles H. Spurgeon called it the greatest hymn ever written in any language. These gripping words form a powerful description of the redemptive suffering of Christ and are unsurpassed in their ability to convey the majesty of the cross.

> When I survey the wondrous cross
> On which the Prince of glory died,
> My richest gain I count but loss,
> And pour contempt on all my pride.
>
> Forbid it, Lord, that I should boast,
> Save in the cross of Christ my God:
> All the vain things that charm me most,
> I sacrifice them to his blood.
>
> See, from his head, his hands, his feet,
> Sorrow and love flow mingled down!
> Did e'er such love and sorrow meet,
> Or thorns compose so rich a crown?
>
> Were the whole realm of nature mine,
> That were a present far too small;
> Love so amazing, so divine,
> Demands my soul, my life, my all.

May all hearts everywhere melt in humble adoration of the great sacrifice made by God's sinless Son, the Lord Jesus Christ, who became sin for us. May such love, "so amazing, so divine," control our lives and lead us to commit ourselves to him.

IV. LIFE APPLICATION

The Centrality of the Cross

The cross of the Lord Jesus Christ is central in the life of the believer. It is also central in worship. That is why Christ instituted the Lord's Supper, a regular time of remembrance when believers reflect on the awesomeness of his death for our sins. This is the purpose of communion at the Lord's table. It is a time to keep the cross central in the life and heart of every disciple of

Christ. Likewise, the cross is central in the believer's daily walk with the Lord. The Christian is to live as he died, selflessly, sacrificially, and with great abandonment to the will of God. As the Lord Jesus remained faithful to the end, so must believers endure in the work that God has committed to us.

Moreover, the cross is central in witnessing for Christ. This is the heart of the gospel—the substitutionary death of God's Son for sins. This is what believers proclaim to the world—the cross. Paul preached "Jesus Christ and him crucified" (1 Cor. 2:2). So must believers declare the dying Lamb of God to a dying world, the only hope of eternal life for sinners.

V. PRAYER

God, we are humbled as we remember the great price paid by our Lord as he acted as our substitute in suffering your wrath on our behalf. How terrible we are that the King of kings and the Lord of lords was sent to die in our place. Lord Jesus, you are worthy to receive glory and honor and power. For you were slain, and with your blood you purchased men for God from every tribe and language and people and nation. To you and you alone be glory now and forever. Amen.

VI. DEEPER DISCOVERIES

A. God (22:1)

This word for *God* (Heb. *el*) is a noun that carries the idea of might and power. It is used throughout the Old Testament in a variety of ways, referring either to men (Job 41:25; Ezek. 32:21), angels (Ps. 29:1), pagan gods or idols (Exod. 15:11; 34:16; Deut. 32:12; Judg. 9:46; Ps. 44:20; Isa. 43:10), inanimate objects of nature (Pss. 36:6; 80:10), and the God of Israel (Gen. 46:3; Exod. 34:6; Deut. 7:9; Job 36:5,22,26; 1 Sam. 2:3; Isa. 5:16; 40:18; 42:5; Dan. 9:4; Nah. 1:2). *El* is an ancient word that was often used of pagan deities in the Near East. It is used throughout the Psalms of the God of Israel: "*el* who arms me with strength" (Ps. 18:32), "*el* who avenges me" (18:47), "living *el*" (42:2; 84:2), "*el* of my life" (42:8), "*el* my rock" (42:9), "*el* sends his love and his faithfulness" (57:3), "*el* who saves" (68:19–20),"my *el*" (89:26; 102:24; 118:28), "*el* who avenges" (94:1), and "a forgiving *el*" (99:8).

B. Forsaken (22:1)

The word *forsaken* (Heb. *azab*) means "to abandon, leave behind, let go, depart." This is the same word used by the Lord in 2 Chronicles 12:1,5 and 15:2 as he vowed to abandon Israel if the nation rejected him. Although this divine abandonment was a complete rejection, it was not always permanent in duration. In Isaiah 54:7, God stated concerning Israel, "For a brief moment

I abandoned (Heb. *azab*) you, but with deep compassion I will bring you back." While on the cross, God forsook Jesus as he placed on him the divine wrath reserved for his people as Jesus acted as a substitute for those who would believe (Isa. 53:4–6,10; 2 Cor. 5:21). This abandonment by God lasted for a short duration and ended when Jesus declared, "Father, into your hands I commit my spirit" (Luke 23:46).

C. Holy (22:3)

See "Deeper Discoveries," 15:1.

D. Despised (22:6)

The word *despised* (Heb. *herpa*) is a noun that occurs seventy times in the Old Testament. It means "to disgrace, scorn, shame, contempt, or rebuke." In some instances *herpa* carries the idea of an accusation or blame that is cast upon someone (Isa. 25:8; Jer. 31:19; Ezek. 36:30). In addition, *herpa* is used of a person or persons who are despised (Gen. 30:23; Neh. 2:17; Isa. 4:1; Joel 2:17,19; Dan. 9:16). It is used to describe the taunting of one's enemies (Judg. 8:15; Ps. 119:42) and of the defamation of a person's character in order to discredit him (Neh. 6:13).

E. Strong Bulls of Bashan (22:12)

The "strong bulls of Bashan" were large cattle located in a fertile plateau east of modern-day Jordan. Bashan was a region known for its great pastures which were used for grazing and growing large, hefty animals (cp. Deut. 32:14; Amos 4:1; Ezek. 39:18).

VII. TEACHING OUTLINE

A. Christ's Separation from God (1–2)
  1. Spurned by God (1)
  2. Silence from God (2)
B. Christ's Strength from God (3–5)
  1. In God's sovereignty (3)
  2. In God's salvation (4–5)
    a. Others trusted God (4a, 5a)
    b. God delivered others (4b, 5b)
C. Christ's Scorn from God (6–8)
  1. Rejected by the people (6)
  2. Ridiculed by the people (7–8)
    a. Mocked (7a)
    b. Insulted (7b–8)
D. Christ's submission to God (9–11)
  1. His birth by God (9)

2. His beginning with God (10)
  E. Christ's Suffering from God (12–18)
    1. His life surrounded (12)
    2. His safety threatened (13)
    3. His bones disjointed (14a)
    4. His heart melted (14b)
    5. His strength gone (15)
    6. His body pierced (16)
    7. His bones exposed (17)
    8. His clothes divided (18)
  F. Christ's Supplication to God (19–21)
    1. Strengthen me! (19)
    2. Save me! (20–21)
      a. Deliver me from dogs (20)
      b. Rescue me from lions, oxen (21)
  G. Christ's Salvation for God (22–31)
    1. Proclaimed to the Jews (22–24)
      a. By the risen Christ (22)
      b. To believing disciples (23–24)
    2. Proclaimed to the Gentiles (25–29)
      a. Worshiped by the nations (25–26)
      b. Believed upon by the nations (27)
    3. Proclaimed to all peoples (30–31)
      a. Served by future generations (30a)
      b. Spoken to future generations (30b–31)

VIII. ISSUES FOR DISCUSSION

1. How do you react when you feel forsaken by God?
2. Since God was willing to reject his own Son because of sin, will he not reject those who are not his children who die in their sins?
3. Do you spend adequate time in prayer, pleading with God to hear your cry and intervene on your behalf?

Psalm 23
The Good Shepherd and Gracious Host

"*I*f He be a shepherd to no one else, He is a Shepherd to me. He cares for me, watches over me, and preserves me."

C h a r l e s   H .   S p u r g e o n

I. INTRODUCTION

"The Shadow of Death"

*A*fter the funeral service of his first wife, the late Donald Grey Barnhouse, distinguished pastor of Tenth Presbyterian Church, Philadelphia, was thinking about how he could convey to his young children the loss of their mother. As he tried to conjure up words of comfort, the shadow of a large van passed over their car as they were driving down the highway. Instantly, Barnhouse thought of the words needed for the moment. "Children," he asked, "would you rather be run over by a truck, or by its shadow?" The children quickly answered, "Well, of course, Dad, we'd much rather be run over by its shadow! The shadow cannot hurt us."

Then Barnhouse, the master illustrator, replied, "The truck of death ran over the Lord Jesus two thousand years ago so that only its shadow now passes over us. That is all that has happened to your mother. Only the shadow of death has passed over her. She is unharmed in heaven."

This is the comforting message of Psalm 23, unquestionably the most-loved song from the inspired pen of David. If there is one psalm that has encouraged more hearts, it is this beautiful masterpiece, probably the best-known passage of the entire Old Testament. As one historian said of this towering psalm: "It has sung courage to the army of the disappointed. It has poured balm and consolation into the hearts of the sick, of captives in dungeons, of widows in their pinching grief, of orphans in their loneliness. Dying soldiers have died easier as it was read to them; ghastly hospitals have been illuminated; it has visited the prisoner and broken his chains, and, like Peter's angel, led him forth in imagination, and sung him back to his home again. It has made the dying Christian slave freer than his master."

Such is the powerful peace that has filled the troubled souls of believers down through the centuries. None who have feasted at the banquet table of this beautiful psalm go away hungry. The great Baptist preacher Charles Haddon Spurgeon called it "the pearl of psalms." Alexander MacLaren, the noted Scottish expositor, said, "It has dried many tears and supplied the mold into which many hearts have poured their peaceful faith." James Montgomery Boice extols it, noting, "Millions of people have memorized this psalm, even those who have learned few other portions. Ministers have used it to comfort people who are going through severe trials, suffering illness, or dying. For some, the words of this psalm have been the last they have uttered in life." This psalm is, indeed, a masterpiece of inspired praise, testifying to the abundant grace and goodness of God to his people.

Here is a testimony by David, the author, of the Lord's faithfulness as he looked back on his life. David wrote out of his own experience as he had spent his early years caring for sheep. The image of a shepherd with his flock was engraved upon his mind to represent his relationship with God. Likewise, David had known what it was to travel and be a weary guest who had enjoyed the care of a loving host. This also pictured his relationship with God. So in this psalm David pulled together both images to convey the abundant provision of God for all believers in need of his peace and protection.

II. COMMENTARY

The Good Shepherd and Gracious Host

> **MAIN IDEA:** *David describes the Lord's loving care for his own people as a shepherd's devotion for his flock and a host's provisions for his guests.*

The Good Shepherd (23:1–4)

> **SUPPORTING IDEA:** *The psalmist represents his relationship to God as a sheep to his shepherd, not lacking any rest, guidance, or safety.*

23:1a. David began this psalm by introducing the first metaphor that describes the relationship between the Lord and his people with the tender analogy of a shepherd and his flock. During his youth David had been a shepherd watching his father's flock (1 Sam. 16:11,19; 17:15), so he was very familiar with this picture. Transferring the image to God, he declared, **The**

LORD **is my shepherd**. The word *my* emphasizes how deeply personal and close was his individual relationship with God. Everything in the next four verses flows out of this shepherd motif.

What is so amazing is that in ancient Israel, a shepherd's work was considered the lowest of all work. A shepherd would actually live with his sheep twenty-four hours a day with unwavering devotion, day and night, both in fair weather and bad, to nurture, guide, and protect his sheep. The shepherd would assume full responsibility for the needs and safety of his flock, even risking his own life for their protection. This is what God has chosen to be to his people (cp. Pss. 28:9; 74:1; 77:20; 78:52; 79:13; 80:1; 95:7; 100:3). He is their everything, their constant protector.

23:1b. Because of the greatness of God and his constant, loving care over his flock, David concluded, **I shall not be in want**. Left to themselves, sheep lack everything, being totally helpless and defenseless animals who cannot care for themselves. But under the shepherd's care, all their needs are abundantly met. So it was for David, as well as for all believers who are under the watchcare of him who is all-sufficient, inexhaustible, and unchanging. All God's sheep, precious to him, **shall not be in want**. They will lack nothing that is good and necessary for enjoying life to the fullest.

23:2. Continuing the shepherd's theme, David boasted, **He makes me lie down in green pastures**. Sheep are fearful animals, easily panicked and, when scared, will not lie down to rest. Only the shepherd can provide the calm assurance to make them lie down in green pastures or grassy meadows. This speaks of the peace and true satisfaction that only God can provide his sheep.

What is more, David said, **he leads me beside quiet waters**. Literally, this refers to waters that have been stilled, further expanding this peaceful scene. Weary and worn sheep need a long, refreshing drink from the rapid stream. But being instinctively afraid of running water, the shepherd must pick up a few large stones and dam up a place, causing the rushing stream to slow its current and create quiet waters. Then the flock may drink with no fear. God gives true, abiding peace to believers who abide in him and drink of his grace.

23:3a. Moreover, this good shepherd **restores my soul**. This statement is subject to different interpretations. It may picture the straying sheep being brought back to the fold (cp. Isa. 49:5; Ps. 60:1). In Hebrew vernacular these words can mean "brings to repentance" or "brings to conversion" (cp. Hos. 14:1–3; Joel 2:12). Psalm 19:7 uses this same wording to picture the spiritual renewal or revival of a believer. But since the word for **soul** (Heb. *nephesh*) is accurately translated "life," this may mean that the Lord restores the psalmist to physical health. Either interpretation is certainly true.

23:3b–c. Furthermore, David wrote, the Lord **guides me in paths of righteousness**. Unlike other animals sheep lack a sense of direction and can become easily lost, even in the most familiar environment. They easily go astray as they are prone to wandering. The shepherd must continually guide them to paths of righteousness, or "the right path," if they are to be moved from field to field without falling into deep crevices or off ragged cliffs.

Likewise, God by his Word and Spirit guides his flock effectively in the right way. All this God does **for his name's sake**, meaning for the honor of his own glory, which is the highest of all his motives. Even when believers sin, God is committed to leading them back to the right path.

23:4a–b. Taking this image a step further, David portrayed the shepherd as being able to protect his sheep in their moments of greatest danger. **Even though I walk through the valley of the shadow of death**, David stated, **I will fear no evil, for you are with me**. The shepherd would lead his flock from one grazing place to another, a move which would often involve passing through a narrow **valley** between high jagged cliffs, often filled with potential dangers such as wild animals. The sun would be obstructed from shining into the valley, creating darkness or a **shadow**. Such a shadow in the valley would often become a place of **death** for wandering sheep, hence a "shadow of death."

Yet even in such danger, the Lord was present to guard and guide his flock, dispelling all **fear** of **evil** as he led them into paths of righteousness (v. 3).

23:4c. Keeping with this shepherd imagery, David declared, **Your rod and your staff, they comfort me**. The shepherd's **rod** was usually an oak club about two feet long. It was used to defend the flock against wild animals such as lions or bears, as well as for counting, guiding, and protecting his sheep. And the shepherd's **staff** was his crook. Bent or hooked at one end, it was used to pry sheep loose from thickets, to push branches aside, to pull fallen sheep out of holes, to lead them along narrow paths, and to drive off snakes.

Such tools were sources of **comfort** for fearful sheep and for David. He lived his life often surrounded by multiple dangers, yet God's Word and loving hand were the most effective means of guiding and guarding his faithful servant David.

𝔹 The Gracious Host (23:5–6)

SUPPORTING IDEA: *The psalmist represents his relationship to God as a guest to a gracious host, not lacking any provision, goodness, or eternal blessing.*

23:5a. David shifted metaphors from the shepherd/flock motif to the host imagery. As a gracious host would attend to the needs of his guests, so David said to God, **You prepare a table before me in the presence of my enemies**. Though surrounded by many **enemies** who sought to harm him, David recognized that God was with him for his good, supplying his needs as a host would care for a guest. Again, the same central theme of this psalm is reinforced. Even under the most adverse circumstances, in the face of threatening enemies, David would lack nothing (cp. v. 1).

23:5b. It was the custom of a loving host to provide oil for the head of his honored guest to refresh him after his travels. Thus David added, **You anoint my head with oil**, speaking of the Lord's ministry to revive his heart, especially when surrounded by many foes who threatened him. The presence of God invigorated him, renewing him for all the demands of life.

23:5c. Further, David testified, **my cup overflows**, referring to the constant supply of drink provided by an attentive host. His cup was always more than filled to the brim, overflowing with the most satisfying drink imaginable. This pictures the abundant supply of divine grace in David's life which was more than sufficient to strengthen and sustain him in the most dangerous circumstances. God is an infinite source of all that believers need to live victoriously in difficult situations.

23:6. Finally, David concluded, **Surely goodness** (Heb. *tob,* that which is pleasant, beautiful, i.e., God's presence and grace) **and love will follow me all the days of my life**, even when he found himself in life-threatening situations. Through thick and thin, in every extremity of **life**, God's blessings were chasing David. Thus, on a triumphant note David wrote, **I will dwell in the house of the LORD forever**.

Even death would serve David's greater good, which would usher him into God's immediate presence where he would enjoy the **goodness and love** of God forever, or literally "throughout the years." Nothing can separate the believer from the love of God, not even death (cp. Rom. 8:38–39).

MAIN IDEA REVIEW: *David describes the Lord's loving care for his own people as a shepherd's devotion for his flock and a host's provisions for his guests.*

III. CONCLUSION

Goodness and Love

The late Harry Ironside, noted preacher at Moody Memorial Church in downtown Chicago, told the story of a troubled woman who once came to him fearful that she was being followed by two men. Whenever she left her apartment, the two men would trail her, or so she thought. Whenever she stepped on the trolley, the two men were at her side. What was she to do?

Ironside quickly sized up that these two men were imaginary figures, figments of her imagination. Wishing to comfort her, he replied, "There's nothing to worry about. Those two men are David's servants, sent to help you." Ironside turned to Psalm 23:6 and showed her in the Bible, "Surely goodness and love will follow me all the days of my life." He assured her, "Those two men are named Goodness and Love and their job is to help you."

"Oh," she said, content with the explanation, never to worry again. Would to God that all believers could be so simple in their faith, believing that the goodness and mercy of God are always present to bless them. Since our Good Shepherd and gracious host is always near to care for us, may our hearts be at peace.

IV. LIFE APPLICATION

Everything We Need

The sufficiency of Christ in the life of any believer is astounding, a matter of great comfort and encouragement. Whenever a person has Christ in his life, he has everything he needs because Christ is everything. Christ is able to meet every need. He is the Alpha and Omega, the Creator and sustainer of all, the infinite God who can meet whatever needs we may have. This is the central theme of this psalm, which is a source of grace to every believer. Because of the indwelling of Christ in believers' lives, they will never lack anything they truly need within the will of God. Christ is their peace and protection in every situation, their guard and guide in all they do.

What a blessing it is for every believer, pictured here as a weak sheep and weary traveler, to know that Christ, the Good Shepherd and gracious host, is sufficient to meet every need. Christ is the full source and abundant supply for meeting every need we have.

V. PRAYER

God, we declare our dependence on you for our spiritual and physical needs. You are the Lord and Shepherd who has provided all that pertains to our life and godliness. For this we bless your name. We know that when death's dark shadows cover us, we have nothing to fear because you are with us. Lord, like a host you provide above and beyond all we could ask or think. Continue to saturate our lives with your goodness and love. In Jesus' name. Amen.

VI. DEEPER DISCOVERIES

A. Pastures (23:1)

This word (Heb. *naweh*) refers to a habitation, a dwelling place, or a pleasant dwelling. *Naweh* was used in the Psalms to speak of the "grasslands of the desert" (65:12) and "the pasturelands of God" (83:12). Here it is used to speak of the pasture where David led and tended his flock (2 Sam. 7:8) and the place where shepherds rested their flocks (Jer. 33:12).

B. Shadow of Death (23:4)

The phrase "shadow of death" (Heb. *salmawet*) is a Hebrew compound word that joins together the two Hebrew words for *shade* or shadow and for *death*. Therefore, *salmawet* refers to the shade of death, terror, or calamity. In Psalm 23:4, the meaning is that God will lead his sheep through dark places, even the experience of death itself. Used numerous times in Job (3:5; 10:21–22; 12:22; 16:16; 24:17; 28:3; 34:22; 38:17), it carries the idea of a thick fog or deep shadow. God is depicted as a God who can extinguish the darkness (Job 12:22; Amos 5:8) and even bring the darkness into judgment (Jer. 13:16). The word is also used in Psalms 44:19; 107:10,14, Isaiah 9:2, and Jeremiah 2:6 as "darkness" or "the shadow of death." The Messiah would be a light to those who lived in such darkness (Isa. 9:2).

C. Fear (23:4)

The word *fear* (Heb. *yare*) is found approximately 330 times throughout the Old Testament and is most often used to speak of reverential awe produced when a person is in God's presence (Exod. 1:17; 1 Sam. 12:14,18; 2 Sam. 6:9; 2 Kgs. 17:28,35–39; Pss. 33:8; 102:15; Jer. 5:22,24; Jon. 1:16). It is also used of those who honor God and take him seriously (Job 1:1; Pss. 31:19; 33:18–19; 34:9; 103:11; 128:1; 145:19; Neh. 7:2) or who fail to do so (Eccl. 8:13). In other instances, as in the context of Psalm 23:4, *yare* is used to describe fear produced by the anticipation of evil (Exod. 14:13; Num. 14:9; Deut. 1:29; 3:2; 7:18; 20:1,3,8; Josh. 10:8,25; Judg. 7:3; 2 Kgs. 1:15; Neh. 4:14; Pss. 27:1,3; 56:3–4,11; Isa. 51:7,12; Ezek. 2:6).

D. Comfort (23:4)

This word (Heb. *naham*) connotes the idea of a person breathing deeply as a physical display of his or her feelings. Sixty-five times in the Hebrew Bible, *naham* is used to speak of comfort and compassion. Perhaps the best known passage that contains *naham*, other than Psalm 23:4, is Isaiah 40:1, "Comfort, comfort my people, says your God." Many passages speak of comforting people in the face of death (Gen. 24:67; 37:35; 38:12; 2 Sam. 10:2; 12:24; 1 Chr. 19:2; Isa. 61:2; Jer. 31:15). Throughout the Psalms, *naham* is used to describe the comfort that God gives his people (Pss. 71:21; 86:17; 119:82; Isa. 12:1; 49:13; 52:9). In Hosea 11:8, the word is used to convey God's tender love for Israel.

E. Anointed (23:5)

The word *anoint* or *anointed* (Heb. *dashen*) literally means "fat or well fed." Metaphorically, it speaks of wealth, abundance, or prosperity. Fat animals were considered the healthiest, and fat was considered the best part of sacrificial animals (Ps. 20:3). This is how the idea of prosperity and wealth became affiliated with fatness (cp. Ps. 92:14; Prov. 11:25; 13:4; 15:30; 28:25). In Psalm 23:5, the reference signifies the abundant blessing of prosperity given by God to David.

F. Goodness, Love (23:6)

These words (or *lovingkindness,* Heb. *hesed*) mean "kindness, mercy, favor, or steadfast love," and they are found many times in the Hebrew Bible (cp. Exod. 20:6; 34:6; Num. 14:18; Ps. 136; Mic. 7:18). *Hesed* is derived from *hasad,* which means "to bend or bow oneself" or "to incline oneself." It denotes a condescending love of God for his chosen people. Here it is used to express David's confidence in the Lord who would be forever favorable toward him. Sometimes *hesed* is called God's covenant love because of its occurrence in Deuteronomy 7:12 and 2 Samuel 7:15.

VII. TEACHING OUTLINE

A. The Good Shepherd (1–4)
  1. The relationship pictured (1a)
    a. God is my loving shepherd (1a)
    b. I am his lowly sheep (1a)
  2. The relationship enjoyed (1b–4)
    a. I shall not lack anything (1b)
    b. I shall not lack rest (2)
    c. I shall not lack life (3a)
    d. I shall not lack guidance (3b)
    e. I shall not lack safety (4)
B. The Gracious Host (5–6)
  1. The relationship pictured (5a)
    a. God is my loving host (5a)
    b. I am his lowly guest (5a)
  2. The relationship enjoyed (5b–6)
    a. I shall not lack provision (5b)
    b. I shall not lack goodness (6a)
    c. I shall not lack eternal blessing (6b)

VIII. ISSUES FOR DISCUSSION

1. Do I demonstrate my total trust in the Lord to provide all of my material and spiritual needs?
2. Do I seek God's guidance to lead me to righteous paths?
3. How have I experienced the guiding hand of God in my life?

Psalm 24
When Worship Is Right

"*T*here should be some preparation of the heart in coming to the worship of God. Consider who he is in whose name we gather, and surely we cannot rush together without thought. Consider whom we profess to worship, and we shall not hurry into his presence as men run to a fire."

C h a r l e s   H .   S p u r g e o n

I. INTRODUCTION

The King Stands for the King of Kings

*G*eorge Fredrick Handel is regarded as one of the greatest composers in the history of the church. His famous oratorio *Messiah* is the most popular of his works; it has moved countless believers to worship God. This masterpiece was first performed in London on March 23, 1743. On this occasion the king of England, George II, was present. All who attended were deeply moved as they heard this inspiring music and biblical text.

When "The Hallelujah Chorus" was sung, containing the powerful words, "For the Lord God omnipotent reigneth," something unexpected happened. King George II himself rose to his feet in an act of homage. This prompted the entire audience to do the same. They remained standing throughout the entire chorus, recognizing the greatness of heaven's one, true King who reigns over all, even over earthly kings. From that time to the present, it has always been customary to stand during "The Hallelujah Chorus."

This is the true heart of worship—a humble recognition of the sovereignty of our triune God and responding appropriately by presenting our praise, devotion, and lives to him. Authentic worship involves beholding God's unveiled glory and responding to his splendor. It requires the pledging of our loyalty to him, ascribing to him his supreme worth, and affirming his incomparable value. True worship is an all-consuming desire to give ourselves to God, yielding all that we are to all that he is.

Psalm 24 is a hymn of praise that directs the hearts of his people to worship God in a manner that recognizes his glory. This psalm has also been labeled an entrance psalm written by David. The possible events that spurred its writing might have been the entrance of the ark of the covenant into Jerusalem, an anniversary of that same occasion, or perhaps a festival commemorating the event. As a royal psalm this song contains several overtones of other royal psalms (Pss. 47; 68; 118; 132), which celebrated God's entrance into the holy city.

II. COMMENTARY

When Worship Is Right

MAIN IDEA: *David describes the Lord's glorious entrance into the holy city of Jerusalem while preparing those who worship the Lord to prepare themselves properly.*

A A Recognition of God's Power (24:1–2)

SUPPORTING IDEA: *David declares the Lord's sovereign authority over his creation and all it contains.*

24:1. This psalm begins with a dramatic declaration, **The earth is the LORD's, and everything in it**. This is to say, everything on the earth, including the earth itself and all that it contains, belongs to God. This universal ownership includes **all who live in it**. All people live under God's sovereign dominion (Exod. 19:5; Deut. 10:14; Pss. 50:12; 89:11).

24:2. God's dominion over the earth and all it contains is established because he has made it: **For he founded it upon the seas and established it upon the waters**. This is not saying that the earth actually floats on a terrestrial ocean. Rather, using poetic language, this pictures the world as an ordered creation founded and established by God (cp. Ps. 135:5–6; 1 Cor. 10:26), a metaphor taken from the founding of a city (cp. Josh. 6:26; 1 Kgs. 16:24; Isa. 14:32). Like a large temple the earth is portrayed as having foundations. This language recalls the act of creation in which God summoned the dry land to rise from the watery surface (Gen. 1:2,9). He is Lord over all the works of his hands, establishing everything in its place, including man.

B A Revelation of God's Purity (24:3–6)

SUPPORTING IDEA: *David prepares the worshiper to enter the holy presence of the Lord by stating the type of worshiper who may come to worship.*

24:3. Since God is sovereign Lord over all creation, who may approach him? This is the reasoning behind the question, **Who may ascend the hill of the LORD?** Who among earth's inhabitants is acceptable and able to come before this sovereign king? Or how must a person prepare himself to approach him? "The hill of the LORD" is a reference to Mount Zion, or Jerusalem, where God dwelled above the ark of the covenant. Asked another way, **Who may stand in his holy place?** This reference was to Jerusalem, which sat atop Mount Zion, "his holy place." The question is, Who is spiritually qualified to fellowship with this awesome king?

24:4. The answer is: **He who has clean hands and a pure heart**. The phrase "clean hands" speaks of the purity of a person's outward actions. A "pure heart" refers to an inner soul that is holy and undefiled, set apart to God without moral defilement. Both the inner life, a person's character, and the outer life, a person's conduct, are represented. In other words, a person's life must be **pure** and **clean** if God is to be approached in worship and fellowship.

Specifically, this requires that a person **not lift up his soul to an idol**. He must have no other gods before his love for and loyalty to the one true God (Exod. 20:3). An idol is anyone or anything that a person loves, fears, or serves more than God. Likewise, this mandates that a person not **swear by what is false**. This would be to place a higher allegiance upon a false god. These requirements do not call for sinless perfection, but the integrity of all of a person's life, including both inward motive and outward manner.

24:5. The person who does come to God in holiness and humility **will receive blessing from the LORD**. This blessing is God's goodness and favor extended to his loyal subjects. Likewise, he will receive **vindication from God his Savior**. Such vindication (Heb. *sedaqa,* "righteousness") refers to God's just treatment of his faithful servants. What is more, here is an Old Testament expression of justification by faith. The person who approaches God through repentance and faith will be declared the righteousness of God.

24:6. The phrase **Such is the generation of those who seek him** refers to true worshipers who seek entrance into the holy sanctuary. These who come, as verse 4 prescribes, are those **who** genuinely **seek your face, O God of Jacob**. There is no hypocrisy here, just genuine and humble faith.

Ⓒ A Realization of God's Presence (24:7–10)

SUPPORTING IDEA: *David calls upon the city of Jerusalem to prepare for the entrance of God into her gates.*

24:7. The phrase **Lift up your heads, O you gates** refers to the entrance of worshipers into the city of Jerusalem. The gates of the holy city are called to open up to prepare themselves for the triumphant entry of God himself. This is a literary device known as personification in which attributes of personality are attributed to inanimate objects. The city gates need to stretch themselves open to make way for the entrance of earth's sovereign King. The psalmist repeated this for dramatic emphasis: **be lifted up, you ancient doors.** The word *doors* is a synonym for gates. Prepare yourself, the psalmist says, **that the King of glory may come in.**

In David's time this referred to the carrying of the ark into Jerusalem. The ark represented the King of glory or the manifested presence of God. This was a call to bring the ark into the sanctuary in triumphant procession. During the first coming of Christ, the greater Son of David, it refers to the triumphant entrance of Christ into Jerusalem on Palm Sunday (Matt. 21:1–11). Ultimately, it refers to the ascension of Christ to the heavenly Zion to be enthroned at God's right hand.

24:8. From within the walls of the city, the rhetorical reply comes, **Who is this King of glory?** The answer follows, perhaps from those who surrounded the ark from outside the walls: **The LORD strong and mighty, the LORD mighty in battle.** This is the One who may enter the city, **the LORD** himself, he who shows himself strong and mighty in defeating all of Israel's foes in **battle.**

24:9–10. Again the request for entrance comes from those carrying the ark, now just outside the city gates: **Lift up your heads, O you gates.** For effect, it is repeated, **lift them up, you ancient doors.** All this heralding occurs so **the King of glory may come in.** From within the city walls, the question comes, perhaps spoken by the guard of the city gates, **Who is he, this King of glory?** The answer comes from those carrying and attending the ark, outside the gates, **the LORD Almighty—he is the King of glory.**

MAIN IDEA REVIEW: *David describes the Lord's glorious entrance into the holy city of Jerusalem while preparing those who worship the Lord to prepare themselves properly.*

III. CONCLUSION

The King of Glory

After Queen Victoria of England had ascended her throne, she went, as is the custom of British royalty, to hear a special presentation of *Messiah.* She had been instructed about her conduct by those who knew the rules of protocol for the royal family, being told that she must not rise when the others stood at the singing of "The Hallelujah Chorus." When that magnificent chorus was being sung and the singers were shouting, "Hallelujah! Hallelujah! Hallelujah! For the Lord God omnipotent reigneth," she sat with great difficulty. It seemed as if she would rise in spite of the custom of kings and queens. But finally, when they came to that climactic part of the chorus, where they proclaimed him as King of kings, suddenly, the young queen rose and stood with bowed head. Breaking all rules of royal etiquette, she felt compelled to rise as if she were taking her own crown from her head and casting it at God's feet.

This is when worship is right. It occurs when the whole person—mind, emotion, and will—responds to God with reverence, humility, praise, and devotion. May all who know him as heaven's King of glory ascribe to him the greatness that is due his name.

IV. LIFE APPLICATION

A Lofty Vision of God

A lofty, transcendent view of God is the most important thing about a Christian. As a person's vision of God goes, so goes his life. One's life will never rise any higher than his thoughts about God. A high view of God will lead to high and holy living. On the other hand, a low view of God will lead to low living. No one can live any higher than his proper understanding of who God is. Charles H. Spurgeon said, "The highest science, the loftiest speculation, the mightiest philosophy, which can ever engage the attention of a child of God, is the name, the nature, the person, the work, the doings, and the existence of the great God whom he calls his Father."

So it is in a believer's life. A person's life will rise no higher than his right vision of God. But the glory of God has been diminished and dimmed in our day. This is why Psalm 24, and other psalms like it, are so important to faith. As our knowledge of God goes, so go our lives. May Christians see afresh the vision of God in this psalm, beholding sovereignty, holiness, and glory. May Christians everywhere ascribe to him the worship due his name.

V. PRAYER

God, you are sovereign over all heaven and earth. The inhabitants and possessions of both are yours to do with as you please. Who may ascend to your holy hill? Who may stand in your holy place? Only those to whom you have given a pure heart and clean hands. You have applied to us the blessing of salvation by giving us the righteousness of the Lord Jesus Christ. We seek your face because you are the King of glory and the Lord Almighty. Lord, hear this prayer and continue to bless us with your sovereign grace. In Jesus' name. Amen.

VI. DEEPER DISCOVERIES

A. Earth (24:1)

This word (Heb. *eres*) is the fourth most frequently used Hebrew noun in the Old Testament, occurring 2,504 times. *Eres* refers either to the entire physical planet (Gen. 1:30; 18:18; Jer. 25:26), the land (Lev. 19:29; Num. 13:20), the inhabitants of the land (Gen. 6:11–13; 1 Kgs. 2:2), soil (Gen. 1:11; Lev. 25:19), or a designated territory (Gen. 4:16; 10:10–11; Deut. 34:2). It refers here to the entire physical planet.

B. World (24:1)

The word *world* (Heb. *tebel*) is used three different ways in the Old Testament. First, it refers to the physical mass of the earth (Ps. 89:12; 1 Sam. 2:8; 2 Sam. 22:16). Second, it refers to the people of the earth (Pss. 9:8; 24:1; 33:8, 96:13; 98:9; Isa. 13:11; 18:3; 24:4; 26:9,18; Lam. 4:12). Third, it is used to refer to the habitable part of the land (Job 37:12; Ps. 90:2; Prov. 8:31; Isa. 14:17; Nah. 1:5). The third usage is its denotation here in Psalm 24:1. *Tebel* and *eres* appear elsewhere in parallelism, or in opposition to one another (1 Sam. 2:8; Ps. 90:2; Isa. 26:9; 34:1).

C. Founded (24:2)

This word (Heb. *yasad*) means "to fix firmly, to build up, to lay a foundation, to set." The real or literal sense of the word is used to refer to the foundation of a structure (Josh. 6:26; 1 Kgs. 5:17; 6:37; 16:34; Ezra 3:6,10,12; Isa. 14:32; 54:11; Zech. 4:9). *Yasad* may be used in a figurative or metaphorical sense of that which is fixed and cannot be moved (Job 26:7; Pss. 78:69; 89:11; 102:25; Isa. 28:16; 48:13; 51:13; 54:11). This is how it is used here.

D. Pure (24:4)

The word *pure* (Heb. *bar*) is an adjective that occurs only a few times in the Old Testament (Job 11:4; Pss. 19:9; 73:1; Prov. 14:4; Song 6:9–10). *Bar* is a derivative of *barar* and refers to that which is pure (2 Sam. 22:27; Ps. 18:26; Dan. 12:10; Zeph. 3:9), cleansed (Jer. 4:11), polished (Isa. 49:2), clear (Eccl. 3:18), clean (Isa. 52:11), chosen (1 Chr. 7:40; 9:22; 16:41; Neh. 5:18).

E. Vindication (24:5)

The word *vindication* or *salvation* (Heb. *yesha*) refers to deliverance, rescue, victory, help, or liberty. In its first usages, *yesha* refers to physical deliverance from one's enemies (Num. 10:9; Exod. 2:17; 3:12; 14:30; Judg. 8:22; Pss.

18:3; 44:7; Jer. 1:8,19), but later it came to have a redemptive meaning (Pss. 51:14; 67:2; 68:19; 79:9; Isa. 45:17,22; 49:6; 52:10; Ezek. 37:23).

F. LORD Almighty (24:10)

See "Deeper Discoveries," 46:7.

VII. TEACHING OUTLINE

A. A Declaration of God's Power (1–2)
1. God controls all (1)
2. God created all (2)
B. A Revelation of God's Purity (3–6)
1. The searching question (3)
   a. Who may approach God? (3a)
   b. Who may abide with God? (3b)
2. The sober answer (4)
   The one who has:
   a. Clean hands (4a)
   b. Pure heart (4a)
   c. Undivided spirit (4b)
   d. Honest words (4c)
3. The sure result(5)
   a. Blessing from God (5a)
   b. Vindication from God (5b)
4. The spiritual reality (6)
   a. These seek God's grace (6a)
   b. These see God's face (6b)
C. A Realization of God's Presence (7–10)
1. First announcement (7–8)
   a. The appeal: the King is coming (7)
   b. The question: who is this King? (8a)
   c. The answer: the mighty Lord (8b–c)
2. Second announcement (9–10)
   a. The appeal: the King is coming (9)
   b. The question: who is this King? (10a)
   c. The answer: the Lord Almighty (10b–c)

VIII. ISSUES FOR DISCUSSION

1. Do I recognize the sovereign reign of God over my life and all creation?
2. Do I properly understand the holy position of God?
3. Do I enter the presence of God with clean hands and a pure heart?
4. What steps do I take to enter the presence of God properly?

Psalm 25

God's Ways in Dark Days

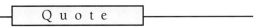

$$\boxed{\text{Q u o t e}}$$

"*I* had rather be in the heart of Africa in the will of God than on the throne of England out of the will of God."

David Livingstone

I. INTRODUCTION

Guiding Lights

F. B. Meyer, noted nineteenth-century British preacher, was sailing from northern Ireland into a seaside port on the coast of England. Nothing could be seen through the thick darkness but a confusing array of lights on shore. Wondering how the captain could possibly navigate the ship safely into harbor, Meyer asked the captain how he could see to steer the ship on this dark night. The captain took him up to the bridge and asked, "Do you see that big light on shore to the left?" Meyer affirmed he could. "And do you see the other big light over there to the right? And now do you see that outstanding light farther still this way? "Keep your eyes on those three lights and see what happens."

As the ship sailed ahead, the large light on the left gradually merged into the middle one. Then the two lights gradually eclipsed the third until the three were merged into one. "There now," said the captain, "all I have to do is see that those three big lights become one. Then I sail straight ahead."

In much the same way, every believer sails through this dark world in desperate need of the guiding light of God's Word. It is incumbent upon all believers to be led by the guiding light of divine relation, which can lead them into the future. This is the central theme of Psalm 25, a psalm "of David." In a time of darkness in his life, he asked for divine guidance to lead him to know God's will (vv. 4–5,8–10,12,21). As the way seemed unclear, David asked to be pointed to the Lord's perfect path.

The historical background of this psalm is not known. But the circumstances involve a painful period when the psalmist was attacked by enemies (vv. 2–3,19), entrapped in a trial (v. 15), isolated from supporters (v. 16), discouraged of heart (v. 17), and hated by foes (v. 19). In his hour of desperation, he needed to be restored according to the Lord's perfect will. So David called out to God for deliverance (vv. 1–3), direction (vv. 4–15), and defense (vv. 16–22). This psalm is an acrostic in which each verse begins with a successive letter of the Hebrew alphabet to aid in memorization and instruction.

II. COMMENTARY

God's Ways in Dark Days

MAIN IDEA: *David offers a prayer seeking deliverance from his enemies, direction into God's way, and defense from dangers.*

A Prayer for God's Deliverance (25:1–3)

SUPPORTING IDEA: *Knowing that God alone is able to deliver him from his enemies, David pleads for the Lord to save him from the shame of defeat.*

25:1–3. First, David affirmed his faith in God by saying, **To you, O LORD, I lift up my soul; in you I trust.** Clearly, the psalmist had a personal relationship with God through a saving faith that sustained him in this crisis. Although David's **treacherous** enemies attempted to put him to **shame** and **triumph over** him, David declared with confidence before the Lord that **no one whose hope is in you will ever be put to shame** (cp. Ps. 35:26). His appeal not to be put to shame is repeated in verse 20 and sets the tone for the psalm.

B A Prayer for God's Direction (25:4–15)

SUPPORTING IDEA: *Seeking divine direction, David asks God to lead him into his divine will while releasing him from the snare of his enemies.*

25:4–5. As God delivered David from his enemies, he asked for general direction into the Lord's will. **Show me your ways,** David prayed, and **teach me your paths. Ways** and **paths** are metaphors for the will of God. David entreated God to reveal his will so it might be pursued and traveled. Not presuming to know God's will, he requested that God **guide** his life moment by moment **all day long,** since he was aware of his sinful nature (v. 18).

Furthermore, David asked God to guide him **in your truth** and to **teach** him. He knew that God's ways are established in truth, or that which is firm and stable. Only **God** who was the **Savior** could deliver David from his enemies according to his ways and paths that David must learn to follow.

25:6–7. Three times in these verses David used the word **remember**. He asked, **Remember, O LORD, your great mercy and love**. David was recalling the mercy and love of God shown to him in the past to secure the same benefits of God for the present. David then asked God, **Remember not the sins of my youth and my rebellious ways**. This was a request for God not to reward him for his sins of the past according to what he deserved but according to what he needed—**mercy**. David then comforted himself by remembering one of the attributes of God—that God is **good**.

25:8–10. In an attempt to discover the will of God, David turned his attention to the greatness of God. **The LORD**, he declared, is **good and upright**, therefore he **instructs**, **guides**, and **teaches**. Furthermore, **he instructs sinners**, those who have gone their rebellious way (v. 7) and strayed from God's way, back into his way. The will of God is something to be pursued, never avoided or treated with suspicion because **all the ways of the LORD are loving and faithful** for those who **keep the demands of his covenant**.

25:11–14. If God's name was to be glorified by his servant, David must regularly ask God to **forgive** his **iniquity**. What is more, the person whom God will **instruct** in his **way** is the one who **fears the LORD** (cp. Ps. 111:10; Prov. 1:7; 3:32). This way is not a random event but **the way** that is **chosen** by God himself. Such holy reverence for God leads to **prosperity** that would continue to David's **descendants**. This covenant is a reference to the promise made by God to Israel (cp. Exod. 20:12; Lev. 26:3; Deut. 4:1). The Lord **confides in those who fear him**, just as a person takes a friend into his confidence and reveals his secret intentions. This personal approach taken by God in revealing his covenant is only for those who reverence him.

25:15. Rather than gazing upon the many dangers that surrounded him, David's eyes were always **on the LORD**, for only he would release David's **feet from the snare**. The Lord alone could overcome the traps set by David's opponents. For David, a Godward focus led to a Godward direction and the divine path.

A Prayer for God's Defense (25:16–22)

SUPPORTING IDEA: *Searching for a defense from his adversaries who seek his life, David appeals for the Lord to remember his character.*

25:16–19. David returned to his initial subject in this psalm which has a chiastic structure (A-B-A). Verses 1–7 and 16–22 are parallel sections (A), prayers for divine protection, while verses 8–15 (B) are a plea for divine direction. This final section (vv. 16–22) contains short, staccato prayer requests, asking for God's defense from his enemies. David was isolated, **lonely**, and **afflicted**, and full of **troubles, anguish, affliction,** and **distress** because he was surrounded by **enemies** who hated him. In this fiery ordeal he pleaded with God to **turn to** him, **free** him from this pain, and **take away all** his **sins.**

25:20–22. In this crisis David asked God **to guard** his life and **rescue** him from his enemies. As he would **take refuge** in God, he determined to walk in **integrity and uprightness** which the Lord would honor. David ended the psalm by asking **God** to **redeem Israel . . . from all their troubles.** This was an intercessory prayer by the king, asking God to redeem or save Israel from its difficulties.

> **MAIN IDEA REVIEW:** *David offers a prayer seeking deliverance from his enemies, direction into God's way, and defense from dangers.*

III. CONCLUSION

Saved by a Web

Frederick Nolan, a believer in Christ, was fleeing for his life from his enemies during a time of religious persecution in North Africa. Pursued by them over hill and valley with no place to hide, Nolan fell exhausted into a wayside cave, expecting his enemies to find him soon. Awaiting his death, he saw a spider weaving a web. Within minutes the spider had woven a beautiful web across the mouth of the cave. The pursuers arrived and wondered if Nolan was hiding there. But on seeing the unbroken spiderweb, they concluded it was impossible for him to have entered the cave without disturbing the web. So his pursuers went on, and Nolan's life was spared. Having escaped, he wrote these words:

> "Where God is, a spider's web is like a wall.
>
> Where God is not,
>
> a wall is like a spider's web."

God's presence was a wall of protection around David, shielding him from his pursuing enemies. Through his trust in God, he was saved. For the believer who reverences God, the Lord remains a constant refuge and shelter.

IV. LIFE APPLICATION

Strength in Weakness

Whether he realizes it or not, every Christian lives in a state of dependency on the Lord. Jesus himself said, "Apart from me you can do nothing" (John 15:5). A person can accomplish nothing of any eternal, lasting value unless he depends on the Lord. In his own strength a person is not able to do anything of any real value for God. But this is a hard lesson to remember and apply. Most believers have a tendency to be self-sufficient and to rely on their own strength when pursuing the Christian life. This was the sin of David in this psalm—the sin of self-sufficiency—and it is the downfall of many modern believers as well.

There is no one too weak for God to use—only people who are too strong in themselves. May believers recognize their human inadequacies and frailties and rest in his infinite strength, knowing that when they are weak they are truly strong.

V. PRAYER

God, teach us to trust you, even though our enemies surround us. Allow us to see your ways, O Lord; teach us your paths and guide us in your truth. For the sake of your name, for your glory, forgive our iniquities and turn to us in mercy that you alone can demonstrate. We reverence you and admit that you are our only refuge from our sins and from those who seek to destroy us. We confide in you alone for our rescue because you alone are gracious. In Jesus' name. Amen.

VI. DEEPER DISCOVERIES

A. God (25:2)

The word *God* (Heb. *elohiym*) is used throughout the Hebrew Bible as a general name for the true God. Although it is sometimes used to refer to pagan gods or deities (Gen. 35:2,4; Exod. 12:12; 18:11; 23:24; Judg. 17:5; Ruth 1:15; 1 Sam 7:3; 17:43; 2 Sam. 7:23; 1 Kgs. 11:2; 2 Chr. 2:5; Ps. 86:8), angels (Pss. 8:5; 97:7), men (Ps. 82:6), and judges (Exod. 21:6), it is used primarily to refer to the one true God who created all things out of nothing. In fact, *elohiym* is often used for God in the early chapters of Genesis. The meaning of *elohiym* is debatable, but it seems to refer to the transcendence of God. The plural form indicates plentitude of power and majesty and also makes allowance for a plurality of persons in the one God. This would certainly allow for the Trinity of the Godhead which is more fully developed later in the Old and New Testaments. This plurality is clearly identifiable in selected passages (cp. Gen. 1:26; 3:22; Isa. 6:8).

B. Truth (25:5)

See "Deeper Discoveries," 51:6.

C. Remember (25:6–7)

David asked the Lord to "remember" (Heb. *zakar*) him three times in Psalm 25. This word is a verb that means "to contemplate, to recollect, to bring to remembrance" when used of past events, but it does not mean that God has actually forgotten something and is now able to recall it. Rather, it is used to convey the idea that God calls himself into action based on his past promises to his servant. This word is used throughout the Old Testament to speak of God remembering, or executing, his covenant promises to his people (cp. Gen. 8:1; 9:15; 19:29; Exod. 2:24; 6:5–6; Pss. 98:3; 105:8,42; 106:45; Jer. 31:34).

D. Covenant (25:10,14)

This is the first usage of the word *covenant* (Heb. *berit*) in the Psalms. A *berit* was a binding pact or agreement between two parties, whether between individuals (Gen. 21:27) or nations (1 Sam. 1:11; Josh. 9:6,15). God often used this word to describe his relationship with Israel, his chosen people. Yet unlike a covenant between people involving a mutual agreement, the covenant between God and his people was a unilateral covenant, or an agreement based on the faithfulness of God alone. This covenant was initiated and instituted by God alone to protect and preserve his chosen ones. The one-sided nature of this covenant is clearly evident in the statement, "I will . . . be your God, and you will be my people" (Lev. 26:12; Exod. 19:5).

E. Guard (25:20)

The word *guard* (Heb. *shamar*) means "to put a hedge around something" or "to set a watch." It is used over four hundred times in the Old Testament in many different contexts, some of which refer to someone acting as an overseer over a garden (Gen. 2:15), flocks (Gen. 30:31), or a gate (Isa. 21:11). In the psalms it speaks of physical protection (Ps. 34:20), the guarding of life (Ps. 86:2), and the Lord's all-encompassing watchcare of his people (Ps. 121:3–4,7).

VII. TEACHING OUTLINE

A. A Prayer for God's Deliverance (1–3)
  1. Protect my life from shame (1–3a)
    a. I trust you (1–2)
    b. I hope in you (3a)

2. Put my enemies to shame (3b)
   a. They are treacherous (3b)
   b. They are without cause (3b)
B. A Prayer for God's Direction (4–15)
   1. He asks for divine guidance (4–7)
      a. Show me your ways (4)
      b. Guide me in your truth (5)
      c. Favor me by your mercy (6)
      d. Forgive me by your love (7)
   2. He affirms divine goodness (8–10)
      a. God will instruct me (8)
      b. God will guide me (9–10)
   3. He asks for divine grace (11)
      a. Forgive me for your sake (11a)
      b. Forgive me by your name (11b)
   4. He raises a probing question:
      Who fears God? (12a)
   5. He receives a promised answer (12b–15)
      a. God will instruct him (12b)
      b. God will bless him (13)
      c. God will confide in him (14)
      d. God will deliver him (15)
C. A Prayer for God's defense (16–22)
   1. Relieve me from attack (16–19)
   2. Rescue me from aspersion (20–21)
   3. Redeem me from adversity (22)

VIII. ISSUES FOR DISCUSSION

1. Do I seek to know the ways and walk the paths of the Lord?
2. Do I keep the covenants and testimonies of the Lord?
3. Am I living a life of integrity and walking in uprightness?

Psalm 26

Walking in Integrity

Psalm 26

I. INTRODUCTION

*T*hose who live godly lives can expect to receive persecution in this fallen world. Often this occurs in the form of a verbal attack by unbelievers. When attacked, believers must be certain that the persecution comes because of their commitment to the Lord and not because of some personal flaw. Such was the experience of David as he reigned as the king of Israel. False charges called into question his ability to lead the nation, challenging his spiritual fitness to approach God in the temple (cp. Pss. 15; 24). What is worse, these charges against David were brought by "deceitful men" (v. 4) and "hypocrites" (v. 4) who were "bloodthirsty" (v. 9), seeking his abdication and death. They would stop at nothing, even resorting to bribery to bring about the king's downfall. The goal was to destroy David and to bring him down.

In the face of such personal attacks, David went to the house of God (vv. 4–6) to focus on the glory of God (v. 8) and to appeal for God's defense. This psalm "of David" is the first of three psalms (Pss. 26–28) which centers on David appearing in the house of the Lord to admire God's glory.

II. COMMENTARY

> **MAIN IDEA:** *David asks God to vindicate and rescue him if, after examination, the king is found to be blameless of the accusations made by his foes.*

A A Prayer for Vindication (26:1)

26:1. This psalm begins with David's cry for exoneration: **Vindicate me, O LORD**, meaning "judge me" in order to prove his innocence of the false accusations made by his foes. He was convinced that he had **led a blameless life** of moral integrity. By a **blameless life**, he meant a sincerity of purpose and single-hearted devotion had characterized his life, not sinless perfection.

He claimed to be innocent of the charges against him, having lived above reproach. He knew the vicious rumors and charges against him were untrue. His life flowed from the fact that he had **trusted in the LORD without wavering**. In the face of men's slanderous charges, David appealed to heaven for God's final verdict, which was all that mattered.

B A Prayer for Examination (26:2–8)

26:2–3. David invited God's close scrutiny of every aspect of his life. **Test me**, **try me**, and **examine my heart and my mind**, he declared to God, believing that such a spiritual inventory would prove him to be blameless. He was confident that such a thorough investigation by God would clear him of his enemies' charges because the Lord's **love** was always **before** him, motivating him to **walk continually** in the **truth** of God's Word.

26:4–5. David pointed to his separation from all the practices of sinners as further proof of his innocence. He pleaded, **I do not sit with deceitful men**. Neither did he seek their worldly advice or **consort with** evildoers. In no way was he identified with the lifestyles of sinful men (cp. Ps. 1:1). David testified, **I abhor the assembly of evildoers**. He rejected their sinful ways and detested everything they stood for.

26:6–8. In contrast to his rejection of sinners, David stated that he loved **the house** of the LORD, where God's people gathered to worship. He washed his **hands in innocence** before the **altar**, the place where God's people came to exalt the Lord's name. His greatest delight in worshiping God was **proclaiming aloud** God's **praise** in **the place where** the Lord's **glory dwells**. God's glory was the revelation of his divine attributes and perfections to these worshipers.

C A Prayer for Salvation (26:9–11)

26:9–10. Finally David prayed, asking God **not** to **take away** his life in the judgment of **sinners**, referring to the same men whom he had rejected (vv. 4–5). These were **bloodthirsty men** who sought to take his life. They were men **full of bribes** who sought to influence others to harm him. David pleaded for God to spare him from their condemnation.

26:11. In contrast to these sinners, David confessed, **I lead a blameless life**, one of moral purity and integrity. He asked the Lord to **redeem** (Heb. *pada,* "to rescue") him from the false accusations and personal attacks of evil men.

D A Prayer of Confirmation (26:12)

26:12. David concluded, **My feet stand on level ground**, or a place of firm footing in the Lord, a place from which he could not slip, as he took his position **in the great assembly** of pubic worshipers. There, in the house of God, he had sure footing as he vowed to stand strong in order to **praise the LORD**.

III. CONCLUSION

The importance of living a life of personal integrity cannot be overstated. A believer's life should always be lived as in the presence of God, as under divine scrutiny. Only by living as before the Lord can a person live without hypocrisy and duplicity. There must be a consistency between a person's convictions and his character. What would such a divine investigation of your life reveal? Could most Christians invite such a thorough examination of their lives by the Lord? David could, and so must Christians today. Perhaps many need to change their ways or restore some part of their life to full integrity. May the study of this psalm be a time of personal restoration to holiness.

When facing difficulties and troubling circumstances, the believer should focus on the glory of God. Corporate worship with like-minded believers is a source of strength for the troubled soul. No greater inner fortitude exists than loving and longing for the glory of God.

IV. TEACHING OUTLINE

A . A Prayer for Vindication (1)
   He claims to be:
   1. Blameless before the Lord(1a)
   2. Bound to the Lord (1b)

B. A Prayer for Examination (2–8)
   1. Examine me (2)
      a. Test my heart (2a)
      b. Try my hand (2b)
   2. Exonerate me (3–8)
      a. I follow where you lead (3)
      b. I reject whom you reject (4)
      c. I hate what you hate (5)
      d. I confess what you forbid (6)
      e. I proclaim what you do (7)
      f. I love what you love (8)
C. A Prayer for Salvation (9–11)
   1. Rescue me (9–10)
      a. From the destruction of sinners (9)
      b. From the deceit of sinners (10)
   2. Redeem me (11)
      a. I am blameless (11a)
      b. You are merciful (11b)
D. A Prayer of Confirmation (12)
   1. A voice of confidence (12a)
   2. A vow of praise (12b)

Psalm 27
Unshakable Confidence

*"**U**nless men see a beauty and delight in the worship of God, they will not do it willingly."*

J o h n   O w e n

Psalm 27

I. INTRODUCTION

*W*hen confronted with mounting adversity, every believer must have resolute faith in God, a trust marked by an unshakable confidence. This was the experience of David as recorded in Psalm 27, a song of hope in the Lord. This is the second of three consecutive psalms—Psalms 26, 27, and 28—in which David focused upon seeking the Lord in the house of God. With triumphant confidence in God, he declared the blessing of being in the Lord's house close to the manifestation of his presence and glory, even when surrounded by trouble.

When confronted with many enemies (vv. 2–3,12) in his day of trouble (v. 5), David sought God in the tabernacle (vv. 4–6) and found in the Lord great courage and strength. Although God had not yet delivered him, he was confident that God's help would surely come. This "psalm of David" is a strong testimony of God's promise to help and defend his people.

II. COMMENTARY

MAIN IDEA: *David cries out to God in the midst of a life-threatening situation, and the light of divine grace shines into his darkness.*

A David's Confidence in God (27:1–3)

27:1. David expressed great confidence in God because the Lord was his **light**, a metaphor of divine holiness, truth, and life, all that is positive and good, and all that dispels the darkness. Furthermore, God was his **salvation**, meaning he was the one who delivered him from harm. Additionally, David knew God was **the stronghold** of his **life** (meaning "a strong fortified place"), the sure defense of his life. Therefore, he need not **fear**, or **be afraid**, of anyone. This personal relationship with God is emphasized by the threefold repetition of **my**.

27:2–3. Even when **evil men**, **enemies**, and **foes** attacked David, and although an army besieged him in **war**, he remained **confident** of God's protective defense. They would **stumble and fall** in utter defeat, for with God one is never outnumbered.

B David's Commitment to God (27:4–6)

27:4–6. David's confidence in God grew out of his commitment to the Lord. He had a living faith that motivated him to seek God's face and favor. The **one thing** for which he asked was that which was most important—God himself. More than anything else, he wanted to live for the glory of God. So he requested that he might **dwell in the house of the LORD**, where he could **gaze upon the beauty of the LORD**. This longing to adore God would occur in **his temple**, which is a reference to the **tabernacle**, not Solomon's temple which was not yet built.

Here in the Lord's dwelling place, David would be kept safe from trouble as if **set . . . high upon a rock**. Thus, God's house would be a place of asylum from the threats of his enemies. Here, he would **sacrifice** and **sing** and **make music to the LORD**.

C David's Cry to God (27:7–12)

27:7–10. Apparently, the Lord's deliverance had not yet come to David, so he cried out to God, **Hear my voice when I call**. The petition, **be merciful to me**, indicates he was in great need of God's help. As David sought the Lord, the delayed answer from heaven gave the appearance that God would turn him away, **reject** him, and **forsake** him. This delay gave the appearance that God had turned away from him **in anger**. But David reminded himself that even if his **father and mother** should forsake him, God would not.

27:11–12. In light of God's faithfulness, David prayed, **Teach me** and **lead me in a straight path**, a firm and secure way without the crookedness of sin. Although many **foes** and **false witnesses** waited by the wayside, seeking to discredit and destroy him, he prayed that God would not turn him over to their evil desires.

D David's Courage in God (27:13–14)

27:13–14. While surrounded by such bloodthirsty foes (cp. 26:9) who sought to take his life, David was **confident** that he would remain among **the living**. God would protect his life. In the meantime, he would **wait for the**

LORD whose timing for deliverance is always perfect. This is David's own encouragement to be bold and courageous while surrounded and threatened. Finally, he repeated, **wait for the** LORD, meaning to have a positive, patient, eager anticipation in the Lord. Further, he exhorted himself to **be strong** in the Lord and to **take heart**.

III. CONCLUSION

When faced with threats and trouble, believers should always seek the Lord, especially in the place of public worship. There is great strength in God's house, where worship is rendered to God and his Word is taught. It is in the house of the Lord that his presence is often realized, in the midst of the congregation where God's glory is revealed. Let the church not forsake the assembling of ourselves together, but encourage one another in the public place of praise.

IV. TEACHING OUTLINE

A. David's Confidence in God (1–3)
 1. God will deliver my life (1)
 2. God will defeat my enemies (2)
 3. God will defend my safety (3)
B. David's Commitment to God (4–6)
 1. I will dwell in God's house (4a)
 2. I will delight in God's house (4b)
 3. I will deepen in God's house (5–6)
C. David's Cry to God (7–12)
 1. Hear me (7)
 2. Help me (8–10)
 3. Teach me (11a)
 4. Lead me (11b)
 5. Protect me (12)
D. David's Courage in God (13–14)
 1. To escape from death (13)
 2. To wait for God (14a, c)
 3. To be sharing in God (14b)

Psalm 28

Rejoicing in Answered Prayer

"*Never was a faithful prayer lost. Some prayers have a longer voyage than others, but then they return with their richer lading at last, so that the praying soul is a gainer by waiting for an answer.*"

William Gurnall

I. INTRODUCTION

*O*ne of the most exhilarating aspects of the Christian life is the dynamic of answered prayer. A direct cause and effect exists between prayer offered on earth and the answer given in heaven. A life of faith lives with the anticipation that God will answer prayer according to his perfect will. Faith believes that God will act in his perfect way.

In this psalm David was endangered by treacherous men (vv. 3–4) who sought to destroy God's work (v. 5). Once again he turned to the Lord, pleading for his divine judgment on the ungodly who showed no regard for God's work. As David waited on God to act, he was concerned that he not share in that judgment but that God would set him apart him from the wicked. In this dark hour God remained David's strength, his shield from all harm, and the shepherd of his soul, protecting and providing for him.

This is another psalm "of David," the third companion psalm of a trio, Psalms 26 and 27 being the other two, which centers around God's house and "the Most Holy Place" (v. 2).

II. COMMENTARY

MAIN IDEA: *David asks the Lord to deliver him from evil men and praises God for hearing his prayer.*

A David's Plea (28:1–2)

28:1–2. David pleaded, **To you I call, O LORD, my Rock**. The Lord was his security. **Do not turn a deaf ear to me**, he prayed. If God was **silent**, giving the appearance that he did not hear his urgent pleas, he would be like those who had gone **down to the pit** (Heb. *bor*), a metaphor for death. In other words, if God failed to answer his prayer, David reasoned, his life would be no different from unbelievers who lived and died without divine deliverance. David's dependence on God is symbolized by his uplifted **hands**, indicating his reaching out toward the **Most Holy Place**. This Holy Place was the innermost part of the tabernacle that housed the ark of the covenant, the symbol of God's presence. David desperately needed God's help!

B David's Petition (28:3–5)

28:3. More specifically, David asked God not to **drag** him **away with the wicked** in judgment. Those who did **evil** deserved divine punishment because, although they spoke **cordially with their neighbors**, giving the appearance of outward godliness, they actually harbored **malice in their hearts**. Thus, he asked not to be judged with hypocritical sinners.

28:4–5. Pleading for divine justice, David petitioned God, **Repay them for their deeds** which are evil. This was a sober imprecation calling for divine wrath exercised on his behalf. He asked God to bring upon them what they deserved—severe judgment. So vile were their works that they showed **no regard for the works of the LORD**. Those who destroy God's works will certainly be destroyed.

C David's Praise (28:6–9)

28:6–7. Suddenly David's mood shifted from deepest concern to highest celebration without his circumstances changing. Believing that God would do right, he anticipated God's vindication. This dramatic difference in David occurred as he realized that God had **heard** his **cry for mercy**. **Praise be to the LORD**, he exulted, whom his **heart trusts**. The Lord was his **strength**. He enabled him to endure throughout this crisis. Likewise, God was his **shield**, protecting him from the assaults of his enemies. His **heart** leaped with joy as he gave **thanks** to God for this help.

28:8. God is **the strength** of all **his people** who trust him, empowering them to persevere through every trial. Similarly, God is **a fortress of salvation for his anointed one**. This is a reference by David to his royal position as the **anointed** king of Israel. God is the one who saves the king.

28:9. David concluded this psalm by offering a personal intercession on behalf of the entire nation. **Save your people** from all their enemies, he pleaded, **and bless your inheritance**, another reference to God's **people** (cp. Deut. 4:20; 1 Kgs. 8:51). He further appealed to God, **their shepherd** (cp. Ps. 23:1; Mic. 5:4; 7:14), to **carry them forever** like a shepherd would carry his sheep.

III. CONCLUSION

The Lord is sufficient for the believer in every circumstance of life, even the most difficult trials. He helps his own with the fullness of his sustaining grace. When believers feel they are so weak that they can advance no further in God's will, the Lord is an ever-present Shepherd who carries forward even the weakest of his sheep, saving them from harm. Let the redeemed call on God. He will not turn a deaf ear to them. Let them not remain silent toward God because one's strength is shown in God's powerful actions on behalf of his weak ones (2 Cor. 12:9).

IV. TEACHING OUTLINE

A. David's Plea (1–2)
   1. Hear me (1–2a)
   2. Help me (2b–d)
B. David's Petition (3–5)
   1. Preserve the innocent (3)
      a. From the wicked (3a)
      b. From the hypocrites (3b)
   2. Punish the impure (4–5)
      a. For their evil deeds (4)
      b. For their indifferent hearts (5)
C. David's Praise (6–9)
   1. God has heard me (6)
   2. God has helped me (7–9)
      a. He is my strength (7a, 8a)
      b. He is my shield (7a)
      c. He is my song (7b)
      d. He is my salvation (8b–9a)
      e. He is my shepherd (9b)

Psalm 29

Sovereign Majesty

Psalm 29

I. INTRODUCTION

*T*he greatness of God's unrivaled, unrestricted sovereignty calls for all creation to give him glory. The reign of his sceptre extends over all. Thus, all who recognize his supremacy should give him praise. This psalm is another song of confidence in God that voices the praise due his name. This is "a psalm of David" in which he saw an awesome electrical storm move across the land. He interpreted it as a theophony, an appearance of God. To this sovereign God who controls the weather, glory and strength should be ascribed.

From heaven where the angelic hosts pay him homage (vv. 1–2), to a violent thunderstorm that sweeps across the Middle East (vv. 3–9), to the universal flood that covered the earth (v. 10), the Lord sits as sovereign king over everything he has made. Orchestrating all events to their appointed end, God governs all peoples, places, and events for the good of his people (v. 11). As a polemic against pagan gods who competed with one another over land and sea, Psalm 29 magnifies the true God who rules over all creation.

II. COMMENTARY

MAIN IDEA: *David calls all creation to worship God who is sovereign over heaven, earth, and people.*

A God's Sovereignty over Heaven (29:1–2)

29:1–2. This psalm begins in the splendor of the heavenly courts as David called upon the **mighty ones**, probably angelic beings, to worship the greatness of **the LORD**. This divine name is used eighteen times in this psalm. One of the chief functions of the angels is to acknowledge God's intrinsic **glory**, or the fullness of his revealed nature, character, **and strength**. Such praise is **due his name** by the heavenly angelic choir of supernatural beings. They are called upon to **worship** him **in the splendor** (outshining) **of his holiness** (Heb. *qodesh*, see "Deeper Discoveries," 15:1).

B God's Sovereignty over Earth (29:3–10)

29:3–4. This psalm shifts from heaven to earth as the awesome sounds of a thunderstorm are viewed as proclaiming the supremacy of God. **The voice of the LORD** was a ferocious thunderstorm that formed **over the mighty waters** of the Mediterranean Sea which **thunders** (1 Sam. 7:10; John 37:4–5; Ps. 18:13; Isa. 30:30–31). This **powerful** storm was a reflection of the omnipotence of God.

29:5–7. This thunderstorm moved inland over the forests of **Lebanon** and broke **in pieces the cedars**, uprooting the tallest and strongest of trees. The towering mountains of **Lebanon**, dominated by **Sirion** (Phoenician name for Mount Hermon), were brought into submission by this storm that was forced to **skip like a calf**, dancing to the Lord's tune. All this was by the decree of the Lord (Isa. 46:9–10) whose **voice** roared in the **flashes of lightning**.

29:8–9. This storm continued to move from the northern Lebanese mountains to the southern **Desert of Kadesh**. As this electrical storm thundered, the **desert** floor shook, and the lightning bolts struck **the oaks**, leaving them mangled. The lightning stripped the forests bare, removing entire sections of trees. Worshipers in the **temple** were moved to **cry, "Glory!"**—echoing the heavenly anthem above (vv. 1–2).

29:10. This thunderstorm was hardly comparable to a far greater storm—the universal **flood** (Heb. *mabbul*, found only in Gen. 6–11) in the days of Noah (Gen. 6–8). In that day, **the LORD** ruled **enthroned** above as **King forever**, judging the earth and drowning the wicked for their iniquities (Gen. 6:5–7).

C God's Sovereignty over People (29:11)

29:11. This sovereign God, presiding over heaven and earth, **gives strength to his people**, working in them to do his will. In an even greater display of his power, **the LORD blesses his people with peace**, even in life's storms, calming their hearts with the abiding assurance that he is God and he works for their ultimate good (Gen. 50:20; Rom. 8:28).

III. CONCLUSION

All creation, both angelic beings and redeemed saints, exist to worship God and to give glory to God (Rom. 11:36). The highest purpose of man is to ascribe strength and splendor to God, who alone is holy. All of life must be lived with this grand theme resonating within our souls as we give glory to our sovereign Lord. Paul understood this when he said to the Corinthian Christians, "So whether you eat or drink . . . do it all for the glory of God" (1 Cor. 10:31). The overriding motivation in the Christian life must be to do everything, both in word and deed, to the glory of God (Col. 3:17). There-fore, let all the saints shout "Glory!" and ascribe to him the honor that is due his matchless name.

IV. TEACHING OUTLINE

A. God's Sovereignty over Heaven (1–2)
  1. Angels worship his strength (1)
  2. Angels worship his splendor (2)
B. God's Sovereignty Over Earth (3–10)
  1. Over the thunderstorm (3–9)
    a. He speaks in the gathering storm (3a)
    b. He speaks in the piercing thunder (3b–6)
    c. He speaks in the lightning strikes (7–9)
  2. Over the universal flood (10)
    a. He sits enthroned above (10a)
    b. He sits enthroned forever (10b)
C. God's Sovereignty Over People (11)
  1. He gives power (11a)
  2. He gives peace (11b)

Psalm 30
Under the Divine Knife

"God uses hardship and affliction as a means of discipline, a means of training His children, of helping them mature in their spiritual lives."

J o h n   M a c A r t h u r

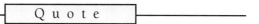

I. INTRODUCTION

Chiseling Away Everything Else

Michelangelo was an extraordinary talent, considered by many to be the most skilled artist who ever lived. He excelled as a sculptor, designer, painter, and architect. To this day his statues of Moses and David, to name a few, are widely recognized and internationally acclaimed. On one occasion Michelangelo was asked how he was able to take a solid block of jagged Italian marble and carve from it a beautiful piece of art like his famous statue of David. "That was easy," the great sculptor said. "I just chiseled away everything that did not look like David."

Throughout the lifelong process of sanctification, this is what God is doing in the life of every Christian. He is chiseling away everything that does not look like Jesus Christ. He delights in taking hardened, jagged blocks of humanity, those who have been flawed by sin, and chiseling away everything that does not conform to the Lord Jesus Christ. This can be a painful process, undergoing God's knife, as he carves away, cutting back all that does not resemble Christlikeness. But it is in loving discipline that God prunes us back, knowing that it will yield righteousness and holiness and enable us to grow into the image of his Son.

This was the experience of David in Psalm 30. This psalm of thanksgiving focuses upon God's loving discipline of David in which he chastened him for his sin of self-sufficiency (v. 6). This divine punishment was no small matter in his life as God brought him under the painful ordeal of a life-threatening illness. Having felt the crushing blows of God's anger and tottering on the brink of death, David cried out for mercy and was forgiven. He was elated to have a new start with the Lord; his saddened soul was restored with rejoicing, dancing, and singing.

This psalm is a "song" of thanksgiving written by David on the occasion of "the dedication" of the temple, literally, the "dedication of the house." Confusion arises at this point as to what the dedication references. Is this a reference to when the property and building materials of the temple were dedicated (cp. 1 Chr. 21:26; 22:1) or the dedication of David's palace? Is it a reference to the location of the property purchased by David from Araunah (2 Sam. 24; 1 Chr. 21), or is it a reference to the dedication of the new palace in Zion (2 Sam. 5:11–12)? As far as the sickness that threatened David's life, history does not record the incident. Many interpreters have used this to deny the accuracy of the psalm title. But an absence from royal records cannot be used to deny the historicity of this event.

II. COMMENTARY

> **MAIN IDEA:** After facing a life-threatening illness because of his sin of self-sufficiency, David cries out to God in repentance, and God hears his cry, forgiving his sin and healing his sickness.

Under the Divine Knife

A The Rejoicing After God's Discipline (30:1–5)

> **SUPPORTING IDEA:** David states his resolve to rejoice in the Lord after he has delivered him from the depths of the pit.

30:1–3. In this psalm David began at the end. He started by looking back on a time of severe but loving discipline from the Lord. He rejoiced that God had delivered him out of this painful ordeal which was brought on by his own sin (cp. v. 6). In this rejoicing, David determined to **exalt** the LORD because he had **lifted** David **out of the depths** of a near-death experience (cp. 71:20; 130:1). The language used here is of drawing water from a well (cp. Exod. 2:16,19). So God had lifted David out of a deep hole.

Apparently, David found himself facing death and knew the occasion would allow his enemies to gloat over him (cp. Pss. 35:19,24–27; 38:16; 2 Sam. 1:17–20). He called to God for help. The Lord healed him from an illness brought on by his sin (v. 6) and spared him from going down **into the pit of death** (Pss. 28:1; 30:3; 88:4). Furthermore, God brought David **up from the grave**, sparing his life from divine justice against his sin which almost led to his death (1 Cor. 11:30; Jas. 5:19–20; 1 John 5:16).

30:4–5. Excited about the Lord's forgiveness, David called on all saints to sing to the Lord and **praise his holy name**. Why? The anger of God's discipline for his sin lasts only a moment while **his favor lasts a lifetime**, enduring forever (cp. Isa. 54:7–8). David drew the reader's attention to the contrasts between God's anger and favor and his own weeping and rejoicing, with the former occurring in the night and the latter in the morning. The weeping under God's chastising judgments lasts only **for a night**, but it will soon be withdrawn when **rejoicing comes in the morning**.

B The Reason for God's Discipline (30:6)

SUPPORTING IDEA: *God disciplined David for his sin of self-sufficiency and self-centered independence from the Lord.*

30:6. In pride David **felt secure** (using a Hebrew word implying a careless ease) and deceived himself into thinking, "**I will never be shaken**." Perhaps David began to enjoy and value the gifts over the Giver, the creation over the Creator (cp. Deut. 8:11–20; 32:15; 2 Chr. 32:2–5; Dan. 4:28–37). In any case he began to trust in his own security and status. His sin was the attitude of self-sufficiency, the sin of independence from the Lord.

C The Reality of God's Discipline (30:7)

SUPPORTING IDEA: *God chastised David by removing his presence from him because of his sin.*

30:7. The Lord disciplined David (cp. Pss. 32:3–4; 38:1–17) by withdrawing from him, allowing him to see his need for God. Previously, the LORD had **favored** him with many blessings. In God's strength David was strong like a mighty **mountain**. But God **hid** his **face** from him. This pictures a withdrawal of his divine fellowship and removal of favor from his life (cp. Ps. 13:1). As a result, David **was dismayed**, terribly shaken, and no longer at ease. David was now suffering under the painful discipline of God.

D The Removal of God's Discipline (30:8–12)

SUPPORTING IDEA: *David, having pleaded his case in repentance, received the forgiveness of God that turned his sadness into shouts of joy.*

30:8–10. To you, O LORD, I called, David declared, as he reacted to the swift chastisement of God. Feeling the pain of discipline, David **cried to the**

Lord, not on the basis of his own merit, but for **mercy.** Humbly he reasoned with God, **What gain is there in my destruction?** David deliberated with God, stating that if his life was taken, the praise he offered God would cease. In other words, "God, how can I praise you from the dust of the grave?"

David, having learned his lesson, pleaded, **Hear, O LORD, and be merciful to me.** This was a cry of repentance, the only way for divine discipline to be removed (cp. Pss. 32:5; 51:4–9).

30:11–12. David demonstrated signs of remorse and repentance by **wailing in sackcloth.** David knew his confession of sin had been heard by God and the divine hand of discipline was now removed. How so? The Lord had **turned** his **wailing,** the result of divinely inflicted pain, **into dancing.** God had removed his **sackcloth,** a sign of mourning, and replaced it with **dancing,** an expression of the rejoicing of his **heart** (1 Sam. 18:6; Pss. 149:3; 150:4). Cleansed, David's heart was able to **sing** to the Lord **and not be silent.**

The mercy of God healed David of his life-threatening sickness, and this filled him with praise (cp. Isa. 38:20, i.e., Hezekiah's recovery). This new-found joy over the forgiveness of his sin was demonstrated by his words, **O LORD my God, I will give you thanks forever.**

> **MAIN IDEA REVIEW:** *After facing a life-threatening illness because of his sin of self-sufficiency, David cried out to God in repentance and God heard his cry, forgiving his sin and healing his sickness.*

III. CONCLUSION

Joy in the Morning

Divine discipline is not God saying, "I'm through with you." Nor is it a mark of being abandoned by him. Rather, it is clear evidence of the Father's love acting for the believer's good, bringing a straying child back to himself. C. S. Lewis said, "God whispers to us in our pleasures; he speaks to us in our work; he shouts at us in our pain." In the life of every Christian, there are times when he fails to listen to God and chooses not to obey his commands. Then the Lord uses his severe discipline to cause the hearts of believers to turn to him and obey his instructions.

Just as David went from the extreme lows of painful discipline from God to the ecstatic highs of knowing divine forgiveness, so the Christian will experience both extremes. Not only will there be sorrowful seasons when the Lord must chasten his children for unconfessed sin in their lives, but there will be triumphant seasons when God will fill repentant hearts with his joy. When sin is confessed, weeping may last for the night, but joy comes in the morning.

IV. LIFE APPLICATION

A Lifestyle of Confession

Every believer must regularly confess his sin to God and repent from his sin. When this humble acknowledgment of personal failure occurs, always to be accompanied by a broken heart, God is quick to forgive. But when sin is concealed, confession is silenced, and repentance is suppressed. Then God's loving discipline is sure to be exercised. But his rod is used with a loving purpose—to restore the believer to personal holiness. Therefore, let every saint be quick to agree with God about his sin, calling out for his forgiveness. When made aware of personal sin by God, the believer must turn to the Lord for forgiveness. The Lord is a Savior to his people. He loves to show himself mighty on behalf of those who belong to him (2 Chr. 16:9).

V. PRAYER

God, we praise you for your gracious interventions in our lives. When we have cried to you, you have heard our cry, bringing spiritual and physical healing. We give thanks to your holy name, knowing that for your people, your anger will last only a moment, but your favor will endure throughout our lifetimes. Thank you for this favor that is ours in the gospel of Jesus Christ. It is because of his sacrifice that our sadness has been turned into gladness. In his name we pray. Amen.

VI. DEEPER DISCOVERIES

A. Grave (30:3)

The word *grave* (Heb. *sheol*) occurs sixty-six times in the Old Testament and is a reference to the realm of the dead, the grave, and the underworld. Both the righteous (Gen. 37:35) and the unrighteous (Num. 16:30) will go to *sheol*. People enter *sheol* because it is God who brings them there (1 Sam. 2:6). It is a place of man's conscious existence (Ps. 16:10) from which no one will return (Job 16:22; 17:14–16). The New Testament equivalent is not the Greek word *gehena*, but rather *hades* (cp. Matt. 11:23, where Jesus quotes Isa. 14:13–15). The body of every person will go to *sheol*, although all souls will not enter into the same final destiny.

B. Favor (30:5)

This word (Heb. *rason*) means "delight, desire, goodwill, or kindness," often shown from a superior to an inferior (Deut. 33:16; Ps. 5:12; Isa. 49:8;

60:10; 61:2). For example, in the Book of Proverbs, *rason* was used of kings toward his subjects (Prov. 14:35; 16:13,15). However, it is also used from one people in general toward another as meaning what is acceptable (Prov. 10:32; 11:27).

C. Dismayed (30:7)

The word *dismayed* (Heb. *bahal*) occurs fifty times in the Old Testament, including the eleven times its equivalent is found in the Aramaic sections of the Old Testament (Daniel). The word means "to be terrified, frightened, perplexed, or confounded." It is used to refer to the distressing reaction God provokes in the nations (Exod. 15:15; Pss. 2:5; 6:10; 83:17; Isa. 13:8; Ezek. 27:35) and in Israel (Ezek. 7:27; 26:18). Likewise, people become distressed or terrified at the thought of God (Job 23:15; Ps. 104:29; Dan. 4:5; 5:6). This word is also used to demonstrate the dread that people may bring on others (1 Sam. 28:21; 2 Sam. 4:1).

D. Mercy (30:8)

This word (Heb. *hanan*) is used seventy-eight times in the Hebrew Bible. It usually means "to supplicate, implore, or beseech." Most often it is extended from a stronger party to a weaker party. It was used, for example, to describe the supplications that Moses presented to God (Deut. 3:23) as well as to describe what Solomon (1 Kgs. 8:33,47,59; 9:3; 2 Chr. 6:24,37) and the psalmist (Ps. 142:1) asked of the Lord.

VII. TEACHING OUTLINE

A. The Rejoicing After God's Discipline (1–5)
  1. David exalted the Lord (1–3)
    a. God raised me (1)
    b. God restored me (2)
    c. God rescued me (3)
  2. David encouraged others (4–5)
    a. Sing to the Lord (4a)
    b. Praise his name (4b–5)
  3. God's anger turns to favor (5a)
  4. Man's weeping turns to joy (5b)
B. The Reason for God's discipline (6)
  1. David felt self-secure (6a)
  2. David grew self-sufficient (6b)
C. The Reality of God's Discipline (7)
  1. God's face was hidden (7a–c)
  2. David's heart was heavy (7d)
D. The Removal of God's discipline (8–12)

    1. David requested from God (8,10)
      a. For mercy (8,10)
      b. For help (10)
    2. David reasoned with God (9)
      a. I cannot praise God in death (9a)
      b. I cannot proclaim God in death (9b)
    3. David rejoiced in God (11–12)
      a. From wailing to dancing (11a)
      b. From sackcloth to singing (11b–12a)
      c. From silence to giving thanks (12b)

VIII. ISSUES FOR DISCUSSION

1. In what ways has the Lord disciplined me for sins in my life?
2. How often do I praise God for his interventions on my behalf?
3. How has the Lord strengthened me and caused me to stand like a strong mountain?
4. Have I ever had my sadness turned into gladness, filling me with the joy that God alone can give?

Psalm 31

God Is My Rock

I. INTRODUCTION

*E*very human weakness is an opportunity to trust in God's strength. The awareness of personal impotence should always lead the believer to cast himself on divine omnipotence. This was David's experience as recorded in Psalm 31. He found himself in yet another painful experience of life, and this ordeal drove him to trust God and his power more fully. In this sense, when he was weak, then he was strong.

On this particular occasion David was confronted with a conspiracy so powerful that even his closest friends and most ardent supporters had abandoned him. Alone and forsaken, he found himself emotionally distressed and physically drained, with no one to turn to but God. Filled with deep anxiety, David had to trust in the Lord. His anguish was transformed into assurance.

This psalm conveys an unwavering trust in God as the psalmist rejoiced in the all-sufficient resources of God. This " psalm of David" was probably to be used by "the director of music" in temple worship, either spoken by the worship leader or by the choir (1 Chr. 23:5,30).

II. COMMENTARY

MAIN IDEA: *David expresses his trust in God to deliver him, although he is surrounded by problems and filled with pain.*

A David's Plea (31:1–5)

31:1–2. This psalm begins with David's urgent plea to God, asking that he listen to his cry and rescue him from his enemies: **In you, O LORD, I have** taken refuge (Heb. *hasa,* "to flee for protection," "to take shelter in"). For David, God was his protection from the assault of his enemies. **Turn your ear to me** was a bold request that God would pay attention to him. David declared, **Be my rock of refuge, a strong fortress to save me.** The repetition of these strong synonyms for God conveys the intensity of the psalmist's trust in him. In asking God to be "a strong fortress" (literally " a house of fortification"), David was trusting in him as his ultimate defense. Although David had often taken refuge among the rocks of the wilderness (1 Sam. 23:25; 24:2), his true security was found in the Lord.

31:3–4. The phrase "Since you are my rock and my fortress" is a restatement of the previous verse. God would guide David after setting him **free** from **the trap** set for him. David asked this so he might pursue God's will. It was to this mighty God that David cried out for deliverance. The grounds of this appeal were not his own goodness, but God's righteousness. He asked this not for his own reputation but **for the sake of your name.**

31:5. In an expression of total trust in God, David prayed, **Into your hands I commit my spirit**, a passage later quoted by One greater than David, the Lord Jesus, as he hung on the cross (Luke 23:46). The psalmist had chosen, literally, to deposit his life into the Lord's hands. This is a picture of total reliance on God. **Redeem me**, he cried out, **O LORD, the God of truth.** God has promised to help his people, and he cannot lie (Titus 1:2).

🅱 David's Passion (31:6–8)

31:6–8. David next revealed the driving passion behind his prayer, a zeal and jealousy for the honor of God's holy name. He declared, **I hate those who cling to worthless idols.** He rejected those who rejected God. In this sense he refused to be associated with the evil lifestyles and wicked beliefs of the godless (cp. Ps. 1:1). He vowed to **be glad and rejoice** in God's **love.** This he did because he knew that God **saw** his **affliction** and **knew** his **anguish.** He believed that God would **set** his **feet in a spacious place**, meaning a large place of firm footing where he could escape the threats and dangers that had hemmed him in.

🅲 David's Pain (31:9–13)

31:9–10. In his troubles David was devastated and drained emotionally, physically, and mentally. His **eyes** were **weak with sorrow**, implying tears; his **soul** and **body** were filled with **grief** and drained of vitality; his **life** was **consumed** with **anguish.** All **strength** had left him. His feeling of confidence had temporarily left him.

31:11–13. What is more, David declared, **I am the utter contempt of my neighbors**, even **a dread**, a reproach to his **friends** and **enemies** alike. His friends had abandoned him like a piece of **broken pottery**; that is, he was cast aside by them. Downcast and disgraced, he stated that the **slander** by his enemies, as well as their attempts to **conspire** and **plot to take** his **life**, were strong. The most frequent weapon used against the psalmist was the tongue.

D David's Petition (31:14–18)

31:14–16. In spite of this persecution, David's **trust in** the LORD was unwavering. He relied on **God** to **deliver** him from his **enemies**. He prayed, **My times are in your hands**, recognizing that all the events and circumstances of his life were under God's sovereign control, which is tempered by his **unfailing love**. Therefore, **let your face shine on your servant** is a request for divine favor (cf. Pss. 4:6; 44:3; 67:1; 80:3,7,9; 119:35).

31:17–18. The phrase **Let me not be put to shame** indicates the dishonor that would result if David's enemies should succeed in their conspiracy against him. David wanted the **wicked** to be **put to shame** and to **lie silent in the grave** rather than allowing him to be silenced in death. Their **lying lips**, which had slandered him, must **be silenced** because they had spoken **arrogantly against** one of **the righteous**, namely himself. Rather than taking vengeance into his own hands, he left the dispensing of wrath to God.

E David's Praise (31:19–22)

31:19–20. As David waited for divine deliverance, his heart was filled with praise for God's **goodness**, a **great**, all-sufficient supply of grace **stored up**, freely shared with **those who fear** him. He was confident that God himself, in the **shelter of** his **presence**, would **hide** him from the plots of evil men.

31:21–22. On the basis of God's goodness, David exclaimed, **Praise be to the LORD, for he showed his wonderful love to me**. When he was under great danger, during his threatening trial pictured as a besieged city, God remained faithful. At times David panicked and cried out to God, "**I am cut off from your sight!**", fearing he would be put to death. Nevertheless, his heart would rally, and he would say, **Yet you heard my cry for mercy**. Thus, David gave praise to God in anticipation of his help and deliverance.

F David's Proclamation (31:23–24)

31:23–24. Having offered praise to God, David next preached to others, calling **all his saints** to **love the LORD** with all their heart, soul, and strength (Deut. 6:5). All God's people should adore God because he **preserves the faithful** when they are abandoned and attacked. But **the proud**, referring to those who rise up in arrogance and harm the godly, refuse to submit themselves to the Lord. But God will pay back those who are proud. Vengeance belongs to the Lord. Therefore, we should **be strong and take heart in the LORD** because he will defend those who hope in him.

III. CONCLUSION

All believers to some degree will be surrounded by evil people who work against them. So we must continually remind ourselves that all the events of his life are being orchestrated and executed in the perfect timing of God. Likewise, we must recall the great goodness of God which is stored up for his elect. The Lord himself will preserve the faithful so they can weather the storm in which they find themselves. The Lord delights in showing his preserving power to the weakest vessels. The believer must not be downcast, but he should take courage, knowing that his infinite God is much larger than the finite people who threaten him.

IV. TEACHING OUTLINE

A. David's Plea (1–5)
  1. Deliver me! (1–2)
  2. Direct me! (3)
  3. Defend me! (4–5)
B. David's Passion (6–8)
  1. Rejecting the godless (6a)
  2. Rejoicing in God (6b–8)
    a. God sees him (6b–7)
    b. God saves him (8)
C. David's Pain (9–13)
  1. He is suffering sorrow (9–10)
  2. He is suffering scorn (11–12)
  3. He is suffering slander (13)
D. David's Petition (14–18)
  1. He prays for victory (14–16)
    a. Save me (14–15)
    b. Shine on me (16)
  2. He prays for vengeance (17–18)
    a. Shame my enemies (17a–c)
    b. Silence my enemies (17d–18)
E. David's Praise (19–22)
  1. God is good! (19)
  2. God is great! (20)
  3. God is gracious! (21–22)
F. David's Proclamation (23–24)
  1. Love the Lord (23)
  2. Look to the Lord (24)

Psalm 32
Straight Talk About Crooked Living

"*Y*ou have not got to the bottom of the blackness of sin until you see that it is a flat rebellion against God himself."

Alexander MacLaren

I. INTRODUCTION

Different Labels, Same Poison

J. Wilbur Chapman, noted Methodist evangelist of the nineteenth century, told of a distinguished minister in Australia who preached regularly on sin. One of the church officers came to him after one sermon to talk with him. He said to the pastor, "We do not want you to talk so plainly as you do about sin. If our boys and girls hear you talking so much about sin, they will more easily become sinners. Call it whatever you will, but do not speak so plainly about sin."

The minister arose from his desk, walked to a utility closet, and brought back a small bottle of strychnine that was marked "Rat Poison." He said, "I see what you want me to do. You want me to change the label. Suppose I take off this 'Poison' label and replace it with some milder label, such as 'Essence of Peppermint.' The milder you make the label, the more dangerous you make the poison."

This is one of the values of Psalm 32. Without changing the labels and minimizing the effect of sin, this psalm speaks directly to the devastating power of unconfessed sin in the life of a believer. As seen in the life of David, sin committed against God led to sorrow and loss of vitality in his life. But as also witnessed in David's life, when he confessed his sin, there was a resurgence of great joy as well as a passion for living to the glory of God. From this magnificent piece of inspired literature, we conclude that confessing our sin is a vital part of vibrant, victorious Christian living.

This psalm reflects the time when David was king over Israel. He sent his troops into battle against the Ammonites while he remained behind. During this time he fell into adulterous sin with Bathsheba (2 Sam. 11:1–5). To make matters worse, he tried to cover up his sin by having her husband, Uriah the Hittite, killed (2 Sam. 11:6–17). For the next year David lived with his guilty conscience in deep agony of spirit. He became emotionally distraught, physically ill, and mentally disturbed.

Nathan the prophet visited the king (2 Sam. 12:1–15) and told him a story of two men, one rich and one poor. One had many flocks, the other just one little lamb. Without warning, the rich man with many flocks took the poor man's one little lamb. When David heard this, he erupted, "As surely as the LORD lives, the man who did this deserves to die!" To this Nathan said, "You are the man!" Exposed, David confessed, "I have sinned against the LORD." When Nathan heard this, he said, "The LORD has taken away your sin. You are not going to die."

This psalm records the joy that David found through the confession of his sin to God. This psalm "of David" was written after his confrontation with Nathan the prophet. It is a *maskil*, meaning that it was intended to instruct and teach. Specifically, this psalm was written by David to teach the people of God to confess their sins to the Lord.

II. COMMENTARY

Straight Talk About Crooked Living

MAIN IDEA: *David, having experienced the forgiveness and blessing of God following the confession of his sin, instructs others in this path of forgiveness.*

David's Cleansing from Sin (32:1–2)

SUPPORTING IDEA: *This psalm begins with the celebration of David over the forgiveness of his sins.*

32:1a. This psalm begins, like the Sermon on the Mount, with the word **blessed**, which can be translated as "happy, joyful, or exuberant." Furthermore, it is in the plural which greatly intensifies the meaning of the word (i.e., abundant or overflowing blessing). David began by announcing and proclaiming the joyful happiness that he discovered in the Lord's forgiveness. This could be translated, "How abundantly richly blessed is he **whose transgressions are forgiven**." The word *transgressions* indicates that a person has willfully departed from and defied God. The word *forgiven* (Heb. *nasa*) literally means "to have one's sin lifted off."

Unconfessed sin is like a great burden on God's people, weighing them down mentally and emotionally. Forgiveness is implied here and stated later because David confessed his sin to God, and this ushered in his forgiveness (cp. Ps. 103:12; Isa. 1:18; 38:17; 43:25; Mic. 7:19; 1 John 1:9). David, in sinning with Bathsheba, was guilty of fornication and defying the authority of God over his life.

32:1b. David also knew that blessing would come to the person **whose sins are covered**. The mountain of sin that David had committed—from adultery to murder to hypocrisy—was now **covered** or concealed by God. In confessing his sin to God, the blemish of sin was put out of sight—out of God's sight. This word *covered* (Heb. *kasa*) is a derivative of the word *kaphar*. It pictures the imagery of the Day of Atonement, the day on which the high priest of Israel took blood from an animal that had been sacrificed in the courtyard of the temple. He carried this blood into the Most Holy Place, where it was sprinkled on the mercy seat of the ark of the covenant.

32:2. David continued, How **blessed** are those **whose sin** ("iniquity," KJV) **the LORD does not count against him**. This sin or iniquity is that which defiles and corrupts a person's character. The Lord graciously chose not to **count** this sin against David, meaning that the debt he owed and the punishment he deserved were no longer on the books. David was polluted and perverted by his sin, but the forgiveness of God moved the Lord not to count David's sin against him. Furthermore, this state of blessedness was reserved for the one **in whose spirit is no deceit**. David had lived many months deceiving himself by rationalizing and covering his sin.

B David's Concealment of Sin (32:3–4)

SUPPORTING IDEA: *David recalls the time when he refused to confess his sin to the Lord and experienced the chastening hand of God, both emotionally and physically.*

32:3–4. Suddenly, the psalm shifts from the present (vv. 1–2) to the past. David suppressed and repressed his sin. He was talking about that time in his life, after he sinned against Bathsheba and Uriah, when he **kept silent** and refused to confess his sin to God. David's conscience brought an awareness of God's moral law. An alarm sounded within his soul when the law of right and wrong, God's law, was violated. The Bible is clear; what a man sows, that he will also reap (cp. Gal. 6:7). If he sows to the flesh, he will reap in the flesh.

David declared that his **bones wasted away**, meaning that his physical stamina and vitality were drained because the Lord's **hand was heavy upon** him. It was God's hand inflicting this physical discipline upon David's body.

Furthermore, David noted, **my strength was sapped as in the heat of summer**. David's failure to confess his sins led to a debilitating and draining weakness. He was also emotionally distraught, because he spoke of his **groaning all day long**. His soul was aching, racked with pain, agonizing, depressed, and downcast. His zest for life was slowly being drained away.

ⓒ David's Confession of Sin (32:5)

SUPPORTING IDEA: *David stops deceiving himself and acknowledges, uncovers, and confesses his sin to the Lord.*

32:5. Verse 5 is the most pivotal verse of this psalm, serving as a climactic turning point for David. Notice that David, in rapid-fire succession, stated the same truth three times in three different ways. This succession is shown in that he **acknowledged . . . did not cover up . . . confess**. David said of this cataclysmic shift, **I acknowledged my sin to you**. He confessed his sin to God because his sin was against God. All sin is ultimately against God, even when it is committed against other persons (cp. 2 Sam. 12:13; Ps. 51:4).

David also wrote, **I . . . did not cover up my iniquity**, meaning that he did not attempt to conceal his iniquity when Nathan confronted him. The phrase "did not cover up" means to bring something out in the open or to reveal something. It is the same word used in verse 1 which is translated "whose sin is covered," but here it is in the negative, "did not cover up." The confession of sin is the uncovering of our sin before God, exposing it for what it is.

David then said to his own soul, "**I will confess my transgressions to the LORD**." To confess (Heb. *yada*) means to speak out openly, even to sing out in public praise. Here it means to declare openly one's sin to God, to speak out openly to him about one's sin. This David did in Psalm 51:3 when he said to the Lord, "For I know my transgressions." David knew that he had transgressed the sovereign rule of God over his life. After David's actions that demonstrated true repentance, he declared of the Lord, **You forgave the guilt of my sin**. The word *forgave* (Heb. *nasa*) literally means "to have the burden of sin lifted off." Before the sin is confessed, it is a heavy burden.

ⓓ David's Counsel About Sin (32:6–11)

SUPPORTING IDEA: *David instructs and counsels God's people on how they may also go about acknowledging their sin to God.*

32:6. Having experienced God's forgiveness, David encouraged true believers to go to God and **pray to** him while he **may be found**. The prayer that the **godly** are urged to offer to God is the prayer in which we confess our sin to God, seeking his forgiveness (v. 5). David continued, **Surely when the mighty waters rise, they will not reach him**. The imagery is of a believer who is overwhelmed in a storm or flood that threatens his life. This flood of mighty **waters** is God's chastening deluge that brings severe consequences.

32:7. David turned to God in faith and trust. In the storms of life, David could say of the Lord, **You are my hiding place.** Interestingly, God was David's hiding place from God himself. It was God who was chastening David. It was his divine hand that was heavy upon him. Forgiveness for the believer is a deliverance from God's chastisement.

Furthermore, David exclaimed, **You will protect me from trouble.** To **protect** (Heb. *nasar*) means "to guard, to protect, to hide," or "to conceal" as a watchman would guard a city, preserving it from trouble (Jer. 31:6). While protecting his servant David, God surrounded him with **songs of deliverance.** From the depths of despair to the heights of praise, this psalm is a song of deliverance. Out of this painful ordeal flowed some of the greatest songs of praise.

32:8–9. David also counseled others: **I will instruct you and teach you in the way you should go.** On the basis of David's own painful experience, he instructed others: **I will counsel you and watch over you. Do not be like the horse or the mule, which have no understanding.** The Lord exhorted the people not to be like the obstinate horse or stubborn mule that refuses to go where its rider leads. Instead, the godly should respond promptly to God on their own accord. David was like a wild horse that rushed into sin, but when it came to confessing his sin, he held back like a stubborn mule.

The warning is clear for the person who will not humble himself before God's sovereign rule. If we do not submit to the Lord, we will be **controlled by bit and bridle.** If the people of God act as disobedient children, he will use severe means to get their attention and gain control (cp. Prov. 26:3). Persistent disobedience by the godly will lead to the chastening hand of God (Heb. 12:5–11).

32:10–11. David contrasted the **woes of the wicked** with the LORD's **unfailing love.** These woes were distresses. At times the term was used to speak of sickness. Because David was trusting in the Lord, he knew that the Lord's **unfailing love** would surround him. This unfailing love (Heb. *hesed*) refers to God's covenant love, a binding, unconditional commitment on God's part to those who trust him (see "Deeper Discoveries," 23:6).

This psalm ends the way it began—with a declaration for the righteous to **rejoice in the LORD** and be glad. This call on the part of David is a call to all believers to rejoice in the Lord's forgiveness. Specifically, it is a call to **sing, all you who are upright in heart!**

MAIN IDEA REVIEW: *David, having experienced the forgiveness and blessing of God following the confession of his sin, instructs others in this path of forgiveness.*

III. CONCLUSION

Straight Talk About Forgiveness

This psalm has provided every believer with what he or she so desperately needs: straight talk about sin. Our world has provided us with a skewed view of sin, and it has penetrated Christian thinking within the church. Let us take counsel from this psalm and be reminded:

> Man calls it an accident;
> God calls it an abomination.
> Man calls it a blunder;
> God calls it a blasphemy.
> Man calls it a chance;
> God calls it a choice.
> Man calls it an error;
> God calls it an enmity.
> Man calls it a fascination;
> God calls it a fatality.
> Man calls it an infirmity;
> God calls it an iniquity.
> Man calls it luxury;
> God calls it leprosy.
> Man calls it a liberty;
> God calls it lawlessness.
> Man calls it a trifle;
> God calls it tragedy.
> Man calls it a mistake;
> God calls it madness.
> Man calls it a weakness;
> God calls it willfulness.

Yet, when sins are confessed to God, he is faithful and righteous to forgive our sin and to cleanse us from all unrighteousness. This is straight talk about forgiveness.

IV. LIFE APPLICATION

Taking Sin Seriously

In applying this psalm, we are reminded of the seriousness of sin, even in the life of a believer. Every sinful attitude, thought, or act is ultimately a revolt against God. It is a direct defiance of God's rule over a person's life, no matter what the sin is, whether large or seemingly small, seen or unseen by human eyes. Sin is a conscious choosing to rebel against God's authority in order to go our own way. It is an uprising against heaven, a conspiracy against God. Consequently, believers must never minimize or trivialize sin as a small, trifling matter. They must deal with it with the same seriousness with which God sees it. That for which Christ died is never trite or insignificant. With deep sincerity and godly sorrow, believers must acknowledge their transgressions to the Lord, never presuming upon God's unmerited grace, but humbling themselves in his presence, seeking his forgiveness.

V. PRAYER

God, how often we fall short of your will. Many times we have corrupted our lives with the pollution of sin. We have rebelled against your sovereign authority and right to rule our lives. We beg you to be merciful to us, forgiving our transgressions and covering our sins. Help us not to be stubborn in refusing to confess our sins which we attempt to cover and hide from you. Teach us in the way we should go so we will know the joy of confessed and pardoned sin. In Jesus' name. Amen.

VI. DEEPER DISCOVERIES

A. Sin (32:1–2)

Four different words for *sin* are used in the first two verses of this psalm: *transgressions* (v. 1a), *sins* (v. 1b), *sin* (v. 2a), and *deceit* (v. 2b). Each conveys an important nuance of the reality of sin.

These verses are an example of Hebrew poetic parallelism, since these four words are placed side by side and cover the entire spectrum of what sin is. Notice that David was tracking the downward progression of sin, first, as a rebellion against God and a revolt against his authority. Then sin is depicted as missing the way God has marked out for man, a departure from righteousness. Then guilt overwhelms him and he becomes polluted within. Finally, man becomes self-deceived as he justifies his own sin to himself and he refuses to deal with its wrongness.

This first word for sin, *transgressions* (v. 1a), is from the Hebrew word *peshah*. This word literally means "a going away from, departure, rebellion, or defiance." A transgression is a willful act of rebellion against God's sovereign authority and a refusal to acknowledge his right to rule the lives of his people. A transgression is not merely against other people whom a person may hurt by his sin, but it is always, ultimately, a treasonous act against God.

The second word is the word *sins* (v. 1b), which is translated from the Hebrew word *hataa*. This word reveals a different nuance of sin and means "to miss the mark, to miss the way, to go wrong, to go astray." This word is an archery term. It pictures a hunter with bow and arrow, aiming at a target or an animal. He shoots the arrow, only to miss the mark and fall short (Rom. 3:23). This is what sin is—life missing the mark of God's Word. It is a person's life falling short of the standard by not measuring up. The standard is the glory of God, the sum total of all his divine perfections, most specifically, God's holiness.

The third word for sin is the word *sin* (v. 2a), or *iniquity* (KJV), which is translated from the Hebrew word *awon*, meaning "corrupt, twisted, bent, perversity, or crooked." While the first word for sin, *transgression*, describes sin in view of our relationship to God and the second word deals with our relationship to God's Word, this word focuses upon a person's relationship to himself. All sin is a self-defilement, a self-corrupting, a twisting of one's own character, and a bending of one's integrity. To the degree that a person sins, he becomes a twisted creature within his own soul. When David sinned, he became unclean and dirty. Psalms 51:2 says, "Wash away all my iniquity and cleanse me." Psalms 51:10 pleads, "Create in me a pure heart." David felt dirty within because his sin had defiled, polluted, and perverted him.

The fourth word used for sin, *deceit* (v. 2a), is translated from the Hebrew word *remiya*, which means "a deception" as in a self-deception. This is precisely what occurred to David for an entire year following his sin of adultery against Bathsheba and murder against Uriah. He lived with sin's deception within his own heart as he attempted to cover over his sin, rationalizing it to his own guilty conscience. Tragically, he did a masterful job of convincing himself that his sin was not that bad, causing him to live a lie. This is what David prayed in his confession in Psalm 51:6, "Surely you desire truth in the inner parts; you teach me wisdom in the inmost place."

B. Acknowledged (32:5)

This word (Heb. *yada*) means "to acknowledge" or "to make known." It emphasizes the recognition and declaration of a fact that is an intimately known reality. This word is one of the most important Hebrew words in the Old Testament, and it occurs 944 times. It means to acquire a deep and thorough knowledge of someone or something, such as a husband would know his wife in a sexual relationship (Gen. 4:1). Here it means to make a full disclosure of that about which one has an intimate knowledge, not a superficial knowledge.

C. Forgave (32:5)

The word for *forgave* (Heb. *nasa*) means "to raise, lift up, bear, carry, take away," "to lift up the head" (i.e., "to take a census"; see Exod. 30:12), "to lift up one's face" (i.e., "to look someone straight in the eyes"; see 2 Sam. 2:22), "to lift up one's hand" (i.e., "taking an oath"; see 1 Sam. 20:23), "to lift up one's voice" (i.e., "to wail or lament"; see Gen. 21:16), "to lift up one's soul" (i.e., "to be entirely dependent"; see Deut. 24:15). But here it is not man who lifts up and removes his sin but God. God rolls our sins away when we confess them to him.

VII. TEACHING OUTLINE

A. David's Cleansing from Sin (1–2)
  1. His defiance is forgiven (1a)
  2. His depravity is covered (1b)
  3. His defilement is not imputed (2a)
  4. His deception is removed (2b)
B. David's Concealment of Sin (3–4)
  1. He suppressed his sin (3a)
  2. He suffered for his sin (3b–4)
C. David's Confession of Sin (5)
  1. He acknowledged his sin (5a)
  2. He uncovered his sin (5b)
  3. He confessed his sin (5c)
  4. He was cleansed of his sin (5d)
D. David's Counsel About Sin (6–11)
  1. Pray to God (6)
  2. Rest in God (7)
  3. Learn from God (8)
  4. Submit to God (9)
  5. Trust in God (10)
  6. Rejoice in God (11)

VIII. ISSUES FOR DISCUSSION

1. What accusing sins do I carry, having failed to confess them to the Lord?
2. What joy could be mine if I would no longer conceal my sin but come clean with God and confess them to him?
3. In what ways does my heart need to be cleansed by God?

Psalm 33

Sing to Our Sovereign

"The sovereignty of God is that golden sceptre in his hand by which he will make all bow, either by his word or by his works, by his mercies or by his judgements."

T h o m a s   B r o o k s

I. INTRODUCTION

Unbroken and incessant praise should characterize the lives of God's people. At the heart of this worship should be a clear declaration of God's sovereignty over everything. In this song of thanksgiving, the psalmist called upon the righteous to sing to the Lord for his absolute control over all the earth. Specifically, he had in mind God's rule over all the Gentile nations. A specific occasion unknown to us prompted the writing of this psalm, one in which God delivered Israel from the threat of an invading nation. Perhaps it was written following a great national victory like what Jehoshaphat (2 Chr. 20) or Hezekiah (2 Kgs. 19) experienced over an encroaching nation.

Whatever the historical background, this psalm is an anonymous hymn of praise, one of only four psalms in Book I (Pss. 1–41) without a superscription. The other untitled psalms are 1, 2, and 10. This psalm is perfectly symmetrical, beginning with a three-verse introduction (vv. 1–3) and climaxing with a three-verse conclusion (vv. 20–22). The main body is divided into two equal sections of eight verses each (vv. 4–11,12–19). The twenty-two verses of the psalm, it has been suggested, were determined by the twenty-two letters of the Hebrew alphabet.

II. COMMENTARY

> **MAIN IDEA:** *The psalmist calls upon the righteous to praise the Lord for his mighty word, perfect attributes, and faithful deeds.*

A The Call to Rejoice (33:1–3)

33:1–2. These first three verses are a call to worship, an invitation to come and worship God. **Sing joyfully to the LORD** is derived from the same Hebrew root as "shouts for joy" (cp. 32:7,11), meaning "to sing aloud with jubilant exultation." Such fervent praise was proper, suitable, and beautiful. The psalmist declared, **Praise the LORD with the harp** and **the ten-stringed lyre**. Let all the instruments declare their praise. These two instruments are representative of an entire orchestra that would be used in the accompaniment of praise. Believers need all the help possible to stir their hearts to praise God (see Psalm 150 for a fuller listing of the instruments to be used in worshiping God).

33:3. A new song is one directed toward God as opposed to an old song sung before a person's commitment of faith to God. An old song was a Canaanite song that would be worldly, meaningless, earthly, and man-centered, reflecting the heart of the writer. But **a new song** was heavenly, eternal, God centered, and reflective of a redeemed heart. Likewise, a new song is a new occasion and a new impulse for expressing praise to God. Every song of praise should emerge from a renewed heart that brings a new awareness of God's grace (cp. Isa. 43:18–19).

B The Causes to Rejoice (33:4–19)

33:4–5. Praise always has its reasons, and those reasons are found in God himself, specifically, who he is and what he has done. Great doxology is always built upon great theology. The phrase **For the word of the LORD is right and true**, means all that God commands is perfectly **right** and absolutely **true** because **he is faithful in all he does.** He never acts out of character but only in ways that are consistent with his holy character. Because **the LORD loves righteousness and justice**, he acts faithfully in the same manner. This is why **the earth is full of his unfailing love.** All his works flow from his unchanging character.

The counsel of the Lord stands forever, the plans of his heart from generation to generation. God's purposes stand, not the heathen's. He is carrying forward his original plan A, never having to change his plans to an alternate plan B or C. He does not change his purposes.

33:6–9. The psalmist declared, **By the breath of his mouth**, he made everything out of nothing, which is to say, he created *ex nihilo*. Omnipotently, he gathered **the waters of the sea into jars** like a farmer who puts his grain into **storehouses**. As a result, **let all the earth fear the** LORD, since he exercises such power over lives. **For he spoke, and it came to be** without any opposition or failure.

33:10–11. In the same way, God rules over human affairs. **The** LORD **foils the plans of the nations** that seek to operate contrary to his sovereign will. **The plans of the** LORD **stand firm forever** as opposed to the plans of impotent men who are always changing. **The purposes of his heart** endure unchanged, unlike the purposes of people. The God who spoke this world into existence continues to rule over it and to order all things by the secret counsel of his will (cp. Eph. 1:11).

33:12–15. Only those **people** who align themselves with God and his revealed plans will know the fullness of his **inheritance**. As God carries out his plans, it is with the full knowledge of our lives, circumstances, and needs. **From heaven the** LORD **looks down and sees all mankind**. From his dwelling place he **watches all who live on earth**. With penetrating gaze God observes every person on the earth. No one escapes his perfect vision (cp. Heb. 4:13). God who forms the hearts of all rules over all things in accordance with his own sovereign purposes.

33:16–19. The psalmist declared, **No king is saved by the size of his army** because, ultimately, the victory belongs to God. The phrase **the eyes of the** LORD **are on those who fear him**, refers to all believers who reverence and trust him, which is another way of saying, **those whose hope is in his unfailing love**. God will work on behalf of his people **to deliver them from death**, from the hands of threatening nations (v. 10), and to keep God's people who trust in him **alive in famine**. God will intervene in the lives of his people at the right moment.

🅒 The Choice to Rejoice (33:20–22)

33:20–22. The people responded in faith to what they had heard in this call to rejoice. The phrase **We wait in hope for the** LORD reaffirms their confident commitment to the Lord. This they can do because **he is our help** (cp. 20:6) **and our shield** (cp. 3:3). In this God the people **trust** (Heb. *batach*, "to attach oneself, depending upon") because he is in control.

The psalm ends with a petition by the people, **May your unfailing love** (Heb. *hesed*, vv. 5,18; see "Deeper Discoveries," 23:6) **rest upon us, O** LORD. He would sustain and support them through every crisis as they put their **hope** in him. Such hope is well-placed and will never disappoint the believer.

III. CONCLUSION

All who have been redeemed and made righteous through their personal faith in God should sing joyfully to the Lord. Praise is the proper response of our hearts to God because of the many good things he has done for us. God calls us to look away from circumstances and trials to him. He invites us to worship him with hopeful hearts. Every believer's song should emerge from a fresh awareness of God's grace, with a fresh voice for the old truth. Charles Spurgeon once wrote, "Let us not present old worn-out praise, but put life and soul and heart into every song, since we have new mercies every day and see new beauties in the work and word of our Lord."

IV. TEACHING OUTLINE

A. The Call to Rejoice (1–3)
  1. Sing joyfully (1–3b)
  a. With praise (1)
  b. With the harp (2a)
  c. With the lyre (2b)
  d. With a new song (3a)
  e. With skill (3b)
  2. Shout jubilantly (3c)
B. The Causes to Rejoice (4–19)
  1. God's Word is all-powerful (4–9)
    a. He commands human history (4–5)
    b. He commands national creation (6–9)
  2. God's will is all-ruling (10–11)
    a. He overrules man's plans (10)
    b. He undergirds his purposes (11)
  3. God's eyes are all-seeing (12–19)
    a. He watches all things (12–14)
    b. He weighs all things (15–17)
    c. He witnesses all believers (18–19)
C. The Choice to Rejoice (20–22)
  1. Wait for God (20)
  2. Trust in God (21)
  3. Hope in God (22)

Psalm 34
An Attitude of Gratitude

"*T*he highest point of all worship and prayer is adoration and praise and thanksgiving."

D .   M a r t y n   L l o y d - J o n e s

I. INTRODUCTION

Not One of Them Thanked Me

*O*ver a century ago Northwestern University, located on Lake Michigan near Chicago, had a voluntary life-saving crew among its students. One of these crews became famous for rescuing shipwrecked sailors. On September 8, 1860, just off the shore of Lake Michigan and near the college campus, the *Lady Elgin*, a crowded passenger steamer, went down. Answering the emergency distress call, a life-saving team at Northwestern University immediately formed themselves into rescue teams and launched out into the waters. Among the students that perilous day was Edward Spencer, a young man who was preparing for the ministry.

Seeing a woman clinging to some wreckage far out in the waters, Spencer threw off his coat and swam out through the heavy waves, successfully rescuing her and pulling her back to the shore. Sixteen more times that day young Spencer braved the fierce waves, saving a host of lives. Exhausted and spent, this heroic young man collapsed from fatigue. Spencer never completely recovered from the exposure of that near-tragic day. With broken health he lived quietly the rest of his life in relative seclusion, disabled, unable to enter the work of the ministry.

Many years later R. A. Torrey, pastor of Moody Memorial Church in Chicago, was telling about this incident at a meeting in Los Angeles when a man in the audience called out that Edward Spencer was present! Torrey invited

Spencer to the platform. An old man with white hair, he slowly climbed the steps to the pulpit as the applause rang out. Torrey asked him if anything in particular stood out in his memory. "Only this, sir," Spencer replied. "Of the seventeen people I saved, not one of them thanked me."

David did not want to fall into such a lapse of ingratitude, so he wrote Psalm 34 to express his thanksgiving to God, specifically for rescuing him from a perilous and threatening situation. Pressures had been very real in his life, mounting and mounting greater, driving him to the point of despair. But David called on the Lord, transferring his trust fully to God, and his fears were relieved. The Lord delivered him out of his desperate situation.

This psalm is a song of praise written by David for the Lord's salvation in his dire circumstances. This was a time when David "pretended to be insane before Abimelech." Sometimes Abimelech is used as a proper name, but the word was also a common title for a Philistine king (Gen. 20; 21:22–34; 26). Thus, it was also used as a dynastic designation, much like the word *Pharaoh* was used in Egypt or *Caesar* in Rome. The latter meaning is probably the case here. If so, the ruler referred to is probably Achish. Information about this king is recorded in 1 Samuel 21:10–15.

This was an incident when David was surrounded by King Saul and the army of Israel. Finding himself in a crisis situation, he pleaded with the Lord to deliver him from this life-threatening experience. As a result of his urgent prayer, God answered David and rescued him from his enemies. Consequently, this psalm expresses David's gratitude to God for his deliverance.

This psalm is an acrostic, the third in the Book of Psalms, in which each verse begins with a consecutive letter of the Hebrew alphabet. The purpose of this literary technique was to help people memorize the psalm and to emphasize the perfection of its structure.

II. COMMENTARY

An Attitude of Gratitude

> **MAIN IDEA:** *Believers should praise God for his mighty deliverance, recognizing that he rescues his people from their fears and out of their distresses.*

A David's Worship (34:1–3)

> **SUPPORTING IDEA:** *All believers are invited to magnify God together in worshiping him.*

34:1–3. Beginning with a strong declaration of praise, David proclaimed, **I will extol the LORD!** He acknowledged all that the Lord had done for him. His worship of God was continuous, stating that praise to him would **always** be on his **lips**. Such praise is contagious. David wanted to **let the afflicted hear and rejoice**.

The phrase **Glorify the LORD with me; let us exalt his name together** is an invitation to other believers to lift high the Lord's greatness in their worship. David acknowledged who God is and what he had done for him. He invited all who would listen to join in God's praise.

B David's Witness (34:4–7)

SUPPORTING IDEA: *David testifies that the Lord heard him and answered him when he called upon him in his time of trouble.*

34:4–5. Recognizing a direct link between what he had prayed and how God intervened, David testified, **I sought the LORD, and he answered me**. The direct result was that God **delivered** him **from all** his **fears**. Although David was traumatized, the Lord flooded his heart with peace. His countenance became **radiant** with joy.

34:6–7. David identified himself as **this poor man**, or one without the resources to bring about his own rescue. When he called upon God, the Lord **heard him** and **saved him out of all his troubles**. The word *troubles* means "to be restricted, tied up, limited, inhibited." But in this impossible situation, David was dramatically delivered by **the angel of the LORD**. This phrase describes a special manifestation of the Lord, probably a Christophany, or an appearance of the preincarnate Lord Jesus Christ (cp. Gen. 16:7; 18–19; 31:11; Josh. 5; Judg. 6; 13), who **encamps around those who fear him**. Just as **the Lord** had protected him, so David was confident that God would deliver **all** who reverenced him with awe and adoration (cp. Dan. 3).

C David's Wisdom (34:8–14)

SUPPORTING IDEA: *David instructs the people in divine wisdom, stating that they are to be satisfied in God himself and to reverence him in order to live a godly life that will be pleasing to him.*

34:8–10. David used several imperatives as he called upon all the people to trust the Lord: **taste** (v. 8), **fear** (v. 9), **come** (v. 11), **keep** (v. 13), **turn** (v. 14), **do** (v. 14), **seek** (v. 14), and **pursue** (v. 14). He declared, **taste and see that the LORD is good**. He summoned all who would listen to discover the same soul satisfaction he had found in God. **Blessed** means "to be happy and content" (see "Deeper Discoveries," 1:1). This describes the person who **takes refuge** in the Lord. The person who is anchored in God knows true happiness.

Those who **fear the LORD** with the deepest reverence will **lack nothing**. Those who fear God will find that he fulfills his word to them. To illustrate this reality, David pointed out that **lions**, the kingly animals at the head of the food chain, would **grow weak and hungry** before **those who seek the LORD**.

Taking refuge in him, they would not **lack** any **good thing**. Because God is **good** (v. 8), his children will receive every good thing from him (v. 10).

34:11–14. Speaking as a wise teacher (Prov. 1:8,10; 2:1; 3:1; 8:32), David entreated his congregation, **Come, my children . . . I will teach you the fear of the LORD**. Even believers must be regularly taught this important lesson (cp. Job 28:28; Ps. 111:10; Prov. 1:7; 9:10; Eccl. 12:13). This fear involves a twofold response. Negatively speaking, David advised, **turn from evil**, especially the evil of **speaking lies**. And, positively, he counseled, **do good** and **seek** and **pursue peace**.

Living in the fear of the Lord is more than a state of heart or mind; it is a life that translates into proper action. These evidences of holiness are the marks of a person who truly fears God.

D David's Wonder (34:15–22)

> **SUPPORTING IDEA:** *David states that the Lord will honor the righteous who are broken and humble of heart.*

34:15–16. The focus of these last verses is **the righteous**, who are mentioned four times (vv. 15,17,19,21). David himself was the epitome of the godly man, and the protection he received from God is the defense offered to all God's saints. David was confident that the Lord's **eyes** and **ears** are open toward the **righteous**, seeing their desperate predicaments, hearing **their cry**, and responding to their distress. So strong was God's defense that the Lord was **against** David's enemies so their **memory** would be **cut off . . . from the earth**. This means his foes would be so defeated that they would soon be forgotten.

34:17–18. David testified from personal experience that the **righteous cry out** to the LORD in their distress and he **hears** and **delivers** them out of **their troubles**. Not distant and removed like pagan gods, **the LORD is close to the brokenhearted**, lowly, and contrite. He **saves** from harm all those who are **crushed in spirit** or weighed down and devastated by their trials.

34:19–21. No matter what **troubles** the **righteous** man may face, **the LORD delivers him from them all**. When surrounded by the world's persecution, he will know the Lord's intervention and protection. He **protects all his bones**, or his whole being, from being **broken**. Evil oppressors who attack the **righteous will be condemned** by the Lord. Such assurance should bolster the faith of all believers when they are persecuted for the sake of righteousness (cp. Matt. 5:10–12; John 15:18–20; 16:33).

34:22. Summarizing this entire psalm, David concluded, **The LORD redeems his servants**. The word *redeem* (Heb. *padah*) means "to ransom or rescue from great harm" and was used to describe Israel's deliverance from

Egypt (cp. Deut. 7:8; 9:26; 13:5; 15:15; 24:18). David was confident that **no one will be condemned who takes refuge in him**.

MAIN IDEA REVIEW: *Believers should praise God for his mighty deliverance, recognizing that he rescues his people from their fears and distresses.*

III. CONCLUSION

Calling on the Lord

What power there is in calling upon the name of the Lord! C. S. Lewis said, "Down through the ages, whenever men might need courage, they might cry out, 'Billy Budd, help me!' and nothing very significant happens. But for nineteen hundred years, whenever men needed courage and have cried out, 'Lord Jesus, help me!' something has happened." Lewis is correct. When believers call upon the name of the Lord Jesus Christ, they grasp the unlimited power of God. This is sufficient to meet any need in life. This is what David came to realize in the experience of this psalm.

Furthermore, God's deliverance is precisely what believers may experience when they find themselves trapped in threatening circumstances. Let the redeemed call with confidence upon the name of the Lord. May the testimony of David in this song of thanksgiving encourage all believers to bring their petitions to God.

IV. LIFE APPLICATION

Closer than a Brother

When believers encounter trials and troubles, they should call to mind the truth of Psalm 34—that "the LORD is close to the brokenhearted" (v. 18). God has promised to be with believers at all times, the bad times as well as the good. Although others may forsake the righteous, God never will. He is a friend who sticks closer than a brother. He abides with his people forever. He "encamps around those who fear him" (v. 7). He is never nearer to believers than when they need him most. The Lord saves those who are crushed in spirit. He redeems his servants. No wonder the soul of believers should boast in the Lord! He delivers them from all their fears. Let the people of God look to him and find strength in time of need.

V. PRAYER

God our Father, you and you alone are good. Our desire is to glorify you at all times, to recognize your preeminence over us. Have mercy on us, and cause your face to shine on us so we may taste and see that you alone are good. Thank you for your providential plan that brings trials into our lives so you may teach us to cry out to you for deliverance. In the name of the Lord Jesus Christ. Amen.

VI. DEEPER DISCOVERIES

A. Delivered (34:4)

This word (Heb. *nasal*) means "to be snatched away, rescued, drawn out of, saved, pulled away" or "to escape." The word was used countless times by David when he petitioned God to rescue him from his enemies who were seeking to take his life. In other psalms the word is used in a salvific sense to speak of a deliverance from one's transgressions (Ps. 39:8) and the grave (Ps. 86:13). Asaph wrote, "Help us, O God our Savior, for the glory of your name; deliver (*nasal*) us and forgive our sins for your name's sake" (Ps. 79:9). The word was also used to ask God for the power to resist sin (Ps. 120:2). Considering the numerous appearances of *nasal* in the Psalms, the theme of deliverance is one of the dominant themes of the Book of Psalms.

B. The Righteous (34:15,17,19,21)

The phrase "the righteous" (Heb. *saddiq*) refers to the person who has put his trust exclusively in God for salvation. The word itself means "conformity to a standard," namely, the perfect holiness of God. It refers both to a positional righteousness, to the forensic right standing of man before God that only God can declare (Gen. 15:6) as well as to a practical righteousness, or the progressive conformity of man to the character of God. Regarding the latter, his life is being lived in increasing conformity to the unchanging standard of God's holy character. This is another way of saying "righteous."

C. Eyes, Ears, Face (34:15–16)

These three words are anthropomorphisms, a literary device that portrays God with human terms. The term itself is derived from two Greek words, *anthropos* ("man") and *morphe* ("form"). Anthropomorphisms are descriptions of God using words that indicate a human physical form and must be taken figuratively. It is the transcendent God repeatedly portrayed in earthly and human terms with such descriptions that are figurative rather than literal. These figurative terms (i.e., eyes, ears, face) are used so that the eternal, incomprehensible God can be made intelligible to finite, fallen man.

Anthropomorphisms are intended to depict the infinite God to the limited minds of human beings. Most occur in Old Testament poetry and prophecy (Gen. 3:8; 6:8; 49:24; Exod. 15:3; 24:11; Josh. 4:24; Num. 12:8; Deut. 11:12; 13:18; 32:10; 2 Chr. 16:9; Pss. 10:17; 17:6; 18:6; Isa. 59:1–2; Jer. 7:13;

Hos. 11:8). These humanlike terms assigned to God are not to be taken literally because the Scriptures are clear that "God is spirit" (John 4:24) and is without bodily form (cp. Deut. 4:12). This is why the Israelites were forbidden from making any image to portray the invisible God (Deut. 4:15–19). No graven image can portray God because he has no physical form. But it should be noted that the second member of the Godhead became incarnate in the person of Jesus Christ.

VII. TEACHING OUTLINE

    A. David's Worship (1–3)
       1. He is continuous (1)
       2. He is contagious (2)
       3. He is corporate (3)
    B. David's Witness (4–7)
       1. God delivered me (4)
       2. God delighted me (5)
       3. God defended me (6–7)
          a. Out of my troubles (6)
          b. By the angel of the Lord (7)
    C. David's Wisdom (8–14)
       1. Taste the Lord (8)
       2. Tremble before the Lord (9)
       3. Turn to the Lord (10)
       4. Turn from evil (11–14a)
       5. Turn to good (14b)
    D. David's Wonder (15–22)
       1. The Lord sees (15a)
       2. The Lord hears (15b–17a)
       3. The Lord rescues (17b–20)
       4. The Lord judges (21)
       5. The Lord redeems (22)

VIII. ISSUES FOR DISCUSSION

1. Do I spend time in private worship as well as corporate worship praising God?
2. Have I tasted and seen the goodness of God in my life?
3. Am I brokenhearted and crushed in spirit by my sins and failures?
4. Do I recount the many times God has delivered me from my enemies?

Psalm 35

A Declaration of War

Psalm 35

I. INTRODUCTION

The righteous will surely be opposed in this world by the unrighteous because of the evil system that is dominated by fallen man's thinking. In such spiritual warfare, the believer must call upon God for victory and protection. David did so in this imprecatory psalm as he called upon God to arise quickly and judge his enemies. It was a plea for divine intervention against David's oppressors who were seeking to destroy his life. David found himself in a dangerous situation, perhaps surrounded by hostile military forces on the field of battle. Possibly it was when David was being pursued by Saul and his men (1 Sam. 23:15). Or possibly David was about to be attacked by a foreign power, one with whom he had previously entered into a covenant.

Some commentators feel that this psalm was written as a companion to Psalm 34 because "the angel of the LORD" is mentioned only in these two psalms in the entire Book of Psalms (34:7; 35:5–6), and both psalms are a cry for deliverance from imminent danger. Regardless of the setting, David pleaded for God to defend him by fighting against his enemies.

II. COMMENTARY

> **MAIN IDEA:** *David calls upon God to destroy his enemies who are attempting to kill him.*

A David's Appeal (35:1–3)

35:1–3. This psalm begins with a fiery appeal to God to judge the psalmist's enemies. Combining legal and military language, David called out, **Contend, O LORD, with those who contend with me**. This was a time for war, so David pleaded with God to attack his foes on his behalf. **Shield, buckler, spear**, and **javelin** were pieces of armor and weapons of war. David wanted God to use them against those who were pursuing him. He summoned heaven's warrior to fight his battle.

B David's Adversaries (35:4–10)

35:4–6. David wanted those who sought his **life** to **be disgraced** and **turned back in dismay** through God's sure defense. He prayed that the angel of the Lord, a designation for the preincarnate Christ (cp. 34:7), would rout his enemies, **driving them away** in a devastating defeat. He asked God to make their path **dark and slippery**.

35:7–10. David's enemies were plotting to capture him with **their net** and **pit**. But their attacks were unjustified. He hoped they would be trapped by their own devices. This section concludes with a vow of praise: **Then my soul will rejoice in the LORD**. With his **whole being** David sought the Lord. In exuberant praise David asked, **Who is like you, O LORD?**, a recognition of the incomparable uniqueness and supremacy of God, who rescues **the poor and needy** from the wicked **who rob them**.

C David's Accusation (35:11–18)

35:11–14. David pleaded his case before God by presenting evidence against his foes. Appealing to God as if he were in a courtroom, David named his adversaries as **ruthless witnesses** and challenged them to come forward and face the record that pointed to their guilt. He presented his formal charges against them, stating, **They repay me evil for good**. Even when his enemies were ill, David sought their good, but in return they had pursued him with unjust hatred.

35:15–18. When David was in difficulty, his enemies **gathered in glee** against him. **They slandered** him and **mocked** him. David pleaded for **the Lord** to be his advocate. This section also ends with a vow of praise from

David's heart as he promised with renewed determination: **I will give you thanks in the great assembly.**

D David's Allegiance (35:19–28)

35:19–21. Coming full circle, David concluded this psalm by calling on God to judge his foes. **Let not those gloat over me who are my enemies,** he asked. The word *gloat* appears three times (vv. 19,24,26) and describes their malicious mocking. They claimed they had seen David doing wrong, but in reality they had not.

35:22–26. Unleashing a series of imperatives, David pleaded for God's defense. **Be not silent,** he urged, but **awake, and rise to my defense.** David asked that God's judgment on his enemies match their evil intent and wrongdoings: **May all who gloat over my distress be put to shame.** This was the malignant destruction they sought for David.

35:27–28. David concluded this section as he did two earlier sections (cp. vv. 9–10,18)—with a declaration of praise. He called upon his faithful supporters to **shout for joy and gladness** because the Lord **delights in the well-being of his servant.** They had good reason to praise the Lord. Likewise, David would magnify the Lord and **speak** of his praises **all day long.**

III. CONCLUSION

It is possible to come to false conclusions in applying this psalm. In seeking to follow any psalm that cries out against one's enemies, a balanced approach is necessary. Far from seeking personal vengeance, David was a man who was known for forgiving his enemies, not harming them. For example, his treatment of Saul when he spared his life was a model of loving one's enemies. Surely, this is how all Christians are to treat those who oppose them—returning evil with good.

But as David prayed, he did ask God to undertake his cause and defeat his enemies. He made this request not for his own gain, but for the advancement of God's glory. We should ask God to deal with anyone who opposes us as we seek to do the work of God for the glory of God. The battle belongs to the Lord, not to us. Leave vengeance with the Lord.

IV. TEACHING OUTLINE

A. David's Appeal (1–3)
1. Contend with my foes (1)
2. Come to my aid (2–3a)
3. Comfort my soul (3b)
B. David's Adversaries (4–10)
1. Disgrace them (4)

2. Drive them away (5)
3. Defeat them (6–8)
  a. May their path be dark (6)
  b. May their plans be doomed (7–8)
  Summation: A Vow of Praise (9–10)
C. David's Accusation (11–18)
  1. They reward evil for good (11–14)
    a. They seek my harm (11–12)
    b. They receive my prayers (13–14)
  2. They rejoice in my harm (15–17)
    a. They slander me when I stumbled (15–16)
    b. They ravage me when I fall (17)
  Summation: A Vow of Praise (18)
D. David's Allegiance (19–28)
  1. He seeks God's vengeance on the ungodly (19–21)
    a. They gloat over me (19a)
    b. They hate me (19b)
    c. They lie about me (20)
    d. They gape at me (21)
  2. He seeks God's vindication of the godly (22–26)
    a. God, be not silent (22a)
    b. God, be not far (22b)
    c. God, be not asleep (23a)
    d. God, contend for me (23b)
    e. God, vindicate me (24–25)
    f. God, put them to shame (26)
  Summation: A Vow of Praise (27–28)

Psalm 36

Man Proposes, God Disposes

Psalm 36

I. INTRODUCTION

*T*here are no limits to the depraved condition to which mankind may fall if left to the ways of their own wicked hearts. But no matter how wicked man becomes, God is greater still, ruling over all for his own purposes. God makes even the wrath of man to praise him. This is the theme of Psalm 36, a song that reveals the utter sinfulness of mankind, but the supremacy of God over all.

Humanistic philosophies and worldly religions minimize such a great divide between these two extremes, elevating man and lowering God to such a point that they are virtually on equal footing. But the Bible will have nothing of such folly. The truth is that God is high and lifted up, infinitely separated from sinful man. This psalm exposes depraved man for who he is—corrupt and condemned—and exalts God for who he is—full of love, righteousness, and wrath. Wise is the reader who puts man in his lowly place—falling short of God's glory—and who puts God in his lofty place—ruling over all.

According to the superscription, this psalm was written "for the director of music" by David, who identifies himself as "the servant of the LORD."

II. COMMENTARY

> **MAIN IDEA:** David contrasts the depravity of wicked sinners with the goodness of God, asking God to elevate the godly and judge the wicked.

A Man's Sinfulness (36:1–4)

36:1. This psalm comes in the form of **an oracle** rising within David's **heart**, a deep burden such as that spoken by the prophets (Isa. 13:1). This deeply felt message is about **the sinfulness of the wicked**. What follows in the first four verses is an apt description of human depravity (cp. Ps. 14:1–3). The ungodly have **no fear** (Heb. *pahad*, "dread") **of God**, meaning they live without any terror of the Lord, as if there is no day of final judgment before God. They refuse to take God into account, and they reject the truth that they will be eternally damned by God for their sinfulness. In other words, the ungodly refuse to take God seriously.

36:2–3. Having disregarded the Lord, the ungodly person **flatters himself**, becoming the center of his own existence, no longer able to **detect**, recognize, or **hate**—that is, reject—**his sin** as he spirals downward into greater depths of degrading depravity. His **words**, arising out of his perverse heart, are **wicked and deceitful**. He speaks out of his own corrupt character. What is worse, he is not **wise** but foolish (cp. Ps. 94:8). As he sinks deeper into sin, he will no longer **do good**; instead, he does what is crooked.

36:4. The wicked person even **plots evil** at night, inventing new ways to sin and rebel against God. No longer just drifting into evil ways, he **commits himself to a sinful course** with deliberate, premeditated resolve. Furthermore, he **does not reject what is wrong** because he has lost all sense of right and wrong and has forfeited the moral resolve to pursue good. In reality, he is totally abandoned to sin, his conscience seared and heart hardened beyond the point of repentance.

B God's Supremacy (36:5–12)

36:5–6. Abruptly shifting focus, David turned from an outward focus upon depraved humanity to an upward focus at the transcendent holiness of God. Itemizing several divine attributes, he affirmed God's lovingkindness by declaring that God's love **reaches to the heavens**. He extolled the unconditional grace and unfailing mercy of God that rises above the quagmire of man's sin, abounding to sinners who repent. David declared that God's **faithfulness** reaches **to the skies**. It knows no limits or boundaries. God's righteousness, or right judgment, **is like the mighty mountains** which cannot be moved. By his divine justice, God can do only what is right, rewarding good and punishing sin.

36:7–10. God's goodness drew David's praise, in contrast to sinful men, who cease to do good (cp. v. 3). By the Lord's **unfailing love**, all **men**—whether **high** or **low**, rich or poor—who trust God will **find refuge** from their sin and from life's storms. **They feast** on the Lord's **abundance** of goodness and **drink from** God's **river of delights**, a constantly flowing **fountain of** abundant **life**. This **river** will always **continue** to satisfy and sustain all who drink from it because its source, God himself, is inexhaustible. Remaining riveted upon God, David pleaded with God, **Continue your love to those who know you**.

36:11–12. Finally, David affirmed the vengeance of God. **May the foot of the proud** slip and fall, he declared. This is probably a reference to the ancient practice of a conquering general placing his foot upon the neck of a defeated general. God would conquer and humiliate all David's foes who were also God's enemies.

III. CONCLUSION

Humanistic, secular philosophies seek to infiltrate and influence the thinking of believers, elevating sinful man and lowering the holy God to their level. But this psalm puts both man and God in their rightful places, condemning man and magnifying God. How can wicked man be received by such a sin-rejecting, sin-judging God? Only through the cross of Jesus Christ. By his death on Calvary's cross, the Son of God bore the sin of the world in his body, paying the due penalty for their transgressions and reconciling them to God through the blood of his cross (2 Cor. 5:21).

This psalm underscores the necessity of the redemption of Christ Jesus, thus glorifying the grace of God. The higher men set God and the lower they place themselves, the greater they will magnify the grace of God in Christ to span this great divide.

IV. TEACHING OUTLINE

A. Man's Sinfulness (1–4)
1. Man is conceited (1–2)
   a. No fear of God (1)
   b. No humility of self (2)
2. Man is crooked (3)
   a. Wicked words (3a)
   b. Tainted wisdom (3b)
   c. Corrupt works (3c)

3. Man is conspiring (4)
   a. Plotting evil (4a)
   b. Pursuing wrong (4b)
B. God's Supremacy (5–12)
  1. God is loving (5)
    a. He is favoring (5a)
    b. He is faithful (5b)
  2. God is righteous (6)
    a. He is immovable (6a)
    b. He is incomprehensible (6b)
  3. God is good (7–10)
    a. He shelters his people (7)
    b. He satisfies his people (8)
    c. He sustains his people (9–10)
  4. God is vengeful (11–12)
    a. He punishes the proud (11)
    b. He eliminates evildoers (12)

Psalm 37
Taking the Long Look

"*S*inners are not, as a general rule, punished here. Their

sentence is reserved until the day of judgment....This is not

the time of judgment. Judgment is yet to come."

Charles H. Spurgeon

I. INTRODUCTION

*I*t may appear that the unrighteous are excelling in this world above and beyond believers. But righteous people must remember that appearances are deceiving. God will have the final say. Psalm 37 is a wisdom poem much like Psalm 1 because it contrasts the two ways of life. There is the way of the godly and the way of the ungodly. A vast chasm lies between the two; they are as far apart as heaven is from hell.

This is a psalm "of David" in which he recorded what he saw all around him—the prosperity of the wicked and the suffering of the righteous. In response, David challenged believers not to become exasperated when the ungodly excelled, often at the expense of the godly, but to remain focused upon God. This song is not addressed to God as most psalms are but is spoken directly to the reader, calling him to trust in the Lord. Its style is similar to the pithy wisdom sayings of Proverbs which differentiate the godly from the ungodly and exhort the godly to trust in the Lord. Such well-placed faith will cause the righteous to inherit the land (vv. 9,22,29) and enjoy God's blessings rather than fret and worry about the wicked who will surely be removed from the earth (vv. 22,28,34,38).

This psalm is an alphabetic acrostic in which every other verse begins with successive letters of the Hebrew alphabet.

II. COMMENTARY

> **MAIN IDEA:** *The godly should trust in the Lord to deliver them from evil because the wicked will ultimately be destroyed, even though they appear to prosper.*

A David's Counsel (37:1–11)

37:1–2. This first section begins with a series of exhortations to the godly. Some of these exhortations are negative (vv. 1,7–8), and some are positive (vv. 3–5,7–8). Each reveals divine wisdom. The psalm begins, **Do not fret because of evil men**, an imperative that is repeated twice more (vv. 1,7–8). The word *fret* translates a Hebrew verb meaning "to be heated," or "to be hot in anger" (cp. Prov. 24:19). David instructed believers not to allow evil men who temporarily succeeded in their plans to become a source of heated worry. Likewise, the righteous should not **be envious** of them, as if wanting to trade places with them. Instead, believers should take the long look into the future when, **like the grass**, the wicked would **wither** and **die away** without hope.

37:3–4. Instead, the righteous should **trust in the LORD**, or depend exclusively on him. They should **delight** themselves **in the LORD**, or find their satisfaction in God, not in the pursuit of evil (cp. Ps. 1:1). Delighting in God will give one righteous desires and thus God will give **the desires of the heart**.

37:5–7a. David advised the righteous, **Commit your way to the LORD**, which means to roll it over onto the Lord. God would make their **righteousness shine like the dawn**, or cause their lives to radiate with the fullness of his divine **justice**. God would vindicate the righteous in the future in his perfect timing, unlike the wicked who sought honor now. The righteous should **be still before the LORD** without taking matters into their own hands and **wait patiently for him**.

37:7b–11. David repeated his original advice: **Do not fret when men succeed**. He returned to the earlier thought of verse 2—sinners who seem to flourish for a season will eventually be destroyed (Eccl. 3:16–17). To point this out, he used a series of contrasts between the godly and the ungodly. **Refrain from anger**, he declared, because these **evil men** in the final day would be cut off and die before entering eternity damned. **But those who hope in the LORD**—the meek—**will inherit the land** (cp. Matt. 5:5). This indicated the fullness of God's blessing.

B David's Caution (37:12–22)

37:12–17. David issued a strong warning about the future of the ungodly. **The wicked** may **plot against the righteous**, scheming to do them harm, but **the Lord** only **laughs** in derision. **Their day** of reckoning with God in the final judgment **is coming**. The wicked may **draw the sword** against the **poor, but** it will be turned against them and **pierce their own hearts**. Their own power **will be broken**. Far **better** is **the little** in this world that **the righteous have than the wealth of many wicked**. Take the long look, David said. **The power of the wicked will be broken**. But the Lord **upholds the righteous** who trust him.

37:18–22. David declared that **the days of the blameless are known to the LORD** (cp. Ps. 90:12). In other words, he is involved with them (cp. Ps. 1:6) to preserve and prosper them. When difficulty comes, whether **disaster** or **famine, they will not wither** like evil men, but they will **enjoy plenty** from his hand. **But the wicked will perish** and pass from the scene **like smoke**. They will suffer great loss and be cast into an eternal hell by the Lord.

C David's Confidence (37:23–34)

37:23–26. David focused more intently on the blessing of the righteous. **The Lord delights in** the **way** of those who trust him, making his **steps firm**. Even if he should **stumble** in the face of difficult adversity, **he will not fall, for the LORD upholds him**. David was obviously advanced in age, looking back on his life that had experienced the faithfulness of God. **I was young and now I am old**, he said, **yet I have never seen the righteous forsaken**. Thus, they have plenty to **lend freely** and abundance overflows to **their children** who are never **begging bread**.

37:27–29. David reminded the righteous to **turn from evil and do good**. This is a call for a lifestyle of repentance, separation, and holiness. A person who does this will always live securely, knowing God's protection and provision. David was assured that God would **not forsake his faithful ones**. **The wicked** would be **cut off** in judgment, but the righteous would be **protected forever** and **inherit** and **dwell in the land** throughout future generations.

37:30–34. The virtues of **the righteous man** are noteworthy. His **mouth** speaks **wisdom** and justice because **the law** of God occupies his heart. God's truth so affects his daily life that **his feet do not slip** into sinful ways. Even when **the wicked** seek to ambush **the righteous, the Lord** will come to their rescue and **not leave them in their power** to be **condemned** with false accusations in court. Thus, the righteous should **wait for the LORD**. Those who do will know God's security though the wicked are cut off. In due time God will exalt his own to **inherit the land**.

D David's Conclusion (37:35–40)

37:35–38. One last time David contrasted **the wicked** and **the blameless**. The wicked may initially flourish **like a green tree**, giving every appearance of strength and success, but he is soon gone. But the blameless and upright have a glorious **future**. All present injustices will be made right by God, whether now or in eternity. His people must wait on him.

37:39–40. Concluding with a positive affirmation, David declared, **The salvation of the righteous comes from the LORD**. This divine rescue comes because **the LORD** is the **stronghold** (Heb. *maoz*, "a strong fortified place") for all who **take refuge in him**.

III. CONCLUSION

President Woodrow Wilson once stated, "I had rather temporarily fail in a cause that will ultimately succeed than temporarily succeed in a cause that will ultimately fail." When assessing any situation, a person should always take the long look. What is most important is not that a cause begins well but that it ends well. This is precisely the wisdom David has given in this psalm. We must not allow the initial success of the ungodly to lead us astray. We should take the long look. Those who trust in the Lord will triumph in the end.

IV. TEACHING OUTLINE

A. David's Counsel (1–11)
  1. Do not fear (1–2)
    a. Evil men may initially prosper (1)
    b. Evil men will ultimately perish (2)
  2. Have faith in God (3–7a)
    a. Trust the Lord (3)
    b. Delight in the Lord (4)
    c. Commit to the Lord (5–6)
    d. Wait on the Lord (7a)
  3. Do not fear (7b–11)
    a. Evil men may initially prosper (7b–8)
    b. Evil men will ultimately perish (9–11)
B. David's Caution (12–22)
  The wicked:
  1. Plot but soon perish (12–13)
  2. Fortify but soon fall (14–15)
  3. Prosper but soon wither (16–17)
  4. Flourish but soon vanish (18–20)
  5. Borrow but soon lose (21–22)
C. David's Confidence (23–34)
  Concerning the righteous, the Lord:
  1. Delights in him (23)
  2. Sustains him (24)
  3. Provides for him (25–26)

4. Protects him (27–28)
5. Prospers him (29)
6. Instructs him (30–31)
7. Delivers him (32–33)
8. Exalts him (34)
D. David's Conclusion (35–40)
   1. The great difference (35–38)
     a. The wicked perish (35–36,38)
     b. The righteous prosper (37)
   2. The great deliverance (39–40)
     a. The Lord delivers the righteous (39a, 40a)
     b. The Lord defends the righteous (39b, 40b)

Psalm 38

The High Cost of Low Living

Psalm 38

I. INTRODUCTION

*S*ickness and suffering in the lives of believers are not always the result of personal sin (cp. Job 1–2), but sometimes they are. For example, Uzziah, king of Judah, was a prideful man who was struck with leprosy when he entered the holy place reserved only for the priest (2 Chr. 26:16–23). The believers in Corinth were suffering physically because of their sin in taking the Lord's Supper in an unworthy manner (1 Cor. 11:29–30). Unquestionably, much of the suffering and sickness that the godly experience is the direct result of sin. Such sins require confession before God (Jas. 5:14–18).

This was the case in the life of David, the author of Psalm 38. This psalm listed as one of the penitential psalms (cp. Pss. 6; 32; 38; 51; 102; 130; 143). David recorded the acknowledgment of his sin to God. He interpreted this sin as the direct cause of his painful experience. This psalm is "a petition," an urgent plea for relief from his painful illness. But far deeper, this psalm contains David's confession of sin (vv. 3–4). He realized his sin had brought the discipline of God.

II. COMMENTARY

MAIN IDEA: *David cries to God under the heavy hand of divine judgment which has brought him much sorrow, acknowledging his sin to God with a broken heart.*

A David's Cry (38:1–4)

38:1–4. Aware that he was suffering because of his sins, David cried out for relief: O LORD, **do not rebuke me in your anger or discipline me in your wrath**. He realized he was suffering under the discipline of God. It was like **arrows** that had **pierced** his body. Most specifically, physical **health** had left his **body** because of his **sin**. Not all sickness is God's punishment, but it was in this case, and David knew it. The **guilt** of his sin was **too heavy to bear**, and he had to find relief.

B David's Chastening (38:5–16)

38:5–10. David described the devastating effect of God's discipline upon him. Noting the direct cause and effect between sin and his suffering, he lamented, **My wounds fester and are loathsome because of my sinful folly**. The physical and psychological effects of his sin were unmistakable. They were marked by sorrow that is described as **mourning**, **searing pain**, **anguish of heart**, **longings**, and **sighing**. So heavy were the crushing effects of these sorrows that his **heart** pounded under duress, his **strength** failed, and the light of his face grew dim as his countenance diminished.

38:11–16. As a result, his **friends** avoided him because of the offensiveness of his **wounds**. At the same time his enemies sought to take advantage of him during this time of weakness as they **set their traps** against him. With deep contriteness of heart, David acknowledged his sin to God. Without justifying himself to others, he chose to be **like a deaf man**, as if he did not hear his enemies' accusations, and **like a mute** who did not answer them. Rather, he would **wait** patiently for God in the presence of those who gloated over his misfortune.

C David's Confession (38:17–20)

38:17–20. At the same time David chose to **confess** his **iniquity**, recognizing that his **sin** was the cause of his suffering. Although he was suffering because of his sin, he was also aware that his **enemies** hated him **without reason** and were repaying his **good with evil**. He was innocent of any wrong against those who were attacking him. But he believed he was suffering under God's chastening hand.

D David's Call (38:21–22)

38:21–22. David concluded this psalm as he began it—by calling upon God to deliver him from his affliction. **Do not forsake me**, he cried out, but **come quickly to help me**. If he was to be rescued, God must do it soon.

III. CONCLUSION

It is important that believers confess their sins to God on a regular basis. In the Lord's Model Prayer, he instructed us to seek God's forgiveness constantly. This requires the acknowledgment of our transgressions to God (Matt. 6:12). Perhaps we would be astounded to realize how much sickness and suffering are inflicted by a loving God, who chastens us for our sins. How necessary it is to ask the Lord, "Search me, O God, and know my heart; test me and know my anxious thoughts. See if there is any offensive way in me, and lead me in the way everlasting" (Ps. 139:23–24). And as God reveals our sin, allowing us to see ourselves as God sees us, we must name our iniquity to him against whom we have sinned (Ps. 51:4). He alone can forgive (Ps. 32:2).

IV. TEACHING OUTLINE

A. David's Cry (1–4)
   1. He requests God's relief (1–2)
     a. Do not rebuke me (1a)
     b. Do not discipline me (1b–2)
   2. He recognizes his sin (3–4)
     a. I have sinned (3)
     b. I am guilty (4)
B. David's Chastening (5–16)
   1. My wounds fester (5)
   2. My spirit mourns (6)
   3. My body burns (7)
   4. My heart groans (8)
   5. My soul sighs (9)
   6. My strength fails (10)
   7. My friends leave (11)
   8. My foes conspire (12)
   9. My hearing and speech fail me (13–16)
C. David's Confession (17–20)
   1. My guilt is before God (17–18)
     a. It is iniquity (17–18a)
     b. It is sin (18b)

2. My pain is from God (19–20)
   a. My enemies hate me (19)
   b. My enemies oppose me (20)
D. David's Call (21–22)
  1. God, come near (21)
  2. God, come now (22)

Psalm 39

Tough Love

I. INTRODUCTION

*G*od disciplines his children when they sin, not because he is unloving but because he *does* love them. True love is tough love. Real love is that which seeks the highest and best in the one who is loved. How a person reacts to the chastening hand of God reveals much about his or her spiritual condition. Wise and mature is the believer who humbles himself under God's discipline and restrains his heart and mouth from rash words.

This was the experience of David as he recorded in Psalm 39 his own response to divine discipline. He chose to humble himself and confess his sin rather than react in stubborn pride. "For the director of music" probably indicates that this psalm was to be used in the temple worship and was to be spoken by the leader of the Levitical choir or by the entire choir. Also, it was "for Jeduthun," one of David's choir leaders (1 Chr. 16:41–42; 25:1,6; 2 Chr. 5:12).

II. COMMENTARY

MAIN IDEA: *David confesses his sins and asks for God's mercy for his failure in not keeping a commitment he made to God.*

A David's Silence (39:1–3)

39:1–3. David determined to guard his mouth as a **muzzle** on an animal so he would not sin against God with his **tongue**. **The wicked** must not hear him respond to God's painful discipline and be led astray. So he remained **silent**, his **heart** burning **hot**, until he could contain himself no longer. His silence did not relieve the pain, but it only made it worse. When he finally **spoke**, it was when he was alone, lamenting to God in private.

B David's Supplication (39:4–6)

39:4–5. David recorded the supplication he poured out to the Lord. He prayed, **Show me, O LORD, my life's end**. In other words, he asked God to make him realize the certainty that his life would eventually end and how short his days on earth really were. The **span of** his **years**, David realized, were as **nothing**. They were a **mere handbreadth**, the smallest measuring unit of ancient times (1 Kgs. 7:26).

39:6. Finite man is nothing but a **phantom**, fragile and frail, dashing **to and fro**. He does so **in vain**, realizing that he **heaps up wealth**, only to lose it at death, and then without **knowing who will get it**. And so David asked God to remind him of the vanity of life.

C David's Sin (39:7–11)

39:7. David turned to God as the only possible source of hope, asking for relief from the painful discipline he was enduring. He asked, **Lord, what do I look for?** The implied answer is, "No one but God." **My hope is in you** (cp. 25:5,21; 33:20; 62:5; 71:5), he declared. He knew his only hope for deliverance was the Lord himself.

39:8–11. David pleaded, **Save me from all my transgressions**. He confessed his sin to God while acknowledging that his suffering must be correcting discipline from the Lord because of his sin. Since this painful process was God's doing, David realized that he must remain **silent**. He prayed for the removal of God's chastening **hand** from him, knowing that God will **discipline men for their sin**. Under such divine chastening, the **wealth** that men work hard for is suddenly removed **like a moth**, and man himself **is but a breath**. This imagery describes the brevity of life.

D David's Submission (39:12–13)

39:12–13. Finally, having called out to God for relief from painful discipline, David submitted himself to the Lord. He pleaded with God to **hear** his

cry for help. He recognized that he lived before God as **an alien** and a **stranger** passing through this world. He had no claims to make upon God. **Look away from me**, David declared, meaning "withhold your discipline from me," so **I may rejoice again**. If not, David feared that he would die under God's chastisement and be no more in the land of the living.

III. CONCLUSION

There is no substitute for spiritual discipline in all areas of the believer's life. The righteous must learn to live his own life meticulously and scrutinize every area by searching for sin and wrongdoing that is constantly revealing itself both inwardly and outwardly. Like a detective, believers must pursue every clue in the process of self-examination. Every word, every thought, and every action must be weighed against the holy, righteous standard of the Lord. Disciplining oneself is no small task, but the rewards that await us as God's people make the struggle worthwhile.

IV. TEACHING OUTLINE

A. David's Silence (1–3)
  1. My mouth is closed (1)
  2. My heart is crushed (2–3a)
  3. My mind is consumed (3b)
B. David's Supplication (4–6)
  1. Show me life's brevity (4–5b)
    a. It is but a few days (4a)
    b. It is but a fleeting life (4b–5c)
  2. Show me man's frailty (5c–6)
    a. But it is a breath (5c)
    b. But it is a phantom (6)
C. David's Sin (7–11)
  1. His confession of sin (7–8)
    a. My hope is in God (7)
    b. My sin is against God (8)
  2. His chastening for sin (9–11)
    a. I am scourged by God (9–10)
    b. I am scolded by God (11a)
    c. I am stripped by God (11b)
D. David's Submission (12–13)
  1. God, hear me (12)
  2. God, help me (13)
    a. Ease your chastening (13a)
    b. Extend your cheer (13b)

Psalm 40

From the Mire to the Choir

"*G*od promises a safe landing but not a calm passage."

A n o n y m o u s

Psalm 40

I. INTRODUCTION

Joy in the Pain

*S*everal years ago Lloyd John Ogilvie, a Presbyterian pastor and chaplain to the U.S. Senate, underwent the most difficult year of his life. His wife underwent five major surgeries, plus the radiation and chemotherapy that followed. Several of his staff members departed. Large problems loomed on every side. All this caused a major emotional discouragement and despondency to come crashing down upon him.

As he reflected back on that crisis, Ogilvie wrote of the abundant joy he found in the Lord: "The greatest discovery that I have made in the midst of all the difficulties is that I can have joy when I can't feel like it. When I had every reason to feel beaten, I felt joy. In spite of everything, [God] gave me the conviction of being loved and the certainty that nothing could separate me from him. It was not happiness, gush, or jolliness but a constant flow of the Spirit through me. At no time did he give me the easy confidence that everything would work out as I wanted it on my timetable but that he was in charge and would give me and my family enough courage for each day: grace. Joy is always the result of that."

This is precisely the joy that is available to all believers in the Lord. The psalmist David found such joy in the midst of one of the most difficult times of his life. He recorded his experience for our encouragement in Psalm 40. We don't know what his excruciating circumstances were, but they were extremely painful to his soul. He compared his ordeal to a horrible pit, a hole into which he had fallen.

Maybe it was the pit of rejection that seemed to engulf him. King Saul's jealous hatred led to a ruthless manhunt. He chased David from place to place and caused him to despair. Perhaps it was a pit of family problems. David certainly knew trouble in his own household as his own son Absalom rebelled against him. Or possibly it was a pit of sin as David may have dug his own hole. Maybe it was a pit of loneliness as David often found himself alone. David may have allowed his problems, though relatively small, to be enlarged disproportionately in his own mind. Whatever the pit, it was real to David.

In the midst of this ordeal, David put his trust in God, calling upon the name of the Lord. The deliverance came and put a new song into David's heart. This psalm looks beyond even David's troubles to the coming of the Messiah (vv. 6–8; cp. Heb. 10:5–10). He looked to the greater David who would be the sacrifice that ended all sacrifice.

II. COMMENTARY

From the Mire to the Choir

> **MAIN IDEA:** *David recalls the Lord's past deliverance from trouble and petitions God to save him from his present ordeal.*

Ⓐ David's Praise (40:1–5)

> **SUPPORTING IDEA:** *David praises God for his past help during a time of trouble.*

40:1–2. David began this psalm by giving a joyful report of his past experiences of God's deliverance. He reflected upon a specific time when he **waited patiently for the LORD** with quiet resignation, being still in the midst of his great distress, awaiting God's intervention. The phrase "waited patiently" is literally, "waiting, I *waited*." God **heard** David's **cry**, implying that David had called out to the Lord and then **waited** for God to rescue him.

David testified that God **lifted** him **out of the slimy pit**. This pictures a distress so severe that he could not escape on his own. This trial is portrayed as a **pit** of **mud and mire**, representing a time in his life when he was trapped and could not escape. Perhaps it was a desolate **pit** of personal sin (cp. v. 12; 2 Sam. 11), adversity (1 Sam. 18:10–17; 23:15–29), family difficulty (2 Sam. 15–18), emotional distress (2 Sam. 18:19–33), or even a literal pit dug by an enemy (Ps. 7:15).

Whatever the **pit**, God graciously intervened, rescuing David, raising him and placing his **feet on a rock**. This gave him **a firm place to stand**. From the sinking sand and silt of the pit, David was placed by the Lord on solid bedrock. Notice the progression of thought of the actions of God: **He turned . . . heard . . . lifted . . . set . . . gave.**

40:3. David also testified that God **put a new song** in his **mouth**, indicating the abundant joy that flooded his heart. This new work of grace prompted a **new hymn of praise**. This singing by David was so open and unrestrained that he acclaimed **many** would **see and fear** the Lord who worked so wonderfully for his people. As a result of David's testimony, many would be encouraged to **put their trust in the LORD**.

40:4. David stated that all who **trust** God would be greatly blessed. To be **blessed** is to be filled with abundant happiness and overflowing joy. This grace belongs to the person who makes a firm, confident commitment to God rather than following the example of **the proud**, who are self-reliant and have no trust in God.

40:5. As David considered his past, he concluded, **Many, O LORD my God, are the wonders you have done.** *Wonders* refers to God's past interventions in David's life. The phrase **The things you planned for us** is a reference to God's providential plan for his people (Rom. 8:28). This is so multifaceted that **no one can recount** the sum of it. It is a sovereign decree full of such blessings that David wrote, **Were I to speak and tell of them, they would be too many to declare.** This is how good God is with his plans of blessing toward those who trust him.

B David's Pledge (40:6–8)

> **SUPPORTING IDEA:** *David was fully surrendered and committed to doing the entire will of God.*

40:6. David wrote, **Sacrifice and offering you did not desire, but my ears you have pierced**, or more literally, "dug," meaning "opened." His ears had been "opened" by God so he would obey his word. David was not lessening the biblical commandments to bring **burnt offerings and sin offerings** to God. But he underscored the attitude of heart necessary as they are offered— a heart eager to hear God's commands and willing to obey them. God desires obedience to his will above sacrifices (cp. 1 Sam. 15:22; Isa. 1:11–17).

40:7–8. David continued, **Then I said, "Here I am, I have come—it is written about me in the scroll."** He remembered his commitment to the Lord, probably at the time of his enthronement, a dedication to keep God's commands. The *scroll* was probably David's personal copy of God's law, the copy which a king received at his coronation that served as his divine charter for governing the land (cp. Deut. 17:18–20; 1 Kgs. 2:3; 2 Kgs. 11:12). Whatever the Word of God required, David pledged to do it. Thus he wrote, **I desire to do your will, O my God; your law is within my heart.** In other words, David pledged to obey God's law with a willing heart. To obey God was the delight of his heart.

David's Proclamation (40:9–10)

SUPPORTING IDEA: *David gave abundant praise to God, publicly proclaiming his righteousness and faithfulness to others.*

40:9–10. The phrase **I proclaim righteousness in the great assembly** shows David's gratitude for God's many blessings that moved him to declare them to everyone in the community of worship. He felt it was his duty to share the good news of God's salvation with others. **I do not seal my lips** meant David was unable to keep silent in the assembly. He could not be silent about God's goodness. Wanting every person of the congregation to know of the Lord's goodness, he stated, **I do not hide your righteousness in my heart; I speak of your faithfulness and salvation.**

David's Petition (40:11–17)

SUPPORTING IDEA: *Even though a person knows the righteousness of God, overwhelming troubles may still come into his life. In these experiences he must seek God for deliverance.*

40:11–12. In this final section of the psalm, David offered a prayer for future deliverance, realizing that trouble is always near. **Do not withhold your mercy from me, O LORD**, David pleaded, having turned to God again for help. He asked that God's **love** and **truth** would be upon him, protecting him from troubles that resulted from his sin. He found himself in another miry pit (cp. v. 2) and again called out to the Lord. The difference now was that the present trial was of David's own making. **My sins have overtaken me**, he acknowledged. He was suffering **troubles without number** as the direct result of his own iniquity. In fact, his **troubles** were **more than the hairs** of his **head**. This admission showed that David had a proper view of God's righteousness derived from the law (v. 10) and was now able to see his own sinfulness.

40:13–15. With urgency David cried out, **O LORD, come quickly to help me**. God was his only source of salvation. Although David waited patiently on the Lord (v. 1), he found himself asking the Lord to **come quickly**. As for the many people who sought to take his life, David asked God to bring them to **shame and confusion**. He requested that they **be turned back in disgrace** and that those who sought to shame him be **appalled at their own shame**. David did not seek to bring his judgment down upon his enemies. Instead, he waited on the Lord to judge those who sought to take his life. This is exemplified best in David's dealings with Saul as he sought to destroy David (cp. 1 Sam. 24:6; 26:11).

40:16–17. **But** to the contrary, **may all who seek God be encouraged** and **rejoice**. Those who trust the Lord will **be glad** in him. This was an effect produced by God's answer to David's prayer. Yet in the meantime, before God acted and intervened, David testified, **I am poor and needy**. This statement conveys David's understanding of his helplessness before his enemies. In his present troubles, David stated, **may the Lord think of me**. Then speaking directly to God, David declared, **You are my help and my deliverer**. He knew that he had no help but God. He ended the psalm by restating the urgency of this prayer: **Oh my God, do not delay**.

MAIN IDEA REVIEW: *David recalls the Lord's past deliverance from trouble and petitions God to save him from his present ordeal.*

III. CONCLUSION

God's Molding Process

God brings trials and troubles into our lives to make us into the people he wants us to be. Whether they are troubles in which we suffer unjustly or the result of our own sin, God uses them to mold us into godliness.

> When God wants to drill a man
> And thrill a man
> And skill a man,
> When God wants to mold a man
> To play the noblest part;
> When He yearns with all His heart
> To create so great and bold a man
> That all the world shall be amazed,
> Watch His methods, watch His ways!
> How He ruthlessly perfects
> Whom He royally elects!
> How He hammers him and hurts him,
> And with mighty blows converts him
> Into trial shapes of clay which
> Only God understands;
> While his tortured heart is crying
> And he lifts beseeching hands!
> How He bends but never breaks
> When his good He undertakes;
> How He uses whom He chooses
> And with every purpose fuses him;
> By every act induces him
> To try His splendor out—
> God knows what He's about!
>
> —Anonymous

IV. LIFE APPLICATION

No Sons Without Sorrow

No Christian is exempt from trials and tribulations. In fact, this is true of all the saints of the Bible. Moreover, it was true of the sinless Son of God, the Lord Jesus Christ. It has been said that God had only one Son without sin, but he has no sons without sorrow. James confirmed this when he wrote, "Consider it pure joy, my brothers, whenever you face trials of many kinds" (Jas. 1:2). This does not say, "*if* you encounter trials," but "*whenever* you experience troubles." The assumption is that all of us will experience difficult times.

Trials are ordained by God according to his perfect plan for the lives of His people. They are for his glory and believers' good. God uses trials to cause the righteous to trust him more fully, to wean them from this world, to purge sin from their lives, and to cause them to live for eternal realities whose fulfillment is in another world. But believers can rest assured that God will deliver them in due time, lifting them to stand on a solid rock while putting a new song in their hearts. No matter what difficulty you may be going through, you may be confident that God has an eternal purpose in it and will not withhold his mercy. He will deliver his suffering servant according to his perfect will, either in this life or in the life to come.

V. PRAYER

God, your ways are not our ways, neither are your thoughts our thoughts. For we all stumble in many ways, yet you have heard our cry and have done many wonderful wonders for your people and for the glory of your name. There is no one like you. We ask you to continue to be faithful to your people and be pleased to deliver us from our enemies. Make our supreme delight the delight to do your will so that your glorious righteousness will be declared to those whom you have placed around us so that all the world may know that you are both a help and deliverer to your people. We pray this all in the name of the only God and Savior of men, Jesus Christ. Amen.

VI. DEEPER DISCOVERIES

A. Waited Patiently (40:1)

The phrase "waited patiently" literally reads, "waiting I waited." This word for "to wait" (Heb. *qawa*) does not mean a waiting to see if something will occur but a waiting with assurance that something will happen, to wait with expectation, to trust confidently in the Lord (cp. Gen. 49:18; Pss. 37:8–9; 119:95; 130:5).

B. Wonders (40:5)

This word (Heb. *pala*) refers to something that is wonderful, miraculous, or astonishing. In Psalm 72:18, Solomon wrote, "Praise be to the LORD God, the God of Israel, who alone does marvelous deeds (*pala*)." These wonders of which David spoke in Psalm 40 were not caused by the actions of men but the providential interventions of the Lord. They are called wonders because of the effect caused within the heart when God's mighty deeds are observed. In other words, it is astonishment and amazement within the heart of a person who observes the powerful intervention of God. The word is used throughout the psalms (Pss. 9:1; 26:7; 75:1; 145:5).

C. Here I Am (40:6–8)

These verses were quoted by the writer of Hebrews in 10:5-7. This New Testament citation is drawn from the Septuagint, an early Greek translation of the Old Testament dating back to before the coming of Christ. Interestingly, these verses appear to be an intertrinitarian conversation between the first and second members of the Godhead. The Son, Jesus Christ, is speaking to the Father, God, and is submitting to the Father's will. He is agreeing to enter the earth and die as a sacrifice for many. "Here I am" connotes the idea of a submissive willingness on the part of the Son to the Father's will which is to enter the world in a human body and act as a sin-bearer on behalf of all who would believe. This was the same response given by Isaiah after he saw the glory in the temple (cf. Isa.6:8).

VII. TEACHING OUTLINE

A. David's Praise (1–5)
1. God heard me (1)
2. God saved me (2)
3. God thrilled me (3)
4. God blessed me (4–5)
   a. As one who trusts him (4)
   b. As one who treasures him (5)
B. David's Pledge (6–8)
1. I will hear God's word (6)
2. I will heed God's word (7–8)
   a. To do your will (7–8a)
   b. To obey your word (8b)

C. David's Proclamation (9–10)
   1. I declare God's righteousness (9)
   2. I declare God's faithfulness (10)
D. David's Petition (11–17)
   1. Protect me (11–12)
      a. From my suffering (12a)
      b. From my sins (12a)
   2. Save Me (13)
   3. Defend Me (14–16)
      a. From those who seek my life (14–15)
      b. With those who seek your love (16)
   4. Remember Me (17)
      a. I am poor (17a)
      b. You are powerful (17b)

VIII. ISSUES FOR DISCUSSION

1. Do I praise God for delivering me from the pit of destruction?
2. Am I faithful to proclaim to others the works of God in my life?
3. When disaster strikes in my life, to whom do I turn for help?
4. Do I delight in doing the will of the Lord?

Psalm 41

Betrayed, Broken, but Blessed

Quote

"*T*he merciful fall into the arms of mercy."

J .   P .   L a n g e

Psalm 41

I. INTRODUCTION

*O*ne of the best tests of any believer's spiritual condition is not what he is when he is succeeding. Rather, the greatest disclosure of what he is occurs as he responds to suffering. Adversity reveals a person's soul. In this psalm, David was at just such a point in his life. He was undergoing much adversity, and yet he was blessed. This psalm is a passionate prayer for God's mercy at a time when David was seriously ill (v. 3) and surrounded by slandering "friends" who longed for his death (vv. 5–8). One close friend especially sought to do him harm (v. 9).

In this perilous predicament, David acknowledged God's blessing in his life (vv. 1–3) and confessed his sin (v. 4). Knowing that he himself had shown mercy to the weak (v. 1), he turned to God and asked for mercy (v. 10). Sensing God's pleasure in his integrity (v. 11), he asked the Lord to uphold him, both now and forever (v. 12).

This "psalm of David" was intended "for the director of music." Its central theme is that those who show mercy will receive mercy.

II. COMMENTARY

> **MAIN IDEA:** *David instructs God's people that those who show mercy and confess their sin will find mercy with the Lord.*

A David's Reward (41:1–3)

41:1. The first line states the general theme of this psalm—blessed will be the believer **who has regard for the weak**. This is, those who show mercy to the helpless will receive mercy from God. Jesus said, "Blessed are the merciful, for they will be shown mercy" (Matt. 5:7). Being blessed means to know the happiness, contentment, and peace that only God can give (cp. Ps. 1:1). In addition, **the LORD delivers** such a merciful person **in times of trouble**. This was true of David as king. As he defended the weak and poor (Prov. 29:14; 31:8–9), God defended him.

41:2–3. More spiritual blessings will come to the merciful person. Specifically, **the LORD will protect him** and **bless him in the land** of promise (Ps. 37:22). Furthermore, David knew the Lord would **sustain him on his sickbed**, a reference to his confining **illness** later referred to as a vile disease (v. 8). These are the blessings of God upon the defender of the weak: happiness, protection, security, and health.

B David's Request (41:4)

41:4. David offered prayer as a person faced with illness, asking for restoration. **Have mercy on me**, David prayed, and **heal me** of sickness. He asked for the mercy he had shown others. This illness he suffered was the result of his own sin. Thus, David confessed to God, **I have sinned against you**. He was familiar with the cause-and-effect connection between his sin and physical illness (cp. Pss. 6:1–2; 32:3–5; 39:1–8). So he confessed his sin to God, believing his illness was God's painful discipline.

C David's Reproach (41:5–9)

41:5–6. While David was in this state of illness (v. 3), his enemies surrounded him like vultures ready to rush in for the kill. In frustration David noted, **My enemies say of me, "When will he die and his name perish?"** They took advantage of his weak condition, slandering him, all the while pretending to befriend him. Perhaps David's adversaries wanted to remove him and his descendants from the throne, causing all to forget his existence. But David saw right through it. When a person came to see him on his sickbed, David knew that he spoke **falsely** about being devoted to him. Instead, this disloyal hypocrite gathered **slander** within his heart, plotting what he would say against David even while standing before him. This slanderer then left and went about spreading tales about David.

41:7–8. David realized that these people **whispered together against** him, plotting his demise. They spread the bad report, **A vile disease has beset him, he will never get up from** . . . **where he lies.** With his illness so serious, they hoped to destroy public confidence in David's ability to carry out the duties and responsibilities of king. Perhaps plans were being made to dethrone David as Israel's king.

41:9. Worse, David declared, even his **close friend**, one whom he trusted and one with whom he **shared** his **bread** in private meals, had betrayed him. This insider, David mourned, had **lifted up his heel** against him, a picture of harm being brought to David. Initially, this refers to the treachery of Ahithophel who betrayed David (2 Sam. 16:20–17:3,23) and prophetically to Judas who would rise up against Christ from among the Twelve (John 13:18).

D David's Renewal (41:10–12)

41:10. David concluded by petitioning God again, asking for **mercy** and health. **Raise me up** from this sickbed, he pleaded, so **I may repay them.** This request was motivated by a desire for justice and for the stability of the nation.

41:11–12. Since David had shown mercy to the weak (v. 1) and confessed his sin (v. 4), he could say to God, **I know that you are pleased with me.** Because his **integrity** remained intact, he knew that God would **uphold** him and **set** him in the Lord's **presence forever** (Ps. 23:5–6). He was both temporarily and eternally secure in God.

E David's Rejoicing (41:13)

41:13. This final verse is a doxology that concludes Book I of the Psalms (cp. Pss. 72:18–19; 89:52; 106:48; 150:6): **Praise be to the LORD, the God of Israel.** What began as blessing for man (Ps. 1) ascends to a blessing for God (41:13).

III. CONCLUSION

This psalm provides a model response for any believer who is undergoing the pain of deep trials. Humility, as demonstrated in David's life, is highlighted as the leading virtue of the person who walks with God. With humility, believers should call upon God in every difficulty, yielding themselves to him. Those who trust God must show mercy to others if they expect to receive mercy from him. Jesus said, "Do to others what you would have them do to you" (Matt. 7:12). When betrayed, the righteous must seek the high road by showing mercy even when they are maligned.

IV. TEACHING OUTLINE

A. David's Reward (1–3)
   1. My happiness is in the Lord (1a)
   2. My help is from the Lord (1b–2)
   3. My health is from the Lord (3)
B. David's Request (4)
   1. Lord, grant me pity (4a)
   2. Lord, give me pardon (4b)
C. David's Reproach (5–9)
   1. His foes belittle him (5–8)
      a. They hate him (5)
      b. They lie to him (6)
      c. They slander him (6b)
      d. They plot against him (7–8)
   2. His friend betrays him (9)
      a. He is close to David (9a)
      b. He is conspiring against David (9b)
D. David's Renewal (10–12)
   1. His power is renewed (10)
   2. His protection is renewed (11)
   3. His purity is renewed (12)
E. David's Rejoicing (13)
   1. God is enthroned (13a)
   2. God is eternal (13b)
   3. God is enduring (13b)

Psalm 42
A Sure Cure for Depression

┌─────────────────┐
│ Q u o t e │
└─────────────────┘

"Instead of muttering in this depressed, unhappy way . . .

remind yourself of God, who God is, and what God is and

what God has done, and what God has pledged himself to do."

D .   M a r t y n   L l o y d - J o n e s

I. INTRODUCTION

God Moves in a Mysterious Way

William Cowper was one of the church's greatest hymn writers, a person mightily used by God. But this gifted composer was not without frequent bouts of deep discouragement, even depression. The first attacks of despair struck him when he was a young man. He was admitted to St. Albans Insane Asylum, where he made several attempts to commit suicide. One of the doctors gave Cowper a Bible, and he began to read it. In learning of the grace of God, he put his trust in Christ and was gloriously saved.

A year after his conversion, Cowper left the asylum and met the famous John Newton, who became his pastor and close friend. Newton and Cowper collaborated to publish a hymnal that included many cherished songs, including Newton's "Amazing Grace" and "Glorious Things of Thee Are Spoken" and Cowper's "God Moves in a Mysterious Way" and "There Is a Fountain Filled with Blood." But in spite of his conversion and expanding ministry, Cowper still struggled with attacks of depression. These often left him discouraged to the point of desiring death.

His attacks of depression drove Cowper to pursue God more deeply. Out of this soul-racking experience he wrote his famous hymn, "God Moves in a Mysterious Way," a song that expresses an unwavering trust in God. The hymn stands as a testimony to the renewed strength and comfort his troubled heart found in God. Here was a man who experienced great disappointment in life, but he learned to trust God.

> God moves in a mysterious way
> His wonders to perform;
> He plants his footsteps in the sea,
> And rides upon the storm.

> Ye fearful saints, fresh courage take,
> The clouds ye so much dread
> Are big with mercy and shall break
> In blessings on your head.

> Judge not the Lord by feeble sense,
> But trust him for his grace;
> Behind a frowning providence
> He hides a smiling face.

> His purposes will ripen fast,
> Unfolding every hour;
> The bud may have a bitter taste,
> But sweet will be the flower.

As seen in the life and writings of William Cowper, even the strongest believers can suffer extreme discouragement and despair. But let it be known that the trust which Cowper exercised in God steadied his soul and brought him peace. It is this faith in God during a time of discouragement that is expressed by the psalmist in Psalm 42. In the face of mounting trials and painful agony, the psalmist rallied his own devastated heart to look to God. In this state of dependence on God, the psalmist found the comfort he needed. Although his discouragement was great, the consolation he received in God was greater. This psalm shows all believers how to overcome their bouts of depression. It describes the upward look of a downcast soul that found peace in trusting God.

Psalm 42 is identified in the title as a *maskil,* meaning a psalm of instruction. In other words, here is wise counsel about trusting God through tough times. Although the author of this psalm is not identified, it was written by "the sons of Korah" and was intended "for the director of music." The "sons of Korah" or Korahites were Levites who were descendents of Kohath, the father of Korah (1 Chr. 6:22–48; 9:17–32; 2 Chr. 20:19). They produced and performed music while the tabernacle was in the wilderness and after the construction of the temple in Jerusalem (cp. Num. 26:11).

This is the first psalm of Book II of the Book of Psalms, and an interesting change occurs in the usage of the divine name. A switch occurs from *Jehovah* being the dominant name used for God in Book I (272 occurrences), to *Elohim* being the dominant divine name in Book II (164 occurrences). What is more, Psalm 43 appears to be a continuation, or extension, of Psalm 42 as the repeated refrain in Psalm 42:5,11 and Psalm 43:5 may reveal.

II. COMMENTARY

A Sure Cure for Depression

> **MAIN IDEA:** *The psalmist, under severe discouragement, longs for the presence of God and exhorts his soul to hope in God.*

A First Causes Of Depression (42:1–4)

> **SUPPORTING IDEA:** *The psalmist looks into his own life and reviews the reasons for his bout with extreme discouragement.*

42:1–2. The psalm begins with a statement of intense longing: **As the deer pants for streams of water, so my soul pants for you, O God.** For the psalmist, this was a time of emotional drought and spiritual dryness. The word *pants* in the Hebrew means "to have a keen, consuming desire for." His driving passion was not for people, possessions, or prosperity but for God. Like a panting deer in desperate need of water, the psalmist cried, **My soul thirsts for God, for the living God.** All the hope, trust, and confidence of the psalmist was in **the living God**, not the lifeless deities of pagan idolatry. His thirst was for the true God who was self-sufficient, independent, autonomous, and willing to come to the aid of his people.

The further desperation of the psalmist is reflected in the question, **When can I go and meet with God?** This was not a denial of God's omnipresence but rather a longing for God's felt presence. The psalmist longed for a deeper personal awareness of God as he suffered the loneliness of his alienation because of his absence from public worship at the temple in Jerusalem.

42:3. This extreme longing for God was intensified by the psalmist's hostile environment created by **men** who said to him **all day long, Where is your God?** These men were the psalmist's enemies (vv. 9–10) who taunted him to doubt, fear, and despondency about the character of God. The enemies actually aimed their attacks not at the psalmist, but at **God.** They were asking, "Where is your God when you need him? Where is your God now? I thought God was with you. So where is he now?" The psalmist's desperation was such that he declared, **My tears have been my food day and night.** The persistent mocking by these oppressors caused him such sorrow that he could not eat.

42:4. As the psalmist reflected on his present condition, his mind was drawn to remember the positive past. He wrote, **These things I remember as I pour out my soul**, reflecting painfully on his separation from Jerusalem (v. 6). These stirring memories were drawn from an exuberant joy experienced by the psalmist during the public worship services in Jerusalem when he **used to go with the multitude, leading the procession to the house of God**. Through the streets of the city, he would lead the parade to the house of God. He had been the rallying point, personally leading this parade to the temple to worship.

Ironically, these pleasant memories from the past became a source of discouragement for the present. This great procession was accompanied **with shouts of joy and thanksgiving among the festive throng**, no doubt involving the singing of psalms and spiritual songs. This would have occurred during the three annual pilgrimage festivals (Passover, Firstfruits, and Tabernacles; cp. Exod. 23:17; 34:18–26; Lev. 23:4–44; Deut. 16:1–17). Also, this may have involved the psalms of assent (Pss. 120–134) that were sung by caravans of pilgrims while ascending to the city of Jerusalem and the temple mount.

Faithful Cure for Depression (42:5)

SUPPORTING IDEA: *The psalmist questions himself to pinpoint the causes of his depression and then asserts his trust in God.*

42:5. The psalmist spoke to his own soul and heart, **Why are you downcast, O my soul? Why so disturbed within me?** These questions were designed to challenge the psalmist, bringing him to a place of self-examination and introspection about his state of sorrow. The psalmist was trying to find the cause of his depression before he sought the needed treatment. This self-contemplation moved the psalmist to command his own soul to **put** its **hope in God**. This is part of the cure for the despairing soul that is spiritually depressed and distraught.

Although he felt isolated from God, the psalmist stirred his mind to override his emotions and feelings by hoping in God. Furthermore, he continued, **I will yet praise him**. This praise flowed from the truth that the Lord was both the psalmist's **Savior** and **God**. He must **hope** in the immutability of God's unchanging character. Relief from depression is found in trusting the immutable character of God.

Further Causes of Depression (42:6–10)

SUPPORTING IDEA: *The psalmist continues to look inward into his soul for the causes of his depression.*

42:6. Although the psalmist sought to evade depression, his soul was **downcast within** him. He recalled the times of worshiping the Lord while in

Jerusalem. He wrote, **I will remember you from the land of the Jordan.** This refers to the region beyond the Jordan River north and east of Jerusalem where Mount Hermon was located. The sons of Korah who wrote this psalm were removed from their place of ministry and usefulness, which was service to God in the temple. They remembered **the heights of Hermon—from Mount Mizar.** The word *Mizar* means "little hill" or "little mountain" and was probably a lesser peak in the Hermon range northeast of Jerusalem. Thus, the psalmist was in the outer edges of his homeland, away from the comforts and conveniences of home.

42:7. The psalmist who sought the flowing streams of water (vv. 1–2) then found a tempest of waters overwhelming his soul. His distress is figuratively portrayed by allusions derived from violent water: **Deep calls to deep in the roar of your waterfalls.** The phrase "deep calls to deep" pictures one wave of the deep calling out to another wave of the deep to coordinate a conspiracy in their efforts to drown the psalmist, figuratively speaking. He continued, **All your waves and breakers have swept over me.** Like a stranded sailor clinging to a piece of driftwood in a raging storm, he was tossed back and forth, taking in water, sinking fast with no hope of rescue.

The **waterfalls, breakers,** and **waves** that overwhelmed the psalmist represent his mounting trials. Nevertheless, these were directed by the Lord. They were under his complete control and were working for the good of the psalmist.

42:8a–b. Although the psalmist was overwhelmed by his predicament, he could say that the Lord directed **his love** toward him. This love was unconditional, covenant love (see "Deeper Discoveries," 23:6), the eternal lovingkindness of God for his people. The psalmist knew that the love of God would not fail his elected ones. **At night,** the psalmist said, God's **song** was with him. The painful ordeal awakened him at night, but he was comforted again by God's love. There was never a time when God was not with the psalmist, although he did not always feel the presence of God.

42:8c–9. The psalmist continued to offer a **prayer** to the **God of** his **life.** He began, **I say to God my Rock.** The psalmist knew that God was an unassailable fortress, a rock (cp. Ps. 18:1–2) in which he could hide from the crashing waves. The question asked in faith, **"Why have you forgotten me?"** was asked because God was not coming to his aid immediately. It appeared that God was not listening and did not care. The psalmist's prayers seemed to be going unanswered, unheard, and unheeded. **Why must I go about mourning, oppressed by the enemy?** he asked. The word *mourning* is a rich Hebrew word (*qadar*) which means literally "to be ashy," "to be dark colored," or "to be black." The psalmist was emotionally devastated and distraught by the taunting enemies of the Lord.

42:10. This oppression began to affect the psalmist physically. He wrote, **My bones suffer mortal agony as my foes taunt me**. The physical pain was caused by the relentless personal attacks of his foes. These people aligned themselves as enemies of God, and thus they were his enemies as well. Literally, this reads, "in murder in my bones," or "a breaking of my bones." The reviling of his adversaries brought about in the psalmist a **mortal agony**. Although his foes did not use sword or spear to take his life, the taunting blows by the sword of the tongue were cutting the psalmist. The specific taunt launched by his enemies was, "**Where is your God?**" To the dismay of the psalmist, this was said **all day long**.

D Final Cure for Depression (42:11)

SUPPORTING IDEA: *In the face of this adversity, the psalmist chooses to praise God through his troubles, trials, and trauma.*

42:11. The psalmist repeated an earlier stanza (v. 5), asking, **Why are you downcast, O my soul? Why so disturbed within me?** He answered these questions by saying to himself, **Put your hope in God**. He meant that he had great confidence in God's ability to handle every situation victoriously. He encouraged his heart to trust God with a positive expectation that he would come through for him, that God would work for his good with perfect wisdom, perfect plans, perfect timing, and perfect power.

To hope (Heb. *yacha*) means to wait upon God's perfect timing with a confident and strong trust in God about the future. The psalmist had already prescribed this cure in verse 5. Now he repeated this simple cure: **hope in God**. While hoping in **God** his **Savior**, the psalmist would also **praise him** for who he is, what he had done, what he was doing, and what he would do.

MAIN IDEA REVIEW: *The psalmist, under severe discouragement, longs for the presence of God and exhorts his soul to hope in God.*

III. CONCLUSION

The Problem of Unbelief

When surrounded by troubles and discouragement, there is a simple but sure remedy for spiritual depression. The cure for the troubled soul is always to hope in God exclusively, knowing that he will never fail.

Speaking to this point, Martyn Lloyd-Jones, in his best-selling book *Spiritual Depression: Its Causes and Cure* (Grand Rapids: Wm. B. Eerdmans Publishing Co., 1965), wrote:

The ultimate cause of all spiritual depression is unbelief. For if it were not for unbelief, even the devil could do nothing. It is because we listen to the devil instead of listening to God that we go down before him and fall before his attacks. This is why the psalmist keeps saying to himself: "Hope Thou in God for I shall yet praise Him. . . ." He reminds himself of God. Why? Because he was depressed and had forgotten God, so that his faith and his belief in God and in God's power, and in his relationship to God, were not what they ought to be . . . Have you realized that most of your unhappiness in life is due to the fact that you are listening to yourself instead of talking to yourself? . . . Now this man's treatment was this: instead of allowing this self to talk to him, he starts talking to himself. Why art thou cast down, O my soul? he asks. His soul had been depressing him, crushing him. So he stands up and says: "Self, listen for a moment, I will speak to you."

IV. LIFE APPLICATION

Turn to God

When a believer finds himself in difficult times, the solution is always the same—hope in God. This is the wise counsel of the psalmist. When faced with demanding circumstances, we should put our confidence and trust in the Lord. This may sound too simplistic in man's eyes, but it is, nevertheless, heaven's solution. But unfortunately, when confronted with encroaching trials, we are tempted to panic and turn to man-made solutions. These can never release us from pain. Some people turn to their work or to a hobby to get them through. Others turn to a new purchase or a new pursuit to numb their sorrow. Still others turn to the bottle or to drugs to ease their pain, only to multiply their agony all the more.

Lasting peace and genuine contentment are found in only one place: Hope in God. We must discipline our minds and direct our wills to hope in God when tempted to dissolve into a pool of despair. Hope in God. Nothing else and no one else can pull us out of the depressing moments of life.

V. PRAYER

God, we praise you for your immutable character; you are our rock. Though the storms of life may rage, your love remains with us through all of life. You are indeed the God of our lives, and we praise and worship you. The supreme desire of our heart is for you to meet with us. Rescue our downcast souls; teach us to remember your faithfulness, and place us again in the festive assembly so that we may worship you. This we ask in the name of Jesus. Amen.

VI. DEEPER DISCOVERIES

A. Disturbed (42:5)

This word (Heb. *hama*) describes a loud sound or noise, a great commotion, or an uproar. It means "to be clamorous" or "to be troubled." The derivatives of the word speak of a person groaning or roaring (Ps. 77:3; Isa. 59:11; Jer. 6:23), waters roaring (Ps. 46:3), waves roaring (Jer. 5:22; 31:35), the heart pounding (Jer. 4:19), and the bowels yearning (Jer. 31:20). Here it refers to the deep groans of a pained, sorrowful heart.

B. Deep (42:7)

The word *deep* (Heb. *tehom*) is used in various ways to speak of water, whether in the form of large bodies of water (Ps. 77:16; Isa. 51:10; 63:13) such as the Mediterranean Sea (Jon. 2:5) or a subterranean water supply (Deut. 8:7; Ps. 78:15). It is often used as an image of destruction and judgment, as an overwhelming flood of divine wrath. It also speaks of the mounting troubles of life, as when David said that the Lord "reached down from on high and took hold of me; he drew me out of deep waters" (Ps. 18:16). The word is used for the water that God brought to judge the evil generation of Noah's time (Gen. 7:11; 8:2). It also speaks of God bringing the ocean depths over the city of Tyre to destroy it (Ezek. 26:19) and the execution of divine destruction against the nations (Hab. 3:10).

C. Mourning (42:9)

The word *mourning* (Heb. *qadar*) occurs nineteen times in the Old Testament. It means "to be dark or black." It was used to describe a state of mourning (cp. Job 30:28; Jer. 14:2) or causing to mourn (Ezek. 31:15). The word is also used in an eschatological sense to describe the darkening of heavenly bodies in the day of the Lord (Isa. 13:10; Jer. 4:28; Joel 2:10,30–31, 3:15; Zeph. 1:15). In this sense, it suggests extraordinary grief because of the impending judgment of God's wrath.

VII. TEACHING OUTLINE

A. First Causes of Depression (1–10)
   1. Missed public worship (1–2)
   2. Verbal ridicule (3)
   3. Pleasant memories (4)
B. Faithful Cure for Depression (5)

       1. The introspective question (5a–b)
         a. Why are you downcast? (5a)
         b. Why are you disturbed? (5b)
       2. The inevitable answer (5c–6a)
         a. Have a patient hope (5c)
         b. Have a praising heart (5d)
   C. Further Causes of Depression (6–10)
       1. Physical separation (6)
       2. Overwhelming trials (7)
       3. Sleepless nights (8)
       4. Unanswered prayer (8c–9)
       5. Difficult people (10)
   D. Final Cure for Depression (11)
       1. The introspective question (11a)
         a. Why are you downcast? (11a)
         b. Why are you disturbed? (11b)
       2. The inevitable answer
         a. Have a patient hope (11c)
         b. Have a praising heart (11d)

VIII. ISSUES FOR DISCUSSION

1. Do I long for God to meet with me?
2. How is this longing expressed in my life?
3. How will I overcome my dismal night of darkness and despair?
4. When facing oppressors and enemies, where do I place my hope?
5. Do I pose questions to myself, seeking to evaluate my spiritual condition?

Psalm 43

Holding On to Hope

I. INTRODUCTION

*T*imes of tribulation either make us or break us. That is, it either drives us closer to God, or it drives us further away from God. But no one remains the same through the experience of deep pain. It all depends upon where a person's faith rests. A time of adversity for the person whose trust is in the Lord becomes a season of increased dependency upon the Lord. So it was for the psalmist, whose ordeal drove him close to God.

Psalm 43 is an epilogue of Psalm 42. In Psalm 42, the psalmist found himself in difficult times, increasingly reliant upon those things that could not be shaken. The psalmist's storm showed no sign of lifting, so in Psalm 43, he continued to seek God in prayer while still oppressed. The source of this trial was an ungodly nation (v. 1), perhaps the Arameans of Damascus, which posed as an enemy (v. 2), and threatened the security of Israel. In this situation, the psalmist was removed from Jerusalem (v. 3), thus this prayer that God would return him safely (v. 1).

He asked that God would lead him back to the holy mountain, Jerusalem (v. 3), so he could worship God again at the altar (v. 4). In the midst of his despair, while endangered by an ungodly nation, he challenged himself to put his hope and trust in God (v. 5). This psalm speaks to every believer, whatever his despair may be. The message is loud and clear: "Put your hope in God" (v. 5; cp. Ps. 42:5,11).

II. COMMENTARY

> **MAIN IDEA:** *The psalmist calls upon God to vindicate him before his enemies while directing him into his holy presence.*

A A Prayer for Vindication (43:1)

43:1. Using courtroom language, the psalmist called out to God, **Vindicate me, O God, and plead my cause against an ungodly nation**. He wanted God to be both his judge, examining him, and his defense counsel, defending him against an ungodly nation that threatened the security of Israel. This is a prayer for vindication from his enemies in which he asked God to plead his cause before them. He wanted God to **rescue** him from the **deceitful** people who threatened his life. The identity of this nation is not mentioned.

B A Prayer of Lamentation (43:2)

43:2. With growing confidence, the psalmist boasted, **You are God my stronghold**, the one who could defend him from all attacks. Nevertheless, as his enemies seemed to be gaining an advantage over him, the situation gave the appearance that God had rejected him. He lamented, **Why have you rejected me?** If God was his sure defense, he wondered, **Why must I go about mourning, oppressed by the enemy?** Seemingly, God had rejected him.

C A Prayer for Restoration (43:3–4)

43:3. God's vindication of the psalmist would be evidenced in the Lord's guidance, which would usher him to Jerusalem to worship. He prayed, **Send forth your light and your truth, let them guide me . . . to your holy mountain**. He was referring to Jerusalem, where the tabernacle was located, the appointed place of public worship. Personified as the psalmist's personal guide, God's **light** was the divine illumination necessary for a person to understand his **truth**. In other words, a God-given understanding of God's Word would lead him back to worship in Jerusalem. The psalmist needed the providential care of God to overturn circumstances before he could go back to Jerusalem.

43:4. Once he got back to Jerusalem, the psalmist pledged, he would go to **the altar of God**, who was his **joy** and **delight**, the satisfaction of his soul. There he would **praise** God with **the harp**.

D A Prayer of Introspection (43:5)

43:5. Repeating the familiar refrain from the previous psalm (42:5,11), the psalmist searched and asked his own heart, **Why are you downcast O my soul? Why so disturbed within me?** He wondered how he could be so emotionally distraught if God was so great. He directed himself, **Put your hope in**

God. In other words, have confidence in the Lord! Rather than focusing outwardly on the enemies who surrounded him, he must look upward to God. With a firm resolve, he determined that he would **praise** the Lord who alone was his **Savior** and **God**.

III. CONCLUSION

In the midst of life's troubles, the believer must direct his heart toward God and anchor his soul in him. Unwavering hope must be placed in God, regardless of the circumstances around us. To do this, the believer must call himself to exercise confident faith in God. The character of God, particularly his faithfulness to his people in times past, should be a strengthening comfort to believers today. God alone is the Savior and sustainer of his people. He alone can rescue us from our darkest trials and troubles.

IV. TEACHING OUTLINE

 A. A Prayer for Vindication (1)
  1. Plead my cause (1a)
  2. Preserve my life (1b)
 B. A Prayer of Lamentation (2)
  1. Why have you rejected me? (2a)
  2. Why must I be repressed? (2b)
 C. A Prayer for Restoration (3–4)
  1. Grant me your truth (3a)
  2. Guide me to your temple (3b–4)
   a. Then I will go to the altar (4a)
   b. Then I will praise you (4b)
 D. A Prayer of Introspection (5)
  1. Question: Why am I downcast? (5a)
  2. Answer: Hope in God (5b)

Psalm 44

One Nation Under Siege

"*Testing is important, inevitable . . . because we must be revealed to ourselves.*"

J .   R u s s e l l   H o w d e n

Psalm 44

I. INTRODUCTION

A sudden, unexpected national crisis is a wake-up call for any people. Whether it is a foreign attack from the outside or internal conflict from the inside, such a time can devastate a people and cause them to seek the Lord. This was the situation with Psalm 44. This *maskil* psalm, written by "the sons of Korah," was a national lament offered to God after Judah suffered a devastating defeat at the hands of a foreign oppressor.

While the actual historical setting is uncertain, this much is known: Israel had enjoyed many victories in her past (vv. 1–8) but found herself reeling under the devastating attacks of a military enemy, perhaps the Assyrian or Babylonian empire (vv. 11,14). So great were these losses that Judah suffered international ridicule (v. 13). The psalmist argued that these national defeats had happened undeservedly (vv. 9–16). He even asked God to point out the failure of his people, not expecting any to be revealed (vv. 17–22). He concluded by calling on God to rise up and deliver his people from their distress (vv. 23–26).

II. COMMENTARY

MAIN IDEA: *The psalmist rejoices in God's past victories on behalf of his people, is perplexed by their current defeats, and prays for God's victory for Israel to return.*

A A Prosperous Past (44:1–8)

44:1–3. The psalmist began by referring to God's past victories on behalf of his people: **We have heard with our ears, O God . . . what you did . . . in days long ago**. The psalmist recalled Judah's fathers telling their sons how the Lord rescued them from the Egyptians (Exod. 15:6; Pss. 17:7; 118:16) and gave them their land under Joshua (Josh. 24:17–18). In so doing, he boasted, God drove out the **nations and planted our fathers** (Exod. 15:17; Ps. 80:8–12; Amos 9:15). So obvious was this divine intervention, the psalmist stated, **It was not by their sword that they won the land**. When Judah had won a battle, the psalmist knew that it was God giving the victory because he **loved them** (Deut. 4:37; 8:17–18; 9:4,6).

44:4–8. Based upon these mighty victories, the psalmist offered praise to God: **You are my King and my God, who decrees victories for Jacob**. The Israelites fought, but God gave the victory. Even in the current generation, God had put their **adversaries to shame**. The psalmist declared, **In God we make our boast** (Ps. 34:2) because he had won the victory for Judah by defeating her foes. Therefore God's people could respond, **We will praise your name forever**. Thanks be to God who had given the victory!

B A Painful Present (44:9–22)

44:9–12. Suddenly, the focus and tone of the psalm shifts. In spite of past victories, the nation was now subjected to devastating defeats. God was seen as opposing his chosen people, having **rejected** that which caused them **to be devoured like sheep . . . among the nations**. The Lord seemed to be driving them from the very land he had given them as a possession.

44:13–16. The psalmist lamented to God, **You have made us a reproach to our neighbors** and **scorn and derision of those around us** (Deut. 28:37; 1 Kgs. 9:7; Jer. 24:10). He added, **My face is covered with shame**, figuratively picturing the humiliation and embarrassment that God had brought on the nation in defeat.

44:17–19. What was most perplexing about these defeats to Judah was that they seemed so undeserved. The psalmist affirmed, **All this happened to us, though we had not forgotten you**. Their loyalty to God was strong and unwavering. Speaking for the people the psalmist noted, **Our hearts had not turned back** nor had **our feet** gone astray, meaning inwardly and outwardly the nation appeared to be blameless. But in spite of this, God had crushed them and covered them **with deep darkness**.

44:20–22. If Judah had forgotten God or gone after **foreign gods**, God certainly would have known it. Instead, the psalmist declared, they had faced **death** continually and were **considered as sheep to be slaughtered**. This same imagery was used by Isaiah in reference to the Messiah (Isa. 53:7). With no explanation, God allowed his people to be destroyed by their enemies.

◖C◗ A Positive Prospect (44:23–26)

44:23–24. In light of their dire predicament, the psalmist called out to God to come to their aid. **Awake, O LORD!** was a call to rouse God to action. While God does not sleep, his apparent inactivity toward them gave this appearance. **Why do you hide your face**, he asked, as if God were withholding his strength from them.

44:25–26. Until God acted, the psalmist lamented, **We are brought down to the dust**. So he cried out in desperation, **Rise up and help us; redeem us because of your unfailing love**. This psalm concludes with this passionate appeal for divine intervention to grant them victory over their enemies as he had done in previous days.

III. CONCLUSION

No matter how threatening a national tragedy may appear to be, there is always hope for the future as people put their trust in the Lord. The God who brought victory to Judah in the past is the same God who can give victory in the present to those who call upon his name. Even the cultural and social upheavals that surround the righteous can be used by God to cause the hearts of people to seek him. The people of God, like the ancient psalmist, should call upon God to redeem them from their nation's moral chaos. No situation is so bleak that it is beyond the redeeming power of God.

IV. TEACHING OUTLINE

A. A Prosperous Past (1–8)
　　1. They had been planted in the land (1–3)
　　　　a. God brought them in (1–2)
　　　　b. God built them up (3)
　　2. They had been protected in the land (4–8)
　　　　a. God decreed victories (4)
　　　　b. God defeated foes (5–6)
　　　　c. God delivered them (7–8)

B. A Painful Present (9–22)
   1. Their military disaster is real (9–16)
      a. They were defeated (9–10)
      b. They were deported (11–12)
      c. They were despised (13–14)
      d. They were disgraced (15–16)
   2. The moral dilemma is reeling (17–22)
      a. They were dedicated (17–18)
      b. They were defeated (19)
      c. They were disillusioned (20–22)
C. A Positive Prospect (23–26)
   1. God, rouse yourself (23–24)
   2. God, redeem us (25–26)

Psalm 45

A Royal Wedding Song

"*There* is no more lovely, friendly, or charming relationship, communion, or company, than a good marriage."

Martin Luther

Psalm 45

I. INTRODUCTION

The first institution that God established was marriage, an expression of his goodness to man. Beginning with the first wedding ceremony in Eden, each subsequent joining of a man and woman together in marriage is a celebration of God's blessing upon his creation. Psalm 45 reflects this divine goodness in marriage. Unique among all the psalms, it is a song of praise to the king on his wedding day.

The identity of the king is not given, although he must have been a member of David's dynasty, and the bride was a foreign princess (vv. 10,12). The wedding ceremony reflects the international prominence of the king. Many dignitaries attended the festive occasion, bringing their extravagant gifts (v. 12). Undoubtedly, this psalm was used during more than one royal wedding. It is a masterful piece of inspired literature that extols the joy and blessings of marriage.

The superscription affirms that this psalm is "a wedding song" as well as a *maskil,* meaning it was intended to teach wisdom about the holy virtue of marriage. As a song "of the sons of Korah," it was written and sung by a member of the Levitical temple choir "to the tune of 'Lilies.'"

II. COMMENTARY

MAIN IDEA: *The psalmist offers praise for the regal splendor of a king on his royal wedding day.*

A The Rejoicing Psalmist (45:1)

45:1. This first verse serves as a prologue of sorts as it gives a rare glimpse into the process of a psalm's composition (cp. 2 Sam. 23:2; Pss. 36:1; 39:1–3; 49:3; 73:2–3; 78:2–3). The psalmist's **heart** was overcome with emotion by the **noble theme** of the royal wedding of the king. He declared, **My tongue is the pen of a skilled writer.** He would convert his feelings on this glorious occasion into words of consecration.

B The Royal Groom (45:2–9)

45:2. The psalmist described the groom in glowing terms. The kingly groom was **the most excellent of men**, meaning literally that he was beautiful, full of splendor. His **lips** (words or decrees) had been **anointed with grace** by the Lord. What this king said under God's control brought blessing to all his people.

45:3–5. As a victorious commander in chief and defender of national security, the king was urged to **gird** his **sword** for battle in order to go forth to do all that was right. He was the **mighty one**, clothed with glorious **splendor and majesty**, who represented God on the earth. He was to adorn himself with true greatness that exceeded even his wedding clothes. He was to advance **victoriously** against the nation's enemies, defending the cause of **truth, humility and righteousness** through awesome, heroic deeds. His **sharp arrows**, under the control of his soldiers, should be aimed and released at the enemy in order to **pierce the hearts of the king's enemies**. He was the defender of the people, the executer of justice.

45:6–7. In this verse either the king is addressed as God, or his throne is addressed as God's throne, or more probably, God's throne is recognized as presiding over the king's throne. Thus, God's sovereign rule over this king's rule is expressed: **Your throne, O God, will last for ever and ever.** Heaven's throne, armed with a **scepter of justice**, was guiding the king's earthly throne. To God the psalmist declared, **You love righteousness and hate wickedness.** These are the two extreme passions of holiness, the one necessitating the other. The heavenly king was recognized as being exalted above his companions and bestowed with **the oil of joy. Anointing** symbolized someone being set apart for a special task (see "Deeper Discoveries," 2:2). The New Testament shows this to be ultimately a messianic reference to the Lord Jesus Christ (Heb. 1:8–9).

45:8–9. As the earthly king put on his impressive wedding robes, they were **fragrant with myrrh and aloes and cassia**. These were expensive fragrances associated with kings (Song 4:14). The king held court in **palaces adorned with ivory** inlays and objects; they were also filled with **the music of the strings**.

C The Radiant Bride (45:10–12)

45:10–11. The psalmist addressed the king's bride as **daughter**. He declared, **Forget your people and your father's house**. The time had come for her to leave her family and cleave to her husband (Gen. 2:24). The psalmist added, **The king is enthralled by your beauty**. She was the object of his desire. So she should freely **honor him** by giving him devotion and respect.

45:12. The phrase **The Daughter of Tyre** is a personification of the Phoenician city famed as a traveling center. Tyre would come to this royal wedding **with a gift** to celebrate this regal occasion.

D The Regal Procession (45:13–15)

45:13–15. The psalmist described the queen's ceremonial arrival before her royal groom. She was **glorious** in her wedding **gown** and **embroidered garments interwoven with gold**. Properly attired, she was led, probably carried, to the king. **Her virgin companions**, either bridesmaids of honor or permanent attendants, followed her as this entourage was **brought to** the waiting king. **Joy and gladness** marked the occasion as the **princess** with her companions proceeded into the royal **palace**.

E The Reigning Offspring (45:16–17)

45:16. Anticipating their prosperous future together, the psalmist addressed the king, **Your sons will take the place of your fathers**. In other words, the offspring of this new union would follow in the illustrious steps of the king and his ancestors, continuing the family line of dynastic succession. These future **sons** would be crowned as **princes** and would reign over **the land**.

45:17. Through this wedding song, the psalmist pledged, **I will perpetuate your memory through all generations**. All who read this psalm would remember this king and rejoice in God's goodness to him. Even the **nations** would **praise** him **for ever**, the psalmist promised, because of this inspired poem.

III. CONCLUSION

We cannot read about the wedding ceremony of this psalm without thinking about another future wedding of a greater son of David, the Lord Jesus Christ, when he will celebrate his eternal union with his redeemed bride (Rev. 19:1–10). The apostle John must have built upon this scene in Psalm 45 when he recorded the account of the marriage supper of the Lamb in Revelation 19. In this coming day the King of kings, Christ himself, will celebrate the joy of his chosen bride, the church, who will clothe herself in a wedding garment made of her righteous acts (Rev. 19:6–8).

This psalm has been applied to the coming Messiah, the future Son of David, who at his second advent will sit on David's throne and rule over all the earth (Rev. 20:1–10). The New Testament applies verses 6–7 of this psalm directly to Christ (Heb. 1:8–9). So there can be little doubt about the messianic fulfillment of this psalm in the risen, reigning Lord Jesus Christ himself.

IV. TEACHING OUTLINE

A. The Rejoicing Psalmist (1)
  1. My passion is stirred (1a)
  2. My pen is skilled (1b)
B. The Royal Groom (2–9)
  1. His gracious words (2)
  2. His girded sword (3)
  3. His glorious majesty (4)
  4. His grand victories (5)
  5. His governing scepter (6–7)
  6. His glad heart (8)
  7. His gathered guests(9)
C. The Radiant Bride (10–12)
  1. Her separation from family (10)
  2. Her submission to her groom (11)
  3. Her supporters from afar (12)
D. The Regal Procession (13–15)
  1. Her attire (13–14a)
  2. Her attendants (14b)
  3. Her approach (15)
E. The Reigning Offspring (16–17)
  1. His sons are princes (16)
  2. His success is perpetuated (17)

Psalm 46

Our Mighty Fortress

Quote

"*We* sing this psalm to the praise of God, because God

is with us, and powerfully and miraculously preserves and

defends his church and his word, against all fanatical spirits,

against the gates of hell, against the implacable hatred of the

devil, and against all the assaults of the world,

the flesh and sin."

Martin Luther

I. INTRODUCTION

A Mighty Fortress Is Our God

*M*artin Luther is one of the key figures in church history, a man mightily used by God to bring reformation to the church. The year 1527 was the most difficult of his life. After ten demanding years of leading the Reformation, a dizzy spell overcame him in the middle of a sermon on April 22 of that year, forcing him to stop preaching. Luther feared for his life. On July 6, while eating dinner with friends, he felt an acute buzzing in his ear and lay down, again convinced he was at the end of his life. He partially regained his strength, but a debilitating discouragement set in as a result. In addition, heart problems and severe intestinal complications escalated the pangs of death.

Of this ordeal, Luther wrote, "I spent more than a week in death and hell. My entire body was in pain, and I still tremble. Completely abandoned by Christ, I labored under the vacillations and storms of desperation and blasphemy against God."

What was worse, the dreaded black plague had entered Germany and spread into Wittenberg. Many people fled, fearing for their lives. Yet Luther and his wife Katy remained, believing it was their duty to care for the sick and dying. Although Katy was pregnant with their second child, Luther's house was transformed into a hospital where he watched many friends die. Then without warning Luther's one-year-old son Hans became desperately ill. With death surrounding him on every side, Luther was driven to seek refuge in God as never before. Psalm 46 became the strength of his soul.

As a result, Luther expanded its truths into the hymn for which he is most famous, "A Mighty Fortress Is Our God." Its majestic and thunderous proclamation of God who is our all-sufficient refuge in our weakest moments has become the enduring symbol of the Reformation.

> A mighty fortress is our God,
> A bulwark never failing;
> Our helper He amid the flood
> Of mortal ills prevailing.
> For still our ancient foe
> Doth seek to work us woe—
> His craft and pow'r are great,
> And armed with cruel hate,
> On earth is not his equal.
> That word above all earthly pow'rs,
> No thanks to him abideth;
> The Spirit and the gifts are ours
> Thru Him who with us sideth.
> Let goods and kindred go,
> This mortal life also—
> The body they may kill;
> God's truth abideth still
> His kingdom is forever.

Like Martin Luther, the author of Psalm 46 found solace and refuge in God during difficult times. The background for this song of praise is unknown, but it was probably written after a military victory over a foreign power that attempted a siege against Jerusalem. It may have been written after the destruction of the armies of Ammon, Moab, and Mount Seir (2 Chr. 20:1–30). Or perhaps it was recorded after the destruction of King Sennacherib and the Assyrian army during the reign of Hezekiah (2 Kgs. 18–19).

According to the superscription, it was written by one of the "sons of Korah" (for background on the sons of Korah, see Introduction, Psalm 42) and was "for the director of music." *Alamoth* may refer to the pitch of the music, denoting that it was to be high for the treble and soprano voices. It may have been implored to refer to certain shrill-sounding instruments (cp. 1 Chr. 15:20).

II. COMMENTARY

Our Mighty Fortress

> **MAIN IDEA:** *The psalmist extols the ability of God to protect the righteous from their enemies by his ever-abiding presence.*

A Our Immovable Refuge (46:1–3)

> **SUPPORTING IDEA:** *The psalmist begins by announcing that God is a strong refuge for his people, providing safety from discouraging and devastating circumstances.*

46:1. When we are attacked and assailed by the discouraging circumstances of life, **God is our refuge** in whom his people will find protection, strength, and stability. God is pictured as a refuge, meaning a strong shelter from danger, an unconquerable fortress, or a walled city where protection is found. Furthermore, when trouble found the psalmist, God was his **strength**, upholding and enabling him to stand through the fiery trials. To have **trouble** means to be in a tight place, to be restricted, tied up, or to be in a narrow, cramped place. The psalmist was between a rock and a hard place with no way out. Yet God was with him, **an ever-present help** in trouble, immediately present and instantly available to his people.

46:2–3. Having understood the all-sustaining power of God, the psalmist wrote, **We will not fear.** This is a bold statement of confidence in God inspired by the greatness of the Almighty. Regardless of what the psalmist and the people of God face, they have no reason to fear. God is in control. The psalmist continued, **Though the earth give way and the mountains fall into the heart of the sea.** This is a picture of confusion, represented as a momentous earthquake that caused an upheaval of the tall, lofty mountains. The mountains, representing stability and continuity, seem to collapse into the sea; and the **waters roar and foam and the mountains quake with their surging.**

This imagery conveys earthshaking circumstances. As the mountains crash into the sea, the sea responds by flooding outside of its assigned barriers. In spite of all this turmoil that pictures devastating circumstances seemingly out of control, **we will not fear.** God is in control.

B Our Inexhaustible River (46:4–7)

> **SUPPORTING IDEA:** *God is the satisfying river who abides in Jerusalem with his protective presence, ready to destroy the enemies of his people.*

46:4. Although the foundations of the earth were shaking and collapsing, **there is a river whose streams make glad the city of God**. Unlike the turbulent waters that roar and foam, the streams of God are continual and make glad the inhabitants of the city of God. *Streams* is perhaps a reference to the stream of Siloam, which was the only water supply for the inhabitants of Jerusalem. This **river** may be the river that flows from the throne of God (Ezek. 47:1–12; Zech. 14:8; Rev. 22:1–2). Jerusalem was often designated as **the city of God** (Pss. 9:11; 48:1–2; Isa. 60:14). It was considered the city **where the Most High dwells**. The **holy place** is a reference to the temple mount where the temple and the ark of the covenant were located.

46:5–7. Perhaps Jerusalem had been under attack from a foreign invader, but the psalmist wrote of the city's fate: **God is within her, she will not fall**. Although enemy forces were in **uproar** and threatened to attack Jerusalem at **break of day**, the time when the city would be most vulnerable, all was well because **God** would **help**.

Although nations might voice brazen threats of invasion and destruction, the Lord would lift up **his voice** to speak, drowning out all other voices, and as a result the earth would melt. Therefore, the sons of Korah could sing with confidence, **The LORD Almighty is with us**. The phrase *LORD Almighty* is literally "the Lord of Hosts." He would guard his chosen city and his holy people (cp. Pss. 24:10; 48:8; 59:5). The psalmist continued, **The God of Jacob is our fortress**, meaning that the Lord of Israel, **God** himself, was a high and safe place, a refuge (Pss. 46:11; 48:3; 59:9,16–17; 62:2,6; 94:22).

C Our Invincible Ruler (46:8–11)

> **SUPPORTING IDEA:** *The battle belongs to the Lord because he will fight the evil forces that threaten his people while bringing glory to his name.*

46:8–9. Following the battle, the psalmist invited the reader to **come and see the works of the LORD, the desolations he** had **brought on the earth**. The works of the LORD were performed throughout the history of Israel, from the conquest of the promised land into the period of the monarchy. Perhaps the **desolations** were the fields that were covered with the mutilated, dead corpses of the enemies of the Lord and his people Israel.

Furthermore, the psalmist declared, God **makes wars cease to the ends of the earth** (cp. Isa. 2:4; Ezek. 39:9; Mic. 4:3; Zech. 9:10), meaning that he would enforce his peace upon his defeated enemies. This imposed peace is inferred by the following statement: **He breaks the bow and shatters the spear, he burns the shields with fire** (cp. Isa. 9:4; Ezek. 39:9–10; Hos. 2:18; Mic. 4:1–4). Be assured that at the end of the day, God would win the victory while delivering his people.

46:10–11. Here there is a shift in the speaker from the psalmist to the Lord himself, who gave a universal command to those who were in uproar: "**Be still, and know that I am God.**" This is not a contemplative call for reflection but a redemptive call to surrender and to know God personally and intimately before his swift judgment is unleashed (Hab. 2:20; Zeph. 1:7; Zech. 2:13). Furthermore, the Lord continued, **I will be exalted among the nations**.

God brought destruction upon the threatening nations so his name might be exalted before them. The psalmist repeated the stanza found in verse 7, telling the reader who this fortress was: **The LORD Almighty is with us; the God of Jacob is our fortress**. This God was the Lord Almighty or literally Jehovah Sabbaoth (see "Deeper Discoveries"). Furthermore, he was the God of Jacob, the God of the patriarchs, the fathers of Israel.

> **MAIN IDEA REVIEW:** *The psalmist extols the ability of God to protect the righteous from their enemies by his ever-abiding presence.*

III. CONCLUSION

In Life and in Death

Martin Luther, by the time of his death on February 18, 1546, was already recognized as a major reformer and one of the leading figures in the history of the church. As he lay on his deathbed in Eisleben, Germany, his last words were, "Our God is the God from whom comes salvation: God is the Lord by whom we escape death." Firm until the end, Luther remained strong in his faith in the Lord. God was his mighty fortress, a bulwark never failing, both in life and in death. May he be so for God's people as they trust him completely in all their trials. God will guide in life; he will guard in death.

An ever-present help in times of trouble, God alone must be the mighty fortress to whom believers run in their most tumultuous hours. Only through faith in God and his Son, Jesus Christ, will believers find eternal salvation from the coming fury of God's wrath.

IV. LIFE APPLICATION

Refuge in the Lord

How easily it is for Christians to become fearful when circumstances and troubles rise up. The storms of life often seem so imposing that our hearts faint within us. Greater and greater a problem can grow, causing us to be discouraged and dismayed. This is why it is important to keep our eyes fixed on God. Focusing upon our problems breeds fear. But looking to God increases faith, bringing peace and comfort.

V. PRAYER

Oh Lord, you alone are our refuge and strength from the pains of life. Though the whole world may crumble around us, to your holy place in Zion we will look. Teach us to look to you so that we may direct others to look and see your works. Oh God of Jacob, open our eyes to see your exalted position above all this day. In Jesus' name. Amen.

VI. DEEPER DISCOVERIES

A. Refuge (46:1)

This word (Heb. *mahseh*) refers to a strong, secure structure that provides shelter from the elements (Isa. 4:6; Job 24:8). In the figurative sense, as it is used here, *mahseh* refers to a shelter from one's enemies who seek to harm and destroy, even kill. The psalmist understood that God was a refuge for his people (Pss. 14:6; 46:1; 61:3; 62:8; 71:7; 91:2,9). This word was used to emphasize God's watchcare over his people.

B. Help (46:1)

The word *help* (Heb. *ezra*) means support or assistance for one who is weak, vulnerable, and helpless. It is widely used in the Psalms to denote the assurance of God's all-sufficient help for the righteous (Pss. 22:19; 27:9; 40:17) as well as a plea for God's help (Pss. 35:2; 44:26). In other passages, it is used in requests by the psalmists for swift action by God when in extreme need (Pss. 22:19; 38:22; 40:13; 70:1; 71:12). By contrast, man's help is useless (Pss. 60:11; 108:12).

C. Strength (46:1)

This word (Heb. *oz*) is used throughout the Psalms to describe the attribute of God's omnipotence (Pss. 62:11; 63:2). It is used to speak of God's mighty voice that rules over all (Ps. 68:33) and his powerful arm that overcomes all opposition (Ps. 89:10). This strength was demonstrated by God in the exodus when he overcame all obstacles to lead Israel out of Egypt through the wilderness into the promised land (Exod. 15:13). This word is used to convey the security, stability, and safety to be found in God (Ps. 30:7), who is a strong tower (Ps. 61:3) and a mighty rock (Ps. 62:7). The strength of God is to be ascribed to him by his people through worship (Pss. 29:1; 96:7).

D. God's Presence (46:5)

The presence of God protected the city of Jerusalem from those who sought to destroy its inhabitants. Conversely, the absence of God, seen as a cloud departing the temple (Ezek. 10), allowed Nebuchadnezzar II and the Babylonian invasion to defeat the Southern Kingdom. This brought about the destruction of Jerusalem and the temple in 586 B.C. and the deportation of a large segment of the population to Babylon (cp. 2 Kgs. 24:1–25:21).

E. Almighty (46:7)

The term *Almighty* (Heb. *sebaot*) refers to a large number of hosts such as human armies (Exod. 7:4; Ps. 44:9), the celestial bodies, i.e., the sun, moon, and stars (Gen. 2:1; Deut. 4:19; Isa. 40:26), or heavenly creatures such as angels (Josh. 5:14; 1 Kgs. 22:19; Ps. 148:2). The title, "the LORD Almighty," or "the Lord of hosts," conveys the idea of the sovereignty of God over all powers in the universe. It also refers to God as the God of armies, both the heavenly army (Deut. 33:2; Josh. 5:14; Ps. 68:17) and the armies of Israel (1 Sam. 17:45). This word occurs 486 times in the Old Testament as a special name for God that speaks of his sovereign rule over the entire created sphere. The Lord is the mightiest warrior and the omnipotent King.

While having military connotations, *sebaot* goes beyond military meanings to encompass the forces of the realms, both heavenly and earthly (cp. 1 Sam. 17:45). Thus, the divine name, "LORD Almighty," or "Lord of hosts," denotes the God who reigns above all, showing himself ready to intervene on behalf of his people (Pss. 80:19; 84:1; Isa. 28:5–6; Amos 4:13; 5:8–9; 9:5–6).

F. Fortress (46:7,11)

This word (Heb. *misgab*) comes from the root *sagab*, which means "to be inaccessibly high." A fortress was a lofty place built on high elevations such as cliffs (Isa. 33:16) and sometimes was surrounded with fortified walls (Isa. 25:12). When used in the figurative sense, as in verses 7 and 11, it means that God was to the psalmist a stronghold of protection, his sure defense from the assaults of his enemies. In the Book of Psalms, *misgab* is connected with other biblical terms that promote the idea of protection such as rock, deliverer, and refuge (Pss. 9:9; 18:2), stronghold, deliverer, and shield (Ps. 144:2).

VII. TEACHING OUTLINE

A. Our Immovable Refuge (1–3)
  1. God is all-powerful (1a)
  2. God is all-present (1b)
  3. God is all-protecting (2–3)
     a. Though the earth moves (2a)
     b. Though the mountains fall (2b)
     c. Though the seas roar (3a)
     d. Though the mountains quake (3b)
 B. Our Inexhaustible River (4–7)
  1. God satisfies his people (4)
  2. God sustains his people (5–6)
  3. God saves his people (7)
 C. Our Invincible Ruler (8–11)
  1. God works judiciously (8–9)
  2. God reigns supremely (10)
  3. God protects powerfully (11)

VIII. ISSUES FOR DISCUSSION

1. What circumstances or people threaten and cause me to fear?
2. In what ways has the Lord Almighty made himself known in my life?
3. Have I spoken with people around me, calling them to come and see the works of the Lord?

Psalm 47

Singing in the Reign

"*T*he world dwarfs us all, but God dwarfs the world."

J . I . P a c k e r

I. INTRODUCTION

*G*od is the unrivaled sovereign over all, ruling all nations and peoples for his own purposes. This position of supremacy should cause all his people to rejoice, offering praise to him who presides over all. This triumphant theme is the subject of this psalm, a dramatic declaration of the kingship of God over all. Everyone and everything are under his rule, whether they acknowledge it or not. This is the essence of the message that is to be declared to the nations of the earth: God is the sole sovereign over all. He alone is God, possessing absolute authority and reigning in the heavens. Here is reason for the people of God to rejoice. God reigns over all the earth (vv. 2,7) including the nations (vv. 3,8), peoples (v. 3), Israel (vv. 4,9), enemies (v. 5), nobles (v. 9) and kings (v. 9).

According to the superscription, this psalm was "for the director of music," possibly meaning it was to be added to the collection of works to be used by the choir director in Israel's worship services. It may have been spoken by the director of the Levitical choir or by the choir itself when the psalm was used in the temple worship. Thus this psalm was "of the sons of Korah" referring to the Levitical choir comprised of descendants of Korah who were appointed by David to serve in temple worship.

II. COMMENTARY

> **MAIN IDEA:** *The psalmist declares that God is the great king over all the earth, reigning and ruling over all.*

A Rejoicing in God's Awesomeness (47:1–4)

47:1. All the **nations** are called to rejoice in **God**, who reigns over all. The phrase **Clap your hands** is an expression of enthusiastic celebration (2 Kgs. 11:12; Isa. 55:12). **Shout . . . with cries of joy** captures the same festive exuberance. This initial call to worship is universal, extended to everyone, inviting the nations into adoration of God. What follows is why God should be so fervently worshiped.

47:2–3. The phrase **How awesome** (a word related to "fear," or "reverence") **is the LORD Most High** describes God's unrivaled sovereignty. His throne is exalted over all. He is **the great King over all the earth**. All earthly kings have limited authority, but God's authority is absolute, universal, and unhindered. The phrase **He subdued nations under us** depicts the free exercise of God's sovereignty to defeat his enemies and bring victory to his people (Pss. 2; 110).

47:4. The phrase **He chose our inheritance for us** means that God has given the promised land to his chosen people, Israel (Gen. 12:7; 17:8; Exod. 3:8; Deut. 1:8). This land of Canaan is described as **the pride of Jacob** or that in which Israel, represented by the patriarch Jacob, takes great delight. It is God's chosen ones **whom he loved**. This **love** represents an expression of his special, elective, covenantal "love" (Mal. 1:2).

B Rejoicing in God's Ascension (47:5–7)

47:5–7. The psalmist declared that **God** had **ascended** victoriously to his throne to rule over the earth amid **shouts of joy** and **the sounding of trumpets**, a reference to the ram's horns, announcing the appearance of God as King (Exod. 19:16,19). Having won the victory for his people in battle, he assumed his place of rightful rule again. **Sing praises to God** is spoken four times in verse 6. This phrase acts as a repetitious call for God's people to give glory to the victorious God. The reason for this boisterous worship is clear. The psalmist declared, **For God is the King of all the earth**. He alone is worthy of our praise because only he reigns over all.

C Rejoicing in God's Authority (47:8–9)

47:8. God reigns over the nations, causing all their efforts—even their evil rebellion—to carry out his eternal purposes predetermined long ago. **God is seated on his holy throne**, executing his sovereign will and doing as he pleases.

47:9. Anticipating the final day, **The nobles of the nations** (national leaders) would **assemble** before God's throne to acknowledge his kingship. They would do so **as the people of the God of Abraham**, meaning they would also surrender themselves to his authority in humble adoration. In the end many Gentiles will believe, be redeemed, and live under God's rule. Thus, let all people rejoice, recognizing his absolute, universal government over all mankind.

III. CONCLUSION

Ultimately, this psalm looks ahead to God's rule through Christ over all the earth during the millennium (Rev. 20). In that glorious day Christ will inaugurate his earthly reign over all the nations immediately following the time of his second coming (Rev. 19:15). Triumphantly, the kingdoms of this world will become the kingdoms of our Lord and his Christ (Rev. 11:15). When that climactic time comes for Christ to establish his kingdom upon the earth, he will descend from heaven and make his grand ascent to his throne in Jerusalem as the unrivaled King of kings and Lord of lords.

In the face of the present uncertainties and international crises, may believers rejoice that God reigns on high and is soon to send his Son back to this earth to inaugurate his kingdom on earth (1 Thess. 4:13–18; 1 Cor. 15:51–58).

IV. TEACHING OUTLINE

A. Rejoice in God's Awesomeness (1–4)
  1. The call to worship (1)
    a. Clap your hands (1a)
    b. Shout for joy (1b)
  2. The causes of worship (2–4)
    a. God reigns over the earth (2)
    b. God reigns over the nations (3)
    c. God reigns over Israel (4)
B. Rejoice in God's Ascension (5–7)
  1. The cause for worship (5,7a)
    a. God reigns from on high (5a)
    b. God reigns over the earth (7a)
  2. The call to worship (5–6,7b)
    a. Shout for joy (5a)
    b. Sound the trumpets (5b)
    c. Sing praises (6,7b)

C. Rejoice in God's Authority (8–9)
   1. The causes of worship (8–9b)
      a. God reigns over the nations (8)
      b. God reigns over the redeemed (9a)
      c. God reigns over the kings (9b)
   2. The call to worship (9c)
      a. Declare God's greatness (9c)
      b. Declare God's exaltation (9c)

Psalm 48

Zion, City of Our God

"*Glorious things of Thee are spoken, Zion city of our God; He whose word cannot be broken, Formed thee for his own abode: On the Rock of Ages founded, What can shake thy sure repose? With salvation's walls surrounded, Thou may smile at all Thy foes.*"

John Newton

I. INTRODUCTION

Jerusalem was the chosen city of God, the place where his divine glory had been most fully put on display. In Jerusalem David united the kingdom and brought the ark of the covenant. In Jerusalem Solomon built the temple, a house for God's glory. In Jerusalem Christ presented himself to Israel, was crucified, buried, raised, and ascended back to heaven. In Jerusalem the gospel of the risen Christ was first preached and the church was launched. And to Jerusalem Christ will return at the time of his second coming.

This psalm, a hymn of celebration, focuses upon God's activity in the holy city, Jerusalem. God is in the midst of the city of David, and she will not be shaken or defeated by enemies. Situated high on Mount Zion, a place of immense beauty and special prominence, Jerusalem is the city of God, the joy of the entire earth. The psalmist offered praise to God who dwelled in Zion to protect her.

According to the superscription, this psalm is "a song," meaning a psalm of praise, probably sung with orchestral accompaniment and was led by "the sons of Korah."

II. COMMENTARY

> **MAIN IDEA:** *The psalmist praises God for the glory of his holy city Jerusalem and the care with which God oversees it.*

A The Description of Zion (48:1–2)

48:1. The greatness of the city of God, Jerusalem, can be explained only by the greatness of **God**. It is **the LORD** who uniquely dwells within, showing his glory **in the city**. Thus, this psalm begins with the declaration, **Great is the LORD, and most worthy of praise**. His presence makes great the city upon the **holy mountain**.

48:2. As an impregnable fortress, elevated above the surrounding terrain, Jerusalem was **beautiful in its loftiness**. As **the joy of the whole earth**, it was admired by other nations (1 Kgs. 10:1–13). Comparable to **Zaphon**, the supposed residence of the chief Phoenician god El, **Mount Zion** was the city of the one true God. Mount Zion was so named because of the ridge upon which Jerusalem was built.

B The Defense of Zion (48:3–8)

48:3. Because God was in Jerusalem's **citadels**, unusually present within her, he was **her fortress** (Heb. *misgob*, "a high safe place"). This means God himself, not her exterior walls, was Jerusalem's true defense. The strength of her **citadels** and **her fortress** was the presence of God within her walls, not chariots or horses, ramparts, or towers.

48:4–7. Invading **kings** may join **forces** to attack the holy city, but they have been defeated. They **fled in terror . . . like that of a woman in labor** overcome with intense **pain**. As great merchants **ships** from **Tarshish** sailing the Mediterranean Sea would capsize and be **shattered by an east wind**, so advancing armies against Jerusalem would be **destroyed** by God.

48:8. Thus, **God** himself **makes** the holy city **secure forever. The LORD Almighty**, literally "the Lord of armies," is the defender of the city (see "Deeper Discoveries," 46:7).

C The Delight of Zion (48:9–11)

48:9–11. Within the protected walls of Jerusalem, worshipers **meditate on** God's **unfailing love** in spite of the threats of advancing foreign armies. When defeated soldiers of the healthier nations are forced to retreat back to their homes, **praise reaches to the ends of the earth** as they report God's victory over them. But more than that, **Mount Zion** herself rejoices, along with the villages of Judah, because their inhabitants know and worship God who performs many awesome judgments.

D The Destiny of Zion (48:12–14)

48:12–14. The psalmist concluded by calling on God's people to consider the lasting security of Jerusalem. They should walk about Zion in order to inspect her towers, ramparts, and citadels. Only then would they discover that her true greatness did not consist of rock or mortar. It was not in what human eyes could see, but in God who was for ever and ever. This unseen defender would be their guide when Jerusalem was under attack.

III. CONCLUSION

Ultimately, this psalm looks ahead to the last days in the time of the great tribulation when Jerusalem will be surrounded by hostile foes. But even in Zion's darkest hour, which is still in the future, God will come to her defense. The Messiah, the Lord Jesus Christ, will descend from heaven and return to the Mount of Olives in order to defend his ancient city (Isa. 24:23; Rev. 14:1). In the last days, God will provide his greatest defense of the holy city in the second coming of his Son, Jesus Christ. Until then, great unrest will characterize the Middle East, and Jerusalem will be a city of perpetual crisis.

IV. TEACHING OUTLINE

A. The Description of Zion (1–2)
  1. It is established by God (1)
  2. It is elevated in glory (2)
B. The Defense of Zion (3–8)
  1. God is her fortress (3)
  2. God is her defender (4–7)
    a. Kings fought the city (4)
    b. Kings fled the city (5)
    c. Kings feared the city (6–7)
  3. God is her security (8)
C. The Delight of Zion (9–11)
  1. She ponders God (9)
  2. She praises God (10)
  3. She rejoices in God (11)
D. The Destiny of Zion (12–14)

Psalm 49
The Poverty of Prosperity

I. INTRODUCTION

*T*he greatest fool is the person who lives for the pursuit of riches in this world, only to lose his soul eternally. The rich may appear to be content, but their prosperity is only temporary. Death is approaching for everyone, and the grave is the great equalizer. Departure from this world will remove all our possessions, never to be enjoyed again. So why live for what you can never keep? The greatest treasure of all is to possess what lasts forever and truly satisfies—eternal life. Only those who put their trust in God will have true riches in this life. Furthermore, only they will be redeemed from death and live forever with God.

This is the theme of this psalm, a song that stands as a warning to all who put their trust in riches. The psalmist counseled the godly not to envy the wicked in their prosperity or to be seduced by their possessions. They will all suffer destruction. Instead, they should live for God and the unseen world yet to come where true riches are found.

II. COMMENTARY

A The Psalmist's Call (49:1–4)

MAIN IDEA: *The psalmist calls on believers not to envy the prosperity of the wicked because they will soon perish.*

49:1–4. The psalmist called upon **all** the **peoples** of the world, both those in **low and high** positions of society. He requested that they **hear** what his mouth would speak. This was a man who had to be heard. He conveyed **words** of wisdom (Heb. *hokma,* "skill in successful living") which would give **understanding** (Heb. *tebuna,* "prudence, insight, discretion"). In words similar to Solomon, the psalmist declared, **I will turn my ear to a proverb** to teach it. Others would hear this psalm sung accompanied by **the harp.**

🅱 The Psalmist's Counsel (49:5–15)

49:5–6. The psalmist was perplexed about why he should **fear when evil days** came—evil days caused by **wicked deceivers.** He knew that the success of those who trusted in their wealth and boasted of their great riches was short-lived. Although they strutted about in pride, God would bring them down in judgment.

49:7–9. Wealth cannot **redeem** (Heb. *pada,* "to ransom, purchase") **the life of another** and provide escape from death. **Life** is such a **costly** commodity that it may not be purchased. **No payment,** even from the wealthiest man, is **ever enough** to deliver from the certain destiny of death and decay.

49:10–12. It is obvious to any observer of life that wise men die just like **the foolish** and **the senseless.** Death is no respecter of persons. All will **leave their wealth to others** when they die (Eccl. 2:19–21). **Their tombs** will become their new **houses,** even though their names are attached to large estates which remain. No matter how much money a person may have, he cannot escape death for he will **not endure.** He will die like **the beasts that perish** (Eccl. 3:19).

49:13–15. The phrase **those who trust in themselves** refers to the proud rich. Their fate will be **like** that of **sheep** being led to **the grave. The upright will** ultimately triumph over the wicked, whether in this life or in the life beyond **the grave.** Regarding the righteous, the psalmist knew God would **redeem** their lives **from the grave,** paying the ransom himself. This is a payment that no man could pay (vv. 7–8). Thus, the psalmist knew that God would take him **to himself** after death (Ps. 73:24), a fate unlike that of those who trusted in themselves.

🅲 The Psalmist's Caution (49:16–20)

49:16–19. Because the wicked would perish in spite of their wealth (vv. 6–14), the godly must not let the prosperity of the rich captivate their hearts. **Do not be overawed when a man grows rich,** the psalmist warned. The rich who die would **take nothing with** them (cp. Eccl. 5:15). Why envy the temporal trappings of a meaningless life? After death the wealthy who trusted in their riches would **never see the light of life.**

49:20. Ending this psalm with dramatic bluntness, the psalmist described a person **who has riches** in this world yet does not understand spiritual truths about God, eternity, and redemption. Such a person **is like the beasts that perish.** They have fleeting riches that will soon be taken away by death. It is far better to fear God.

III. CONCLUSION

The fleeting pleasures of worldly riches are seductive and deceptive, able to pull people away from God. Instead of being duped and defrauded, the righteous must look to God for true satisfaction. Jesus reasoned, "What good will it be for a man if he gains the whole world, yet forfeits his soul? Or what can a man give in exchange for his soul?" (Matt. 16:26). The implied answer is so obvious that our Lord did not even need to answer it. Clearly, it is unprofitable to gain this world but lose heaven in the exchange. Such is eternal loss.

So powerful is the deceitfulness of riches that Jesus declared, "It is hard for a rich man to enter the kingdom of heaven" (Matt. 19:23). The righteous, whether poor or rich, must trust God, not earthly gain. People should be rich in faith and not seek to lay up treasure in heaven.

IV. TEACHING OUTLINE

A. The Psalmist's Call (1–4)
   1. He calls to all peoples (1–2)
     a. To the low and high (1–2a)
     b. To the rich and poor (2b)
   2. He cries out with prudence (3–4)
     a. Dispensing wisdom (3a)
     b. Giving understanding (3b)
     c. Speaking proverbs (4a)
     d. Explaining riddles (4b)
B. The Psalmist's Counsel (5–15)
   1. Fear not the ungodly (5–14)
     a. They cannot redeem themselves (5–9)
     b. They cannot rescue themselves (10–12)
     c. They cannot rule themselves (13–14)
   2. Focus upon the God of life (15)
     a. He alone can redeem us (15a)
     b. He alone can reunite us (15b)
C. The Psalmist's Caution (16–20)
   1. The rich will leave everything (16–17)
     a. His riches (16a,17a)
     b. His splendor (16b,17b)
   2. The rich will never see life (18–19)
     a. Prosperity now (18)
     b. Perdition forever (19)
   3. The rich will perish like beasts (20)

Psalm 50

Worthless Worship

"The dearest idol I have known, Whatever that idol be,

Help me to tear it from thy throne, And worship only thee."

W i l l i a m   C o w p e r

Psalm 50

I. INTRODUCTION

There will be times when worship may seem by all outward appearances to be proper and acceptable, even skilled and beautiful. But as God observes it, he sees it for what it really is. Halfhearted, apathetic praise is an abomination to God. Such worthless worship flows from external ritual and empty routine and is devoid of right heart attitudes. God detests such meaningless activity because the heart of such worshipers is far from him (cp. Isa. 1:11–15; Matt. 15:7–9; Rev. 3:15–16).

This psalm provides insight into those times when worship is wrong. A courtroom setting is represented in which God summons his people to appear before him to answer for their lukewarm worship. He does not condemn them for failing to provide sacrifices to him but for approaching him with self-sufficient attitudes, devoid of thanksgiving (vv. 14–15). God rejects such worship.

"Asaph," the author of this psalm, was one of David's three choir leaders, a leader of the Levitical choir and director of music for Israel's corporate worship (1 Chr. 6:31–40; 15:17–19; 16:5,7,37). This is the first of twelve psalms written by Asaph (Pss. 73–83). It is prophetic and pointed in tone. This psalm calls the people of God to fervent, focused worship.

II. COMMENTARY

> **MAIN IDEA:** *The psalmist states that those who go through the motions of worship without heartfelt praise and obedience will be judged by God.*

A God Summons to Judgment (50:1–6)

50:1–2. This psalm begins with Asaph, the psalmist, describing a heavenly courtroom scene in which God himself, the Judge, comes to preside and render his verdicts. Three names are used for God: **the Mighty One, God**, and **the LORD**. This is the God who **summons the earth** to appear in the judgment before him.

50:3–6. God comes to act in judgment over the earth **and will not be silent**. When the Lord speaks, **a fire devours** those **before him** who await his decree. **He summons** heaven and earth to his courtroom to **judge** them, even his own people **who made a covenant with** him. As he speaks, **the heavens** speak with one voice, proclaiming his righteous judgments, because **God** is **judge**—and none other.

B God Speaks in Judgment (50:7–15)

50:7–13. The actual words of God speaking to his people in judgment, correcting and reproving them, are recorded: **Hear, O my people, and I will speak** and **testify against you**. What is the divine charge? He did **not rebuke** the people for their **sacrifices** but because they wrongly assumed that the Lord had **need** of their **bull** or **goats**. All the sacrificial animals already belonged to God, even **the cattle on a thousand hills**. **Every bird** and all **creatures of the field** belong to God. Even if God **were hungry**, he would **not tell** his people, as if he were dependent on them. Such is not the case. God does not eat the flesh of animals as if he needed them for sustenance.

50:14–15. God wants his people to acknowledge their dependence on him, not vice versa. They must offer **thank offerings** to God for his abundant mercies to them, fulfill their **vows** to him, and call upon God when in trouble. The thank **offerings** and **vows** were not commended but voluntary offerings offered in gratitude (Lev. 7:12; 22:29). These offerings were to be eaten by those giving the offerings because they symbolized communion and fellowship with God. Only after these prerequisites were fulfilled would God **deliver** his people because they had honored him.

C God Sentences to Judgment (50:16–23)

50:16–17. With increasing intensity God rebuked the wicked who recited his **laws** and agreed to his **covenant** without any genuine conviction. These religious hypocrites, in spite of their presence in public worship, actually hated God's **instruction** and rejected his word.

50:18–21. God exposed several examples of sin in these religious pretenders. They joined in the sinful practices of **a thief** and **adulterers** and those who spoke against their **brother**. Chief among their sins was the tragic illusion that God was **like** sinful man, a blasphemous trivialization of a holy God. Such desecration of God's flawless character draws his rebuke.

50:22–23. God addressed those **who forget God**. The stinging indictment of these pseudo-worshipers is that God will **tear** them **to pieces** and leave no one to **rescue** them. But the true worshiper who **sacrifices thank offerings** will be honored by the Lord.

III. CONCLUSION

Scripture makes plain that God seeks worshipers who give him authentic praise from a pure and contrite heart. Not just any worship will do. Specifically, God seeks those who will worship him in spirit and truth (John 4:24), meaning inwardly with the proper heart attitude, yielding humbly to the truth of Scripture. Such worship is to be a lifestyle, a way of living, an ongoing pattern of absolute surrender to God (Rom. 12:1). If God detests fleshly worship, he delights in true worship from holy and humble hearts (Phil. 3:3). May true worshipers offer praise that glorifies God. He alone is worthy.

IV. TEACHING OUTLINE

A. God Summons to Judgment (1–6)
  1. He calls all people (1–2)
  2. He confronts all people (3–6)
B. God Speaks in Judgment (7–15)
  1. He challenges worshipers (7)
    a. I will speak (7a)
    b. I am sovereign (7b)
  2. He convicts worshipers (8–13)
    a. Not for their animals (8)
    b. But for their attitudes (9–12)
  3. He corrects worshipers (14–15)
    a. He wants grateful hearts (14a)
    b. He wants obedient wills (14b)
    c. He wants dependent lives (15)
C. God Sentences to Judgment (16–23)
  1. The evidence presented: disobedience (16–20)
    a. They recite God's Word (16)
    b. They reject God's Word (17–20)

2. The execution spoken: destruction (21–22)
   a. God has been silent (21a)
   b. God now speaks (21b)
   c. God now sentences (22)
3. The expectation required: delight (23)

Psalm 51
True Confessions

━━━━━┤ Q u o t e ┝━━━━━

"*A*Christian must never leave off repenting, for I fear

he never leaves off sinning."

C h a r l e s   H .   S p u r g e o n

I. INTRODUCTION

Wet, Dry, but Not Clean

A college freshman went to the dorm laundry room with his dirty clothes bundled into an old sweatshirt. Embarrassed by how dirty his clothes were, he never opened the bundle but just pushed the clump of dirty clothes into the washing machine. When the machine stopped, he pushed the bundle into the dryer. Finally, he took the still-unopened bundle of clothes to his room—only to discover that they were not clean.

There is a moral to this story for Christian lives. God says, "Don't keep your sins in a safe little bundle. Bring them out in the open one by one and confess them so they may be cleansed." Confession of our sins to God is essential. What is confession? The word means "to say the same thing." Confession is agreeing with God about our sin. It also involves repentance, or a turning away from the sin confessed, no longer embracing it.

Psalm 51 is one of the most graphic pictures of confession of sin found anywhere in the Bible. This psalm contains David's humble prayer for forgiveness as he sought cleansing from God after a massive moral breakdown in his life. As the superscription of the psalm suggests, it was written after David's sin of adultery with Bathsheba which was followed by the sin of murder against her husband Uriah (2 Sam. 11). Almost a year after this sin, God directed the prophet Nathan to confront David with his sin, and only then was David quick to repent.

This psalm contains David's confession of sin, and it emphasizes the importance of true repentance. It provides insight into the nature of genuine confrontation of sin in a believer's life. When a Christian sins, he must confess his sin immediately with deep contrition. Only then can he enjoy the forgiveness of God that leads to a restoration of his walk with the Lord. A study of this psalm reveals the characteristics of genuine repentance.

II. COMMENTARY

True Confessions

MAIN IDEA: *David confesses and repents of his sin against God, pleading for divine forgiveness and mercy.*

A A Cry for Forgiveness (51:1–2)

SUPPORTING IDEA: *David begins by entreating God to forgive his sin, pleading for God to be compassionate.*

51:1a–b. David understood that forgiveness with God was based solely on divine mercy, **unfailing love**, and **compassion** (Heb. *rehem*, "the bowels," i.e., sympathy), not human merit. The opening appeal, **Have mercy on me, O God**, was a request not for what he deserved—painful discipline—but for what he desperately needed—divine grace. David was aware of his need to have God's mercy **according to** his **unfailing love** and **great** compassion. He appealed to God to act in accordance with his loving nature.

51:1b–2. This appeal for forgiveness is pictured in three ways. First, the phrase **Blot out my transgressions** means to wipe away David's sinful acts of rebellion and willful deviation. As if David's sins were accurately written by God in a book, he pleaded that his acts of sinful rebellion would be removed from record (cp. Exod. 32:32; Num. 5:23). Second, comparing himself to a foul garment stained with filth, David prayed, **Wash away all my iniquity**, as a person would wash dirty clothes. Third, he pleaded, **cleanse me from my sin**. This pictured the purification necessary for temple worship under the ceremonial law. This threefold request expressed David's desire for complete forgiveness by the Lord.

B A Confession of Sin (51:3–6)

SUPPORTING IDEA: *David confesses the heinousness of his sin by acknowledging that he understands the seriousness of his wrongdoing.*

51:3. Painfully aware of his sin, David acknowledged, **I know my transgressions**. His conscience pressed guilt from his sin to his mind, so much so that his sin was **always before** him, haunting his mind.

51:4. David recognized that his sin was against God, not just against others, including Bathsheba, Uriah, and the nation. He confessed, **Against you, you only, have I sinned**. David's sin was treason against God, since David had **done what** was **evil in** God's **sight**. Fully acknowledging his sin, David called it what it was—not weakness but wickedness, not an accident but an atrocity. He accepted God's verdict, admitting that God was **proved right** when he spoke against David's sin **and justified** when he judged him. No alibis or shifting of blame here. David offered no lame excuses to God, only a full confession of his own guilt that deserved divine justice.

51:5. Delving deeper into the source of this matter, David stated that his problem was a corrupt heart, saying, **Surely I was sinful at birth**. He entered this world a sinner in nature long before he became a sinner in actions. In fact, this internal corruption predated his **birth**, actually beginning nine months earlier when he was **conceived** in the womb. It was at conception that the Adamic sin nature was transmitted to him. The problem of what he did—sin—arose from what he was—a sinner.

51:6. David knew that he fell short of God's desire for his life. His words **Surely you desire truth in the inner parts** indicate that David had been living a lie before God by attempting to cover up his sin. But he went on to say, **You teach me wisdom**. Wisdom should lead us to act honestly and openly with our sin against God. Only a fool would try to hide his sin before the Lord. This was a tragic role David had been playing.

𝕮 A Call for Cleansing (51:7–9)

SUPPORTING IDEA: *David asks that God remove the stains of his sins while bringing spiritual renewal.*

51:7. This verse expresses another plea for pardon. **Cleanse me with hyssop** alludes to the image of a leper seeking cleansing. In such a case, hyssop would be dipped in blood and sprinkled seven times on the leper at the altar (cp. Lev. 14:6). Accordingly, David saw himself as a spiritual leper in need of divine cleansing. The removal of his sin would occur through the shed blood of the coming Messiah, Jesus Christ (cp. Heb. 9:22). Only then would he **be whiter than snow** (cp. Isa. 1:18).

51:8. David's words **Let me hear joy and gladness** would be the result of the forgiveness he sought (cp. Ps. 32:1–2). **Let the bones you have crushed rejoice** indicates how crushed he was by Nathan's indictment (cp. 2 Sam. 12:1–14). His whole body ached under the heavy burden of sin.

51:9. David asked God to **hide** his **face from** his **sins**, which were ever before him. In other words, "Forgive me so you will not look upon **my sins** any longer." Returning to the accounting imagery, he prayed, **Blot out all my iniquity**. Only then could David be right with God.

D A Commitment to Holiness (51:10–12)

SUPPORTING IDEA: *David asks God to renew his steadfast spirit and restore the joy of his salvation while not punishing him according to his transgressions.*

51:10. Having confessed his sin and received God's forgiveness, David prayed for a pure heart so he would not fall back into sin. **Create in me a pure heart** is something that only God could do. Only God could **renew** his **heart** with a **steadfast spirit** of purity.

51:11. David's words **Do not cast me from your presence** do not indicate that he feared he would lose his salvation. Rather, it was a plea that God would not remove his divine power from David's life. Thus, he asked God not to take his **Holy Spirit** from him. He feared being set aside in serving God, a severe discipline he deserved and would suffer if God did not accept his confession.

51:12. David pleaded with God to **restore** to him the joy of his **salvation**. Sin and joy cannot exist in the same heart at the same time. The two are mutually exclusive. Note that David did not request that his salvation be restored but the *joy* of his salvation. He wanted a **willing spirit** so he could obey God's Word and persevere in holiness.

E A Consecration of Life (51:13–17)

SUPPORTING IDEA: *David vows to teach sinners the ways of God while reaffirming his commitment to God.*

51:13. Once forgiven, David promised God that he would **teach transgressors your ways.** He would communicate the truth that God would afflict them for their sin. This would also include the pardon they would receive when they confessed their sin. Psalm 32 is the fulfillment of this vow. As a result of such teaching, **sinners** would **turn back to** God by acknowledging and forsaking their sin.

51:14–15. David prayed, **Save me from bloodguilt, O God**. The enormity of his sin continued to burden David. He knew that he deserved the death penalty for his sins. This sobering reality caused him to seek forgiveness. Once pardoned, David declared, **My tongue will sing of your righteousness** to others who needed to seek the same forgiveness.

51:16–17. David knew that God did not desire only an animal **sacrifice** or **burnt offerings** from him for his sin. **The sacrifices** that God required were a **broken spirit** and a **contrite heart**. Humility before God and brokenness over sin are expressions of genuine confession, and David knew it.

F A Concern for God's Glory (51:18–19)

SUPPORTING IDEA: *David requests that God's blessings will rest upon Jerusalem and the sacrifices offered within the walls of the city.*

51:18. David was aware of the close connection between his personal holiness as the king of Israel and the national blessings from God which the people would enjoy. Character does count. The sins of leaders affect other people as well as themselves. Thus, he prayed, **Make Zion prosper** by strengthening and protecting **the walls of Jerusalem** from foreign attack. Now that David had been renewed, he prayed that the nation would be renewed. First personal renewal, then corporate renewal.

51:19. Only **then**, once forgiven, would David present **righteous sacrifices** to God with a right heart. Only **then** would **whole burnt offerings** and **bulls** be offered in order to **delight** God. The heart must be right before sacrifices can be right.

MAIN IDEA REVIEW: *David confesses and repents of his sin against God, pleading for divine forgiveness and mercy.*

III. CONCLUSION

What's Wrong with the World?

Many years ago there was a famous correspondence in the *London Times* under the subject, "What is wrong with the world today?" In this editorial the writer researched and reported on the various moral and social ills plaguing the world. The article called for an answer rhetorically from the readers. The best letter mailed to the editor was a reply from the distinguished G. K. Chesterton.

> Dear editor:
> What's wrong with the world?
> I am.
> Faithfully yours,
> G. K. Chesterton

Unquestionably, the heart of the world's problems is the sinfulness of man. But more than that, the source of each person's problems is sin, most specifically, one's *own* sin. Every Christian must set a watch over his own life. Once sin is made known to his heart, confession must follow immediately. The good news of Jesus Christ is that a full forgiveness of sin is offered for all who will repent of their sin and come to him. The apostle John declared, "If we confess our sins, he is faithful and just and will forgive us our sins and purify us from all unrighteousness" (1 John 1:9).

Such confession involves repentance; the two are inseparably bound together. May all who are aware of their sin come to the one and only fountain filled with blood drawn from Immanuel's veins, plunge beneath that flood, and lose all their guilty stains.

IV. LIFE APPLICATION

A Broken and Contrite Heart

When believers come before God to confess their sin, the inner spirit they desire is brokenness and humility. All sin grows from the root of pride, which is the exaltation of our will over the will of God. Likewise, pride always involves a hardening of our hearts. They become less pliable and less responsive to the things of God. But when the righteous confess their sin to God, these aspects of sin must be reversed. Instead of hardness of heart, there must be brokenness, or a shattering of ego and a crushing of pride. The hardened soil of the soul must be broken up if it is to receive God's commands and respond to him.

Rather than self-exaltation, there must be a contrite heart, one that is crushed and lowered in the presence of God. This is the sacrifice that God desires—a broken and contrite heart. From such a life arises the sacrifice of a sweet-smelling aroma that is acceptable and pleasing to God. Let believers clothe themselves with humility as they confess their sins to God. The Lord is opposed to the proud, but he gives grace to the humble.

V. PRAYER

Oh God, we entered this world estranged from you, enslaved to sin from the womb. Yet you in your grace rescued us for yourself. You made us a people to be called by your name, a royal priesthood, a holy nation. Lord, we ask you to shower your mercy upon us by blotting out our transgressions, washing away our iniquities, and cleansing us from our sins. Against you alone have we committed treason and acted in a way that is not worthy of our calling. Restore the joy of our salvation and give to us a willing spirit so we will be sustained in your way. May we offer to you the proper sacrifices of a broken spirit and a contrite heart. In the name of our Lord Jesus Christ. Amen.

VI. DEEPER DISCOVERIES

A. Truth (51:6)

This word (Heb. *emet*) is a derivative of *aman*, which denotes the idea of certainty, dependability, firmness, or sureness and is often translated as "truth" or "faithfulness." This word is used 127 times in the Old Testament, often to speak of the divine attribute of truthfulness (cp. Gen. 24:27; Exod. 34:6; Pss. 25:5; 31:5; 71:22; Jer. 4:2; 42:5). It is also applied to the words and commandments of God because he possesses truth (cp. 1 Kgs. 17:24; 2 Chr. 18:15; Pss. 26:3; 30:9; 43:3; 69:13; 86:11; 91:4; 108:4; 117:2; 119:142,151; 138:2). Likewise, it is a characteristic of those who know God (Exod. 18:21; Neh. 7:2; Ps. 15:2; Zech. 8:16). Here in Psalm 51:6, the word *truth* means "moral integrity and reliable living" or that which conforms to the standard of God's truth.

B. Wash (51:2,7)

The word *wash* (Heb. *kabas*) occurs fifty-one times in the Old Testament. It was commonly used by the Hebrew people to speak of laundering or washing clothes. Thus, this word compares the forgiveness of sin with the washing of clothes, removing what is dirty and defiling. *Kabas* also refers to ceremonial cleanness (Exod. 19:10,14; Num. 8:7; 19:7; Lev. 11:25). It occurs thirty-one times in Leviticus where the ceremonial cleansing of the worshiper, or cleansing from idolatry, is mentioned (cp. Jer. 2:22; 4:14). David uses the word in a spiritual sense, requesting that he be cleansed as with hyssop (v. 7), an intentional reference to the instruction of lepers to use a hyssop for cleansing their dreaded disease (Lev. 14:6–7). To David, his sin had defiled and stained him to the point that he had to be cleansed within. This was something that only God could do.

C. Pure (51:10)

The word *pure* or *clean* (Heb. *tahor*; KJV) is an adjective that occurs ninety-four times in the Old Testament and is a derivative of the verb *taher*. The word is used either in the material, ceremonial, or ethical sense. David uses the term in its moral sense in asking God to purify his heart, meaning to take away his impurity, filth, and defilement. The cleaning of the pollution or spiritual contamination that enters the heart of man is impossible with man. Job asked, "Who can bring what is pure from the impure?" (Job 14:4). In contrast to the sinful pollution within man, God's words are absolutely pure (Ps. 12:6), and his eyes are "too pure to look on evil" (Hab. 1:13). The Lord alone can make sinful man clean (cp. Jer. 13:27; 33:8; Ezek. 36:25,33; 37:23).

D. Broken (51:17)

This word (Heb. *shabar*) occurs 147 times in the Old Testament. It means "to bring destruction," "to break, shatter, or ruin." It was used of the breaking of nations and peoples in divine judgment (Jer. 28:2,11; Ezek. 30:21; Amos 1:5) and destroying, or dashing to pieces, certain objects or idols (Exod. 32:19; 34:1; 2 Kgs. 11:18; Jer. 43:13). Here it is used metaphorically to describe a condition of the heart in which a person is shattered by sin or by the scorn of others (Ps. 69:20).

VII. TEACHING OUTLINE

A. A Cry for Forgiveness (1–2)
　1. Blot out my sin (1)
　2. Wash away my sin (2)
B. A Concession of Sin (3–6)
　1. My sin is before me (3)
　2. My sin is against God (4)
　3. My sin is within me (5–6)
C. A Call For Cleansing (7–9)
　1. Cleanse me of guilt(7)
　2. Cheer me with gladness (8)
　3. Clear me of charges(9)
D. A Commitment to Holiness (10–12)
　He desires from God a:
　1. Pure heart (10a)
　2. Steadfast spirit (10b)
　3. Empowered life (11)
　4. Joyful heart (12)
　5. Submissive will (12b)
E. A Consecration of Life (13–17)
　1. I will teach others (13)
　2. I will praise God (14–15)
　3. I will humble myself (16–17)
F. A Concern for God's Glory (18–19)
　1. May God's work prosper (18)
　2. May God's pleasure be full (19)

VIII. ISSUES FOR DISCUSSION

1.　Do I have a proper view of myself and my sin nature?
2.　Do I spend adequate time confessing sin to the Lord each day?
3.　When confessing my sin, do I identify the specific sins that I am guilty of committing?
4.　Do I praise God after having confessed my sins?

Psalm 52

Divine Intervention

"*L*et us lean on God with all our weight. Let us throw

ourselves on his faithfulness as we do on our beds, bringing

all our weariness to his dear rest."

C h a r l e s   H .   S p u r g e o n

Psalm 52

I. INTRODUCTION

A psalm of exhortation, this is the first of four consecutive psalms written by David "for the director of music" (Pss. 52–55). In these psalms David expressed confidence in God when under attack by an evil enemy. As indicated by the title, David was running from Saul and fled to the priest Ahimelech and the priests of Nob for provisions and guidance (1 Sam. 21:7). This psalm was written "when Doeg the Edomite had gone to Saul and told him: 'David has gone to the house of Ahimelech.'" Saul was so angered by the report that he had the entire community massacred by Doeg.

In this psalm David declared the kind of man Doeg was, as indicated by his slaughter of so many people. As the psalmist took refuge in God, as in a high tower of safety, he awaited the total destruction of his enemy by the Lord. Here is a song of bold, confident trust in God in spite of the threats of Doeg.

II. COMMENTARY

MAIN IDEA: *David denounces the perversity of his enemy and pledges himself anew to God.*

A David's Foe (52:1–4)

52:1. David began with a question of accusation, **Why do you boast of evil?** Castigating his enemy Doeg, the leader of Saul's men, he lamented, **Why do you boast all day long?** His foe, mighty in doing evil, bragged about his constant rebellion against truth and right. But he was **a disgrace in the eyes of God**, David declared—an embarrassment to heaven, a violation of everything God desired.

52:2. Rebuking the depravity of his opponent, David chided, **Your tongue plots destruction**. He was conspiring and organizing harm to destroy others. Full of perversity, Doeg's mouth was like **a sharpened razor**, cutting, penetrating, and killing. What he said brought the bloody destruction of others (Jas. 3:6,8). His words were consistent with his deceitful practices.

52:3–4. The reality of the problem, David said, was his wicked heart: **You love evil rather than good, falsehood rather than speaking the truth.** His sense of morality was wrong. His affections were corrupt and twisted by his depravity. He loved what he should hate and hated what he should love. Thus, his words were deceitful.

B David's Fury (52:5–7)

52:5–7. David pronounced the ultimate destruction of God upon his arrogant enemy. He declared, **God will bring you down to everlasting ruin**. This would be a just punishment for his ruthless dealings. Death would remove him forever. So devastating would his destruction be that **the righteous** would **see** it and be motivated to **fear** God. The godly would **laugh** in derision at the absurdity that anyone would oppose God's will.

C David's Faith (52:8–9)

52:8–9. In contrast to Doeg, David's faith was in God. He was **like an olive tree flourishing in the house of God**, meaning productive, prolific, and prosperous (cp. Hos. 14:6). Expressing his reliance on God's grace, David vowed that he would **praise** God **forever** for his many exploits and **hope** in God's **name**. God's name represents the sum total of all God's holy attributes. Repeating his vow, David determined, **I will praise you in the presence of your saints**.

III. CONCLUSION

In this psalm David placed his confidence in the name of God when under attack from Doeg. He relied on God with a heart full of praise. Every believer today must do the same. When surrounded by troubles and under attack, we should claim God as our stronghold, fortress, and refuge. God will protect those who call on him and hide themselves in him. May all trials and dangers serve to drive God's children deeper into his presence. He will destroy the unrighteous while giving victory to his people.

IV. TEACHING OUTLINE

A. David's Foe (1–4)
1. His pride is disgraceful (1)
2. His plotting is destructive (2)
3. His perversity is deceitful (3–4)

B. David's Fury (5–7)
1. The destruction of the ungodly (5)
   a. God will bring you down (5a)
   b. God will snatch you up (5b)
2. The derision by the godly (6–7)
   a. The righteous will fear (6a)
   b. The righteous will jeer (6b–7)

C. David's Faith (8–9)
1. His trust is in God (8)
   a. He is rooted in God (8a)
   b. He is fruitful for God (8b)
2. His thanks is to God (9)
   a. For what God does (9a)
   b. For who God is (9b)

Psalm 53

The God Who Rules Fools

"To be an atheist requires an infinitely greater measure of faith than to receive all the great truths which atheism would deny."

Joseph Addison

I. INTRODUCTION

Foolish Unbelief

D. L. Moody, the great evangelist of the nineteenth century, was preaching to a large gathering of people, proclaiming the gospel of Christ. In the crowd that day was an obstinate atheist who decided to disrupt the meeting. This unbeliever wrote down one word on a piece of paper—*Fool*—folded it and handed it to the usher, saying he had an urgent message to be delivered to Moody. The usher carried it to the platform in the middle of the sermon and placed it on the pulpit. Assuming an emergency, the evangelist stopped his message and read the note. There it was, one word—*Fool*. He looked and saw the atheist waving at him. Without missing a beat, Moody announced, "A most remarkable thing has just occurred. Many times I have received a letter in which the sender has forgotten to sign his name. But this is the first time anyone has signed his name but forgotten to write the letter."

This word *fool* is also God's appraisal of anyone who tries to live without him. It is nothing short of spiritual insanity to attempt to live apart from God. Yet so many people around the world live without God and depend on themselves for all their needs. The person who spurns the truth of his Word, God says, is a fool. This was David's appraisal of the entire human race apart from the grace of God. Unbelief makes a person a fool—not a person who is mentally deficient but one who is morally depraved and spiritually destitute.

An amazing similarity exists between Psalm 14 and Psalm 53. Psalm 14 was probably written first and then later adapted into Psalm 53 as a result of a dramatic victory that God had given to his people. In this psalm, "a *maskil* of David," the author lamented the total depravity and moral foolishness of the human race. The superscription reveals that it was to be sung "according to *mahalath*," possibly the first word of a well-known tune to which this psalm was to be sung.

II. COMMENTARY

The God Who Rules Fools

MAIN IDEA: *David sees the total depravity and final destruction of the human race; this prompts his longing for the deliverance of God's people.*

A The Fool Described (53:1)

SUPPORTING IDEA: *The corruption of the human race and its denial of God flows from a corrupted nature that is inherently evil and void of good.*

53:1a. Here is David's accurate assessment of the human race. **The fool** does not mean a person of mental incompetence, but a person of moral insensitivity and spiritual ignorance. He rejects and ignores God and says, **There is no God**. The problem lies deep within **his heart** (Heb. *leb*, "the totality of man's inner nature")—the seat of his mind, emotions, and will. At the very center of his being, in the depth of his soul, he rejects the knowledge of God. He is a practical atheist, not necessarily an intellectual one. He lives as if there were no God with whom he has to deal. He orders his life as if there is no heaven, no hell, no final judgment, no eternal punishment.

53:1b. The result of this blatant rejection of God is a corrupt life. The refusal of God always leads to the corruption of a person's life; the two are inseparably bound together. Lumping together all unbelievers, David declared that **they all are corrupt** in their inner person or essential being. That is, their nature is totally depraved (cp. Jer. 17:9). Thus, **their ways are vile**, meaning "injustice or iniquity." In other words, all their dealings are an abhorrence to a holy God because they are so unjust, lacking a sense of what is right. Because their personal character is corrupt, their practical conduct is inevitably the same.

53:1c. Consequently, David's summation is, **There is no one who does good**. No one apart from God's grace practices what is pleasing to the Lord. All their deeds are displeasing to God, even their best efforts to do good works. All their righteous deeds are as "filthy rags" in God's sight (Isa. 64:6).

B The Fool Discovered (53:2–4)

SUPPORTING IDEA: *The entire human race lacks spiritual insight and therefore has turned away from God to evil activities.*

53:2. Following David's insight, God's perspective is now given. **God looks down from heaven on the sons of men**, which means that he is investigating the human race, judging lives, scrutinizing hearts, auditing actions, and weighing motives. No creature is hidden from his sight (Heb. 4:13). God looks to **see if there are any who understand** the insanity of their rejection of him. Are there any who grasp the seriousness of their rebellion against God? Have they carefully considered the ramifications of their unbelief?

The implied answer is *no*. Lost sinners do not understand what awaits them as they continue in their evil ways. Furthermore, God surveys the earth for **any who seek** him. It is implied that there are none who seek him, not even one (Ps. 14:1–3; Rom. 3:10–12). Without the Holy Spirit all people are running away from God.

53:3. Rather than seeking God, the opposite occurs. **Everyone has turned away** from God to go his own way. Left to themselves, lost people will always run away from God, never to him (cp. Isa. 53:6). **They have together become corrupt** like soured milk. Repeating verse 1, David stated, **There is no one who does good, not even one**. God's thorough investigation reveals that there are no exceptions to vile wickedness that has infected the human race.

53:4. David now reasoned, **Will the evildoers never learn** that their ways are an offense to God? Do they not understand that their end is eternal destruction? This is another rhetorical question implying the negative answer, "No, left to themselves, they will never learn." These **evildoers** are **those who devour my people**, bringing great persecution and opposition to true believers. With a voracious appetite for harm, they devour and consume God's **people as men eat bread**. Therefore, it is not surprising that from this state of spiritual deadness, they **do not call on God**.

C The Fool Destroyed (53:5)

SUPPORTING IDEA: *Ultimately, God will defeat and destroy the godless who attack his people.*

53:5. David anticipated the judgment of the wicked, a devastation so certain that the verbs are recorded in the past tense as if it has already occurred.

There they (the godless who oppose God) **were overwhelmed with dread** (Heb. *pahad,* "terror, panic"). They will be terrified with great fear because God will unleash his fiery judgment and wrath upon them. Those who do not fear God will be filled with great **dread** because he will come in destructive power to rout his enemies.

Regarding this outpouring of divine wrath, David stated to true worshipers, **God scattered the bones of those who attacked you.** The scene pictures a battlefield in which God defeated his enemy's advance. No disgrace was considered greater for a foreign power than to have the **bones** of their defeated army **scattered** across the battlefield rather than buried. This is how overwhelming God's devastating judgment of the wicked will be.

D The Faithful Delivered (53:6)

SUPPORTING IDEA: *The awaited Messiah from Zion will deliver Israel, restoring the fortunes of the past.*

53:6. David concluded on a positive note by asking God to rescue his people from all his enemies. **Oh, that salvation** (Heb. *yeshua,* "help, deliverance, victory") **for Israel would come out of Zion!** The salvation requested here is God's temporary rescue from the onslaught of fools that were previously mentioned (vv. 1–4). **When God restores the fortunes of his people,** David declared—looking to the distant future when the Messiah would establish his millennial reign upon the earth (cp. Rev. 20)—**let Jacob rejoice and Israel be glad.** This jubilation would be the result of God's victorious reign over the **fortunes** of **Israel.**

MAIN IDEA REVIEW: *David sees the total depravity and final destruction of the human race; this prompts his longing for the deliverance of God's people.*

III. CONCLUSION

Lower and Lower

C. S. Lewis once quipped, "No clever arrangement of bad eggs will make a good omelet." The same can be said about the total depravity of mankind. No matter how cleverly man may try to arrange his life, he is still inherently evil and incapable of being good on his own. The Bible says that man was created a little lower than the angels. One thing is clear—he has been getting lower and lower ever since. There is only one known cure for the deadly plague of sin—and that is the Lord Jesus Christ. He alone can remove the heart of stone and replace it with a heart of flesh. May all whose hearts are prepared by God's Spirit call upon the name of the Lord.

IV. LIFE APPLICATION

The Problem of the Human Heart

If we are to understand the world rightly, we must have an accurate understanding of human depravity. No Pollyanna view of mankind will suffice. The truth is that man's nature is corrupt, perverse, and sinful. "The heart is deceitful above all things and beyond cure. Who can understand it?" (Jer. 17:9). This inborn corruption extends to every part of man. As a result of the fall of Adam and the spread of sin to the entire human race, his mind, emotions, and will have been polluted by sin. Consequently, "there is no one who does good" (Ps. 53:1,3). All people have turned away from God. This is the fundamental problem of all mankind.

It has been said that "the heart of the human problem is the problem of the human heart." So it is. Man's problems are not external, such as a need to change his environment. The point at issue is internal; the problem is his heart. This is why all people must be born again. They need a new heart, a new nature that loves God and seeks to pursue holiness. We must proclaim the gospel and serve as witnesses for Christ if people and society are to be changed. The only way to authentic, lasting change is through the power of the gospel of Jesus Christ (cp. 1 Cor. 15:1–5).

V. PRAYER

God, we praise you for redeeming us for yourself. Though we were corrupt, vile, and evil and were traveling away from you, you saved us and called us to yourself. You made us a people when we were not a people, adopting us into your family by the blood of Jesus Christ. Our salvation is in him alone because he is our salvation that has come out of Zion. Therefore we rejoice in Jesus Christ. We pray this in the name that is above all other names—the name of the Lord Jesus Christ. Amen.

VI. DEEPER DISCOVERIES

A. Corrupt (53:1)

This word (Heb. *shahat*) occurs 151 times in the Old Testament and is used to speak of decay, ruin, destruction, waste, or death. The word describes the total devastation of Sodom and Gomorrah (Gen. 13:10; 19:29), cities (Judg. 20:42; 2 Sam. 24:16), the destruction of Amaziah (2 Chr. 25:16), the utter defeat of the pagan nation Babylon, causing its collapse and demise (Jer. 51:11), crops (Judg. 6:4), the slaying of enemy soldiers (Judg. 20:21,25,35), the destruction of the Syrians (2 Chr. 24:23), and the destruction of Israel (Hos. 13:9). Here the term is applied to the self-destruction caused by sin and spiritual decay of sinful hearts.

B. Understand (53:2)

The word *understand* (Heb. *sakal*) means "to comprehend" or "to grasp." It was often used to speak of one's spiritual understanding of God and the things of God. The prophet Isaiah recorded, "They know nothing, they understand (*sakal*) nothing; their eyes are plastered over so they cannot see, and their minds closed so they cannot understand" (Isa. 44:18; cp. Ps. 14:2; Isa. 41:20, 52:15; Jer. 9:23–24). Here it implies the spiritual blindness of those who are corrupt within their own hearts.

C. Evildoers (53:4)

This word *evildoers* or the phrase "workers of wickedness" (Heb. *awen*; NASB) is one of the many Hebrew words used in reference to sin. It covers a wide range of sinful acts, including falsehood, idolatry, iniquity, and unrighteousness. Thus, the word emphasizes all aspects of sin, including its planning, expression, and consequences.

D. Shame (53:5)

The word *shame* (Heb. *bosh*) means "to be confounded, disappointed, ashamed, disgraced, or perplexed." The root occurs 155 times in the Old Testament, mostly in Psalms and Isaiah. This word conveys the idea of the public embarrassment a person feels after a plot to sin has failed and ended in disgrace. It means to become pale or to blush when one's sin is exposed and judged by God. It conveys the total defeat and utter humiliation of the evildoer. Disenchantment and despair follow those who are put to shame (Ezra 9:6; Isa. 1:29; 30:5; Dan. 9:7).

VII. TEACHING OUTLINE

A. The Fool Described (1)
  1. His heart rejects God (1a)
  2. His life refuses good (1b,c)
    a. He is morally corrupt (1b)
    b. He is ethically vile (1c)
B. The Fool Discovered (2–4)
  1. He is observed by God (2)
  2. He is offensive to God (3–4)
    a. All have turned away (3a,4c)
    b. All have turned corrupt (3b)
    c. All have turned evil (3c,4a,b)

C. The Fool Destroyed (5)
    1. He is scattered by God (5a)
      a. Their dread is increased by God (5a)
      b. Their bones are strewn by God (5a)
    2. He is shamed by God (5b)
D. The Faithful Delivered (6)
    1. His salvation is by God (6a)
    2. His restoration is by God (6b)
    3. His celebration is in God (6c)

VIII. ISSUES FOR DISCUSSION

1. Why does the entire human race not seek God?
2. To whom does the Lord give spiritual understanding?
3. If the corruption of mankind is universal, why do some people trust the Lord while others refuse to trust him?

Psalm 54

With Help from Above

"*I* sometimes think that the very essence of the whole Christian position and the secret of a successful spiritual life is just to realize two things. . . . I must have complete, absolute confidence in God and no confidence in myself."

D .   M a r t y n   L l o y d - J o n e s

I. INTRODUCTION

*L*ife's trials strip away any vestiges of self-confidence and anchors the soul to a deeper confidence in God. In such a humbling dependence, the believer calls on the name of God and finds strength in the midst of his weaknesses. Again and again in life, this is precisely where David found himself, calling on the Lord for help in a crisis too big for him to solve on his own. Psalm 54 is the record of his intentional reliance upon God, the third in a cluster of four psalms written by David (Pss. 52–55) in which he prayed for divine deliverance when he was pursued by Saul.

In this situation David had rescued an Israelite border town from the Philistines but was still considered a traitor to Saul (1 Sam. 23; 26). This "*maskil* of David" was for the "director of music" and was to be accompanied by "stringed instruments." This psalm was written "when the Ziphites had gone to Saul and said, 'Is not David hiding among us?'" (cp. 1 Sam. 23:19–23; 26:1–5). The Ziphites were men from David's own tribe, the tribe of Judah. Although he was being hotly pursued by ungodly men who sought to take his life, David trusted in the Lord to deliver him.

This psalm is a confession of confidence in God that he would protect David from his enemies. Amid much disillusionment, David turned to the Lord who was his help (v. 4). Here is encouragement for any believer who has been wrongly accused.

II. COMMENTARY

MAIN IDEA: *David petitions God to deliver him from his enemies who want to kill him.*

A David's Trial (54:1–3)

54:1–2. Surrounded by many enemies, David cried out, **Save me, O God, by your name**. It was an urgent prayer for deliverance from life-threatening danger. God's **name** represents all that God is, the sum total of his perfect attributes. **Vindicate me by your might** is a call by David for God to prove David's innocence by rescuing him. **Hear my prayer** was a pressing appeal that God would not just **listen to the words** of David's prayer but actually answer his prayer.

54:3. The word **strangers** means either foreigners or apostate Israelites. In this case it was the latter, Saul and the Ziphites (cp. 1 Sam. 23:19; 26:1). David stated, **Ruthless men seek my life**. They were attacking David because they were **without regard for God** (cp. John 15:18–20) and thus no regard for God's man.

B David's Trust (54:4–5)

54:4. With unassailable confidence, David declared, **Surely God is my help**, the one who would deliver him from the threats of his enemies (Pss. 30:10; 72:12; 118:7). In the midst of this attack, the Lord would sustain him until rescue came.

54:5. David asked, **Let evil recoil**, or come back and harm **those who slander me**. May they be harmed by their own wicked devices, he prayed. David appealed to God to **destroy them**, according to his **faithfulness**. God must react against evil, and David left it to God to do so, not taking vengeance into his own hands.

C David's Triumph (54:6–7)

54:6. Anticipating the certainty of divine help, David burst forth in spontaneous praise: **I will sacrifice a freewill offering to you** (cp. Lev. 3; 7:16; Num. 29:39). This offering was for what had already been and what would yet be received from God: In exultation, David noted, **I will praise your name, O LORD, for it is good**. He did not allow his bleak circumstances to color his knowledge of God, but he remained convinced that God was good, even in the midst of his adversity. Such is the focus of strong faith.

54:7. David had the assurance that he had been heard, even before God rescued him. He acknowledged that he had been **delivered from all** his **troubles** in the past. Surely God would do so again in the present. Confident of victory David stated, **My eyes have looked in triumph on my foes.** Once again, as he found himself in yet another dire straight, he trusted in God, believing he would grant the victory.

III. CONCLUSION

In every painful ordeal, God is a help to his people. He is the all-sufficient one who sustains them through deep waters. God is his people's deliverer who, according to his perfect timing, rescues the righteous from harm. God is good all the time and is to be trusted in every stormy trial. Even when attacked by others, believers should praise God who rescues his people from trouble. One of the secrets to trusting God is to remember his faithfulness in past times. Like David in this psalm, we should remember that the many triumphs God has given us over our foes in the past is proof that we may trust him in the present.

IV. TEACHING OUTLINE

A. David's Trial (1–3)
  1. My appeal is to God (1–2)
    a. Save me (1a)
    b. Vindicate me (1b)
    c. Hear me (2a)
    d. Listen to me (2b)
  2. My Attack is by the godless (3)
    a. By strangers (3a)
    b. By sinners (3b)
B. David's Trust (4–5)
  1. God is my help (4)
  2. God is my sustainer (5)
C. David's Triumph (6–7)
  1. I will praise God's name (6)
  2. I have reason to praise God (7)
    a. He delivered me (7a)
    b. He defeated my foes (7b)

Psalm 55

Betrayed by a Friend

"It is infinitely better to have the whole world for our enemies and God for our friend, than to have the whole world for our friends and God for our enemy."

John Brown

Psalm 55

I. INTRODUCTION

Perhaps no greater pain racks the human heart than to be betrayed by a close friend or confidante. The capacity for emotional injury is far deeper in such a case than if the attack had been instigated by an avowed enemy. So it was with David in this individual lament, Psalm 55. He had been betrayed by a former close companion, one who was previously an intimate friend. Because of the treachery of this traitor, he responded in prayer to God, expressing deep, personal anguish (vv. 1–8) and righteous anger, (vv. 9–15), as well as assurance that God would deal with this matter (vv. 16–23).

This psalm is described as "a *maskil* of David." This threat had absorbed his thoughts, ultimately leading to his confidence in God to protect him and right the wrongs he had suffered.

II. COMMENTARY

> **MAIN IDEA:** David laments his betrayal by an intimate friend and expresses confidence that he will be delivered from harm by God.

A David's Anguish (55:1–8)

55:1–3. With a deep sense of urgency, David pleaded, **Listen to my prayer, O God.** He was **distraught at the voice of the enemy.** The reference is to a powerful conspiracy in Jerusalem under the covert leadership of someone previously close to David, much like that of Absalom (cp. 2 Sam. 15–18). These rebels had brought **suffering upon** him, David lamented, and had reviled him **in their anger.** Rather than seeking his own vengeance, he turned to God while suffering the persecution and slander aimed at him.

55:4–8. David's **heart**, or his entire inner being, was **in anguish** (Heb. *hul*, "to turn in a circle," "to whirl, twist"). He was torn up on the inside, or tied in knots, figuratively speaking. Apparently he feared that his own **death** was close at hand. With graphic language, he declared that **fear** (Heb. *yare*, "adject terror"), **trembling** (Job 21:6; Isa. 21:4; Ezek. 7:18), and **horror** (Heb. *pallasut*, "fearfulness") had **overwhelmed** (Heb. *kasa*, "to cover up, clothe") him.

He wished for **the wings of a dove** that he might **fly away** from this predicament and escape to a remote place of **rest**, even if it were a **desert**. Living in an isolated wilderness, yet at peace, would be better than being in the king's palace in turmoil. Longing for quiet relief, David confided, **I would hurry to my place of shelter**, meaning a place far away from conspiring, corrupt people.

B David's Anger (55:9–15)

55:9–11. Motivated by righteous anger, David prayed for God to overturn the plots of his foes. **Confuse the wicked, O LORD**, he petitioned. In other words, throw their plans into disarray. This request was prompted by a desire for the common good, since he saw **violence and strife in the city** caused by these enemies. Like wild animals they were prowling about, looking for innocent and helpless people to prey on. **Malice and abuse, destructive forces**, and **threats and lies** were left in their wake.

55:12–15. If David had been opposed by **an enemy** or a known **foe**, he could have defended himself. But he had been betrayed by a close **companion**, he who was a **close friend**, one with whom he had **enjoyed sweet fellowship** in the **house of God**. This made this threat exceedingly difficult and painful. Thus, speaking with holy indignation, David prayed, **Let death take my enemies by surprise**. He desired God's swift destruction of all his **enemies** who were opposing God's leadership through him.

ℂ David's Assurance (55:16–23)

55:16–19. In spite of this mounting threat to his life, David expressed confidence that the Lord had heard him. He vowed to **call to God**, knowing that **the** LORD would save him. The Lord would ransom (Heb. *pada*, meaning "rescue") David from the battle waged against this once-close friend and his duped followers. Now more than ever, David rested in **God**, **who is enthroned forever** as a sovereign ruler over all circumstances (Pss. 103:19; 115:3). The Lord would hear the evil threats of these malicious people who had **no fear of God**.

55:20–21. David reflected further on the treachery of his former **companion**, now turned betrayer. He described this turncoat as one who had violated **his covenant**, meaning he had broken all oaths of loyalty to David. **His speech** was **smooth as butter** and **oil**, slick and soothing, yet **war** was **in his heart** (Ps. 52:2). What hypocrisy belonged to this so-called friend—this snake in the grass!

55:22–23. Addressing those who had maintained their integrity and remained loyal to him, David encouraged them to cast their **cares on the** LORD and he would sustain them. When believers commit themselves and their burdens to the Lord, they will be upheld by God's mighty hand (1 Pet. 5:6–7).

David was certain that God would **bring down** his enemies to **the pit of corruption**. Perhaps this alluded to the grim deaths of Absalom (2 Sam. 18:9–15) and Ahithopel (2 Sam. 17:23). He expressed his conviction that these men would **not live out half their days**, meaning they would die premature deaths. **But as for me**, David pledged, **I trust** (Heb. *batah*, "to attach oneself to") **in you**.

III. CONCLUSION

Whatever a person sows, that will he also reap. If he sows to the flesh, he will reap the flesh. If he sows seeds of deceit, treachery, and betrayal, he will reap a bitter harvest of destruction and death. God is not mocked. This psalm serves as a sobering reminder that God hears everything—not only the prayers of the righteous but the perversity of the ungodly. Because God is holy and just, his saints who are often betrayed and afflicted will find a sure defense in the Lord. Rather than seek their own revenge, believers need only trust in God.

IV. TEACHING OUTLINE

A. David's Anguish (1–8)
 1. He is under siege (1–3)
  a. By troubling thoughts (1–2)
  b. By threatening enemies (3)
 2. He is under sorrow (4–8)
  a. Anguish fills his heart (4–5)
  b. Escape fills his mind (6–8)
B. David's Anger (9–15)
 1. God, confuse the wicked (9–11)
  a. They spread violence (9)
  b. They suffer abuse (10)
  c. They speak lies (11)
 2. God, confound the traitor (12–14)
  a. A foe can be endured (12)
  b. A friend cannot be endured (13–14)
 3. God, condemn the wicked (15)
C. David's Assurance (16–23)
 1. God saves (16)
 2. God hears (17)
 3. God ransoms (18)
 4. God afflicts (19–21)
 5. God sustains (22)
 6. God destroys (23)

Psalm 56

Delivered from Danger

"Faith is a living and unshakable confidence, a belief in the grace of God so assured that a man would die a thousand deaths for its sake."

Martin Luther

I. INTRODUCTION

*O*nly God can save his people, not only from their sins but from suffering as well. When surrounded by troubles, believers should call upon God for deliverance, trusting that he will rescue them out of their distress. Psalm 56 is such a song of trust, one in which David prayed to God to save him when he was under attack by enemies.

The historical background is an incident in David's life when he fled from Saul to Gath, the hometown of Goliath. In Gath he took up temporary residence among the Philistines (1 Sam. 21:10–15), only to escape to the cave of Adullam when hunted by his foes (1 Sam. 22). The enemies in this psalm were not the Philistines but Saul and his men who dogged his steps in an attempt to take David's life. Understanding this, David's first reaction was to be fearful (vv. 3–4,11). But through it all, David put his trust in the Lord, who prevailed on his behalf.

According to the psalm's title, it was to be sung according to a tune commonly known as "A Dove on Distant Oaks."

II. COMMENTARY

> **MAIN IDEA:** *David calls upon God to deliver him from his enemies, drawing comfort from his trust in the Lord.*

A David's Troubles (56:1–2)

56:1–2. David voiced an urgent appeal for God's help when he was attacked by his enemies. **Be merciful to me**, he cried out, **for men hotly pursue me**. These were fierce foes who pressed their **attack** against him. Thus, his life was in great danger as **slanderers** pursued him, **attacking . . . in their pride**.

B David's Trust (56:3–4)

56:3–4. Under this attack David acknowledged his human frailty by saying, **When I am afraid, I will trust in you**. In the midst of this trouble, David was resolute in his trust in God. **What can mortal man** (Heb. *basar*, "flesh," man in his weakness) **do to me?** This was a rhetorical question implying the negative answer: nothing except what God in his sovereignty permits. David reasoned that man is powerless to thwart God's eternal purposes in his life.

C David's Trials (56:5–6)

56:5–6. The problem was that **all day long** evil men were twisting his words, David declared, **plotting to harm me**. He was the object of their slanderous smear campaign as they misrepresented his words. They lurked in the shadows, ready to strike at a moment's notice. They were watching his **steps**, **eager** to pounce and **take** his **life**. This trial was real, painful, and potentially devastating.

D David's Triumph (56:7–9)

56:7–9. Do not **let them escape** divine retribution, David pleaded. He wanted God in his anger, which is just and vengeful, to deal with them according to their sin. **Bring down the nations** in judgment, he asked, because of their evil dealings. Thus, this threat must have come from men who belonged to foreign nations outside Israel. David asked that God would **record** his **lament**, which means to take note of his sorrow. God would surely act on his behalf. **List my tears on your scroll** was a request for God to **record** them in his register in heaven. Such injustice would scream for God's actions to defend and deliver David. His **enemies** would **turn back** because God would come to his aid.

E David's Thanksgiving (56:10–13)

56:10–11. David concluded with a strong declaration of praise to God, even in the face of mounting troubles. **In God** and his **word**, David would trust without being afraid. **What can man do to me?** he asked. Again, the implication is that man can do nothing except what God in his sovereignty permits.

56:12–13. David declared that he was **under vows** to **present** his **thank offerings** to God. No matter what might happen, David resolved to offer thanks to God. He had every reason to praise God in the present because God had delivered him from death in the past. Surely God would rescue him in the future. This deliverance would serve a great purpose, namely, that David would walk before God **in the light of life**, another way of saying abundant life, or the full blessedness of life in **God**.

III. CONCLUSION

Whenever the believer finds himself surrounded by those who wish him harm, he must put his trust in the Lord. Only then will anxiety be replaced with assurance and panic with peace. Terrifying circumstances will come into the life of every believer. In such hours of desperation, David can serve as an example of confident trust. In the Lord we have contentment, composure, and peace in the face of overwhelming troubles.

IV. TEACHING OUTLINE

A. David's Trouble (1–2)
  1. Men pursue me (1–2a)
  2. Men persecute me (2b)
B. David's Trust (3–4)
  1. I courageously trust God (3)
  2. I confidently trust God (4)
C. David's Trials (5–6)
  1. Men distort my words (5)
  2. Men devise my harm (5b)
  3. Men dog my steps (6a)
  4. Men desire my life (6b)
D. David's Triumph (7–9)
  1. God, rout my enemies (7,9)
  2. God, record my tears (8)
E. David's Thanksgiving (10–13)
  1. Praise God for his Word (10–11)
  2. Praise God for his working (12–13)

Psalm 57

Soul Refuge

"*As* sure as God puts his children in the furnace, he will

be in the furnace with them."

C h a r l e s H . S p u r g e o n

Psalm 57

I. INTRODUCTION

*T*he God who permits believers to fall into fiery trials is the same God who can deliver them from these troubles. When surrounded by adversity, God's people should call upon him to rescue them out of their troubles. This was the experience of David in Psalm 57, a heartfelt prayer for deliverance when he was threatened by Saul. This lament psalm was a *miktam* written by David "when he had fled from Saul into the cave." The psalm was "for the director of music" and was to be sung "to the tune of 'Do Not Destroy.'" Though threatened by Saul, David expressed unwavering confidence that God would rescue him from this desperate situation.

Psalm 57 is connected to the previous psalm, Psalm 56, in its historical background and poetic language. A soul-stirring refrain is repeated in this psalm, "Be exalted, O God, above the heavens" (vv. 5,11), much like the chorus that connects Psalm 42 with Psalm 43. This refrain calls upon God to exalt himself, to exercise his sovereignty by reversing David's troublesome circumstances and to show himself to be Lord over all. Here is a humble appeal for God's mercy by David.

II. COMMENTARY

> **MAIN IDEA:** *Confident that the Lord will answer, David petitions God to deliver him from the danger of his enemies.*

A David's Petition (57:1–3)

57:1. David began with the passionate plea that God would **have mercy** on him. His petition is repeated twice to express urgency and is an identical opening to Psalm 56. Ultimately, it was in God that his **soul** took **refuge** for protection. As David trusted in God, he realized he was under **the shadow of God's wings**. This pictures the divine care he sought that was compared to the care of a mother bird for her young (cp. Ps. 17:8).

57:2–3. God Most High is a divine name which emphasizes that God is lifted up above all his creation, over all circumstances, and that he rules over all. This sovereign God, lifted up and transcendent, **fulfills his purpose** without any wavering, according to his eternal decree. God can be trusted, David said. He sent from **heaven** and saved him, rebuking those who hotly pursued him. He was referring to Saul and his skilled warriors. God's overruling purposes are always a great motivation for prayer.

B David's Persecutors (57:4–6)

57:4–5. Detailing his persecutors, David lamented, **I am in the midst of lions** and **ravenous beasts**. He pictured these **men** with **teeth** like **spears and arrows**, meaning they had **tongues** which were like **sharp swords**. They were able to inflict disabling, deadly harm. Such is the power of the tongue! In the midst of describing these attackers, David's mind suddenly turned to God: **Be exalted, O God, above the heavens; let your glory be over all the earth**. This God-centered focus on divine supremacy was the strength of his life in every adversity, a sure anchor for his soul in the midst of trouble. David requested that **God** show his sovereign **glory** by coming to his rescue.

57:6. Returning to the detailed portrayal of his foes, David continued exposing them before God. Like a hunter seeking prey, they had **spread a net** for his **feet** to trap him (Pss. 7:15; 9:15). But God had promised to keep the feet of the righteous from slipping (Pss. 37:24; 55:22). Instead of ensnaring David, **they** had **fallen into** the **pit** they had dug for him.

C David's Praise (57:7–11)

57:7–8. Still looking heavenward, David steadied his heart in God. **My heart is steadfast**, he repeated twice, underscoring the firm resolve of his soul to trust in God. Rather than pouting about his plight, he declared, **I will sing**

and make music in worship of almighty God. He roused his own heart, **Awake, my soul!** as if to say, "Let not my soul be sluggish or dull toward God." David vowed to awaken before **dawn** to begin the day by offering fervent praise to God.

57:9–10. Looking beyond the confinement of the cave in which he found himself, David vowed, **I will praise you, O LORD, among the nations** and **the peoples**. Once he was delivered from his trouble, his worship of God would be his public witness to the unbelieving Gentile **nations**. David must praise God because his love was great, **reaching to the heavens**. Because God's name was high and lifted up, so David's praise must be.

57:11. Repeating the earlier spoken refrain, David concluded, **Be exalted, O God, above the heavens**. This was an appeal for God to demonstrate his sovereignty by intervening in David's life, reversing his plight and turning back his enemies. Such a rescue, a deliverance, would display God's **glory over all the earth**.

III. CONCLUSION

No matter what difficulty may come to believers, they must take refuge in God, calling upon him for mercy. God is a Savior who delights in rescuing his people, not only from their sin but also from their suffering and sorrow. In an hour of trouble, let the righteous lift to God the petition for him to exalt himself above the heavens. He will display his sovereignty over their lives by causing all things to work together for his glory and their good. May hearts be awakened to sing his praise!

IV. TEACHING OUTLINE

A. David's Petition (1–3)
  1. God, have mercy (1)
  2. God, hear me (2–3)
    a. God serves his purposes (2)
    b. God sends his love (3a)
    c. God saves his people (3a)
    d. God scatters his enemies (3b)
B. David's Persecutors (4–6)
  1. Enemies slander his name (4)
  REFRAIN: Be exalted, God (5)
  2. Enemies spread their net (6)
C. David's Praise (7–11)
  1. I will sing to God (7–8)
    a. Purposefully (7)

      b. Passionately (8a)
      c. Preeminently (8b)
2. I will sing about God (9–10)
      a. Among the nations (9)
      b. To the heavens (10)
REFRAIN: Be exalted, God (11)

Psalm 58

Character Counts

Quote

"*Character is what you are in the dark.*"

D . L . M o o d y

Psalm 58

I. INTRODUCTION

An inseparable connection exists between a person's character and his conduct. The former is the source of the latter. Some people claim that a leader's private life does not matter, that we should be concerned only about his public performance. But what a leader is internally will always show up externally. This is the focus of Psalm 58, a lament psalm filled with righteous anger about corrupt leaders who lord it over the people. This psalm is a passionate prayer of David for God to judge corrupt judges and to make right every wrong suffered at their hands. This psalm is a *miktam* written "for the director of music" and "to the tune of 'Do Not Destroy.'" God, the supreme judge over heaven and earth, must destroy them swiftly.

Contained in this psalm is David's outcry against human injustice on the earth and his earnest plea that God would devastate and destroy those ungodly rulers and judges who harmed the righteous. David was confident that God would eventually punish all wrongdoers and reward good. This is the only hope in a day when persecuted believers find themselves in a polluted world suffering oppression for righteousness' sake. In such dark hours, believers must call out for God to exalt himself and demonstrate his sovereignty over ungodly leaders.

II. COMMENTARY

> **MAIN IDEA:** *David denounces ungodly rulers and petitions God to judge them while protecting the godly.*

A David's Indictment (58:1–5)

58:1. In the first verse David set the subject and tone of this psalm; it is a scathing indictment of unjust rulers. **Do you rulers** (Heb. *elohim,* "gods"; in this passage it is a reference to "earthly rulers who govern the affairs of men") **indeed speak justly?** This is a rhetorical question implying a negative answer. **Do you judge uprightly among men?** Again the implied answer is negative, clearly stated in the next verse.

58:2–3. David answered his own question: **No, in your heart you devise injustice.** This diagnosis indicates that the problem was within depraved human nature (cp. Jer. 17:9; Pss. 14:1–3; 53:1–3). As a result, the evil fruit of their life showed up when their **hands** meted **out violence on the earth.** In other words, their hands did **violence** because their hearts were vile. This heart problem went back to their **birth** in sin. Thus, **from the womb they** were **wayward** and spoke **lies.** These evil leaders were acting consistently with their inherited sin nature (cp. Ps. 51:5).

58:4–5. The phrase **Their venom**—referring to the speech issuing from their mouth—was **like the venom of a snake,** poisonous and deadly. They were **like . . . a cobra that has stopped its ears,** meaning deaf to sound reason. They were stubborn and incorrigible, and they ignored all calls for justice.

B David's Imprecation (58:6–11)

58:6–7. In the face of such human injustice, David had no choice but to call on God to intervene. Appealing for divine wrath, David prayed, **Break the teeth in their mouths, O God.** That is, let the very weapons they use— their mouths—be destroyed as one would **tear out . . . the fangs of the lions.** Further, **let them vanish like water that flows away.** That is, let them be absorbed into the ground and utterly vanish from the scene. **When they draw the bow** to pronounce their decisions, **let their arrows** be blunted to do no more harm.

58:8–9. Using two more potent metaphors, David declared, let these ungodly rulers be **like a slug melting away as it moves along,** or drying up to nothing. Likewise, let them be **like a stillborn child,** dying before further harm can come from them. David's request was that they **not see the sun,** or no longer be allowed to live and cause harm to God's people. Speaking about the swiftness of God's judgment, David declared that these wicked leaders would be **swept away**, suddenly removed by God.

58:10–11. The righteous who had suffered under these unjust leaders **will be glad** at their destruction because God will bring justice. Then, once God intervenes, the godly will **bathe their feet in the blood of the wicked**. This pictures a victorious army walking through the battlefield to inspect the carnage of the defeated foe. In the end, men will say, **Surely the righteous still are rewarded**. God's people will exclaim, **Surely there is a God who judges the earth**. When God has judged the unjust leaders, people will see that sin cannot win and right will prevail.

III. CONCLUSION

Government leaders are appointed by God for the good of the people. They are to serve as his agents through whom he works to provide law and order for society (Rom. 13:1–6). But leaders often become corrupt, and they minister injustice to good people. What are God's people to do in such a situation? The Bible calls them to leave vengeance with the Lord in the face of wicked leaders. They are to pursue peace with all men, submitting to those over them as much as possible. They must not take matters into their own hands. Ungodly leaders is an issue with which God must deal. But we can pray that the Lord will rebuke and remove such people.

IV. TEACHING OUTLINE

A. David's Indictment (1–5)
  1. Wicked rulers are prevailing (1–2)
    a. They speak unjustly (1a)
    b. They judge unrightly (1b)
    c. They devise injustice (2a)
    d. They spread violence (2b)
  2. Wicked rulers are perverted (3–5)
    a. They speak their lies (3)
    b. They spread their venom (4)
    c. They scatter their deceit (5)
B. David's Imprecation (6–11)
  1. Shatter their teeth (6)
  2. Strip away their presence (7–8)
  3. Snuff out their lives (9)
  4. Spill their blood (10)
  5. Satisfy the righteous (11)

Psalm 59

Special Delivery

"*H*ow can I look to be at home in the enemy's country,
joyful while in exile, or comfortable in a wilderness? This is
not my rest. This is the place of the furnace and the forge
and the hammer."

C h a r l e s   H .   S p u r g e o n

I. INTRODUCTION

*G*od specializes in special deliveries, rescuing his children from troublesome situations. Always in his own perfect timing, according to his own perfect plan, God rescues his people from harm when they call on him. In this psalm David offered this kind of prayer to God, asking for divine deliverance from evil men who sought to do him harm. The historical setting is the occasion "when Saul had sent men to David's house in order to kill him" (1 Sam. 19:11). But in spite of this sinister threat, David remained strong in his faith toward God, anchored with unshakable trust.

In this imprecation psalm that is emotionally charged and full of lament, David prayed that God would keep him secure from the life-threatening advances of evil men and defeat their attempts to take his life. God answered this prayer through David's wife Michal, who helped him escape through a window (1 Sam. 19:11–14). As king of Israel, David wrote this *miktam* and looked back upon the time of his deliverance that occurred in earlier days. In so reflecting, David responded with praise and gratitude to God.

II. COMMENTARY

> **MAIN IDEA:** *David pleads with God to defend him from his adversaries while offering praise for the divine deliverance he had received in the past.*

A David's Cry (59:1–5)

59:1–2. This psalm begins with an emergency call to God as David prayed, **Deliver me from my enemies, O God**. This was a fervent plea to be rescued by the Lord from those who rose up **against** him. Again, he asked to be delivered **from evildoers** and **bloodthirsty men** who wanted to take his life. Obviously, David found himself in a life-threatening situation.

59:3–4. Calling for God's attention and intervention, he pointed to these men and said to God, **See how they lie in wait for** ambush. They were **fierce men** who conspired **against** him, in spite of the fact that he had committed **no offense or sin**. This lack of offense was not a claim of sinless perfection by David but one of personal holiness, innocence, and integrity. Having examined his own life, David concluded that he had **done no wrong**, certainly nothing that would justify this kind of vicious **attack** against him. Under their mounting opposition, he blurted out, **Arise to help me; look on my plight!** This advance of his persecutors gave the outward appearance that God was indifferent and needed to be aroused from slumber.

59:5. David called out to God with a string of divine names, indicating the God-centered focus of his faith: **O LORD God Almighty, the God of Israel**. Each name revealed a unique feature of God's grace. David wanted God to **rouse** himself **to punish all the nations** that had come against Israel. His plea was that God would show **no mercy to wicked traitors**. This implied that they were fellow Jews who had turned against Israel in the attack, or they were from a nation that had once pledged its allegiance to Israel but now had broken their agreement.

B David's Confidence (59:6–13)

59:6–8. These evil enemies returned **at evening**, **snarling like dogs** or wild scavengers feeding off trash, and were thus unclean. They would **prowl about**, looking for prey. **They spew from their mouths** much harm, their tongues being like swords. They would say, **"Who can hear us?"** taunting God that even he must not know their evil plot. But God mocked such blasphemy. **You, O LORD, laugh at them** in derision (cp. Ps 2:4) and **scoff** at their feeble efforts. How absurd it was to oppose God! The psalmist was confident that his enemies would not succeed.

59:9–10. David addressed God as **my Strength** because of the Lord's past work of sustaining and strengthening David. He knew that God saw his plight and would surely intervene, watching him at all times. The Lord was his **fortress**, the one who protected him when attacked, and his **loving God**, the one who tenderly cared for him. This same loving, powerful God would **go before** David (cp. 2 Sam. 5:24), ensuring victory **over those who** were slandering him.

59:11–13. David prayed for God to spare the lives of his enemies, at least initially, so they would **wander about** in humiliation and defeat for all to see. David gave the reason for such an ignominious existence: this defeat would be **for the sins of their mouths** in slandering and conspiring against him. For this, he appealed to God to **consume them in wrath**. Once these enemies were defeated, David's victory would be a resounding testimony to a watching world **that God rules over Jacob** as the one true God.

C David's Celebration (59:14–17)

59:14–17. In spite of the advancement of these enemies, David remained certain of their defeat. Like **snarling dogs**, they **prowl** and **wander about for food**. He declared that he would sing of God's **strength** because the conquering power of God would surely defeat his enemies. He confessed that God was his **fortress** and **refuge**, protecting him from harm. Again, he identified God as **my Strength**, the one to whom he sang praise. David's faith in God's sovereignty transformed his heart from initial anxiety to triumphant assurance.

III. CONCLUSION

Whenever the believer is surrounded by dangers, he must run to God, who is a fortress for those who trust him. "The name of the LORD is a strong tower; the righteous run to it and are safe" (Prov. 18:10). As the one sure defender of his people, God is, according to David's testimony, "my rock, my fortress and my deliverer . . . my shield and the horn of my salvation, my stronghold" (Ps. 18:2). All these images of God are intended to convey that the Lord is a strong protector and a sure defense from everything that threatens his people. God's people must always call upon him. He alone is a fortress of protection from troubles.

IV. TEACHING OUTLINE

A. David's Cry (1–5)
  1. He calls for God's deliverance (1–2)
    a. From my enemies (1)
    b. From evildoers (2)

2. He calls for God's defense (3–5)
   a. See my conspirators (3–4a)
   b. Save me from them (5a)
   c. Show them no mercy (5b)

B. David's Confidence (6–13)
  1. God will disregard them(6–8)
   a. They snarl like dogs (6)
   b. They spew out words (7a)
   c. They scoff at God (7b)
   d. God scoffs at them (8)
  2. God will defend me (9–10)
   a. He is my fortress (9a)
   b. He is my fighter (9b–10)
  3. God will devastate them (11–13)
   a. Spare them (11a)
   b. Scatter them (11b)
   c. Smite them (12–13)

C. David's Celebration (14–17)
  1. His danger is amid foes (14–15)
   a. They return like dogs (14)
   b. They roam for prey (15)
  2. His delight is in God (16–17)
   a. He sings of God's power (16a)
   b. He sings of God's mercy (16b)
   c. He sings of God's defense (17)

Psalm 60
Transforming Trials into Triumph

I. INTRODUCTION

*T*here are times when God's people suffer defeat, giving the appearance that God has forsaken them. But such times of difficulty should not drive believers into despair. Rather, this should cause them to experience a deeper dependency on the Lord. This was the experience of David as recorded in Psalm 60. He prayed an urgent prayer for victory after suffering a devastating defeat.

The historical background is identified in the superscription as a time when David fought in the north against "Aram Naharaim" (Mesopotamia) and "Aram Zobah" (between Damascus and the Upper Euphrates) when another nation, Edom, invaded the southern part of Judah and brought defeat to Israel. This conflict may be included in the recorded list of David's wars which he fought against surrounding nations. In response to this invasion, David dispatched Joab, one of his chief commanders, to subdue this Edomite aggression (2 Sam. 8:13–14; 1 Chr. 18:3–4,12–13). Joab returned to David with the good report that he had "struck down twelve thousand Edomites in the Valley of Salt," and thus Israel had prevailed in victory.

Psalm 60 was "a *miktam* of David" (cp. Pss. 16; 56; 57; 58; 59), and it was to be sung "to the tune of 'The Lily of the Covenant.'" It contains David's shock at the nation's devastating military defeat as well as the confident hope that God would bring victory to David and the people. David realized that both victory and defeat come from the Lord.

II. COMMENTARY

MAIN IDEA: *David is shocked that the people of God have suffered a devastating defeat, but he petitions the Lord to bring victory.*

A David's Devastation (60:1–4)

60:1. This psalm begins with David's painful outburst, **You have rejected us, O God.** This was his lament upon learning of the devastating military defeat that Israel had suffered at the hands of their enemies, the Edomites. This defeat **burst** upon them like an overwhelming flood, giving the impression that God had cast them aside because he was **angry** with them and had judged them with this event. Out of a desperate heart, David cried to God to **restore** them to victory and prosperity.

60:2–3. As if struck by a devastating earthquake, David lamented, **You have shaken the land.** This referred to this shocking defeat by the foreign invaders (cp. v. 9). Furthermore, God's anger had **torn** the nation as a thin garment would be ripped to pieces. Thus, David pleaded that God would **mend its fractures** because the nation was still reeling under the **quaking.** God had sent **desperate times** by these enemies, causing the nation to **stagger** like a person who had been given too much **wine,** signifying the cup of God's wrath.

60:4. Realizing that this defeat had ultimately come from God's hand, David knew that only God could restore them to victory. Thus, he interceded on behalf of the nation, reminding God that **for those who fear you, you have raised a banner to be unfurled before the bow.** In ancient warfare a **banner** was a visual rallying point for troops who were under attack. It acted as a point of reference for soldiers who were startled and confused by a surprise attack. After suffering defeat by the Edomites, the Israelite warriors were perplexed and disoriented. They needed a standard—the **banner** of truth, the Word of God—to rally them and lead them into battle.

B David's Intercession (60:5–8)

60:5. So David prayed, **Save us** from our enemies **and help us with your right hand.** This was the hand of greatest strength which was able to overcome all opposition. The phrase **those you love** is an expression of tender endearment. God's people might **be delivered** if God would act. Only God could save them, and David knew it.

60:6–8. Remembering what **God** had already **spoken**, perhaps referring to what was recorded in the "Book of the Wars" (Num. 21:14), David declared, **In triumph I will parcel out Shechem and measure off the Valley of Succoth.** He meant that God would distribute to his people the land promised in the Abrahamic and Palestinian covenants—**Shechem** and **Succoth**—two territories east and west of the Jordan River taken by Israel. Furthermore, God declared, **Gilead is mine** as well as **Manasseh** and **Ephraim** and **Judah.** These lands ultimately belonged to God, and he would give them to his people in victory, a conquest pictured by the divine **helmet** and **scepter.**

This **triumph** would be over enemies who inhabited the promised land, including **Moab** and **Edom** and **Philistia**, foes who would become their servants. Thus, figuratively speaking, Moab would use a **washbasin** to cleanse their feet. To Edom God would **toss** his **sandal** so they would stoop to serve Israel's needs. This pictures God's overwhelming victory over their enemies.

ⓒ David's Expectation (60:9–12)

60:9–10. Transitioning to his final appeal, David asked three rhetorical questions. The first was, **Who will bring me to the fortified city?** This is to say, who would lead King David into battle against Israel's enemies? The anticipated answer is *God.* The one who had defeated their enemies was the same God who would defend them. Second, David asked, **Who will lead me to Edom?** In other words, who would go before the king into battle and guarantee the victory over the nation's enemies? Third, David asked, **Is it not you, O God?** Clearly, it was **God** who would lead them into victory. The God who had **rejected** them and **no longer** marched **with** their **armies** into battle would lead them to triumph over their enemies.

60:11–12. Petitioning God's intervention, David pleaded, **Give us aid** (literally, deliverance) **against the enemy.** David realized that the **help of man** was useless and would only lead to further defeat. But strengthened with unshakable confidence, David declared, **With God we will gain the victory.** God alone could reverse the outcome of their last defeat, and he would surely do so. He would **trample down** their enemies like a triumphant warrior.

III. CONCLUSION

The timeless lesson of this psalm is clear: only God can give victory in the face of defeat. When believers are suffering harm, God can rout their foes and win an overwhelming victory. No matter how great the setback may be, defeat is never final as long as the grace of God is available. But to be sure, the righteous are not without responsibility. Like David in this psalm, they must call out to God and ask for the victory. And like David, they must use spiritual tactics such as prayer, faith, and God's Word, acting with determined resolve.

God will not turn a deaf ear to such an urgent plea for help. He will answer in perfect timing according to his perfect will.

IV. TEACHING OUTLINE

A. David's Devastation (1–4)
  1. God has rejected them (1a,2a,3)
  2. God must restore them (1b,2b)
  3. God will rally them (4)
B. David's Intercession (5–8)
  1. God, deliver us from defeat (5)
    a. By your right hand (5a)
    b. For your loved ones (5b)
  2. God, give us our enemies (6–8)
    a. Shechem and Succoth (6)
    b. Gilead and Manasseh (7a)
    c. Ephraim and Judah (7b)
    d. Moab, Edom, and Philistia (8)
C. David's Expectation (9–12)
  1. God must triumph (9–11)
    a. The important question (9)
    b. The inevitable answer (10)
    c. The intercessory request (11)
  2. God will triumph (12)
    a. He will gain the victory (12a)
    b. He will defeat my foes (12b)

Psalm 61

Like a Rock

"Faith, like a muscle, grows by stretching."

A .   W .   T o z e r

Psalm 61

I. INTRODUCTION

Faith is a living, active confidence in God, a firm reliance upon him in every circumstance and crisis. This is how David met the trials and troubles thrown against him. He did so with a firm trust in God, and Psalm 61 is the inspired record of another such occasion in his life. David wrote this prayer at a time when he was removed from Jerusalem and surrounded by troubles. He was probably fleeing from his rebellious son Absalom (2 Sam. 15–18), hiding in the Judean wilderness among the rocks. In the higher ground among the rocky crags, he was safe in their protection. But David looked beyond the physical rocks to the Lord as his ultimate protection. God was his rock of safe hiding.

This idea of God as a rock is a common image that appears twenty times in the Book of Psalms. This song of trust was intended to be sung "with stringed instruments" and was written "for the director of music." Psalms 61–64 form a unit of psalms with the common theme of trust in God in times of troubles.

II. COMMENTARY

MAIN IDEA: *David prays for strength and security, and he praises God for hearing his prayer.*

A David's Appeal (61:1–2)

61:1–2. Petitioning God's help, David cried out, **Hear my cry, O God; listen to my prayer.** With a fiery passion and deep fervency, he lifted his voice to the Lord. The location from which he called, **from the ends of the earth,** hints that David, at the time of this experience, was in a foreign land, away from the presence of God in his homeland of Israel. His words, **I call as my heart grows faint,** indicated that he was becoming discouraged and weak, and he felt estranged from God's presence.

With focused request, David pleaded, **Lead me to the rock that is higher than I.** This rock was a secure place of safety where he could escape his oppressors, a place of protection. The truth is that this asylum was not a place but a person, God himself. David wanted to be renewed and restored in the close intimacy of his personal relationship with God.

B David's Assurance (61:3–5)

61:3. David cited the all-sufficient power of God to protect him by using four figures of speech, each representing God: **refuge** (v. 3), **strong tower** (v.3), "tent" (v. 4), "shelter" (v. 4). First, he spoke with resounding confidence about God: **You have been my refuge** meaning "a shelter from danger." When attacked by men and surrounded by threatening circumstances, God himself was David's refuge. Second, David identified God as **a strong tower against the foe,** a figure that pictured the high part of a walled city, as opposed to a wilderness refuge behind which people hid when attacked. The idea here is not of a person fleeing from place to place but of a person defending himself in his walled city when attacked by foes. This is what God was to David, his defender from all harm.

61:4. Third, David pictured God as a **tent** in which he longed **to dwell . . . forever.** The word *tent* (Heb. *ohel*, "covering, dwelling place") is also translated "tabernacle" and refers to the wilderness tent where the ark of God was kept. Thus, David asked **to dwell** where God himself dwells (cp. 27:4), a place of intimate fellowship. Fourth, David portrayed God as a place of **shelter,** literally the sheltering **wings** of a mother bird shielding her young from harm (cp. Pss. 17:8; 36:7; 57:1; 63:7; 91:4).

61:5. David then gave the reason for his intense longing for God. His **vows** to **God** had arisen from his troubled heart in the midst of this crisis. These vows spoke of an unwavering commitment to God, even in the face of overwhelming trouble. Confident that the Lord had heard his pledges of firm commitment, he declared, **You have given me the heritage** promised to God's people. David was referring to a restored place in the promised land. This inheritance is a recurring theme in the psalms (Pss. 16:6; 37:18; 135:12; 136:21–22).

C David's Allegiance (61:6–7)

61:6–7. David next made several specific requests of God. First, he asked God to **increase the days of the king's life**. He prayed that God would preserve him and keep him alive while he was abroad until he could return to the safe confines of the promised land. Second, he asked that **his years** be extended **for many generations**. In other words, may God extend his dynasty for many years, even long after his death. Ultimately, in this request, David looked ahead to the coming of the Messiah, the greater Son of David who would come through his lineage (2 Sam. 7). Third, David asked to **be enthroned in God's presence forever**. This was a request for special favor with God throughout eternity. Fourth, he asked God to **appoint** his **love and faithfulness**. David sought God's steadfast love **to protect him** from his enemies, perhaps Absalom.

D David's Adoration (61:8)

61:8. In spite of his troubling circumstances, David chose to worship and praise God. Although the outlook was threatening, the uplook remained glorious. Anticipating God's deliverance, David declared, **Then will I ever sing praise to your name and fulfill my vows day after day**. This was a promise of daily obedience to the Lord, the desired lifestyle of all true worshipers (cp. Rom. 12:1).

III. CONCLUSION

As David hid himself in the rock, he placed his trust in God. The Lord is the solid rock on whom all believers must build their lives; all other ground is sinking sand. This rock is Jesus, the Rock of Ages, in whom believers must hide themselves by faith. Christ alone is a refuge in the storms of life. He protects his people from human foes and adversaries. But more than that, Christ is the only refuge from the wrath of God that will be poured out on sinners in the last day. May all come to the Rock, the Lord Jesus Christ, and hide in him.

IV. TEACHING OUTLINE

A. David's Appeal (1–2)
  1. God, listen to me (1)
  2. God, lead me (2)

B. David's Assurance (3–5)
1. God is my sure refuge (3a)
2. God is my strong tower (3b)
3. God is my secluding tent (4a)
4. God is my sheltering wing (4b–5)
C. David's Allegiance (6–7)
1. Extend my days (6a)
2. Extend my dynasty (6b–7a)
3. Extend your devotion (7b)
D. David's Adoration (8)
1. I will sing praise (8a)
2. I will fulfill promises (8b)

Psalm 62

God Alone

"The character of God is a perfect

and glorious whole."

W i l l i a m   S .   P l u m e r

I. INTRODUCTION

No person, pursuit, or possession should ever take preeminence over God. God *alone* must be the believer's trust. As David wrote this song, he declared that in the midst of his troubles he was not looking to anyone or anything other than God to deliver him. In the opening verses, the key word is *alone,* a word that occurs four times in relationship to God (vv. 1-2,5-6). David stated that his faith rested solely in God, the singular object of his trust. This solitary reliance upon the Lord was the firm foundation for David's life.

Concerning the background of this psalm, David was surrounded by evil conspirators who wanted to dethrone him. Perhaps the setting was the treason he faced during Absalom's rebellion (2 Sam. 15–18), or it could have been Saul's jealous rage. David committed himself to God, placing his trust in God who was his salvation. The message of this psalm is clear: No matter how difficult the trial, trust in God *alone.*

This "psalm of David" was written "for Jeduthun," who apparently was "the director of music."

II. COMMENTARY

MAIN IDEA: *David trusts exclusively in God to protect him from his enemies, who were conspiring to remove him from the throne.*

A David's Trust (62:1–2)

62:1. David began by reaffirming to his own **soul** who God is. The word *soul* (Heb. *nepesh*) refers to one's entire being, one's whole inner self, encompassing the mind, emotion, and will. Thus, David's entire inner person, or his whole heart, found **rest in God alone**. This particular word for God (Heb. *elohiym;* see Deeper Discoveries, 25:2) is in the plural form, indicating plentitude of power, majesty, and dominion (cp. Gen. 1:1,3,6). David vowed to trust in God, who was his **salvation** and who would deliver him from all harm. This word *alone* (Heb. *ak*) is used with a fourfold, intentional repetition (vv. 1–2,5–6) to underscore the exclusivity of David's reliance on God. It is difficult to wait on God when danger lurks, yet David chose to do so. Refusing to take matters into his own hands, he waited on God to act.

62:2. The psalmist's trust was well placed. He boasted that God **alone** was his **rock**. Although David's world was quaking, his hour was dark, and his circumstances were difficult, he was sustained by God, who was rock-solid and immovable, David's **salvation** and **fortress** (Heb. *misgab*, "high place," "a refuge set high up"; cp. 18:2; 144:2). Although he had reasons to fear, he wrote with confident resolve, **I will never be shaken**. In this time of mounting difficulty, the psalmist's faith rose still higher. He was safe in God's care (cp. 10:6; 37:24)

B David's Troubles (62:3–4)

62:3. Addressing his assailants, David asked rhetorically, **How long will you assault a man?** The **man** to whom he referred was himself. He accused them of trying to **throw him down** like a **leaning wall** or **tottering fence**. These two metaphors show how he saw himself—in a weakened state, ready to fall.

62:4. These conspirators intended **to topple** David **from his lofty place**. David was probably referring to an attempted coup to remove him from his royal throne. The people who plotted to do so were those around him who posed as his friends. **With their mouths** they were blessing David and praising him, but **in their hearts** they were cursing him and plotting evil plans against him. Their slanderous lies threatened to turn the tide of public opinion against him and undermine his leadership.

C David's Testimony (62:5–8)

62:5–7. Reaffirming his confident trust in God (vv. 1–2), David instructed his heart to **find rest . . . in God alone**. By repeating the opening refrain, he called upon himself to have faith in God, a reliance that was full of **hope**, a Hebrew word meaning an eager waiting upon God that looked forward to his intervention. His natural tendency would be to act impetuously, taking these matters into his own hands. But David understood that God alone was his **rock**, **salvation**, and **fortress**, the one who could protect and defend him. God was his sole deliverance. God **alone** would uphold his **honor**.

62:8. David invited others to share his confident faith in God: **Trust** (Heb. *batah*, "to attach oneself to another object") **in him at all times, O people**, even in the midst of difficult times. As a parallel synonymn for **trust**, David called out to the people, **pour out** their **hearts to him**. This was a reference to earnest prayer, or the unburdening of oneself to God who alone **is our refuge**. True faith will express itself in fervent prayer to God.

D David's Truth (62:9–12)

62:9–10. David concluded by contrasting the weakness of man (vv. 9–10) with the power of God (vv. 11–12). David's unwavering testimony was to trust God, not man. **Lowborn men**—meaning those of low rank and social standing—as well as **the highborn**—those born into privilege—**are but a breath**, meaning futile, empty, and **a lie**, representing those who are not anchored to God's holy truth. They are **weighed on a balance**, helpless to deliver themselves out of trouble. Mortal man must not trust in his own devices such as **extortion**, **stolen goods**, or **riches**. All of these will surely fail.

62:11–12. In contrast to mortal man, God alone can be trusted. Only he is **strong** and **loving**. In other words, he is able to deliver his people who trust him, and he is willing to take into account their best interests and highest good. Unquestionably, God **will reward each person** who trusts him, **according to what he has done**. The believer who trusts God will be rewarded by him. It is futile to initiate our own deliverance. We must wait patiently on God to act.

III. CONCLUSION

When fear, worry, anxiety, and panic come to a believer's heart, he must remember that God is *strong* and *loving* toward him. These two divine attributes are the twin towers of every believer's trust in God. Because God is strong, he is over all the events of history, even our own lives. Thus, he is able to deliver his believers out of all their troubles. We may rest assured that nothing is impossible for God, who rules and overrules all. Likewise, God is loving and merciful, a kind King who uses his omnipotence with infinite tenderness, coming to the aid of his people in their darkest hour. Believers can confidently call out to God for help, knowing that he loves them perfectly and will use his power wisely when they are attacked and endangered.

IV. TEACHING OUTLINE

A. David's Trust (1–2)
　1. God alone is my rest (1a)
　2. God alone is my rescue (1b)
　3. God alone is my rock (2a)
　4. God alone is my refuge (2b)
B. David's Troubles (3–4)
　1. He is assaulted by man (3–4a)
　2. He is lied about by man (4b)
　3. He is cursed by man (4c)
C. David's Testimony (5–8)
　1. He speaks to himself (5–7)
　　a. Rest in God (5)
　　b. Rely upon God (6–7)
　2. He speaks to others (8)
　　a. Trust in God (8a)
　　b. Pray to God (8b)
D. David's Truth (9–12)
　1. Man is unreliable (9–10)
　　a. Temporal (9)
　　b. Truthless (10)
　2. God is unshakable (11–12)
　　a. Strong (11)
　　b. Loving (12)

Psalm 63

One Holy Passion

"*Glory is essential to the Godhead, as light is to the sun. Glory is the sparkling of the Deity.*"

T h o m a s   W a t s o n

I. INTRODUCTION

One Thing Only

Stranded in the open sea, a man was afloat on a small raft, dying without any water. His weakened and cramping body was about to collapse. His lips were parched. His eyes were seeing spots. His stomach was in knots. There was only one thing he wanted—water. He had no interest in watching television or any desire for amusement or entertainment. He was not daydreaming about his many possessions back home. Nor was he fantasizing about the stock market or his favorite sports team. He had only one thing on his mind—water. He had to have water, and until he received it, nothing else mattered.

This is precisely where David was, both physically and spiritually, as he wrote Psalm 63. He was in the dry and barren wilderness of Judea without water. His body ached for liquid replenishing. Yet the deepest thirst of his life was for *living* water. David's soul yearned for God! He did not want money or any material thing. He wanted God for who God was. With all the passion of his soul, he thirsted to know and experience the greatness of God.

The historical circumstances of this psalm "of David" are revealed in the title, "When he was in the Desert of Judah" either fleeing from King Saul (1 Sam. 19–31) or Absalom (2 Sam. 15–19). David was in the desert wilderness of Judah. He must have been fleeing from Absalom because in verse 11 David refers to himself as "the king." He was not yet king when Saul chased him.

The story of Absalom's rebellion against David is told in 2 Samuel 15–19. Estranged from his father because he felt mistreated by him, Absalom spent four years winning over the hearts of the people, making himself conveniently available to the complaints of the people by sitting beside the road. When Absalom thought he had a majority of support, he was ready to set up a rival kingship in the nearby city of Hebron.

David was caught off guard and feared an attack on Jerusalem. He fled the city with many loyal soldiers and headed east for the Transjordan region. He left weeping and crying in the night as Absalom moved into Jerusalem. So David crossed the Jordan River and hid in the desert region of the Judean wilderness with Absalom in hot pursuit.

II. COMMENTARY

One Holy Passion

> **MAIN IDEA:** David declares the true and deepest longing of his soul as one who seeks God.

A David's Passion for God (63:1–2)

> **SUPPORTING IDEA:** David affirms his soul's consuming passion to behold God.

63:1a. David began by declaring, **O God, you are my God.** He identified God as "my God," reflecting the intimate relationship he had with the Lord. More than just believing in the existence of God, and more than just knowing about God, David actually knew him personally as "my God." Therefore, David stated, **Earnestly I seek you,** revealing his longing to pursue the knowledge of God by taking the initiative.

63:1b. Finding himself in a barren wilderness, a **dry and weary land where there is no water,** David felt more than a physical thirst for water. He experienced an intense inner longing for God: **My soul thirsts for you, my body longs for you.** He knew that he must maintain a close, vibrant walk with God to be sustained, strengthened, and satisfied. His soul could no more live without God than his body could live without water (cp. Pss. 42:1–2; 84:2; 143:6; Matt. 5:6; John 7:37).

63:2. David's passionate longing for God was intensified because of a past encounter he had back in Jerusalem **in the sanctuary.** In this experience he beheld God in his power and glory. Perhaps this was similar to Isaiah's vision of God's holiness (Isa. 6:1–8). This high view of God, leading to a deeper knowledge of God, had gripped David's soul at a time before his enemies drove him into the wilderness. It was David's experience of God's glory in his life that led him to seek God so passionately. He had **beheld** the great King of the universe, exalted in absolute power, undiminished in blazing glory, awesome and transcendent.

David's Praise for God (63:3–5)

> **SUPPORTING IDEA:** *David declares his commitment to praise God in whom his soul delights.*

63:3. Having encountered God so dramatically, David was moved to praise him. **My lips will glorify you**, he vowed, **because your love** (Heb. *hesed*; see "Deeper Discoveries," 23:6) **is better than life**. This steadfast love by which God had committed himself to David was more valuable to him than **life** itself. He knew that God was not only with him but *for* him through thick and thin, in good times and bad times, both on and off the throne, in the royal court as well as in the rugged wilderness.

63:4. Because of God's unconditional love, David pledged, **I will praise you as long as I live**. God's steadfast love for David prompted the same kind of love in David for God. In the midst of this wilderness experience, his lips were active in praising God. **In your name I will lift up my hands**, he declared, assuming a humble posture in prayer. He was ready to receive every good gift through personal trust in God alone.

63:5. In God, David declared, **my soul will be satisfied as with the richest of foods**. He used the metaphor of a royal banquet prepared with the choicest of **foods**. David probably remembered the stately feasts he enjoyed as Israel's king. With this regal background, he reminded his own heart that only God could satisfy the true yearnings of his soul (John 4:13–14; 6:35). As a result, David stated in jubilation, **With singing lips my mouth will praise you**.

C David's Pursuit of God (63:6–8)

> **SUPPORTING IDEA:** *David remembers how his mind was consumed with thoughts of God.*

63:6. **On my bed I remember you**, David declared, recalling what he had seen "in the sanctuary" (v. 2). He thought of God **through the watches of the night**. When David awoke in the night, his first and best thought was about God. He was a man with a mind that sought the Lord. No wonder he had a God-satisfied soul.

63:7. David explained why he was so preoccupied with God: **Because you are my help**. Because of this, he was singing **in the shadow** of God's **wings**. David was surely baking under the hot sun of the wilderness. He found occasional relief in the shade that brought comfort and peace. This cooling shade was precisely what God was to his troubled soul. Under the fiery heat of trials, he found relief in the shadow of God's presence. This divine shadow, able to shield him from all fear and anxiety, is compared to the way a mother bird shelters her young beneath her wings. God was David's strength and encouragement in this scorching trial.

63:8. David stated that his **soul** was clinging to God with a strong grasp of faith. But at the same time, God's **right hand** was holding him up. Who was holding whom? While David was clinging to God, God was upholding him.

D David's Protection from God (63:9–11)

SUPPORTING IDEA: *David confirms God's watchcare over him as his enemies seek to kill him.*

63:9–10. The final movement of this psalm is David's recognition that God was the one who would protect him from his enemies. **They who seek my life will be destroyed,** David testified. **They will go down to the depths of the earth.** Here he referred to the realm of the dead or the grave. **They** would **be given over to the sword,** presumably by God, **and become food for jackals.** Their dead bodies would be left in the battlefield to be eaten by these scavenging desert animals. Those who sought David's life would have their own lives taken.

63:11. In the face of such protection, **the king**—David himself—would **rejoice in God.** Such praise for God is only natural because of the divine victory on David's behalf. In fact, **all who swear by God's name,** meaning all who trust and fear God, would **praise him** when they learned what God had done for David. But **the mouths of liars**—those who opposed David and believed Absalom's lies—would **be silenced** by God in utter shame.

MAIN IDEA REVIEW: *David declares the longing of his soul as one who seeks God.*

III. CONCLUSION

Seeking the Savior

In his book, *Seeing and Savoring Jesus Christ,* John Piper wrote about seeking the Lord:

> The deepest longing of the human heart is to know and enjoy the glory of God. We were made for this. "Bring My sons from afar and My daughters from the ends of the earth . . . whom I created *for My glory*" (Isa. 43:6–7). To see it, to savor it, and to show it—that is why we exist. . . . We were made to know and treasure the glory of God above all things; and when we trade that treasure for images, everything is

disordered. The sun of God's glory was made to shine at the center of the solar system of our soul. And when it does, all the planets of our life are held in their proper orbit. But when the sun is displaced, everything flies apart. The healing of the soul begins by restoring the glory of God to its flaming, all-attracting place at the center.

We are all starved for the glory of God, not self. No one goes to the Grand Canyon to increase self-esteem. Why do we go? Because there is greater healing for the soul in beholding the splendor than there is in beholding self. Indeed, what could be more ludicrous in a vast and glorious universe like this than a human being, on the speck called earth, standing in front of a mirror trying to find significance in his own self-image? It is a great sadness that this is the gospel of the modern world.

But it is not the Christian Gospel. . . . The Christian Gospel is about "the glory of Christ," not about me. And when *it is*—in some measure—about me, it is not about my being made much of by God, but about God mercifully enabling me to enjoy making much of him forever" (John Piper, *Seeing and Savoring Jesus Christ,* Wheaton, Ill: Crossways Books, 2001, pp. 20-22).

May this one holy passion for God's glory thrill our souls and dominate our lives throughout all our years upon this earth. May we seek to glorify God by enjoying him forever.

IV. LIFE APPLICATION

Growing Closer to the Lord

Eternal life consists of knowing God and experiencing a close and personal relationship with him through the Lord Jesus Christ (cp. John 17:3). Scripture is full of exhortations calling believers to draw closer to God (cp. Ps. 73:28; 2 Chr. 15:2; Zech. 1:3; Mal. 3:7; Heb. 7:19). Daniel understood the importance of an intimate relationship with God when he wrote, "The people that do know their God shall be strong" (Dan. 11:32 KJV). The word of the Lord spoken through the prophet Jeremiah is true: "Let not the wise man boast of his wisdom or the strong man boast of his strength or the rich man boast of his riches, but let him who boasts boast about this: that he understands and knows me, that I am the LORD" (Jer. 9:23–24).

Likewise, the apostle Paul knew of this surpassing importance when he wrote, "I want to know Christ and the power of his resurrection and the fellowship of sharing in his sufferings" (Phil. 3:10). The Christian life should be continuous progression in which believers "grow in the grace and knowledge of our Lord and Savior Jesus Christ" (2 Pet. 3:18). This is the focus of Psalm 63, a passionate call to know more intimately this great and glorious God.

V. PRAYER

God, you alone quench our thirsty souls. As we live in this dry and weary land, we will continually seek your face. We long to see your power and glory in our lives because your lovingkindness is better than life. Therefore, we will praise you with our lips as our thoughts are saturated with you. Lord, please continue to uphold us; be our help from those who seek to destroy our lives. For the glory of your name we pray. Amen.

VI. DEEPER DISCOVERIES

A. Seek (63:1)

This word (Heb. *shahar*) denotes the time before sunrise, the morning dawn, or the breaking of day. The KJV translates this as "early will I seek thee." The idea being conveyed here is that the psalmist would pursue God before all else. First and foremost in his life, he would seek God. This speaks of the priority of his pursuit of God. Accordingly, Christ said, "Seek first his kingdom and his righteousness, and all these things will be given to you" (Matt. 6:33).

B. Beheld (63:2)

The word *beheld* (Heb. *haza*) means "to see, look, observe" and in certain contexts "to prophesy." The word is mostly found in the poetry literature of the Old Testament. Sometimes it is used to speak of actually seeing a manifestation of the divine presence of God (Exod. 24:11; Job 19:26). The word is often used of visions of revelation given by God (Num. 24:4,16; Isa. 1:1; 2:1; 13:1; 30:10; Lam. 2:14; Ezek. 13:6–8; Amos 1:1; Hab. 1:1; Mic. 1:1; Zech. 10:2). It is also used to speak of spiritual understanding, as when Job spoke with Elihu: "All mankind has seen (*haza*) it; men gaze on it from afar. How great is God—beyond our understanding! The number of his years is past finding out" (Job 36:25–26). It is difficult to know how this verb is used here. Either David had a dramatic encounter with God that involved a vision, much as Isaiah had with God (Isa. 6), or it meant a renewed spiritual insight into God's greatness.

C. Think (63:6)

The word *think* (Heb. *haga*) denotes a low sound such as muttering, murmuring, or moaning. The word is found mainly in the poetry literature of the Old Testament, particularly in Psalms and Isaiah. The term was used to refer to righteous ponderings (Pss. 35:28; 37:30; 71:24; Prov. 15:28) and reflective meditation (Josh. 1:8; Pss. 1:2; 63:6; 77:12; 143:5). Some interpreters believe that "thinking" or "meditating" upon the Scriptures means they were read audibly to help people process and ponder their message.

D. Upholds (63:8)

The word *upholds* or *uphold* (Heb. *tamak*) is used twenty times in the Old Testament. It means "to grasp, lay hold of, support, hold up, or maintain." It was often used of moral matters and spiritual truths. Here it is used of the inner support David received from God when he was confronted by his enemies. God would support him in this trial. The word was used by David when he said to the Lord, "In my integrity you uphold me" (Ps. 41:12), meaning he would be strengthened by God to walk in holiness. David used *tamak* in Psalm 17:5, "My steps have held to your paths." The word is also used to represent God upholding the coming Messiah (Isa. 42:1) and upholding Israel with his "righteous right hand" (Isa. 41:10). These statements describe God's overruling strength.

E. Destroyed (63:9)

This word (Heb. *shoa*) means "to be rushed over," as in ruin and swift destruction. It was used to speak of a desert wasteland as if it had been destroyed (Job 30:3; 38:27). It described a consuming storm that brought great destruction (Prov. 1:27; Ezek. 38:9). Thus it was used to speak of divine judgment. Isaiah asked the inhabitants of Israel, "What will you do on the day of reckoning, when disaster comes from afar?" (Isa. 10:3). The impending divine judgment and ruin that awaited Babylon is described as "a catastrophe (*shoa*) you cannot foresee will suddenly come upon you" (Isa. 47:11). The word describes the terrible judgments associated with "the great day of the LORD" (Zeph. 1:14). Those who sought to harm David in this psalm would be completely destroyed.

VII. TEACHING OUTLINE

A. David's Passion for God (1–2)
  1. His desire is personal (1a)
  2. His desire is preeminent (1b)
  3. His desire is powerful (1c)
  4. His desire is provoked (2)
    a. In God's house (2a)
    b. By God's power (2b)
    c. By God's glory (2b)
B. David's Praise for God (3–5)
  1. I will sing to God (3–4,5b)
    a. To glorify God (3)
    b. To praise God (4,5b)

2. I am satisfied in God (5a)

C. David's Pursuit of God (6–8)

   1. I remember God (6)

   2. I rejoice in God (7)

   3. I remain with God (8)

D. David's Protection from God (9–11)

   1. My enemies will be destroyed (9)

   2. My enemies will be devoured (10)

   3. My enemies will be devastated (11)

VIII. ISSUES FOR DISCUSSION

1. Do I seek God above all other earthly pursuits?
2. Is the love of God better to me than all of life?
3. Do I spend sufficient time meditating on the character of God?
4. Do I cling to God and depend on his power to uphold me?

Psalm 64
Ambushed by Adversity

"*N*othing influences the quality of our life more than

how we respond to trouble."

E r w i n   G .   T i e m a n

Psalm 64

I. INTRODUCTION

*A*s the righteous seek to do the will of God in a world that hates God, the enemies of God are always rising up against his people. Because David was a man after God's own heart, he had many enemies. Whether they were people close to him—men like Saul or Absalom and their cohorts—or foreign nations that threatened Israel's borders, David was often surrounded by many foes. But in the midst of these stressful situations, David called to God and found the protection and deliverance he needed.

Psalm 64 is another "psalm of David" in which he requested God's protection from his enemies (vv. 1–2). They were poised and ready to do him harm (vv. 3–6). But he believed that God would fight for him (vv. 7–9). This caused him to lead others to rejoice in God (v. 10). This is another individual lament of David in which he prayed for God's protection from the conspiracy of those who waited to ambush him. With mounting confidence he was assured that a divine defense would shield him from his enemies.

II. COMMENTARY

MAIN IDEA: *David requests that God protect him from his enemies by fighting on his behalf.*

A David's Request (64:1–2)

64:1. David launched this psalm by raising a **complaint** to God against the danger of his enemy (cp. vv. 3–6). He pleaded with God, **Hear** (Heb. *shama,* "to give undivided attention") **me, O God . . . protect my life from the threat of the enemy.** This threat produced the kind of fear that can have a paralyzing effect. Perhaps the threat was as destructive as the attack itself.

64:2. David asked God to **hide** him **from the conspiracy** (Heb. *sod,* "secret plots") **of the wicked** who were plotting to do him harm. This was a request that God would conceal him with divine protection so he could escape their threats. Those who sought to do him harm were a **noisy crowd of evildoers** who conspired and planned an uproar against him.

B David's Reproach (64:3–6)

64:3. Describing the destructive attacks of his enemies, David declared, **They sharpen their tongues like swords.** They were lashing out with cutting, slanderous words that inflicted great harm (cp. Pss. 55:21; 57:4). Moreover, they were aiming **their words** at him **like deadly arrows** (cp. Ps. 59:7). Their words pierced and destroyed. Clearly the main weapon of this enemy was their tongue.

64:4. Furthermore, these enemies were shooting **from ambush** (Heb. *mistarim,* "hidden places"), lurking in the shadows, waiting for an advantage to strike him. The fact that David was an **innocent man,** blameless in character, meant that such a personal attack was unprovoked and unjustified. Nevertheless, **they shot at him—suddenly,** without any warning. These men, without the restraint of **fear,** assumed they would not be exposed.

64:5. What is more, they encouraged each other in **evil plans** to harm David, bolstering one another as they talked about **hiding their snares.** Brazenly they mocked the all-seeing eyes of God, presuming they would never be found out.

64:6. In addition, they were plotting **injustice** by pronouncing, **We have devised a perfect plan.** They thought they had a conspiracy that would never be defeated. From all this, David concluded, **Surely the mind and heart of man are cunning.** The truth is that the unregenerate heart of man is evil and depraved through and through (cp. Jer. 17:9; Pss. 39:11; 62:9).

C David's Retribution (64:7–9)

64:7–8. But David was confident that **God** would reverse the situation and do to his enemies precisely what they intended to do to him. These enemies intended to shoot him with arrows (v. 3), but God, in turn, would **shoot them with arrows** (cp. 7:13). God would bring judgment on the ungodly. He would **turn their own tongues against them** and **bring** them to **ruin**. The plans plotted by these enemies for David would surely come back upon them.

64:9. When God acts in vengeance to vindicate his own servants, **all mankind will fear.** In that day all who observe this triumph of divine justice **will proclaim** the mighty acts **of God and ponder what he has done.**

D David's Rejoicing (64:10)

64:10. In conclusion, David encouraged all **the righteous** to **rejoice in the LORD.** Believers should glorify God for his acts of judgment on the wicked (cp. Rev. 19:1–10). In so doing, they should also **take refuge in him** who alone can protect his people. Only God can deliver the righteous from the attacks of the wicked. **Let all the upright in heart praise him,** David declared. God alone is worthy of praise.

III. CONCLUSION

The great Baptist preacher Charles H. Spurgeon wrote, "Even now the thirsty arrow longs to wet itself with the blood of the persecutor. The bow is bent, the aim is taken, the arrow is fitted to the string. . . . Remember, God's arrows never miss the mark, and are every one of them, instruments of death." Spurgeon's remark is true, because God is full of vengeance and will protect his servants. David wrote, "[God] has prepared his deadly weapons; he makes ready his flaming arrows" (Ps. 7:13).

Be assured that the wicked will be exposed in due time and defeated. Such overwhelming victories cause God's people to fear the Lord and rejoice in his grace.

IV. TEACHING OUTLINE

    A. David's Request (1–2)
       1. Hear me (1a)
       2. Help me (1b)
       3. Hide me (2)
    B. David's Reproach (3–6)
       1. My enemy's weapons are cutting (3)
       2. My enemy's ambushes are concealed (4)
       3. My enemy's plans are cunning (5–6)

C. David's Retribution (7–9)
   1. God's weapons are deadly (7)
   2. God's warfare is destructive (7b–8)
   3. God's works are dreadful (9)
D. David's Rejoicing (10)
   1. Rejoice in the Lord (10 a,c)
   2. Reside in the Lord (10b)

Psalm 65

Dynamic Devotion

"The Christian ought to be a living doxology."

M a r t i n   L u t h e r

Psalm 65

I. INTRODUCTION

A high view of the supremacy of God causes believers to trace their blessings to his heavenly throne. Every good thing comes from God above. This truth was often expounded by the psalmist. This song of praise extols this fact, pointing to the many blessings God will pour out upon his people who are in need of his sustaining grace. God, who is infinitely good, delights in favoring his loved ones with good things. This praise psalm highlights some of these choice blessings.

Written by David, this psalm's historical setting was a festive celebration at the tabernacle, probably at the Feast of Tabernacles, the longest and most joyful feast of the Jews. After the crops were brought in and the firstfruits were offered to God (cp. Lev. 23:33–43; Num. 29: 12–39), the people celebrated the harvest, recognizing that all their blessings came from God's hand. This psalm was probably sung in connection with this harvest feast, although it could also have been sung in Israel at any time. In the same way today, this psalm should turn hearts to the Lord in humble gratitude for his bountiful blessings.

MAIN IDEA: *David expresses praise to God for his spiritual and physical blessings.*

A Praise God for His Grace (65:1–4)

65:1. David introduced this psalm with a declaration of praise to God, the central theme that runs throughout this song. Praise awaited God **in Zion**, the city of God, or Jerusalem, the place where God's people gathered for worship. In this **praise** song, David acknowledged that their **vows** or promises made to God in an earlier time of need would **be fulfilled**. Perhaps it was a vow made by farmers, a promise to bless God when the harvest was gathered.

65:2. David addressed God with these words: **O you who hear prayer**. This set God apart from the idols of the pagan nations—gods who were deaf. He acknowledged that all people would **come** to him. Prophetically, this statement looked ahead to the future millennial kingdom when all flesh would come to worship the Lord (cp. Zech. 14:16–19).

65:3. The primary blessing for which David offered praise was God's forgiving grace. Looking back at their past disobedience, he declared, **When we were overwhelmed by sins, you forgave our transgressions**. He was referring to their sinful acts of moral anarchy against God's law. Graciously and kindly, God removed their sin and stopped the consequences of their sin.

65:4. The phrase **Blessed are those you choose** and **bring near to live in your courts** is a tender reference to Israel as God's chosen people. These people, God's chosen ones, were selected by sovereign grace to be a royal priesthood (Exod. 19:6) who enjoyed God's presence. Speaking on behalf of the entire nation, David acknowledged, **We are filled with the good things of your house**. Great spiritual blessings flowed from being in God's presence. These blessings would include a deeper knowledge and enjoyment of God, divine peace, and abundant grace.

B Praise God for His Greatness (65:5–8)

65:5. David progressed in his praise to another dimension of God's blessings—his providential sovereignty that brings order to the world. God performs **awesome deeds of righteousness** in **all the ends of the earth**, even to **the farthest seas**. This distinguished **God our Savior** from the local, heathen idols who worked only in one region. God works in all the earth, and he alone is **the hope** of all people.

65:6–7. God **formed the mountains** out of nothing, but he also controls all that he created, having **stilled the roaring of the seas** and their waves. In addition, God calms the chaotic **turmoil of the nations**. His sovereignty rules over all, over inanimate objects and living beings, over believers and unbelievers alike.

65:8. David pointed out that **those living far away** in a pagan land would **fear** God's **wonders**. This referred to God's saving acts on behalf of his people that produced fear and amazement even in those who did not know him. The phrase **Where morning dawns and evening fades** means either "all day long" or "those nations in the east where the sun rises and those peoples in the west where the sun sets." Either way, God calls forth **songs of joy** from all people at all times. This manifestation to all people did not occur in David's day. The psalm looks forward to the spread of the gospel to the ends of the earth (Acts 1:8) and ultimately to the millennial reign of Christ (Rev. 20).

C Praise God for His Goodness (65:9–13)

65:9–10. This final section of praise focuses upon the goodness of God, specifically his bountiful provision in the promised land. David acknowledged that God cared **for the land**, meaning Palestine; he watered it with **streams**; and he enriched it with **grain**. All this occurred because God had **ordained it**. He even sent **the showers**, or gentle rains, to **bless** the **crops** with abundant harvests.

65:11–13. Carts, or farm wagons, overflowed because they could not contain the bountiful harvest. God's blessing even extended to **the grasslands of the desert**, to **the hills**, resulting in **gladness** to **the meadows** with its **flocks**, and to **the valleys** with its **grain**. Because of those many expressions of God's goodness, his people shouted for **joy** and sang. God is an overflowing source of blessing to his people.

III. CONCLUSION

Theology, which is the proper study of God, should always lead to doxology, the proper worship of God. Learning the truth about God, that he is the giver of all good things, should produce praise for God in the life of the believer. This psalm reveals God to be the source of all good things in life. Believers should offer joyful praise that acknowledges this reality. As divine blessings flow from heaven's throne to earth, thankful worship should flow from our hearts to God. Let all people ascribe to the Lord the praise due his name, shouting and singing for joy.

IV. TEACHING OUTLINE

A. Praise God for His Grace (1–4)
  1. He answers prayer (1–2)
  2. He atones for sin (3)
  3. He accepts worshipers (4a)

    4. He assigns blessings (4b)

B. Praise God for His Greatness (5–8)

    1. He causes great things (5)

    2. He created the world (6)

    3. He calms the nations (7)

    4. He calls for praise (8)

C. Praise God for His Goodness (9–13)

    1. He waters the land (9a–10c)

    2. He blesses the crops (9b,10d–11)

    3. He clothes the hills (12)

    4. He covers the meadows (13a)

    5. He fills the valleys (13b)

Psalm 66

Shout to the Lord

Quote

"*S*ing lustily and with a good courage. Beware of singing as if you were half dead, or half asleep; but lift up your voice with strength."

John Wesley

I. INTRODUCTION

*P*raise offered to God must be expressed heartily. Worship is never to be offered with apathy. It should be energetic and fervent in its adoration of God. This psalm demonstrates such dynamic praise. It is a psalm of thanksgiving in which the psalmist, probably the king of Israel, invited all the people to shout with joy to God. He encouraged everyone to declare that God had been with them. He had performed mighty deeds in the midst of their threatening trials, both to chasten them and to rescue them. Through it all, God was faithful to hear their prayers and to answer when they cried to him in the face of an enemy's threat. No wonder the psalmist called on God's people to be passionate in their praise of God.

It is possible that this deliverance of which the psalmist spoke was from the Assyrians, Israel's dreadful foe (2 Kgs. 19). This is the second psalm in a series of four (Pss. 65–68) that call God's people to worship him for rescuing them from foreign oppression.

II. COMMENTARY

MAIN IDEA: *The psalmist offers thanks for God's mighty deliverance in a time of crisis and invites others to join him in this praise.*

A A Call to Sing (66:1–4)

66:1–3. The psalmist began by summoning **all the earth** to **shout with joy to God** with a cry of adoration (1 Sam. 10:24). He invited everyone to **sing the glory** (Heb. *kabod*, "greatness") **of his name**. In the Bible a person's name represents his personality. God's name represents his awesome character and holy attributes. The people were to recognize and rejoice in the mighty acts through which God had made his **enemies cringe before** him.

66:4. Anticipating a favorable response to his invitation, the psalmist declared that **all the earth bows down to** God in humility and homage. They longed for a future time when great numbers from throughout the world would worship God.

B A Call to See (66:5–7)

66:5–7. The psalmist extended his invitation to all people: **Come and see what God has done**. This was an appeal to behold and consider the saving acts that God had performed for his people. Specifically, he urged all the earth to behold how God had **turned the sea into dry land**, recalling the time when God delivered Israel from the Egyptian army at the Red Sea (Exod. 14). In this mighty rescue, God's people **passed through the waters on foot** in an extraordinary demonstration of God's power. In response to this awesome deed, the psalmist invites the reader to **come, let us rejoice in him** because **He rules forever**, demonstrating **his power** over **the nations** who **rise up against him**. All peoples could see this mighty salvation by coming to the temple (cp. vv. 13–14), where his power was made known and celebrated through worship.

C A Call to Shout (66:8–12)

66:8. With growing intensity the psalmist called for God's people to shout to the Lord. God should be praised by his **peoples** for what he had done in the past (vv. 5–7), as well as for what he was doing in the present (vv. 8–12). **The sound of his praise** was to be heard among worshipers in the temple (v. 13).

66:9–12. The psalmist declared that God had **preserved our lives and kept our feet from slipping** into the grave. Thus, God's people had every reason to praise him. Even in the midst of their distress, God was working for their good because he had **tested** them and **refined** them **like silver**. Like a metalsmith heating precious metals in a furnace to remove all impurities, so God worked in trials to refine his people. Thus, God worked for their good, even in their suffering. Israel's enemies meant it for evil, but God worked it for good (cp. Gen. 50:20). The phrase **You brought us into prison** is a reference to being taken as prisoners of war. **Laid burdens on our backs** pictures forced slavery by the foreign armies who rode over the **heads** of Israel's fallen soldiers. Through **fire and water** is a metaphor for severe troubles. **But** God **brought** his people **to a place of abundance** (literally, an overflowing, cf. Ps. 23:5) or prosperous circumstances.

D A Call to Sacrifice (66:13–15)

66:13–14. The psalmist came to the temple to offer **burnt offerings**, serving as an example for the people to do likewise. Further, he would **fulfill** his **vows** which were **promised** to God **when** he **was in trouble**.

66:15. In this act of worship, he vowed to God, **I will sacrifice fat animals to you**. This included **rams**, **bulls**, and **goats**. The lavishness of these gifts presented to God could scarcely do the occasion justice. God had acted graciously on behalf of his people; only the best gifts should be brought to him.

E A Call to Savor (66:16–20)

66:16–20. **Come and listen**, the psalmist appealed to the gathered worshipers, and **let me tell you what he has done for me**. He indicated that he **cried out to** God with **praise . . . on his tongue**. But he knew that if he had unconfessed **sin** in his **heart, the Lord would not have listened**. He was aware that sin disqualifies the person who cries out to God from being heard (cp. Ps. 66:18). But a blameless heart gives assurance that **God has surely listened and heard** the psalmist's . . . **prayer** (cp. 1 John 3:21). This was an invitation to all worshipers to search their own hearts, knowing that unconfessed sin prevents God from hearing and honoring **prayer**. Because the psalmist's praise was offered from a pure heart, God did not withhold **his love**.

III. CONCLUSION

A true worshiper comes to God in humility, recognizing the majesty of God, and offers praise to his name. This psalm describes many components of authentic worship. Genuine worship will cause the believer to lose sight of himself in the light of God's glory. This will move the worshiper to sacrifice his life for the glory of God. The believer should offer his entire being to God as a living sacrifice (Rom. 12:1).

Moreover, the authentic worshiper offers God a spotless sacrifice that is without blemish. The worshiper should scrutinize every area of his life to see that it is in line with the holiness of God. This can be done only as the believer renews his mind in the Word of God so he does not become conformed to the world system that is steeped in sin (Rom. 12:2).

IV. TEACHING OUTLINE

A. A Call to Sing (1–4)
  1. Shout joyfully to God (1)
  2. Sing loudly to God (2)
  3. Speak graciously to God (3)
  4. Submit gladly to God (4)

B. A Call to See (5–7)
  1. Behold God's deeds (5)
  2. Behold God's deliverance (6)
  3. Behold God's dominion (7)

C. A Call to Shout (8–12)
  1. God preserves us (8–9)
  2. God purifies us (10)
  3. God punishes us (11–12a)
  4. God protects us (12b)

D. A Call to Sacrifice (13–15)
  1. I will fulfill my vows (13–14)
  2. I will bring my best (15)

E. A Call to Savor (16–20)
  1. God has helped us (16)
  2. God has heard us (17–20)

Psalm 67

Let the Nations Be Glad

I. INTRODUCTION

*A*n exalted view of God should compel the believer to do great things for God. At the heart of this is the desire to reach the world with the saving message of God's truth. The higher a believer's view of God, the stronger should burn his passion that others will come to know this glorious God. Psalm 67 inspires this kind of fervor—a holy zeal that more and more unconverted people from among the nations will become worshipers of the one true God. In order that such global missions be extended, the psalmist asked that God's blessing be poured out upon his people. In other words, he prayed that God's people would be blessed so they could extend God's blessings to the unconverted world. He asked for God's blessing so they might carry out this noble task of world evangelization.

This is the highest motive for outreach and missions. God will receive greater glory by an increasing number of worshipers who are glad in the Lord and who declare his greatness on a global scale.

II. COMMENTARY

MAIN IDEA: *The psalmist petitions God's blessing for God's people so all the nations will praise God.*

A The Psalmist's Petition (67:1)

67:1. The psalmist asked, **May God be gracious to us and bless us.** It was a request for a fuller measure of God's grace to be showered upon them. Using a synonymous phrase, he added, **and make his face shine upon us.** This imagery is a reference to the Aaronic blessing (Num. 6:24–26) in which the high priest of Israel asked the blessing of God to be extended to his people, as a king would smile on a subject with pleasure. This favorable countenance of the sovereign pictured the granting of their requests (cp. Pss. 4:6; 31:16; 80:3,7,19; 119:135). In like manner the psalmist made this request that God's favor would rest upon his subjects.

B The Psalmist's Purpose (67:2)

67:2. The purpose for such a petition was that God's **ways** might **be known on earth.** He wanted God's blessing to empower and enable his people in their spiritual lives. The psalmist also asked that God's blessing would be upon his people so they would spread his **salvation among all nations.** Intentionally, God chose Israel to serve as his instrument to reach a lost world with the saving message of his name (cp. Gen. 12:1–3; 22:18).

C The Psalmist's Passion (67:3–5)

67:3. The psalmist reinforced the global outreach of the previous verse. His words **May the peoples praise you, O God,** invited their worship with the passion of the psalmist himself. His passionate zeal was that more and more people, presently unconverted, would be added to the company of those who magnified God's name. This implies that God's people would carry the truth of divine redemption and forgiveness to **all the peoples,** leading to their conversion.

67:4. The psalmist exulted, **May the nations be glad and sing for joy.** This worldwide worship of God would become a reality only as God's people proclaimed to **the nations** the message of God's kingdom. Their salvation would usher in gladness and **joy.** This is the ultimate goal of evangelism and missions—that a greater number of worshipers will praise God. Praise would be prompted as they came to realize that the Lord rules the people **justly** and guides **the nations of the earth.**

67:5. The psalmist repeated verse 3, using a literary device known as inclusio, a technique that emphasizes the truth contained in a statement. **May**

the peoples praise you, O God, he reiterated, desiring that God would be adored by more and more worshipers.

D The Psalmist's Prospect (67:6–7)

67:6–7. As he had asked for God's blessing (v. 1), the psalmist was confident that such blessings would surely be extended. Thus, he concluded, **Then the land will yield its harvest**. He anticipated the bountiful harvest of food in the promised land, an expression of God's goodness that would strengthen their bodies and enable them to serve him. Looking forward to this harvest, he declared, **God, our God, will bless us**. He would do so for the purpose of advancing God's kingdom. His blessing would come to his people so that **all the ends of the earth** would **fear him**. God would bless his people so they might be a blessing to the unconverted nations.

III. CONCLUSION

Rightly does John Piper write in *Let the Nations Be Glad:* "Missions is not the ultimate goal of the church. Worship is. Missions exists because worship doesn't. Worship is ultimate, not missions, because God is ultimate, not man." Piper continues, "Worship, therefore, is the fuel and goal in missions. It's the goal of missions because in missions we simply aim to bring the nations into the white-hot enjoyment of God's glory. The goal of missions is the gladness of the peoples in the greatness of God" (John Piper, *Let the Nations Be Glad: The Supremacy of God in Missions*, Grand Rapids: Baker Books, 1993, p.11).

May the people of God be used by him in the work of missions to bring countless people to faith in Jesus Christ so that they, in turn, will become worshipers of the true God. May God bless his people, not for their sakes, but so this increase in worship may occur.

IV. TEACHING OUTLINE

A. The Psalmist's Petition (1)
  1. Show your grace to us (1a)
  2. Shine your goodness upon us (1b)
B. The Psalmist's Purpose (2)
  1. May God's revelation be known (2a)
  2. May God's salvation be received (2b)
C. The Psalmist's Passion (3–5)
  1. May all peoples praise God (3,5)
  2. May all nations rejoice in God (4)
D. The Psalmist's Prospect (6–7)
  1. Then God will bless his people (6–7a)
  2. Then God will build his kingdom (7b)

Psalm 68

Persistent Praise

"*In* prayer we act like men; in praise we act like angels."

Thomas Watson

Psalm 68

I. INTRODUCTION

*A*ll people have been created by God for the ultimate purpose of giving him glory. Nowhere is this reason for one's being more heard than in the vocalized praises of his people. It is this purpose for living that forms the heartbeat of this psalm, a song in which David ascribes greatness to God. This psalm is a victorious song of celebration that extols God's triumphant ascent to Mount Zion to rule over Israel and the earth. David probably wrote this psalm when he conquered the holy city Jerusalem (2 Sam. 5:6–9) or when he moved the ark of the covenant from the house of Obed-Edom to Jerusalem (2 Sam. 6). Appropriately this psalm would have been used at subsequent victories of Israel, leading the people to rejoice in God for the victory he gave to his people.

This inspired hymn reviews the history of Israel from their leaving Mount Sinai, through their wilderness wanderings, to their entrance into and conquest of the promised land. David focused upon Mount Zion as the chosen abode of God in this new land, the place where the Israelites would take many captives and receive many spoils of victory. David invited the Lord's people to join him in praising the God who performs righteous acts.

II. COMMENTARY

> **MAIN IDEA:** *David rejoices that God is a mighty warrior and victor over his enemies, inviting praise from all people.*

🅰 David's Rejoicing in God's Purposes (68:1–6)

68:1–3. With an opening fanfare of fervent passion, David prayed that God would **arise** in power and that **his enemies** would **be scattered** in devastating defeat (cp. Num. 10:35). Then God's **foes** would be **blown away** like **smoke** and would melt like **wax** before a hot fire. In this display of divine power, **the righteous** would **be glad and rejoice**.

68:4–6. David invited the people to praise God for his tender care. **Sing to God . . . who rides on the clouds**, he declared. This pictures the Lord coming to the aid of his people. The words refuted a similar claim made of Baal, the pagan god. The name of the one true God was **the LORD** (Heb. *Yah*, an abbreviation for Yahweh), the self-sufficient, eternal God. He was **a father to the fatherless**, caring for orphans, **a defender of widows**, protecting the defenseless. He **leads forth the prisoners**, those who suffer for the sake of righteousness, **with singing** while **the rebellious live** without God's loving care.

🅱 David's Recollection of God's Providence (68:7–18)

68:7–10. David looked to the past, reflecting on the faithfulness of God to his people in order to bolster his heart in the present. He did so by reflecting on Israel's march from Mount **Sinai through the wasteland**. There **the earth shook**, a manifestation of God's majesty (Exod. 19:18), and the clouds **poured down rain** to refresh God's people. Forty years later God's people **settled in** the promised land, where the Lord promised to provide for his people, even **the poor** (Josh. 5:11–12).

68:11–14. Before the battles were fought, **the Lord announced** that he would be victorious over Canaanite **kings and armies** (cp. Exod. 23:22–31; Deut. 7:10–24; Josh. 1:2–6), and it came to pass. The phrase **Even while you sleep** indicates their most vulnerable and defenseless moment. God would still fight for Israel, and their enemies would be scattered like fresh **snow**. God promised to protect his **dove**, an affectionate term for Israel.

68:15–18. As Israel occupied the promised land, God chose Mount Zion to be the place of his earthly abode, making jealous the **mountains of Bashan** (Mount Hermon). The other **mountains** of Israel were filled with **envy** because God chose **to reign** in Zion **forever**. God's entrance to Zion when

David moved the ark to Jerusalem is pictured as being attended by **the chariots of God** with **thousands of thousands** of the angelic host.

In this triumphant ascent God **ascended on high**, taking his place on Mount Zion. He was victorious over his enemies, taking as **captives** those who were once **rebellious** toward God's rule but were now subdued. The apostle Paul used this verse to speak of Christ's triumphant ascension to the Father's right hand following his resurrection (Eph. 4:8–10).

C David's Realization of God's Power (68:19–27)

68:19–20. A major shift occurs at this point in the psalm. Up to now, David had recounted what God had done for Israel in the past. Now he praised God for his activity in the present: **Praise be to the Lord, to God our Savior, who daily bears our burdens**. This daily care by God, their **Sovereign LORD**, included their **escape from death** at the hands of their enemies.

68:21–23. Surely God would **crush the heads of his enemies**, utterly defeating them, David declared, just as he had done in the past. The Lord said, "**I will bring them from Bashan**," the place where they fled to hide at the victorious march of God into Jerusalem with the ark of the covenant. God would cause Israel to be victorious, and the nation would **plunge** its **feet in the blood** of its **foes**.

68:24–27. David's focus returned to Israel's triumphant **procession . . . into the sanctuary** in Jerusalem. It was a march attended by **singers** and **musicians** and **maidens** with **tambourines**, all leading the people to **praise God**. From **the little tribe of Benjamin**, to **the great throng** of Judah in the south, to **Zebulun** and **Naphtali** in the north, all God's people should join in praising God.

D David's Request for God's Protection (68:28–31)

68:28–31. David prayed that God would continue to triumph over his foes. **Summon your power** and **show us your strength**, he prayed, **as you have done before**. When they came to Jerusalem, foreign **kings** would bring **gifts** as a tribute. He called upon God to **rebuke** the mighty pharaoh of Egypt who was pictured as **the beast among the reeds**. Likewise, God should **rebuke** other powerful princes, who are represented as **the herd of bulls among the calves**—the strong among the weak. These **humbled** leaders should **bring bars of silver** in tribute because God would **scatter the nations** that threatened war, making them submit to him.

E David's Reaffirmation of God's Praises (68:32–35)

68:32–35. David called upon all the foreign nations to **sing praise to the Lord**. He was the awesome God who rode the **ancient skies** in majestic glory. He thundered with a **mighty voice** in unrivaled authority. Let the one true

God be praised! David concluded, **You are awesome, O God, in your sanctuary,** a reference to where the ark rests in Jerusalem.

III. CONCLUSION

One of the most interesting features of this psalm is that Paul applied verse 18, which referred to the arrival of the ark of the covenant at Mount Zion, to the triumphant ascension of the Lord Jesus Christ following his resurrection. Ultimately, this psalm points prophetically to the enthronement of Christ Jesus at the right hand of God the Father (Eph. 4:8–10). While God is represented in this psalm as receiving gifts from men, even rebellious men, in the New Testament he is revealed as giving gifts to his people, the church.

The point is clear: a victorious king would both receive and dispense gifts, especially the spoils of victory. This sovereign is the King of kings and Lord of lords, Jesus Christ. Through his work at the cross, he delivered sinners from slavery to sin and ushered them into his presence.

IV. TEACHING OUTLINE

   A. David's Rejoicing in God's Purposes (1–6)
     1. May God defeat his enemies (1–2)
       a. Let God arise (1a)
       b. Let God attack (1b–2)
     2. May believers delight in God (3–6)
       a. Let them rejoice in God (3)
       b. Let them sing to God (4–6)
         (1) He rides on the clouds (4)
         (2) He cares for the needy (5–6)
   B. David's Recollection of God's Providence (7–18)
     1. God's march through the wilderness (7–10)
       a. He went before them (7)
       b. He blessed them (8–9)
       c. He guided them (10)
     2. God's Victories over Canaan (11–14)
       a. He gave the word (11)
       b. He routed the kings (12–14)
     3. God's ascent to Mount Zion (15–18)
       a. He chooses Mount Zion (15–16)
       b. He conquers Mount Zion (17–18)
   C. David's Realization of God's Power (19–27)
     1. God's reign is continuous (19–23)
       a. He will daily bless his people (19–20)
       b. He will diligently crush his enemies (21–23)

2. God's reign is celebrated (24–27)
   a. His procession arrives (24–25)
   b. His procession acclaims (26–27)
D. David's Request for God's Protection (28–31)
  1. God, demonstrate your power (28)
  2. God, devastate your enemies (29–31)
   a. He receives gifts (29)
   b. He rebukes kings (30–31)
E. David's Reaffirmation of God's Praises (32–35)
  1. Sing praises to God (32–33)
   a. From all the earth (32)
   b. To him who reigns above (33)
  2. Proclaim power to God (34–35b)
   a. He is majestic (34)
   b. He is awesome (35a)
   c. He is powerful (35b)
  3. Praise be to God! (35c)

Psalm 69

Hated Without a Cause

I. INTRODUCTION

*S*uffering unjustly in this fallen world is a painful experience for believers, but one that should be expected. This evil world system is no friend to grace, and it seeks to destroy those who live according to righteousness. In Psalm 69 David stands as a model for all saints who suffer opposition and persecution for doing what is right. Finding himself persecuted because of his zeal for God, David pleaded with God to rescue him from wicked people who wanted to kill him. To make matters worse, his own brethren had schemed this conspiracy against him. In his desperate plight, David pleaded with God to deliver him and asked that the Lord's wrath be poured out upon his enemies. With renewed faith, he ended this psalm with resounding praise to God, who would deliver him from his distress.

This psalm "of David" is one of the most quoted psalms in the New Testament. It was often applied by the apostles to Christ (Matt. 27:34,48; Mark 15:23,36; Luke 23:36; John 19:29; Rom. 11:9–10) and unbelievers (2 Cor. 6:2). Thus, as David suffered for the sake of righteousness, it was a foreshadowing of the coming of Jesus Christ, who would be hated and rejected by his own people. This psalm provides encouragement for all believers who suffer persecution for their faith by a hostile world.

II. COMMENTARY

> **MAIN IDEA:** *David petitions God to deliver him from his foes and to punish those who taunt and accuse him.*

A David's Crisis (69:1–4)

69:1. David began this psalm abruptly with **Save me, O God**, pleading for God's deliverance from his troubles. He described his predicament as **waters which had come up to his neck**. Deep waters was a common metaphor for threatening problems. David was up to his neck in trouble and was about to drown. He called out for God's rescuing mercy.

69:2–4. Stringing together more watery synonyms that described his trial, David prayed, **I sink in the miry depths**. He was drowning in the depths of despair. The phrase **I have come into the deep waters**, pictures him overwhelmed by his troubles. **The floods engulf me**, he declared, referring to the many attacks of his enemies. Exhausted from crying, he was **worn out calling for help**, so much so that his throat was **parched**, or hoarse.

Surrounded by many enemies to whom he had done no wrong, he acknowledged, **Those who hate me without reason outnumber the hairs of my head**. They were seemingly too numerous to count. **Without cause**, they had spread false accusations against him, turning the people against him.

B David's Confession (69:5–12)

69:5–6. Ready to confess his sin which had brought on his troubles, David declared, **You know my folly, O God; my guilt is not hidden from you**. The word *folly* indicates a sin against truth, a moral insolence, and *guilt* is the filthy conscience that results. David was not admitting that there was truth in the false charges of his enemies. But his troubles had caused him to search his heart in order to purify it. He feared that his persecution might weaken the faith of others. So he prayed, **May those who hope in you**—referring to those who truly believe in God—**not be disgraced because of me**.

69:7–12. David recognized the larger issue of spiritual warfare in this situation. He confessed that his present **scorn** was **for** God's **sake**, meaning for the cause of righteousness (cp. Matt. 5:10–12). He was a **stranger** to his own **brothers** because his **zeal** for God's **house** had ostracized him from others, causing him to be misunderstood. David knew he was suffering **insults** that were directed toward God. This persecution had caused him to **weep and fast**, suffer **scorn**, and **put on sackcloth**—a symbol of remorse and humiliation. People made **sport of** him and mocked him. **Drunkards** made him the theme of their **song** by belittling him.

C David's Cry (69:13–18)

69:13. In the face of this unjust persecution, David declared, **I pray to you, O LORD, in the time of your favor.** This refers to a time when God would demonstrate his saving mercy (cp. Ps. 32:6). This appeal was based on God's mercy, specifically his **great love**, not on David's merit.

69:14–18. Thus, David cried out, **Rescue me from the mire**, or "deliver me from **those who hate me**." Again he appealed to **the goodness** of God's **love** and his **great mercy** as the basis for God to **answer** his cry. **Rescue me**, he pleaded, knowing that God was his only hope for deliverance from his adversaries.

D David's Conspirators (69:19–21)

69:19–21. Appealing to God, David stated, **You know how I am scorned, disgraced and shamed**. These terms conveyed the persecution he had suffered from his enemies. This rejection had **broken** his **heart**, leaving him **helpless**. No **sympathy** from **comforters** was to be **found**. They had **put gall**, a poisonous herb, in David's food, and they had given him **vinegar** to drink. These are metaphors for the bitter betrayal he had suffered. These enemies had inflicted great harm upon David.

E David's Charge (69:22–28)

69:22–26. Motivated by righteous indignation, David prayed for God's **retribution** to fall on his foes. The phrase **The table set before them** refers to the meal that his adversaries shared when they met to make their evil plans. David wanted their **eyes** to **be darkened** so they would not be able to carry out their conspiracy against him. Further, he asked God to **pour out** his **fierce anger** and to bend their **backs**, permanently disabling them. He wanted these people wiped out, leaving **no one**, not even their families, **to dwell in their tents**. In other words, David wanted those who sought his life to be removed by God. The reason for this punishment was that they had persecuted God's people.

69:27–28. David pleaded with God, **Charge them with crime upon crime** and **do not let them share in your salvation**. Let their names **not be listed with the righteous**. This does not mean he wished for their eternal damnation, but he desired the full punishment of their sins if they did not repent. Hypothetically speaking, David asked that they be **blotted out of the book of life**. Yet he knew their names were **not . . . listed with the righteous**.

F David's Celebration (69:29–36)

69:29–33. In much **pain** and **distress**, David asked God to **protect** him which means to raise him to a place that is both elevated and guarded. Then, as a man who trusted God, David abruptly shifted from his pain (v. 29) to **praise** (v. 30). He rose above his circumstances and looked to heaven to **praise God's**

name in song. In confident faith he looked forward to the time when he could record his deliverance by praising God. This joyful worship, especially in the midst of trials, would **please the LORD**. David offered to God more than the prescribed sacrifices of an ox or a bull. He offered his wholehearted praise.

69:34–36. Building to a crescendo, David called on all **heaven and earth** to praise the Lord because God would save Zion. In that day God would rebuild the devastated cities of Judah, allowing **the children of his servants** to **inherit it**.

III. CONCLUSION

This psalm is distinctly messianic, as it finds its ultimate fulfillment in the coming of the Lord Jesus Christ. One of the most quoted psalms in the New Testament, it was applied by the apostles to the rejection suffered by Christ. From this psalm we see a foreshadowing of our Lord's persecution by the world (v. 4; cp. John 15:25), zeal for God (v. 9; cp. John 2:17), and circumstances of the cross (v. 21; cp. Matt. 27:48). From this prophetic vantage point, we learn in this psalm that Christ is the perfect embodiment of righteousness that was persecuted by evil men for doing God's will and God's work. Likewise, all believers today who live godly lives in Christ Jesus will suffer persecution (2 Tim. 3:12).

IV. TEACHING OUTLINE

A. David's Crisis (1–4)
 1. He is drowning (1–2)
 2. He is drained (3)
 3. He is despised (4)
B. David's Confession (5–12)
 1. He has sinned (5–6)
 2. He has suffered (7–12)
  a. Dishonor (7)
  b. Disassociation (8)
  c. Despite (9)
  d. Depression (10–11)
  e. Degradation (12)
C. David's Cry (13–18)
 1. Answer me, God (13)
 2. Deliver me, God (14–15)
 3. See me, God (16–17)
 4. Ransom me, God (18)
D. David's Conspirators (19–21)
 1. They shame him (19)
 2. They sicken him (20)

3. They scorned him (21)

E. David's Charge (22–28)
　1. Bind my enemies (22)
　2. Blind my enemies (23)
　3. Blast my enemies (24–26)
　4. Bury my enemies (27)
　5. Blot out my enemies (28)

F. David's Celebration (29–36)
　1. I will praise God (29–33)
　　a. This will glorify God (29–30)
　　b. This will gratify the Lord (31)
　　c. This will gladden others (32–33)
　2. May all praise God (34–36)
　　a. Let all peoples today praise him (34–35a)
　　b. Let people tomorrow praise him (35b–36)

Psalm 70

Lord, Come Quickly!

Psalm 70

I. INTRODUCTION

*T*he best prayers are often the shortest prayers, quick distress calls offered to God in the heat of a crisis. Without time for formality or structure, these pleas are desperate cries for God to intervene quickly. Such a short, passionate plea is this brief psalm "of David," only five verses in length. It was a short but urgent prayer offered by David at a troubling time when he was surrounded by evil men. So perilous and pressing was this crisis that David pleaded with God for a quick rescue. There was no time to waste or he would surely perish. This prayer is nearly identical to Psalm 40:13–17, the only exception being that this psalm substitutes "God" (Heb. *elohim*) for "LORD" (Heb. *yahweh*) (vv. 1,4–5).

The title of this psalm identifies it as "a petition" which means literally "to bring to remembrance" (cp. Ps. 38). This psalm reminds God's people of their urgent need for the Lord.

II. COMMENTARY

> **MAIN IDEA:** *David offers an urgent prayer for God's immediate help when threatened by his enemies.*

A David's Cry (70:1)

70:1. With a desperate heart, David cried out to God, **Hasten, O God, to save me.** Finding himself surrounded by threatening enemies, he called on God to deliver him. The word *hasten* is not a part of the original Hebrew text, but has been supplied by the translators for clarity. Instead, the original text reads, literally, "God, to save me." These are the words of a person under great pressure. David continued to implore God by asking, **O LORD, come quickly to help me.** This was no time to be eloquent with words. Some of the greatest prayers in the Bible are short and to the point, reflecting a crisis situation.

B David's Concern (70:2–4)

70:2. The psalmist acknowledged that there were those who sought his life, revealing that he was in a life-threatening situation with bloodthirsty men. He asked that they would **be put to shame and confusion** or be exposed and fail. Further, **may all who desire my ruin**, a reference to the attempts of these same evil men, **be turned back in disgrace.**

70:3–4. The word **Aha** is an expression of scorn. David asked that his enemies be turned **back because of their shame** and brought to naught because of their evil actions. But he wanted **all** who sought God to **rejoice and be glad.** The reason for their celebration was their belief that God was enthroned and was in control, even in a crisis. And when God did deliver his servant David, it would be a cause for great joy for all believers **who love** his **salvation.** David knew that his rescue by God would bolster the faith of his people and move them to say, "Let God be exalted!"

C David's Confidence (70:5)

70:5a. Putting no confidence in himself, David confessed, **Yet I am poor and needy.** This statement shows that he understood his protection from his enemies would not come from his own human resources but from God. Thus, he cried out all the more, **Come quickly to me, O God.** Unlike verse 1, in this instance **come quickly** is actually found in the original text. Its inclusion emphasizes the urgency of this situation.

70:5b. Declaring his firm confidence in God, David stated, **You are my help and my deliverer.** There was no one to rescue him but God. Without a moment to spare, David pleaded for God's intervention: O LORD, **do not delay.** Without a moment to spare, David pleads for God's immediate intervention.

III. CONCLUSION

When God's people find themselves in desperate situations, God must be their first recourse, never their last resort. Like David in this psalm, they must turn to the Lord and not petition him casually but urgently. Believers should call out to God in their hour of trouble with desperate pleas. They should press straight to the point and plead for God's attention. May the Lord, through this psalm, encourage the hearts of all who seek him.

IV. TEACHING OUTLINE

A. David's Cry (1)
   1. Save me completely (1a)
   2. Help me quickly (1b)
B. David's Concern (2–4)
   1. May the godless be exposed (2–3)
      a. Disgrace them (2–3)
      b. Disorient them (2a)
      c. Defeat them (2b,3b)
   2. May the godly be enthused (4)
C. David's Confidence (5)
   1. I have no self-confidence (5a)
   2. I have only God-confidence (5b)

Psalm 71
Finishing Strong

"*It* would be a good thing if young people were wise and old people were strong, but God has arranged things better."

M a r t i n   L u t h e r

I. INTRODUCTION

Saving the Best for Last

*T*hroughout the pages of Scripture, God called many of his choicest servants to do their greatest work in their latter years. Abraham was one hundred years old when Isaac was born, and Sarah was ninety when she delivered. Moses was eighty when God enlisted him to lead Israel out of Egyptian bondage. Caleb was eighty-five when he requested the tallest mountain with the largest giants to fight. Zacharias and Elizabeth were both advanced in years when God chose them to have a son, John the Baptist. The apostle John was ninety, or perhaps older, when God commissioned him to write the Book of Revelation. With each of these saints, God saved the best for last.

This quality of steadfast endurance in one's final years is the central theme of Psalm 71. This song is the prayer of an anonymous saint, one advanced in years, who had trusted God all his life. Now in old age, he still sought divine help as he was attacked by enemies. His adversaries saw that his strength was waning and assumed that God had abandoned him. But the psalmist called on the Lord to deliver him again. This psalm should make believers aware that God will surely deliver them, no matter how old they might be.

While this psalm has no superscription, it has been suggested that it couples with Psalm 70 which, if this is the case, serves as its introduction.

II. COMMENTARY

Finishing Strong

> **MAIN IDEA:** *The psalmist, an old man, finds himself afflicted and attacked by adversaries and cries out to God for deliverance.*

A A Prayer of Confidence (71:1–8)

> **SUPPORTING IDEA:** *The psalmist reaffirms to God his trust in him alone; from his youth until his old age, he has trusted him.*

71:1–2. With a bold confession of faith in God, the psalmist affirmed, **In you, O LORD, I have taken refuge**. He relied not on his own human ability but chose to rely upon divine sovereignty. **Let me never be put to shame**, the psalmist asked, as he placed his trust in God. This would occur if he were to be humiliated by his enemies and should suffer loss while resting in God. He pleaded not his own goodness but for God's **righteousness**. How much better to appeal to God based on God's perfect character rather than on man's flawed character.

71:3. The psalmist cried, **Be my rock of refuge** (Heb. *maon*, "dwelling place"; cp. Pss. 90:1; 91:9). He reaffirmed that God was the permanent home for his soul to which he could **always go** to find strength and protection. The word *always* is emphatic here, not found in Psalm 31:1–3 from which it is believed these verses are drawn. Over his long life, the elderly psalmist had found God to be always faithful to him. Now more than ever, he had reason to trust God who had been reliable and sufficient in every trial. These many years had not diminished his confidence in God, his **rock** and **fortress**, the stability and strength of his life.

71:4. The psalmist asked God to deliver him **from the hand of the wicked**. These enemies were **evil and cruel men** who opposed all that was good and holy. Although it is not directly stated, the psalmist possibly suffered this injury for doing right in a fallen world (cp. Matt. 5:10–12; John 15:18–20; 2 Tim. 3:12).

71:5–6. Since his **youth**, the psalmist had put his **hope** in God and had never been disappointed in his **Sovereign LORD**. He had every reason to praise God in his twilight years. Over these many decades—**from birth** to this point—his **hope** in God had been unwavering.

71:7–8. Now in his golden years, the psalmist still had need to trust God. He had not outgrown his need for the Lord. He declared, **I have become like a portent** ("wonder" KJV; "marvel" NASB), meaning people were amazed at the troubles in which he, an older man, still found himself. Nevertheless, he was unshaken in his confidence in God. **You are my strong refuge** (Heb. *mahseh*, "shelter from danger"; Pss. 14:6; 46:1; 61:3; 62:7–8; 73:28; 91:2,9), he testified. With renewed fervor, the psalmist vowed to declare his praise for God, declaring his **splendor all day long** for all people to hear.

B A Prayer of Contrition (71:9–13)

SUPPORTING IDEA: *The psalmist lifts to God the wicked plots of his adversaries, asking God to intercede on his behalf by judging his enemies.*

71:9–11. In his advanced years, now more than ever, the psalmist needed God not to **cast** him **away** or **forsake** him because he is **old** and weak. He indicated that he was growing weaker with each passing year. He especially needed God's strength, since his age made him more vulnerable to attack. His increased years had increased his **enemies**. They spoke slanderous lies against him, he lamented, saying, **God has forsaken him**. His enemies supposed they could **pursue him and seize him** without anyone to rescue him. But in planning their sinister plots, they forgot God.

71:12–13. In response to these threats, the psalmist prayed, **Be not far from me, O God**. If God should delay or not **come quickly**, he sensed that it would be too late to help him. Consequently he requested, **May my accusers . . . be covered with scorn and disgrace** in humiliating defeat and open shame.

SUPPORTING IDEA: *The psalmist reaffirms his commitment to praise and proclaim the mighty acts, power, and righteousness of God.*

C A Prayer of Commitment (71:14–21)

71:14–15. In the face of this personal threat, the psalmist remained anchored in God. Rather than destroying his faith, these trials actually deepened his reliance on God. Instead of turning bitter, he remained buoyant, abounding in positive confidence in God. With deepening resolution, he asserted that his mouth would tell of God's righteousness **all day long**. He declared that God's **salvation** was so great that it could not be measured. God's inexhaustible mercies could not be counted.

71:16. In the face of this mounting threat against his life, the psalmist vowed, **I will come and proclaim your mighty acts, O Sovereign LORD**, especially God's **righteousness**. He would extol God's greatness, no matter what. He would do so because God always worked to right wrongs. God could be trusted to act on behalf of his people.

71:17–18. From his **youth** to the present (cp. v. 9), the psalmist testified that God had taught him the way of life. For God's enduring faithfulness, he would declare the Lord's **marvelous deeds**. Now old, he recognized that he needed the Lord's help more than ever. If God would preserve him through this trial, he promised he would declare his **power to the next generation**.

71:19–21. God in his righteousness is transcendent and majestic, high and lifted up, towering over man's injustices, always doing **great things**. The psalmist remained confident that God ruled over his troubles. Not only had God made him see his troubles, but God would also restore his life out of these troubles, specifically **from the depths of the earth**. This imagery represents the grave, specifically this near-death, life-threatening situation from which God would deliver him. God would restore his reputation before men, and they would again know that God was with him.

D A Prayer of Celebration (71:22–24)

SUPPORTING IDEA: *The aging psalmist ends the psalm by praising God with harp, lyre, and lips.*

71:22–24. Concluding with a strong vow of **praise**, the psalmist pledged that he would praise God with loud singing accompanied by **the harp** and **the lyre**. His lips would **shout for joy** because he had been redeemed by God from his enemies and their threats. His tongue would tell of God's **righteous acts** on his behalf. This magnification of God would last **all day long** because God had **put to shame** his enemies.

MAIN IDEA REVIEW: *The psalmist, an old man, finds himself afflicted and attacked by adversaries and cries out to God for deliverance.*

III. CONCLUSION

Faithful unto Death

At the age of eighty-six, Polycarp, the second-century pastor of the church of Smyrna, was summoned before the Roman proconsul. There he was ordered to take an oath, renouncing Christ and claiming allegiance to Caesar. Polycarp responded, "Eighty-six years have I served the Lord Jesus. He has been faithful to me. How can I be faithless to Him and blaspheme the name of my Savior?"

Enraged, the proconsul sent a messenger into the city of Smyrna to proclaim that Bishop Polycarp had committed high treason against Rome by admitting to being a Christian. A bloodthirsty mob gathered in the arena of the city. There they built a pyre of boards and planks while they clamored that Polycarp be handed over to them. They had brought nails to fasten Polycarp's hands and feet to the stakes.

Polycarp then uttered these famous words:

> Put away those nails and let them be. The One who gives me strength to endure the flames will give me strength not to flinch at the

stake. You threaten me with a fire that burns for a short time and is quickly quenched. For you do not know the fire that awaits the wicked and the judgment to come and an everlasting punishment. Why are you waiting? Come do what you will to me.

With that, the fire was lit and Polycarp was martyred for his faith in Christ. Even in his advanced years, he was faithful to God until death. May it be so with us. May we grow bolder and more committed to God, even as we grow older.

IV. LIFE APPLICATION

Seeking the Lord in Old Age

As we grow older, life's problems do not go away, but often they actually increase. New troubles must be faced in our latter years. Physical ailments with their pains and limitations must be faced. Loss of power and income can be sobering. Retirement can provide additional spare time, allowing the wandering mind to be too active in analyzing potential problems. Loneliness and discouragement can quickly settle in. The loss of a spouse through death can lead to despair. Loss of lifelong friends can compound these feelings of despondency. Watching a changing world that is disintegrating and becoming increasingly evil adds to the frustration.

Likewise, the constant reminder that our own death is looming on the horizon can add a sense of panic. All of these issues can accelerate in old age, bringing tests to our faith as never before. In the latter years of life, we need the Lord more than ever.

V. PRAYER

Oh sovereign Lord, in you we have taken refuge because you are our rock and fortress. From our birth we have been dependent on you for everything. You have never failed us. From the beginning of our salvation until the days of our old age, we declare your infinite worth. Lord, teach us to praise you more and more by telling of your righteousness and salvation. Teach us to speak of your mighty acts to the next generation. In the blessed name of our Lord. Amen.

VI. DEEPER DISCOVERIES

A. Old (71:9)

The word *old* (Heb. *ziqna*) means "advanced in years" or "old age." It was used of Sarah (Gen. 24:36), Solomon (1 Kgs. 11:4), and Asa (1 Kgs. 15:23).

God says, "Even to your old age and gray hairs I am he, I am he who will sustain you. I have made you and I will carry you; I will sustain you and I will rescue you" (Isa. 46:4). This word is a derivative of *ziqna*, which was used to speak of those who were "old and full of years" (Gen. 25:8; 35:29; Job 42:17). The Old Testament places great value on the testimony of the aged (1 Kgs. 12:6; Ezek. 7:26; Jer. 26:17). Furthermore, "Children's children are a crown to the aged" (Prov. 17:6) and "gray hair the splendor of the old" (Prov. 20:29).

B. Perish (71:13)

This word (Heb. *kala*) occurs 237 times in the Old Testament in various forms. It means "to be completed, finished, destroyed, or at an end." The meaning derived from the root is to bring a process to completion. So the best corresponding English word is "finished." This completion or ending may have negative or positive connotations. Obviously, the connotation in this psalm is negative and points to the complete destruction of the psalmist's wicked adversaries. In this sense, this word was used to describe the judgment of God that will fall upon the wicked (Pss. 18:37; 37:20; 78:33; 90:7; Isa. 1:28; 29:20; Jer. 5:3; 14:12; Ezek. 5:13; 7:8; 13:14; 22:31; 43:8). At times God threatened to consume or finish off the rebellious Israelites (Exod. 32:10; Num. 16:21; Lam. 3:22). The word is also used to describe the devastating effects of war (Deut. 7:22; 1 Sam 15:18; Jer. 16:4).

C. See (71:20)

The word *see* (Heb. *raa*) means "to understand," as if one would see intellectually what had not been previously understood; other denotations are "to behold, perceive, view with right understanding." Here it means to be made to see and understand with divine enlightenment that only God can give (Num. 8:4; Deut. 4:36; 5:24; 34:4; 2 Kgs. 8:10,13; 20:13,15; Pss. 60:3; 78:11; Jer. 24:1; 38:21; Ezek. 11:25; Amos 7:1,4,7; 8:1).

D. Sing Praise (71:22)

The phrase *sing praise* (Heb. *zamar*) occurs exclusively in the Hebrew poetry sections of the Old Testament and means "to make music" or "to celebrate." This phrase expresses great joy directed toward God and is prominent in the Psalms (Pss. 7:17; 9:2,11; 18:49; 21:13; 27:6; 30:4,12; 33:2; 47:6–7; 57:7,9; 59:17; 66:2,4; 68:4,32; 71:22–23; 75:9; 92:1; 98:4–5; 101:1; 104:33; 105:2; 108:1,3; 135:3; 138:1; 144:9; 146:2; 147:1,7; 149:3). It usually has a positive connotation, that of praising God; only two passages are exceptions to this (Isa. 25:5; Amos 5:23).

VII. TEACHING OUTLINE

A. A Prayer of Confidence (1–8)

1. God is my habitation (1–3)
   a. My refuge (1)
   b. My rescuer (2)
   c. My rock (3)
2. God is my hope (4–7)
   a. My saving deliverer (4)
   b. My sure confidence (5)
   c. My steady reliance (6)
   d. My strong refuge (7)
3. God is my happiness (8)
B. A Prayer of Contrition (9–13)
   1. God, do not forsake me (9–11)
      a. For I am aged (9)
      b. For I am attacked (10–11)
   2. God, do not be far away (12–13)
      a. Come quickly (12)
      b. Consume completely (13)
C. A Prayer of Commitment (14–21)
   1. I will praise you (14–15)
      a. Increasingly (14)
      b. Continually (15)
   2. I will proclaim you (16–18)
      a. Your mighty acts (16a)
      b. Your majestic character (16b)
      c. Your marvelous deeds (17)
      d. Your mighty power (18)
   3. I will pursue you (19–21)
      a. Because of who you are (19)
      b. Because of what you do (20–21)
D. A Prayer of Celebration (22–24)
   1. With musical instruments (22)
      a. With the harp (22a)
      b. With the lyre (22b)
   2. With my lips (23–24)
      a. With shouts of joy (23a)
      b. With songs of praise (23b–24)

VIII. ISSUES FOR DISCUSSION

1. Do I find myself increasing in godly wisdom as I grow older?
2. Do I regularly declare to God my total dependence on him?
3. Do I faithfully teach the next generation the truths of God?

Psalm 72
One Greater Than Solomon

| Q u o t e |

"We see on the shore of time the wrecks of the Caesars,

the relics of the Moguls, and the last remnants of the Otto-

mans, Charlemagne, Maximillian, Napoleon, how they flit like

shadows before us! They were and are not; but Jesus forever is."

C h a r l e s   H .   S p u r g e o n

I. INTRODUCTION

Two Towering Mountain Peaks

Two towering mountain peaks rise up from the surrounding plains. One is immediately before you, close and near; the other looms on the horizon. A considerable distance separates the two peaks, causing the second to appear smaller. But as you approach them, you realize that the second peak is not the smaller of the two but actually larger. In fact, the closer you get to the peaks, the more the second peak towers over the first. The second mountain rises up into the clouds and disappears; the first remains easily in full view. The second peak is snowcapped; the first is not. The closer you draw to the two peaks, the more it becomes obvious: the grandeur of the second mountain far exceeds the first.

This is the dual effect presented in Psalm 72. Two towering mountain peaks of truth stand before the reader in this psalm. Each summit represents the reign of a mighty king. One is near and great; the other is far away yet even more grand. The first is the reign of Solomon who ruled over Israel; the second is the reign of Christ who reigns over all the earth. The first kingdom is temporal; the latter is eternal. The first is regional; the latter is universal. The first is the son of David, Solomon; the latter is the Lord Jesus Christ, a greater Son of David than Solomon.

Immediately evident in Psalm 72 is the reign of Solomon, the king of Israel. But a careful reading of this psalm reveals another kingly reign, a second mountain peak that looms on the horizon. It is the reign of a promised descendent of Solomon, a greater son of David, the Lord Jesus Christ. This dual focus must be maintained when studying Psalm 72. One kingly reign stands immediately before the reader; the other is still in the future at the time of its writing.

The superscription of this psalm designates it as a psalm "of Solomon." Not only was it written *by* Solomon; it was probably written *for* Solomon, specifically on the occasion of his succession to the throne of his father David. Thus, this is a coronation psalm written probably by Solomon on the occasion of the beginning of his reign as king over Israel (1 Kgs. 2). Likewise, this psalm was also used at the time of the inaugurations of other future kings of Israel. Psalm 72 is an intercessory prayer by the people on behalf of their newly installed king, petitioning God that his reign would be marked by divine favor and holy virtue.

But one greater than Solomon emerges from the shadows of this psalm. It also points to the glorious reign of the Lord Jesus Christ, who would govern all the earth (vv. 8,11). This dominion far exceeds Solomon's forty-year reign over Israel. A greater than Solomon is revealed in this royal psalm.

II. COMMENTARY

One Greater Than Solomon

MAIN IDEA: *Solomon prays for the earthly, temporal blessings of God to rest upon his reign but looks ahead to the Lord Jesus Christ, who will reign forever.*

A An Equitable Reign (72:1–4)

SUPPORTING IDEA: *Solomon prays that the king's reign will be marked by righteousness and justice for all people.*

72:1–2. Solomon began by interceding, **Endow the king with your justice, O God, the royal son with your righteousness**. The words *justice* and *righteousness* are used synonymously as requests for God-given abilities to be granted to this king that would lead to equity, fairness, and rightness. Solomon's duty was to dispense divine justice as a **judge**, defending righteous

people who were unjustly attacked by evil men. Prophetically, Jesus Christ is the divine protector of his people, both in this age and in the age to come.

72:3. **The mountains**, which represent the most dominant aspects of the kingdom, as well as the little **hills**, meaning those lesser parts, would know peace or a sense of **prosperity**. If the king reigned in **righteousness**, blessings would result for everyone under his rule.

72:4. As the divinely appointed guardian of God's people, the king would **defend the afflicted** who suffered unjustly and **save the children of the needy** who were attacked by ungodly men. He would **crush** all evil leaders and their ruthless followers who tried to harm God's people. In the end, Christ would crush Satan, the greatest **oppressor**.

B An Eternal Reign (72:5–7)

SUPPORTING IDEA: *Solomon prays for the unending reign of the king; this points to the eternal reign of Christ.*

72:5–6. Looking beyond time to eternity future, the people boasted that this king would endure **through all generations**. This looks far beyond the reign of Solomon, a mortal man, to an eternal reign that would never end (cp. Dan. 4:34–35; Luke 1:30–33)—the reign of Christ Jesus. He would **be like rain falling on a mown field**, pouring his blessing on his people, refreshing, renewing, and replenishing them **like showers watering the earth**.

72:7. In Solomon's time the righteous would flourish and know divine blessing. Prosperity would be theirs. This divine favor would abound until **the moon** was **no more**. Again this refers to a time beyond Solomon's day, or the regime of any human ruler. It looks ahead to the eternal reign of God's Son, Jesus Christ (Rev. 11:15).

C An Expansive Reign (72:8–11)

SUPPORTING IDEA: *Solomon prays that the dominion of the king's reign will extend to all peoples.*

72:8–9. The people were glad that their king would rule **from sea to sea**. This refers to the Red Sea, the Mediterranean Sea, and beyond. Likewise, this king would reign from the Euphrates **River to the ends of the earth**. Ultimately, this points to the universal kingdom of Christ over all the earth during his millennial reign (Rev. 20:1–10) and eternal state (Rev. 21:1–22:5). Even **the desert tribes** of the Arabian desert would **bow before him** and **lick the dust**.

72:10–11. **The kings of Tarshish** (present-day Spain), **Sheba** (southern Arabia), and **Seba** (northern Africa) would bring him **tribute** and **gifts**. This homage did occur in Solomon's day (1 Kgs. 4:21; 10:1,23–24; Isa. 60:4–7), but it also looks ahead, ultimately, to the worship of kings in the eternal state

(Rev. 21:24). In that day all kings as well as all nations over which they rule will come before the glorified Christ and **bow down** and **serve him** (cp. Phil. 2:10–11).

D An Excellent Reign (72:12–14)

SUPPORTING IDEA: *Solomon intercedes for the loving expressions of God to be demonstrated through the king to the people.*

72:12–14. With divine love guiding him, this king would **deliver the needy.** He must undertake their cause because they had no one to speak for them. This king would **take pity on the weak and the needy.** In fact, he would save **the needy from death** at the hands of ungodly men. He would **rescue** innocent, godly people who had suffered **oppression** and who had been victimized by **violence.** Heaven's righteous king will come to their aid because **precious is their blood** that has been shed in martyrdom for his kingdom.

E An Exalted Reign (72:15–20)

SUPPORTING IDEA: *Solomon petitions God that divine blessing will be bestowed upon the king's reign.*

72:15. Anticipating his own reign, as well as future kings of Israel, Solomon shouted to God, **Long may he live!** This verbalized the desire of the people. Further, he asked for tribute **from Sheba** and prayer and blessing from the people.

72:16–17. The phrase **May his name endure forever,** is a request that the name of Christ might be honored **as long as the sun. All nations will be blessed through him,** a promise that finds fulfillment in Christ alone.

72:18–19. The psalmist exclaimed, **Praise be to . . . the God of Israel, who alone does marvelous deeds.** These wonderful deeds had been performed by God on behalf of the king. With a worldwide vision for God's greatness, Solomon concluded, **May the whole earth be filled with his glory.** The supremacy of this king and the greatness of his kingdom deserved the greatest praise. **Amen and Amen** are the heartfelt affirmations of Solomon and the people.

72:20. The phrase **This concludes the prayers of David son of Jesse** is an editorial notation that marks not only the end of Psalm 72 but the conclusion of the second section of the psalms (Pss. 42–72). This conclusion corresponds to the shorter endings of the other four books (Pss. 41:13; 89:52; 106:48; 150:6).

MAIN IDEA REVIEW: *Solomon prays for the earthly, temporal blessings of God to rest upon his reign but looks ahead to the Lord Jesus Christ, who will reign forever.*

III. CONCLUSION

Jesus Shall Reign

The glorious reign portrayed in this psalm points to the future kingdom of Christ, a reign far greater than the rule of Solomon. In the last day Christ will govern the entire world. Isaac Watts expressed this truth in one of his hymns:

> Jesus shall reign where'er the sun
> Does his successive journeys run,
> His kingdom spread from shore to shore
> Till moons shall wax and wane no more.
>
> From north to south the princes meet
> To pay homage at His feet,
> While western empires own their Lord
> And savage tribes attend His word.
>
> To Him shall endless prayer be made
> And endless praises crown His head;
> His name like sweet perfume shall rise
> With every morning sacrifice.
>
> People and realms of every tongue
> Dwell on His love with sweetest song,
> And infant voices shall proclaim
> Their early blessings on His name.

May all hearts glory in the coming reign of Christ over all the earth.

IV. LIFE APPLICATION

The Final Word

In this fallen world, believers are subject to many injustices. It may be suffering at the hands of an unfair boss. Or it may be enduring the persecution of an unsaved spouse. Perhaps it is being misunderstood by others because of biblical convictions. Whatever the injustice may be, a King and Judge who will rule with perfect fairness and justice is coming. This King will have the final word.

V. PRAYER

God, we are grateful for your Messiah who is greater than David and Solomon. He is the one to whom all kings will bow and the one who will be served by all generations. Lord Jesus, we acknowledge your rule over our lives as our Messiah. Praise be to your glorious name forever; may the whole earth be filled with your glory. Amen.

VI. DEEPER DISCOVERIES

A. Rule (72:8)

The word *rule* (Heb. *rada*) means "to reign, rule, or subjugate" and occurs twenty-three times in the Old Testament. One time it means "to trample" (Joel 3:13), and twenty-two times it means "to reign over" (Lev. 25:43,46,53; 26:17; 1 Kgs. 8:16; 9:23; 2 Chr. 8:10; Pss. 68:27; 110:2; Isa. 14:2,6; 41:2; Jer. 5:31; Ezek. 29:15; 34:4;). This word is generally used of human rule and not divine rule.

B. Bow Down (72:11)

The phrase "bow down" (Heb. *shaha*) means "to prostrate oneself," especially before a superior (Gen. 18:2; 19:1; 43:26,28; 1 Sam. 24:8; 2 Sam. 9:8; 15:5), although rarely it is before an equal (Gen. 23:7; 1 Kgs. 2:19). The word occurs over 170 times in the Hebrew Bible, most often of prayer (Gen. 22:5; 1 Sam. 1:3). It is used most often of worshiping God (Exod. 11:8; 24:1; 33:10; Deut. 26:10; 1 Sam. 15:30; Isa. 27:13), but sometimes it describes idol worship (Deut. 8:19; 11:16; 30:17; Josh. 23:7; Judg. 2:19; 2 Chr. 7:19; 25:14). This word speaks of submission and of adoration to be given to God.

VII. TEACHING OUTLINE

A. An Equitable Reign (1–4)
   This king will:
   1. Preside fairly (1–2)
   2. Prosper abundantly(3)
   3. Protect mercifully (4)
B. An Eternal Reign (5–7)
   1. As long as the sun shines (5)
   2. As long as the rain falls (6)
   3. As long as the moon exists (7)
C. An Expansive Reign (8–11)
   This king will be worshiped:

1. By near nations (8a,9)
2. By distant nations (10)
3. By all nations (8b,11)
D. An Excellent Reign (12–14)
This king will show mercy to:
1. The pitied (12)
2. The poor (13)
3. The persecuted (14)
E. An Exalted Reign (15–20)
This king will receive:
1. Generous tribute (15a)
2. Grateful prayers (15b)
3. Glad praise (15c)
4. Growing prosperity (16)
5. Great fame (17a)
6. Global worship (17b–19)
   a. By all nations (17b)
   b. For his awesome works (18)
   c. For his glorious name (19)
CONCLUSION (20)

VIII. ISSUES FOR DISCUSSION

1. Do I live my life under the sovereign reign of Jesus Christ?
2. Do I help the needy, afflicted, and weak?
3. Do I defend those who are unable to defend themselves?
4. Do I live to praise the name of Jesus Christ and to fill the whole earth with his glory?

Psalm 73

Myopic Faith

I. INTRODUCTION

A Seeing Problem

*M*yopia is a visual problem that keeps people from seeing objects at a distance. They can see only what is immeditely before them. Without the aid of glasses or contacts, they cannot see where they are going or what is on the distant horizon. What is even worse is *spiritual* myopia. The person with this problem can see only what is immediately under his "spiritual nose," that which is temporal, physical, and earthly. He can only see the here and now.

"Asaph," the author of Psalm 73, suffered a severe bout of myopic faith. This gifted man was an outstanding musician in the time of David (Ezra 2:41) and an appointed minister of music in the temple as the leader of one of David's Levitical choirs (1 Chr. 15:19; 16:5). As a writer of inspired Scripture, Asaph and the body of musicians who descended from him (cp. 2 Chr. 35:15) wrote Psalm 50 and Psalms 73–83. This psalm was written during a time when he took his eyes off the Lord and focused on the prosperity of the wicked around him. This look caused him to struggle and lose sight of the eternal because he was giving full attention to the temporal.

This psalm addresses one of life's most difficult problems: How is it that the wicked so often prosper while the godly suffer so much? This is the dilemma of myopic faith.

II. COMMENTARY

Myopic Faith

MAIN IDEA: *It is not possible for a person to see and trust in the eternal while his focus is on the temporal.*

A The Disturbing Problem (73:1–3)

SUPPORTING IDEA: *Asaph remembers a time in his life when he envied the prosperity of the wicked and nearly fell into doubt about the goodness of God to the righteous.*

73:1. Asaph began this psalm with his bottomline conclusion: the goodness of God. **Surely God is good to Israel**, he declared. He affirmed the benevolence of God who was constantly good to his people who trusted him and those who were **pure in heart** (cp. Ps. 24:4). This is one of the most fundamental truths about God—he is good (Heb. *towb*) (cp. Pss. 25:8; 34:8; 86:5; 100:5; 106:1; 107:1; 118:1,29; 119:68; 135:3; 136:1; 145:9).

73:2–3. But Asaph confessed that he came close to abandoning this confidence in God's goodness. The phrase **But as for me** occurs four times in this psalm. It was a device used by Asaph to confess his error. He continued, **my feet had almost slipped**, meaning that he had nearly turned aside from the right way. By his own admission, he **had nearly lost** his **foothold** and could have suffered a monumental fall in his spiritual life. What caused it? Asaph allowed his focus to shift from the goodness of God to **the prosperity of the wicked**, and this caused him to doubt God. Why should people who disregard God be the recipients of his goodness more than those who trust him? This was the question in Asaph's mind.

B The Distorted Perspective (73:4–12)

SUPPORTING IDEA: *Asaph recalls his envious thoughts produced by a poor outlook.*

73:4–5. Asaph described the troubling contradiction that he saw all around him—the prosperity of the wicked who had **no struggles** (cp. Mal. 3:15). Of course, they did have problems, but they were hidden from Asaph's gaze. In his eyes, they were **healthy and strong** and were **free from the burdens common to man**. From the psalmist's vantage point, they were not **plagued by human ills**, but they died seemingly painless deaths. This reveals the envy and self-pity that almost developed in Asaph's heart.

73:6–9. The speech of the wicked was corrupt, and this added to Asaph's bewilderment. They scoffed at what was good and spoke with **malice** toward

God and his kingdom. Full of **arrogance**, they acted as if they controlled **heaven** and owned **the earth**.

73:10–11. Under the sway of this madness, **people** were turning to the wicked and drinking **up** the **waters** that spewed from their mouths. In other words, others were drinking up what they said, as if it were wise. The wicked were saying, **How can God know? Does the Most High have knowledge?** In their pride they assumed that God could not see their sin because it went unpunished.

73:12. Drawing a summary of the previous verses, Asaph lamented, **This is what the wicked are like—always carefree, they increase in wealth**. The ungodly, so he thought, were peaceful and prosperous, healthy and wealthy. Although this view was grossly distorted and exaggerated, this is how the discouraged psalmist saw it.

ℂ The Debilitating Pain (73:13–16)

SUPPORTING IDEA: *Asaph's wrong perspective leads him to question his pursuit of righteousness.*

73:13–14. Spiraling downward, Asaph dissolved into self-pity. He lamented, **Surely in vain have I kept my heart pure**. In other words, it seemed to do him no good to follow God and obey his word. So what good was it to remain **pure**? **All day long** he felt **plagued** and **punished** for doing right. Why remain loyal to God if this was his reward?

73:15–16. Asaph's thoughts, if they had been expressed, would have been a stumbling block to the congregation. He simply could not **understand all this**. It remained an enigma why God seemed to prosper the wicked and punish the righteous. It was an **oppressive** source of inner conflict that caused him much heaviness of heart.

𝔻 The Dawning Perception (73:17–20)

SUPPORTING IDEA: *When Asaph is reminded of God and the eternal, he remembers the eternal punishment that awaits the wicked.*

73:17. In the midst of his spiritual crash, something changed the psalmist's outlook on life. Negative thinking had engulfed him. But he came to a turning point and had an eye-opening experience when he **entered the sanctuary of God**. He who ministered in the house of God was confronted with the eternal perspective. No doubt, the Word of God was brought to bear upon his life, correcting his misjudgment. Through the prism of divine truth, he saw the **final destiny** of the wicked and comprehended their final judgment.

73:18–20. Gripped with God's perspective, Asaph affirmed, **Surely you place them on slippery ground; you cast them down to ruin**. The final destruction of the wicked was sure. **Suddenly**, when they least expected it, they would be **destroyed**. They would be **swept away by terrors**, suffering a dreadful death that led to everlasting punishment. God would **arise** as from sleep and remove the ungodly.

🄴 The Dynamic Praise (73:21–28)

SUPPORTING IDEA: *Asaph regrets the marred perspective he once held and reaffirms his faith in God.*

73:21–22. Asaph's inner pain was the result of the envy that had sprung up in his embittered spirit. As a result, he was **senseless and ignorant**, without any spiritual discernment or understanding. Comparing himself to a wild animal, he admitted to God, **I was a brute beast before you.** This means he was devoid of clear thinking.

73:23–24. Asaph attributed the restoration of his spiritual sight to the faithfulness of God who was **always with** him. God would not let go of him, even when he drifted into spiritual apathy. It was God holding on to his **right hand**, not vice versa, that made the difference. He now received guidance from God's Word that enabled him to overcome his foolishness with sound **counsel**. In spite of his period of unfaithfulness, he remained confident in God's lovingkindness that would receive him into his heavenly **glory**.

73:25–26. Speaking with the right spiritual perspective, Asaph boasted with renewed faith, **Whom have I in heaven but you?** This rhetorical question implies a negative answer. No one but God could help him. Asaph desired **nothing** but God, who alone was his chief passion. **My flesh and my heart**, his whole being, fails, but God is the **strength** of his **heart** and his **portion**—the sum total of his inheritance—**forever**. The Lord was his sustainer, his very life.

73:27–28. Asaph concluded that the **unfaithful** people who were **far from** God would **perish** in this life, as well as forever. **But as for me, it is good to be near God**, he declared. This was the only vantage point that provided the right perspective on life.

MAIN IDEA REVIEW: *It is not possible for a person to see and trust in the eternal while his focus is on the temporal.*

III. CONCLUSION

Jesus, Our Only Hope

Much like Asaph, Charles Wesley was a man gifted by God to write spiritual songs. Wesley was a famous eighteenth-century hymn writer who wrote more than seven thousand hymns, many of which are still sung in Christian worship. His classic works are among the finest in the English language. His hymns include "Hark, the Herald Angels Sing," "Christ the Lord Is Risen Today," and "O For a Thousand Tongues to Sing." Born in England, he was educated at Christ Church College at Oxford University in the 1720s. He helped his brother John shape the Methodist movement.

Lying on his deathbed in March 1788, Charles Wesley was fixed upon the greatness of God. His last thoughts were about Psalm 73, specifically verses 25–26: "Whom have I in heaven but you? And earth has nothing I desire besides you. My flesh and my heart may fail, but God is the strength of my heart and my portion forever."

As he reflected on these verses, he called his wife to his side and dictated his last words:

> In age and feebleness extreme,
>
> What shall a sinful worm redeem?
>
> Jesus, my only hope thou art,
>
> Strength of my failing flesh and heart.
>
> O could I catch a smile from thee,
>
> And drop into Eternity.

This is how to overcome myopic faith—by looking away from the charms of this world and focusing on the glories of Christ. May we look exclusively to the Lord and consider the beauty of his holiness. May all who trust in God take the long look into eternity and consider the end of the ungodly.

IV. LIFE APPLICATION

The Right Outlook

In a world where the wicked seem to prosper more than the righteous, the believer's eyes must be fixed on God and his goodness. God can give the believer a proper outlook on life and eternity. This perspective will dominate the believer's life only when he constantly focuses on God, trusting in him alone.

V. PRAYER

God, you shower unmerited blessings on those who are pure in heart. Keep us from envying the possessions of those around us. Grant us contentment with what you give us. It is good to be near you in your sanctuary because you are the strength of our heart and our portion forever. In Jesus' name. Amen.

VI. DEEPER DISCOVERIES

A. Prosperity (73:3)

The word *prosperity* (Heb. *shalom*) is a noun used 237 times and is most often tranlated as "peace." It connotes a satisfied, complete, harmonious condition and complete fulfillment in life. This state of peacefulness leads to a comfort that is both internal and external (Pss. 4:8; 29:11; Prov. 3:2,17).

B. Sanctuary (73:17)

See "Deeper Discoveries," 15:1.

C. Guide (73:24)

This word (Heb. *naha*) means "to lead or to direct someone down the right path" (Exod. 13:21; 32:34; Num. 23:7; Neh. 9:12; Job 38:32; Isa. 58:11). It occurs thirty-nine times in the Old Testament. Nowhere is this verb more vividly demonstrated than in the Book of Exodus, where God guided Israel with a cloud by day and fire by night (Exod. 13:21; Ps. 78:14). In the Psalms, this guidance describes God guiding his servant (Pss. 27:11; 31:3; 61:2; 77:20; 139:24; 143:10). This guidance leads a person down the path of righteousness (Pss. 5:8; 23:3; 67:4).

D. Perish (73:27)

See "Deeper Discoveries," 1:6.

VII. TEACHING OUTLINE

A. The Disturbing Problem (1–3)
1. I am confident in God's goodness (1)
2. I am confused about God's goodness (2–3)
   a. My feet almost slipped (2)
   b. My eyes envied sinners (3)
B. The Distorted Perspective (4–12)
1. The wicked are always healthy (4–5)
   a. They have strong bodies (4)
   b. They have no burdens (5)
2. The wicked are always haughty (6–11)
   a. They have conceited hearts (6a)
   b. They have cruel hands (6b)
   c. They have callous hearts (7a)
   d. They have careless minds (7b)
   e. They have corrupt mouths (8–11)
3. The wicked are always happy (12)

a. They are carefree (12a)
b. They are wealthy (12b)
C. The Debilitating Pain (13–16)
  1. I have kept pure (13–14)
  2. I have been plagued (14)
  3. I withheld my words (15)
  4. I suffered much oppression(16)
D. The Dawning Perception (17–20)
  1. I entered the Lord's sanctuary (17a)
  2. I saw the wicked's final destiny (17b–20)
    a. God casts them down (17b–18)
    b. God sweeps them away (19)
    c. God despises them (20)
E. The Dynamic Praise (21–28)
  1. I was previously self–focused (21–22)
    a. I was self–despairing (21)
    b. I was self–deceived (22)
  2. I am now God–focused (23–28)
    a. God holds me (23)
    b. God guides me (24)
    c. God captivates me (25)
    d. God strengthens me (26)
    e. God protects me (27–28)

VIII. ISSUES FOR DISCUSSION

1. Do I envy the prosperity and possessions of the wicked?
2. Do I ever doubt the goodness of God in my life?
3. Do I ever doubt the need for the pursuit of righteousness in life?
4. Do I desire God above all earthly possessions?

Psalm 74
Rise Up, O God

Quote

"*God's* wounds are better than Satan's salves."

J o h n   T r a p p

I. INTRODUCTION

Few ordeals in life are more excruciating than suffering defeats while serving God. When God's work is met with setbacks, his people agonize over these losses and long for God's kingdom work to be reestablished. And until God's kingdom is again prospering, distress fills the hearts of his servants. In these times of devastation, they must call out to God for relief and restoration. This is the focus of Psalm 74, a song of lament that expresses the agony of God's devastated people. Israel's enemies had destroyed the temple (2 Kgs. 25), but even worse it seemed that God had forgotten them.

This psalm is a "*maskil* of Asaph," meaning a contemplation recorded by one of Asaph's descendants. In this psalm God's exiled people wept over the destruction of the temple and the devastation of Jerusalem in 586 B.C. In their pain and agony, the psalmist called out to God to remember them and bring divine relief in this distressing hour.

This psalm was probably written after the Babylonian invasion of Judah and Jerusalem in 586 B.C. This national catastrophe left the city in ruins. Most of those who were not killed were exiled to Babylon. The psalm is a powerful plea for God to reestablish his covenant people in their land.

II. COMMENTARY

MAIN IDEA: *Asaph mourns the destruction of Jerusalem and the temple as he recounts God's past deeds and calls for God to rise up on behalf of his people.*

🄰 A Prayer of Desperation (74:1–3)

74:1. Feeling spurned by God, Asaph began by asking the searching question, **Why have you rejected us forever, O God?** But God had not **rejected** them; he had withdrawn the power of his presence from them. The psalmist asked about the duration of this rejection, an abandonment demonstrated by the ransacked city and ruined temple (cp. Ps. 79:1). He also asked, **Why does your anger smolder against the sheep of your pasture?** The image of the smoldering city that had been ravaged by a foreign oppressor is symbolic of God's rejection and abandonment of his sheep, Israel, who lived in God's pasture, Jerusalem (cp. 80:4).

74:2. The psalmist cried out for God to **remember** his past intervention in the history of Israel, the **people** whom he had **purchased** from Egypt (Exod. 20:2). Furthermore, the nation was God's chosen **inheritance** (cp. Deut. 4:20; 9:26,29; Ps. 28:9; Jer. 10:16), or those whom he had redeemed (Exod. 15:13,16). Furthermore, God **dwelt** among his people on **Mount Zion** (1 Kgs. 6:12–13) which was God's holy hill (Ps. 2:6) and dwelling (Ps. 132:5,7).

74:3. Because of God's gracious dealings in the past, the psalmist pleaded for God to **turn** his **steps toward** the **everlasting ruins** of God's sanctuary. Asaph longed for God's presence to return and restore the **destruction the enemy** had **brought** to the temple.

🄱 A Prayer of Lamentation (74:4–9)

74:4. The psalmist turned to the hostile invaders and detailed the devastation they had inflicted on the temple in Jerusalem. Describing the advancing Babylonians, he stated that their **foes roared** like lions into the sanctuary, the **place** where God **met** with his people. These fierce barbarians **set up their standards as signs**, polluting the holy place. **Standards** may refer to military banners which functioned as emblems of victory.

74:5–8. The desecration of the temple involved the smashing of the **carved paneling** of the inner sanctuary. These wicked invaders **wielded axes** in the say way as they would **cut through a thicket of trees.** Then they **burned** the **sanctuary to the ground.** They conspired to crush God's people by burning **every place where God was worshiped in the land.**

74:9. To add to the chaos, God had alienated himself by giving **no miraculous signs**, nor had he left Israel with any **prophets** to warn of this unexpected disaster. The absence of signs and a reliable prophetic voice made the people unsure about **how long this** tragedy would continue.

🄲 A Prayer for Retribution (74:10–11)

74:10–11. Attempting to provoke God to respond to this desperate situation, the psalmist asked, **How long will the enemy mock you, O God? Will the foe revile your name forever?** The insults that were made against God and his sanctuary inflamed the righteous indignation of the psalmist (Ps. 69:9; John 2:17). The apparent inactivity of God provoked the psalmist to request him to use his strong **right hand** to strike Israel's enemies and **destroy them**.

D A Prayer of Exaltation (74:12–17)

74:12. Remembering God's past actions on behalf of his people, the psalmist broke into an anthem of praise, magnifying and exalting the Lord. The loyalty of Israel was still to her **king** (cp. Pss. 5:2; 10:16; 24:7–10; 29:10; 44:4; 47:2,6–7; 68:24) who was **of old** (cp. Ps. 55:19; Mic. 5:2; Hab. 1:12) and who brought **salvation upon the earth** (Gen. 49:18; Exod. 14:13; 1 Sam. 14:45; 2 Chr. 20:17; Pss. 14:7; 20:5; 35:9; 68:19; 98:2–3; Isa. 12:2; 52:10; Jonah 2:9).

74:13–15. The psalmist also remembered that it was God who **split open the sea by** his **power**. This refers to the parting of the Red Sea as Israel left Egypt (Exod. 14:13–22). Likewise, it was God who **broke the heads of the monster in the waters** (Exod. 14:23–31), a reference to the Egyptian pharaoh (Isa. 51:9; Ezek. 29:3). The washed-up corpses of the Egyptian army became food for **the creatures of the desert**. The psalmist acknowledged that it was God **who opened up springs and streams** in the barren wilderness so Israel had water (cp. Exod. 17:6). Moreover, God dried up the Jordan River (cp. Josh. 4:23) so Israel could enter the promised land.

74:16–17. The psalmist also acknowledged God's sovereign rule and possession of **day** and **night** (cp. Gen. 1:5), as well as and the celestial bodies of the **sun** and **moon** (cp. Gen. 1:15; Isa. 45:7). The **boundaries of the earth** were set by God, who marked off the lines of the continents (cp. Gen. 1:9; Prov. 8:29; Job 38:8) and fashioned the seasons of **summer and winter** (cp. Gen. 8:22).

E A Prayer for Restoration (74:18–23)

74:18–20. Having reflected upon God's sovereign rule, the psalmist then asked the Lord to **remember how the enemy** had **mocked** him and how **foolish people** had **reviled** his sacred **name**, Yahweh (Exod. 6:6–8). The psalmist pleaded that God would **not hand over the life** of his covenant people to these barbarous people, whom he portrayed as savage **wild beasts**. At stake was the existence and future of the nation, as well as God's **covenant** (Gen. 17:1–22) that pledged to preserve them as a great nation. The **violence** these invaders brought had filled **the land** with **dark places**, a reference to the grave (Pss. 88:6; 143:3; Lam. 3:6).

74:21–23. The psalmist pleaded on behalf of the **oppressed, poor**, and **needy** for God to **rise up** and **defend** their **cause**. The psalmist ended this lament by asking God to **remember** and **not ignore** the **uproar** of his **enemies**.

III. CONCLUSION

As long as God reigns, defeat of his kingdom is impossible. Because God rules for his own glory, God's people have an assured future. When the disappointing setbacks of life occur, especially in serving God's kingdom, believers should turn to the Lord. No matter how devastating the defeat may be, failure is never final as long as the grace of God is available.

IV. TEACHING OUTLINE

A. A Prayer of Desperation (1–3)
    1. God, receive us (1)
    2. God, remember us (2)
    3. God, return to us (3)
B. A Prayer of Lamentation (4–9)
    1. They shouted their defiance (4a)
    2. They set up their banners (4b)
    3. They swung their axes (5)
    4. They smashed the paneling (6)
    5. They smoked the sanctuary (7a)
    6. They shamed your name (7b)
    7. They spoke their pride (8)
    8. They silenced our prophets (9)
C. A Prayer for Retribution (10–11)
    1. How long will you be shamed? (10)
    2. How long will you be still? (11)
D. A Prayer of Exaltation (12–17)
    1. God, you saved the earth (12)
    2. God, you split the sea (13)
    3. God, you subdued sea monsters (14)
    4. God, you spread out the streams (15a)
    5. God, you shut up the rivers (15b)
    6. God, you stationed the planets (16)
    7. God, you set earth's boundaries (17a)
    8. God, you situated the seasons (17b)
E. A Prayer for Restoration (18–23)
    1. Remember their taunts (18)
    2. Recall our trials (19)
    3. Regard your testimonies (20)
    4. Reward the troubled (21)
    5. Repress their threats (22–23)

Psalm 75

The Divine Disposer

I. INTRODUCTION

*L*iving in a fallen world, believers are faced with injustices on every side. These inequities can cause the spirit to become discouraged, leading to dismay. In these times of widespread wrongs, believers must remain focused on God, who promises to judge rightly. In spite of the many inequities of the arrogant, the godly must give praise and worship to God, who punishes wrong and rewards right. This sense of divine justice was the hope of ancient Israel when they found themselves threatened by foreign powers. Their confidence remained fixed on God, who humbles the proud and honors the humble.

This is the message of this "psalm of Asaph." It was probably written by a descendent of Asaph in the days before the Assyrian invasions (2 Kgs. 18–19). The superscription is addressed to "the director of music," instructing him to have this psalm sung to the tune of "Do Not Destroy." This tune title probably refers to the opening words of a familiar song (cp. Pss. 57; 58; 59). It is a thanksgiving hymn that expresses deep gratitude for God's justice in the world.

II. COMMENTARY

MAIN IDEA: *Asaph is confident in divine justice and knows that God will destroy the wicked.*

A A Word of Thanksgiving (75:1)

75:1. In this first stanza the people of God spoke with a burst of jubilant thanksgiving: **We give thanks to you, O God . . . for your Name is near.** As one voice lifted heavenward, this was spoken by the entire congregation in unison. The phrase *your Name* refers to the fullness of God's person, a revelation of who he was, the representation of God's holy character and infinite being. The entirety of God's awesome person is said to be **near**, meaning close to his people, always ready to intervene for their good. He is always close at hand, presiding over the affairs of his people.

B A Word of Triumph (75:2–3)

75:2–3. With this second stanza, God speaks (vv. 2–5): "**I choose the appointed time; it is I who judge uprightly.**" God would not fail to **judge**, but he would do so in his own **appointed time.** He holds the earth's **pillars firm** and stabilizes world orders and crumbling societies through his common grace.

C A Word of Threat (75:4–5)

75:4–5. In this stanza God continues to speak, issuing a warning to the wicked: **To the arrogant I say, "Boast no more," and to the wicked, "Do not lift up your horns."** The lifting up of an animal's horns pictures stubborn resistance toward its master, holding its head high so a yoke could not be put on it. God declares that his people are not to lift up their **horns against heaven** in prideful rebellion.

D A Word of Trust (75:6–8)

75:6–7. The worship leader, possibly a Levitical song leader, added his personal observations to what God had just spoken. **No one from the east or the west or from the desert** could exalt a man. Only God can **exalt a man.** In other words, whether a person is lifted up or brought down, such promotion or demotion belongs to God. **He brings** some people **down** in retribution, and he **exalts** others in reward.

75:8. The LORD is portrayed as holding **a cup.** This symbolizes God's judgment upon the proud. The cup was **full of foaming wine mixed with spices,** potent and powerful. God poured it out, as though forcing his wrath down the throats of the wicked, making them **drink it down** to the **dregs**. They would drink the cup of divine wrath down to the last drop.

🄴 A Word of Testimony (75:9–10)

75:9. In this closing section, an individual worshiper responded to what had been previously spoken in this psalm. Perhaps it was the Levitical song leader speaking for all the people. Or perhaps it was a descendent of Asaph. He declared, **I will sing praise to the God of Jacob**. This was a vow of praise to God for his righteous judgments which would exalt the humble and bring down the proud.

75:10. This individual worshiper concluded by aligning himself with God. He would **cut off the horns of all the wicked** in order to humble them, he pledged, just as God promises to do. But **the horns of the righteous** would be **lifted up**, or promoted and rewarded by the hand of God. In other words, God will do as he promises in matters of judgment.

III. CONCLUSION

God will never abandon the righteous. He is always near, ready to step forward to help them. In spite of the many injustices that fill the earth, he has not abdicated his sovereign rule and judgment. Whether this punishment upon the wicked is to be inflicted in this life, or in the final day of judgment, divine justice will be served. So believers may rest in the Lord and rely upon his protection. Judgment is coming. God will put down the wicked and lift up the righteous. Thanksgiving should be offered continually to God. Only he is worthy of our praise.

IV. TEACHING OUTLINE

A. A Word of Thanksgiving (1)
  The congregation says:
  1. God, we give thanks for your name (1a–b)
  2. God, we give thanks for your deeds (1c)
B. A Word of Triumph (2–3)
  God himself says:
  1. I will judge uprightly (2)
  2. I will uphold securely (3)
C. A Word of Threat (4–5)
  God himself says:
  1. Do not speak out your pride (4a)
  2. Do not lift up your horns (4b–5a)
  3. Do not stretch out your neck (5b)

D. A Word of Trust (6–8)

   The worship leader says:

   1. No one can exalt a man (6)
   2. God alone can exalt a man (7–8)
      a. God alone judges (7a)
      b. God alone debased (7b)
      c. God alone exalts (7b)
      d. God alone punishes (8)

E. A Word of Testimony (9–10)

   An individual worshiper says:

   1. I will sing praise to God (9)
   2. I will serve the purposes of God (10)
      a. I will cut off the horns of the wicked (10a)
      b. I will lift up the horns of the righteous (10b)

Glossary

confession—Admission of personal sin and seeking forgiveness from God and others

conversion—God's act of changing a person's life in response to the person's turning to Christ in repentance and faith

covenant—A contract or agreement expressing God's gracious promises to his people and their consequent relationship to him

creation—God's bringing the world and everything in it into existence from nothing

cross—Two wooden beams shaped as a letter *t* or *x* used as an instrument to kill criminals by the Roman government; the wooden beams on which Jesus was killed and thus a prominent symbol of Christian faith

discipline—Corrective instruction used by God to promote righteous living in his children

evangelism—The central element of the church's mission involving telling others the gospel of salvation in Jesus Christ with the objective of leading them to repentance and faith in him

evil—Any person or action that opposes the plan of God

exile—Israel's life in the Assyrian kingdom after 722 B.C. and Judah's life in Babylon after 587 B.C.

exodus, the—The most important act of national deliverance as chronicled by Moses in the Book of Exodus when God enabled the Israelites to escape Egypt

faith—Belief in and personal commitment to Jesus Christ for eternal salvation

fall, the—The result of the first human sin which marred the image of God in all humans and enslaved the entire human race in sin (Gen. 3)

firstborn—The oldest son born into a Jewish family or the first offspring of livestock. The firstborn were dedicated to God in a special sense

forgiveness—Pardon and release from penalty for wrongdoing; God's delivery from sin's wages for those who repent and express faith in Christ; the Christian act of freeing from guilt and blame those by whom one has suffered wrong

glorification—God's action in the lives of believers, making them able to share the glory and reward of heaven

Godhead—The unity of the triune God: Father, Son, Holy Spirit

grace—Undeserved acceptance and love received from another, especially the characteristic attitude of God in freely providing salvation for unworthy sinners

hell—The place of everlasting punishment for the lost

holy—God's distinguishing characteristic that separates him from all creation; his transcendence above all; the moral ideal for Christians as they seek to reflect the character of God as known in Christ Jesus

holy of holies—The innermost and most sacred area of the tabernacle and temple, where God was present and where sacrifices were made by the high priest on the Day of Atonement

idolatry—The worship of that which is not God

intercession—A prayer presenting one person's needs to another as Christians presenting the needs of others to God or as Christ or the Holy Spirit representing believers before God

Jerusalem—Capital city of Israel in the Old Testament; religious center of Judaism in the New Testament; also name of the heavenly city John describes in Revelation (New Jerusalem)

joy—The inner attitude of celebrating one's salvation regardless of outward circumstances

judgment—God's work at the end time involving condemnation for unbelievers and assignment of rewards for believers

law—God's instruction to his people about how to love him and others; when used with the definite article *the*, *law* may refer to the Old Testament as a whole but usually to the Pentateuch (Genesis through Deuteronomy)

mercy—A personal characteristic of care for the needs of others; the biblical concept of mercy always involves help to those who are in need or distress

Messiah—the coming king promised by the prophets; Jesus Christ who fulfilled the prophetic promises; Christ represents the Greek translation of the Hebrew word *messiah*

millennium—A thousand-year period when the righteous will reign on earth

Passover—The Jewish feast celebrating the exodus from Egypt (Exod. 12); celebrated by Jesus and his disciples at the Last Supper

perseverance—The response of enduring even in the face of difficulty; Christians develop this trait by facing and overcoming hardship and adversity

repentance—A change of heart and mind resulting in a turning from sin to God that allows conversion and is expressed through faith

righteousness—The quality or condition of being in right relationship with God; living out the relationship with God in right relationships with other persons

sacrifice—According to Mosaic Law, an offering to God in repentance for sin or as an expression of thanksgiving; Christ as the ultimate sacrifice for sin

saints—Those holy or set apart to God; any person in Christ

Glossary

salvation—Deliverance from trouble or evil; the process by which God redeems his creation, completed through the life, death, and resurrection of his Son Jesus Christ

sin—Actions by which humans rebel against God, miss his purpose for their lives, and surrender to the power of evil rather than to God

sovereignty—God's freedom from outward restraint; his unlimited rule of and control over his creation

total depravity—The condition of all humanity after the fall, polluting with sin every dimension of man's being—mind, emotion, and will

trials—Afflictions and hardships permitted in our lives by God to develop stamina and endurance in us (Jas. 1:2-4)

Trinity—God's revelation of himself as Father, Son, and Holy Spirit unified as one in the Godhead and yet distinct in person and function

truth—That which is real and reliable; opposite of falsehood and error; descriptive of the divine Father, Son, and Spirit as the full revelation of the one true God

worship—Reverence, honor, praise, and service shown to God

wrath of God—God's consistent, holy response opposing and punishing sin

Yahweh—The Hebrew personal name of God revealed to Moses (Exod. 3:14); this name came to be thought of as too holy to pronounce by Jews; often translated LORD or Jehovah

Zion—Another name for Jerusalem

Bibliography

Popular Expositions

Beisner, Calvin. *Psalms of Promise.*
Boice, James Montgomery. *Psalms.* 3 vols.
Maclaren, Alexander. *Expositions of Holy Scripture.* Vol. 4.
Phillips, John. *Exploring the Psalms.* 2 vols.
Stedman, Ray. *Psalms of Faith.*
Swindoll, Charles. *Daily Grind.* 2 vols.
Wiersbe, Warren. *Meet Yourself in the Psalms.*

Devotional Commentaries

Alexander, J. A. *The Psalms Translated and Explained.*
Henry, Matthew. *Matthew Henry Commentary.*
Lockyer, Herbert, Sr. *Psalms: A Devotional Commentary.*
Scroggie, W. Graham. *A Guide to the Psalms.*
Spurgeon, Charles H. *Treasury of David.* 7 vols.

Exegetical Commentaries

Davidson, Robert. *The Vitality of Worship.*
Dickson, David. *Psalms.* Geneva Series of Commentaries.
Harman, Allan. *Psalms.*
Kidner, Derek. *Psalms.* 2 vols.
Leupold, H. C. *Exposition on the Psalms.*
Perowne, J. J. Stewart. *The Book of Psalms.*
Ross, Allan P. *Psalms.* Bible Knowledge Commentary.
Unger, Merrill. *Psalms.* Unger's Commentary on the Old Testament.
Wilcock, Michael. *The Message of Psalms 1–72.*
Wilcock, Michael. *The Message of Psalms 73–150.*

Technical Commentaries

Calvin, John. *Calvin's Commentaries.* Vols. 4–6.
Craige, Peter C., Marvin E. Tate, and Leslie C. Allen. *Word Biblical Commentary.* Vols. 19–21.
Delitzsch, Franz. *Keil-Delitzsch Commentary on the Old Testament.* Vol. 5.
Gameren, Willem Van. *Psalms.* The Bible Expositor's Commentary. Vol. 5.

Hebrew Tools

Armstrong, Terry A., Douglas L. Busby, and Cyril F. Carr. *A Reader's Hebrew and English Lexicon of the Old Testament.*

Brown, Francis, Samuel R. Driver, and Charles A. Briggs. *A Hebrew and English Lexicon of the Old Testament.*

Even-Shoshan, Abraham. *A New Concordance of the Old Testament.*

Gameren, Willem Van, ed. *New International Dictionary of Old Testament Theology and Exegesis.* 5 vols.

Harris, R. Laird, Gleason L. Archer Jr., and Bruce K. Waltke. *Theological Wordbook of the Old Testament.* 2 vols.

Owens, John Joseph. *Analytical Key to the Old Testament.* 4 vols.

Ringgaren, Butterweck, ed. *Theological Dictionary of the Old Testament.* 10 vols.

The Englishmen's Hebrew and Chaldee Concordance of the Old Testament.

Torrey, R. A. *Treasury of Scripture Knowledge.*

Weingreen, Jacob. *Practical Grammar for Classical Hebrew.*